Coaching Today's Athlete

A Football Textbook

Coaching Today's Athlete

A Football Textbook

by
John Ralston
and
Mike White
of Stanford University

with Stanley Wilson

NATIONAL PRESS BOOKS / PALO ALTO / CALIFORNIA

Contents

231.9

334-339

366

Foreword

Innumerable books on football have been written by men pre-eminent in their profession. None has been more ambitious an undertaking than *Coaching Today's Athlete*. The combination of textual matter and drill book represents a completeness and thoroughness that make it a ready reference for students of the game, whether they are on the threshold of their careers or have devoted a good portion of their lives to it.

Football coaching is a lot more than a few X's and O's and some amateur psychology. There is a definite need for an all-encompassing study of this complex game, its coaches, its players, its systems. I can think of no two men more qualified than Coaches John Ralston and Mike White to provide this necessary, knowledgeable information. I was privileged to know and to coach John Ralston when he was a player; he was on my coaching staff at the University of California; and I have followed his career closely during the intervening years. He is one of the most competent football men in the nation today. Mike White played on the University of California squad during my tenure as coach, and I also have followed his professional coaching career closely. There are few coaches of my acquaintance who are as technically sound or possess the "feel" for the game as Coach White.

Because of the combined backgrounds and talents of Coaches Ralston and White, they have produced a textbook and a practical workbook that will be beneficial to students, teachers, and coaches.

Lynn Waldorf

Preface

In planning the contents of this textbook, the authors set out to produce something more than "just another football book" or to relate in detail our experiences in the coaching profession. We were intent upon writing a textbook that would take into consideration the needs of the prospective and the beginning coach; we also recognized the requirements of the experienced coach whose needs are considerably more sophisticated. To fill these voids, the authors canvassed high school and college coaches, students and teachers in the classroom, and athletes who still are competing. We discussed current football trends and problems during a multitude of football clinics throughout the nation. We then drew on our coaching experiences that took us from high school to major college programs. The results of our search are dual: we have produced a comprehensive textbook that studies our philosophical and technical beliefs and relates *what* programs are successful and *why*; we then found it necessary to produce a drill book to implement that knowledge into *how* a program succeeds. The result is an effort to bridge the gap between the philosophical and the practical, the classroom and the on-the-field teaching and learning experience.

It is not our notion that the "Stanford system" or the "Ralston system" is the only effective way to play football. We realize fully that what is workable for one coach might be entirely wrong for another. We therefore have compiled basic, sound information and techniques that have been tested thoroughly and are applicable to *any* system at *any* level.

The key to the successful implementation of this information is the knowledge and the accompanying ability of a prospective or practicing coach to be flexible. Throughout the text, we recommend flexibility in the selection of a system of play and urge that the system be adjusted to the personnel of the squad. It is our purpose to provide the necessary understanding of the game and to suggest alternate methods of reaching coaches' goals.

We realize that before gaining sufficient confidence in themselves, most young coaches follow the same pattern as we did at the beginning of our careers: we coached the way we were coached in college. Our playing and early coaching backgrounds were with the Waldorf T formation. We followed it in high school and college coaching, and it was successful for us for many years—perhaps too many years before adjustments were made. We were guilty at times of attempting to fit the players into the system rather than of adjusting the system to fit the players. However, upon reflection, we realized that to gain the necessary knowledge to properly assess a system, it is a fundamental requisite to develop as much expertise as possible. Therefore, we wish to share with all other present and prospective coaches the knowledge we have gained through failure and success, through winning and losing, and through twenty years as students of the game.

Acknowledgements

It is customary in a textbook of this nature to extend appropriate credit to those who aided in making it possible. When we considered this responsibility, we realized that it would require the names of perhaps thousands of coaches, players, students of the game, and authors. The game of football as we know it today is the result of an evolutionary process. It is common knowledge that the first intercollegiate football game was played in the United States on November 6, 1869, between Princeton and Rutgers. However, if the football historian delves deeply enough, he finds that the ancient Greeks played a form of football known as *harpaston,* and the Romans a similar game, *harpastum.* A form of the game was known in England as early as the Twelfth Century.

Perhaps this heritage and wide participation results in the familiar saying, "There is nothing new in football, only variations." However, we recognize that there have been, and are, outstanding innovators with imaginative and inventive minds who make the game more exciting and more complex with the arrival of every Autumn season. We do not claim to present anything unique, nor do we possess a mystique that sets us apart. Indeed, we do present some different approaches, some distinctive techniques, some exciting philosophies that we believe make Stanford football atypical. Some of the subtle differences are ours; some have been built upon the innovators of past and present years who have contributed so greatly, yet humbly, to the game.

To these many coaches, players, students of the game, and authors we acknowledge and give our thanks. We likewise give our thanks to the game itself.

More specifically, we do extend our appreciation to those who have gone before us, our teachers, and our colleagues. We would be remiss if we did not pay tribute to those who aided us materially as we grew and those who continue to contribute to us and thousands of others in our profession.

Introduction

Our philosophy of the game of football has become so intertwined with our personal concepts of conduct that it is difficult to consider them as two distinct and separate entities. One element of our philosophy is bound up in our personal world as it applies to our associations with our fellow man in day-to-day living. The other component is our football philosophy in which we determine what it takes to win and then alloting the necessary time in which to accomplish the mission.

Upon analysis, the two philosophies become intertwined—we have implicit faith that the lessons that are taught and learned on the football field are articles of faith that comprise the framework of day-to-day living regardless of periodic social modifications or violent upheavals. Similar to the leaders of our nation or our communities, the coaches' primary purpose of existence is to affect responsibly and positively the persons with whom we work and those we lead. To accomplish both our personal and coaching goals, it is our inherent principle to impart to young people attitudes and codes of conduct that will be incorporated into their lives and forever be an integral and influencing part of their future existence.

There are five precepts by which we attempt to pattern our personal lives; they have become important components of our profession which we diligently attempt to impart to our players:

1. A burning desire to win or to be successful;
2. The creation of a compulsion to improve at all times, either through direction or self-improvement;
3. To possess a singular virtue of stick-to-itiveness;
4. To be honest, possess integrity, humility, and to observe spiritual values;
5. To be flexible in meeting the desires, needs, and individual requirements for fulfillment.

Because the coaching profession provides an outlet for the practice of these philosophies, it is imperative for coaches to perform periodic self-evaluations and to determine their own basic philosophies for existence. The key elements in character building of today's youth are an intelligent approach to the solution of the problem and a tireless devotion to work hard enough, long enough, to accomplish the job. Life situations can be created for athletes by coaches who possess well-ingrained philosophies of life coupled with consistency of purpose.

Coaching Today's Athlete

A Football Textbook

1

Competition

During the past several years, particularly, our civilization has been accused of being materialistic, pragmatic. However, competition continues to be the core of our way of life. Sports and physical education are dedicated to support and to perpetuate the humanistic, moral, and ethical principles that are basic to the human being and to society. Competition is the backbone of American society. It is democracy at its very best. It is an expression of the historical free enterprise system and our inherited competitive nature.

Competition is not new or unique in the world's history. Long before the modern days of the bow and arrow, the hunter practiced his skills on the mountain tops and the plains. Children learned the ways of survival when they were taught to hunt and to fish, to swim and to ride. These skills meant life, and much of the culture of ancient civilizations was embodied in the competitive sphere of natural survival.

From the beginning of time, athletics more often than not were part of religious ritual and constituted a competitive preparation for life. They started as part of man's history and established themselves as cornerstones of his heritage. Athletic contests were fundamental features of man's existence rather than merely vehicles of amusement or recreation. They gratified a basic desire of accomplishment and of surmounting challenging foes. Sports then evolved into a natural desire to compete with others, an all-consuming love of play.

Man was forced to be a fighter from the very beginning in order to exist; strength and alertness aided him in the repulse or conquest of his enemies. He learned endurance and courage, essential qualities in a fighter; we require these qualities of today's athlete. Many sports were the results of "accidents." They were not deliberately invented but arose from man's quest to exist and overcome his countless enemies. The Greeks were the first to assert that sport molded character. They were convinced that only regular exercise could produce a well-rounded personality. It taught them self-control and promoted a strong physique and physical courage.

Some of the distinctive features and social qualities of the British relate directly to their high regard for sports. This is why it often is said that the battle of Waterloo was won on the playing fields of Eton. Probably recollecting this, Adolph Hitler declared during World War II, although mockingly, that the fight was between those who had been through his schools and those who had been at Eton.

Early American settlers faced a formidable task on an inhospitable continent. Physical activity was an integral part of the struggle for existence, and pleasures from physical activities had to come almost wholly from productive efforts in their daily routine.

As man continued to practice these skills—dictated by practical considerations—he acquired a liking for them quite independent of their primary aim, and he continued to pursue them even after their original purpose no longer applied.

Because of our heritage and our desire to engage in profitable pursuits, we have incorporated competition as a way of life in America. We compete for food, for housing, friends, jobs, a better community and nation, education, and government. Further, we compete with ourselves, perhaps the most demanding type of all.

Because of its manifestations, competition has become the American way of life—perhaps to its salvation. Important persons entrusted with channeling healthy competition are the coaches who hold in their trust the cherished heritage of improving and building on thousands of years of competitive endeavor. These are difficult times in which we live; because of our rapidly changing ideals and ideas, coaches and physical education teachers must assume a new and stronger role in leadership. Today's student-athlete is far different from the one we knew and coached even two years ago. They ask questions and want answers. They want to be involved. They want to know the reasoning, the explanation for decisions, and methods of accomplishing missions. We welcome sincere inquiries because the student should have an opportunity to be an essential cog in the machinery of learning through competition. It then becomes the lot of the conscientious coach to teach the competitive athletic skills, and if at all possible, to aid in transferring those competitive lessons into tools of life values. To *hope* that the athletic program will have values in the formation of character is not enough; a coach must *teach* these values as he teaches a skill; and he must set by example their necessity and their worth.

The coach who is aware of the lessons of athletics as related to life values will make a highly significant contribution to the development of moral and ethical behaviors of generations to come. But the practice of this philosophy works both ways: the coach, too, must be a competitor. Although all coaches do not have the same approach to the teaching of the game of football, the distinctive mark that all of us possess is that we like to compete. Otherwise, we would not be in the profession. If for no other reason, we compete because we know there always is a more proficient person ready to take our places if we fail in our programs.

So it boils down to the coach's ability to transfer his competitiveness to the player, who in turn uses that quality to enhance his future life. But it is essential for a coach to evaluate himself regarding the manner in which competitiveness is instilled in the players. The tyrannical coach often is controlled by his own demands of emotion or ego. He attains stature in a relative sense by reducing the size of his associates and squad members. He achieves satisfaction by subjugating those who are weaker or less knowledgeable than he. It does not require a professional analyst to determine the weakness and ultimate failure in this approach. This is one of the primary reasons that we devote considerable text discussion to the role of the coach and the coach-player relationship. Competition is a medium, a way of expressing oneself, a way of doing something. However, competition can be good or bad depending on the manner in which it is conducted. This places the burden squarely on the leader, the coach.

It is his duty to develop in his players the love of competition —the mainspring of the American system. Youngsters who are imbued with the spirit of competitiveness seldom are swayed by insidious propaganda. We believe they withstand this technique because sports essentially are based on honesty, fair play, and by competing according to definitive rules. Athletes also are taught to think on their feet, make spot decisions, and are not fearful of competing against overwhelming odds. It aids them in making intelligent decisions involving themselves, their neighbors, their families, their communities, and their countries. They have a very sound foundation on which to base their lives.

The obvious question that arises concerns the youth who does not have the ability, or does not seek, varsity competition. A national survey recently showed that more male students across the nation are interested and active in sports than ever before in the country's history. They are turning out by the hundreds of thousands for intramural and club sports. William P. (Dutch) Fehring, Director of Stanford's Intramural and Club Sports program, points out:

"Although I have no specific statistics to prove it, I firmly believe that a disciplined athlete is a much more disciplined person. I can only generalize and say that of the hundreds of thousands of students who participate in sports and recreation nationally, only a small ratio engage in anti-social actions."

The morals are obvious:

It is the coach's responsibility to channel the athlete's self-esteem and confidence so the fear of failure will not inhibit his performance in the game of football or in the game of life. The coach holds the trump card because he is able to instill these competitive ingredients in his athletes:

1. The desire to get better. The athlete himself must want to improve and to succeed in whatever else he does. He will not settle for mediocrity;
2. He must satisfy himself and will not be happy being second best;
3. He must develop concentration. The mind quits long before the body loses its efficiency. The mind must be disciplined to respond to the body;
4. He must possess intensity;
5. He must possess courage. We rarely have met "two o'clock in the morning courage"—that which is necessary on an unexpected occasion;
6. Above all, integrity and tough-mindedness are essential to perform under adversity. Intensity, in our frame of reference, is spelled out in the illustration, written for Coach White by his close friend Larry Gardner, trainer with the Dallas Cowboys.

It is only appropriate to close a chapter on competition with some thoughts from the late Vince Lombardi. Coach Lombardi possessed one of the most incisive minds in the history of football; however, he additionally practiced self-discipline, humility, and at all times worked diligently to upgrade the coaching profession. He believed in playing to the fullest both the game of football and the game of life. And he held high his regard for the Almighty, both in his professional and personal pursuits.

Coach Lombardi declared that winning is an all-the-time thing, not a sometime thing. He also pointed out that winning is a habit; similarly, so is losing. There is no room for second place, according to Coach Lombardi, because the second place bowl game is for losers played by losers. The fire and passion of America and Americans are to be first in anything that we attempt to accomplish.

Coach Lombardi placed a lot of faith in a lot of things, but one of his highest priorities was in the heart of the athlete and of man. Although a competitor plays with every inch of his body, he has to possess a lot of heart to come off the field first. So does man.

The immortal coach noted that running a football team is not so different from running a government, an army, a business, or one's personal life—the name of the game is to win. And it is the competitive man who wins—he is drawn to the field of combat, whatever it is, because of its competitive nature.

Coach Lombardi was known for his deep belief in God and human decency, but it didn't deter him from advocating the value of

INTENSITY

I - "Intestinal Fortitude," or more emphatically, just plain American "guts." This is what made America what it is today and what can make your team and you the best in your endeavor.

N - "Noise," not by mouth, but through action. The name of the game is still "knock" no matter how complex it gets due to our new varied offenses and defenses. If you knock the other guy or team down more times than he or they do you, YOU WIN!

T - "Training." If you are going to participate in a team sport, live by it; if not, get out of it. This will be better for the sport, your team and you.

E - "Energy." Every living substance on this earth lives by its energy. Without this ingredient there is no life, whether it is on the football field or in the life of a protozoan. The amount of energy correctly applied in an effort is directly proportional to the result obtained. There is no dishonor in being blocked; the dishonor is in having such a deficiency of energy that you allow yourself to stay blocked.

N - "Need." The greatest "need" in this game or in life itself is pride. Taking enough pride in your team and yourself so that you acquire the knowledge through your coach or through your own efforts and therefore can honestly say, "Under the prevailing circumstances, I, physically and mentally, offered my team and my coach 100% of my talent."

S - "Sacrifice." If you are not willing to sacrifice enough of yourself to give your team your best effort, then strengthen your team by getting out and letting someone participate who will.

I - "Intelligence." To play this game you have to be smart -- not smart alec. Between these two, there is a tremendous difference. You are first a scholar, and second an athlete. You do not play ball to go to school; you go to school to play ball. If you are not eligible scholastically, whether All American or not, you are of no benefit to your team.

T - "Thoroughness." If you are thorough in execution no one can criticize you. If you are not--there is a teammate on the bench who should be where you are.

Y - "You." If you don't have the desire to win and to practice to win, no coach or employer, whichever the case may be, needs you or wants you. Most of all, however, without this need for self satisfaction your life will be a fruitless, unrewarding one. Nature endowed us with the mobility and brain to do with ourselves what we wish. If you do not use it to the best of your advantage you are not a very good athlete, but even more disappointing, you are not much of a man.

combat. He believed with all of his heart that combat, developed through discipline and grinding, repetitious preparation, readies a man for the field of battle whether on the playing greens or in the fight for life where victory or defeat is based on a man's willingness to work his heart out to realize his finest hour.

2

Why Coach?

Looking back over twenty years of coaching, one of my truly great thrills came in the 1968 University of Southern California-Stanford game played in Palo Alto before some 80,000 fans. It was a seesaw battle, as is the case in most Stanford-Trojan games, with USC ultimately winning 27-24. The great USC tailback, O. J. Simpson, was the difference in the battle, but his heroics did not totally dominate the game. Although USC was driving for what ultimately was the winning field goal, it was during this series of plays that I received my greatest football thrill and made me realize upon reflection that these are the things that add up to why men coach — at the very least, why we coach.

During the fourth-quarter USC drive, Stanford was using a five-man line and one of our tackles was Bob Bittner, a young man from Lodi, California. The story had its beginning when we recruited Bob in high school and we were impressed with his six feet three inch height and one hundred eighty-five pound frame. We were certain that he could build to two hundred and twenty-five pounds by his senior year. To the contrary, Bob played his senior year at one hundred and eighty-one pounds; he actually had lost four pounds during his collegiate career. Under normal circumstances, and by current standards, a man six feet three inches tall and one hundred and eighty one pounds could not play defensive tackle in the tough Pacific-8 Conference. But the current standards did not consider Bittner's nine-pound heart. He was a mild-mannered young man off the field but one of the most intense, toughest players that I have ever seen perform. He had learned well the lesson of getting the most out of the mental and physical equipment he possessed.

To set the stage a little more clearly, the previous year Bittner was paired off with Ron Yary, later a number one professional draft choice. Yary was about six feet five and weighed two hundred and seventy pounds. The two players hit head-on play after play and finished the game in a stalemate. It was much the same situation in the 1968 game; this time Bittner was paired off with the fine Southern California tackle, Sid Smith, who carried two hundred and forty five pounds on a six feet four inch frame. They had been going at it all day, and sometime just prior to the memorable play, Bittner took a hard blow over his eye. It later required five stitches, although I'm sure he was oblivious to either the pain or the blood that was rolling down his face.

On the next play, O. J. Simpson faked into the line away from Bittner's position and Steve Sogge, the USC quarterback, started to roll back to Bittner's side. In an Oklahoma defense, this means a leverage assignment and I still can see Bittner coming off Smith's block and chasing Sogge to our near sideline. At the moment of decision of the leverage assignment, Bittner snapped his head around to pursue Sogge, and my eyes caught his. It is difficult to describe that look; it was all there—knowledge of responsibility, realization of his responsibility to the team, all the intensity and emotion that a young man is capable of mustering, and the characteristic of never giving up. Bittner made his pursuit angle down the line and knocked Steve Sogge clear over our bench. The emotion displayed in Bittner's eyes, his intensity of purpose, and his subsequent successful pursuit were worth all of my years in coaching.

Bob Bittner personifies the athletes who get the most out of what they have, both mentally and physically: perseverance, determination, and a willingness to work. These are the athletes who are not necessarily blessed with outstanding talent, but who will not take a backward step under any circumstances.

A more recent example was evident in the 1971 Rose Bowl game against Ohio State University. We had studied from 15,000 to 20,000 feet of their films and particularly researched their goal line defense. We noted that, at all times in their goal line defense, their defensive end was in a stack with either their strong safety or weak safety on the outside shoulder of our tight end. We noted that at no time did their opponents utilize a slight three to four-foot flex of the tight end or just how they would adjust to this deployment. Further, we felt confident that if we aligned in a set with the left half behind the short side tackle and a fullback at home, their rover, Jack Tatum, would set to the weak side. This meant that the free safety Mike Sensibaugh would stack behind the OSU defensive end. During our practice sessions, we assumed that if Bob Moore, our tight end, would flex some three to four feet, that their defensive end would take the gap and allow us to pin him.

We felt strongly that we could run our forty-one fullback play with the fullback faking over the strong guard and pull our four guard in a sweep action around the tight end. We felt that Sensibaugh would be held with the inside fake, and our strong guard, Dan Lightfoot, should be able to run a path leading our ball carrier, Jackie Brown, on the strong sweep. The tackle's block was not anticipated to be a problem because it was just one-one-one with an inside fullback fake. The center overblock was not considered a problem, especially with the fake of the fullback. The flanker block was a stalk block, because of the predicted man coverage and his past threats. Consequently, everything was dependent on the tight end's block. As the play was called for the first time in a second and four situation, we were driving to our first score and all eyes of the coaching staff were fixed intently on our tight end. We watched Bob Moore flex about three feet from the strong tackle and assumed the defensive end would take the gap. To our utter frustration, he stayed on the outside shoulder of Bob. Bob then moved another foot; the defensive man didn't budge from that outside position. All of our plans and preparation, it appeared, were voided by a matter of a step or two that the defensive man refused to make. It was only natural to assume that our quarterback would check off the play. On the contrary, he proceeded with the play that on the drawing board would appear to have no chance for success. In running the far back sweep, it would be too much—and virtually impossible—to ask the tight end to block a man aligned on his outside shoulder. However, Moore, through countless hours of coaching and preparation, also realized that something was wrong with our plan. Now it became a matter of the success or failure of the human equation. He knew what his job was: it was not defined to pin the defensive end to his inside because he took the gap alignment; rather, it was to tie him up and perhaps finish a block that would place him between the defensive end and the ball carrier. He performed the classic block: face right into the letter, with tremendous extension. He knocked the defensive man back off the line and then whipped his right elbow around to get what we refer to as the wall-off, or finished position, in maintaining that block until Jackie Brown and Dan Lightfoot had skipped around the corner and into the end zone for our first score.

This not only was the answer to the human equation; it was a lesson in self-expression. Although the definition of exactness was not all that the coaches had told Moore it would be, he nonetheless had the ability to recognize his assignment and get the job done.

The ingenuity conceived and carried out by Bob Moore reflects his ability to think on his feet. It was fulfilling to our coaching staff that he put into practice the coach's philosophy, "No matter what the circumstances, adjust to them and *get the job done*."

The story of Jim Plunkett, All-American and Heisman and Maxwell trophy winner, is a reflection of all five of the precepts in which we believe. Jim is an outstanding athlete of Mexican-American extraction who was born and who grew up in the most humble of circumstances. Although it was necessary for him to aid his family financially by working after school, weekends, and during vacations, he found time to excel in football, wrestling, and baseball while in high school. He was honored as an All-Northern California high school quarterback, went to the state finals in two successive years as a 191-pound wrestler, and pitched solid baseball for James Lick High School in San Jose. With all of these activities and home responsibilities, he compiled a 3.3 overall grade point average. As a reflection of his outstanding ability, he was chosen, along with another Northern California quarterback, to participate in the North-South Shrine High School football game held in Southern California each Summer. After the players reported for practice, the coaches determined that the other quarterback was better equipped to lead the North team, and Jim was assigned the position of defensive end — a spot unfamiliar to him. The coaches made a wise decision because Jim's competitor for the job was a better quarterback at that time. The sequel to the story is that five years later Jim was the finest football player in the nation; the boy who played ahead of him in the all-star game failed to win a starting collegiate assignment. What caused the Plunkett transformation?

To begin with, Jim's freshman year was rather mediocre. Going into Spring practice, he was a fourth-string quarterback. Although invited back early with the varsity squad during his sophomore year, we decided to "redshirt" him. This gave him a year to mature physically and an opportunity to improve his technical skills through observation and practice. His intensity was such that if he were told to throw the ball two hundred times, he threw it five hundred times. While running the scout squad, he was dumped by on-charging linemen innumerable times; he resolutely got up and was ready to call a vulnerable pass/run option on the succeeding play. In my total coaching experience, no one worked so hard or so long at his trade than Jim Plunkett in his quest for excellence.

Returning to competition during his "redshirt" sophomore year, Jim was an instant success and at the conclusion of the season was named to the Pacific-8 All-Conference team. He did not become complacent; rather, he continued to work more diligently. Plunkett worked on such routine practice drills as the five-step drop and throwing the ball into a net until he was near exhaustion. His willingness to sacrifice and to pay the price to improve made him the top athlete on the West Coast during his junior year, and he further was mentioned on several All-America teams. Rather than riding the crest, this recognition appeared to give Jim renewed intensity; at the start of his senior year his goal first and foremost was a dual team goal: to win the conference and to take Stanford to the Rose Bowl for the first time in nineteen years; and second, to be the number one football player in the nation. His dedication, attitude, willingness to learn, and team leadership took us to the Rose Bowl; those same qualities made it possible for him to reach his secondary goal of winning both the Heisman and Maxwell trophies.

We cite these vivid illustrations to point out some of the reasons young men choose coaching as a profession. It should not be a choice based on hoped-for fame, glory, or financial return. The satisfactions usually come from the athletes themselves and the lessons that they learn and "give back" to the coach on the athletic field. We often refer to these lessons as "indelible impressions" that will guide a young man through his entire life. Having an opportunity to be a part of creating some of the indelible impressions is the cherished responsibility of a football coach, and it probably is the prime reason he is in coaching and working with today's athletes.

Many young men have incorporated sports as an integral part of their lives; yet they are not certain that they have the motivation or qualifications to become coaches. There are a number of avenues that a young man may explore to determine whether he would enjoy coaching as well as he does playing. Enthusiastic and dedicated young men always are in demand to work after school, weekends, and Summers at public playgrounds and recreation areas; most Summer camps employ recreational and sports counselors; Little League, American Legion baseball, Pop Warner leagues, and church and civic groups generally welcome young athletes to help with their programs. When a student reaches the college level — particularly when he is in graduate school — he often can obtain a position as a teaching assistant to a coach or physical education teacher. All of these outlets, or any one of them, should give a young man sufficient exposure to determine whether he likes coaching or whether coaching likes him. It is a two-way street. The prospective or practicing coach must realize that the game essentially belongs to the players. The primary justification for including sports in the educational development of young people rests upon the dual premise that it provides both physical and character values for those who are engaged in the game. The burden of determining that these values become a reality rests primarily with the men in the profession.

3

What Is Coaching?

In the past six years, American educational institutions have faced crises of greater magnitude than ever before in history. Militant student and liberal, restless, faculty members have engaged in a variety of activities ranging from peaceful dissent to overt rebellion. Although relatively few in number, the dissident factions have altered, if not changed, the face of American education.

The era has produced a new breed of students and a new breed of athletes. Open hostility and dissension have been manifested by a significant sub-culture of students. The coach's authority has been questioned in such diverse areas as personal appearance and competitive values. Some high schools and colleges have experienced racial crises, accompanied by demands for admission of more black and other minority athletes. Similar ultimatums have been made in relation to the hiring of coaches from representative ethnic groups.

The academicians have responded in reshaping and modifying curricula. Whole new programs of study have been instituted. Accordingly, the role of the coach has changed significantly. He no longer stands alone as a coach, the entity; his position has become that of teacher first, coach second.

We agree with the necessity and appropriateness of new philosophies and programs embraced by educational institutions. We also agree that coaches must react to new trends. He must not become locked into outdated attitudes, prejudices, or outmoded social structures. As sociological changes emerge, so must the coach be aware of the necessity of altering, modifying, or revamping his long-practiced philosophy of the human and technical aspects of football.

However, notwithstanding concessions on what may appear to be radical changes in response to social requisites, the coach's authoritative and responsible competence must prevail. For the coach to ascertain success, he is tested in nine, ten, or perhaps eleven two-hour sessions on either Friday afternoon, Friday evening, or Saturday during the Fall of the year. His teaching will be put to a test in front of a multitude of judges. He must have the necessary insight and understanding to be able to communicate openly and effectively with the athletes who come under his direction. He must have the athlete totally prepared physically and mentally as he readies himself for the final exam which comes on game day.

The teaching of physical skills relates to the mind more than ever before in sports' history. Today's student-athlete must be motivated to learn with greater efficiency and flexibility primarily because outside pressures and demands never have been greater. He who motivates is a teacher. It is the teacher-coach who captures the essential spirit of an athletic program in a manner that is marked by integrity, imagination, and understanding.

All too often in this era of stress and turbulence, the coach does not take the time nor effort to evaluate himself, particularly in terms of the athletes with whom he works. Educators generally agree that coaches should be judged by the same criteria as other members of the faculty. As long as forty-six years ago Knute Rockne recognized the coach's role as a teacher and expressed evaluations succinctly: "The coach has to be a super teacher. He must see to it that the class learns what he has to teach. If he flunks half the class, he flunks with them. It is not what a coach knows, it is what he can teach his boys, what he can make them do." (Knute Rockne, *Coaching*, 1925, p. 209)

Teaching aids and methods of evaluation have improved immeasurably since Coach Rockne's observations. They will continue to improve. Already we rely heavily upon television, sophisticated scouting and recruiting techniques, and refined staff and player personnel procedures. These products of technology contribute to increased efficiency in learning and in freeing coaches to give more individual attention to their players and detailed planning. But they are not the total and final answers.

Perhaps Emerson was looking to this Age of Technology when he advised, "Not he is great who can alter matter, but he who can alter my state of mind." In this context, we are making large and significant demands of the teacher-coach, but we will have a successful program only when we make these demands and when we require him to assume a primary role as an educator.

In a 1959 report by the American Council of Education, it was found in a survey that there was unanimous agreement among students in a variety of institutions that they value far more highly the faculty member who is willing to make known his own commitments. It, therefore, is axiomatic that teachers should understand themselves and their goals as well as their students. We often neglect to consider that the psychology of the teacher is equally as complex as that of the learner. What occurs on the practice or game field is the process of interaction of student and teacher, and between the individual athlete and squad as a group. The teacher-coach is a vital element in this process of interaction. Developing an understanding of the athlete or student essentially is a problem of understanding human motivation.

What, then, constitutes and enhances interaction between the teacher-coach and his players? "He, [the teacher] must first of all be aflame with interest himself, at least in his own specialty. So aflame, indeed, that it is easy for him to light the torches of youth. If he possesses enthusiasm which grows out of abundant and sound knowledge, he is likely to be successful."[1]

This quality or characteristic in modern sports is not the "do or die" half-time rhetoric that was appropriate and effective forty years ago, or even more recently. Rather, it is a sincere, deliberate, and enthusiastic outcry for something of value. Real enthusiasm, faith, and quiet confidence are contagious.

An aware teacher-coach must realize the enormity of the task before him. He must recognize the tremendous influence he has on the athletes that come under his direction. The lessons he teaches on the athletic field will carry over into later life and will provide guidelines for a young man to accept his responsibility in his chosen profession, his family, and the community in which he lives. We have referred previously to these lessons as "indelible impressions." They take the form of pursuit of purpose, teamwork, dedication, perseverance, and the vital lesson that ultimate success in any endeavor comes through the willingness to sacrifice and pay the price to excel.

Coaching is a painfully slow process even under the best of conditions. It often may appear all the slower because of the coach's familiarity with his subject. How many times must this drill be repeated? When will that blocking assignment become instinctive? There is no miracle for the teacher-coach. A thoughtful and perceptive teacher-coach knows the limitations as well as the capabilities of his team members, and he does not unnerve and confuse his players by attempting to force them to assimilate and digest more rapidly than is possible with their mental and physical equipment. A successful teacher-coach becomes a living reflection of what he teaches. He must believe in what he is doing, why he is doing it, and the direction in which he is going. He must exude enthusiasm, dedication, interest, and faith. He must be flexible in what he teaches and the manner in which he teaches. He must be

---

[1]Briggs, T. H. *Secondary Education,* The Macmillan Company, 1933, p. 533.

a winner all the way and strive for excellence in everything he does. *He must want to win as badly as a coach as he did as a player.* A coach must possess a pride in his responsibility which, in turn, will carry over to his players.

Because a coach is such a vital part of a young man's life, he must always set the proper examples. Not only must we inspire our athletes to perform their best, but we must inspire their best behavior. A coach must practice personal integrity, not only in his associations with the team, but in his personal life both on and off the football field. At the same time, a coach must develop early in his career the ability to cope with adversity and not to blame his staff or players. If one is to take the bows and applause, he must learn to accept defeat with humility. However, the ability to bounce back from extreme adversity and to hit the practice field with renewed enthusiasm is a constant requisite. A coach must realize that the only way to reverse the tide and to get back on the positive side is to work even harder in his teaching, preparation, and attention to detail.

Following a discussion of why a young man should or should not seek the coaching profession for his life's work, it only follows that one must determine just what *is* a coach.

Here is at least a partial list of what we consider to be the basic ingredients that a coach should have:

1. An inspiration to students and an ability to command faculty respect.
2. Friendly and helpful to team members and students.
3. Tireless worker.
4. Colorful and imaginative—ability to operate under the public's eye with dignity, gentlemanly appearance, and sportsmanlike conduct.
5. Good disciplinarian—helpful attitude but respectful control.
6. Capacity for organizing recruiting program if coaching at the college level.
7. Commitment to operate program within the rules of his league or conference.
8. Ability to fit into the athletic department organization and cooperate in overall program.
9. Understanding of the role of students and respect for students in nonathletic activities.
10. A good organizer and administrator. Must have executive ability to get the most out of those employed by him.
11. Flexibility in his coaching methods, techniques, system.

4

Responsibilities and Spheres of Influence

The title of "Football coach" at all levels carries with it responsibilities and spheres of influence that are unending, and the prospective or practicing coach must be willing to "pay the price" that accompanies these obligations. It would appear that no single person is answerable to so many. However, all of his "constituents" are integral parts of the total football program. The coach's circle of interested persons and agencies includes the players, the institution's administration, his fellow coaches, the academic faculty, the various media that cover sports events, the community, and the alumni.

Before delineating the coach's responsibility and sphere of influence, it is necessary to consider the basic principles that apply in this unique profession. It all begins and ends with the adoption and application of a sound code of ethics. The profession continually must advance and earn the respect of participants, the institution, the community, and the active participants in the sport. Rules and regulations are designed to govern as well as to advance the sport. This is a cherished responsibility that a coach must foster on behalf of himself, his associates in the department, and his colleagues in the profession. Without genuine and wholehearted acceptance and practical application of the tenets which that responsibility represents, it cannot become an effective instrument in the solution of the problems which have brought occasional criticism and discredit to the game. The reputation of the coaching profession, and the fine influence that the game of football can exert upon the American people, depends in large measure upon the manner in which coaches live up to both the letter and the spirit of the code of ethics. High trust and confidence is placed upon coaches, and this position is typified by the comment of one of the nation's outstanding college presidents when he said: "The coach is an important person in every hamlet, village, and city throughout the land, oftentimes a better known and more influential teacher of the young than his colleagues in other branches of teaching."

Every present or prospective coach doubtlessly has formed his own personal code of ethics. However, he additionally should learn well the stated objectives of the American Football Coaches Association: "To help maintain the highest possible standards in football and the football coaching profession, to work together for the improvement of conditions in American football, and to promote the coaching profession." (Article I, by-laws.)

A coach first must be aware continuously of the great power of influence that he wields in his relationship with his players. He must recognize that this powerful influence will have a long-standing effect, either positively or negatively, depending upon the coach himself. Society entrusts to coaches its dearest possessions—the youth of America—and through his own example, the coach always must be certain that the athletes who have played under him are finer and more decent men for having that exposure. The ability to instill the highest desirable ideals of character traits in players is a heavy responsibility that rests on the shoulders of the coach, and it is through his teaching that the youths should develop foundations of healthy competition and respect for one another. Coaches must be sincerely interested in their players, not only as athletes on the field, but as students and individuals off the field. Often a player will take a personal problem to his coach when he wouldn't consider approaching his parents or school counselor. The coach must be ready to accept this responsibility and to be ready and qualified to give aid and counsel. The coach should keep an open-door policy and be available to discuss sports, courses of study, jobs, personal or adjustment problems, and just *be there* as someone with whom to talk. At the college level, the coach should be knowledgeable regarding majors, courses of study, new programs; he should be familiar with graduate programs, and he should work closely with the school's placement office in aiding seniors to obtain interviews for possible employment when they graduate.

Because a coach is a member of the academic community, he accepts the responsibility of keeping his program in the proper perspective and within the total scope of the school or university. An awareness of the department's standards, budgets, objectives, and policies will create harmony and improve working conditions and personal relationships. An individual coach should not feel that his is the only sport in the department; rather, he should support all athletic programs and encourage his athletes to participate in more than one sport if they wish.

In too many instances, the athletic department is isolated from the rest of the school community either because of geographic location or by philosophy. The head coach should make every conceivable effort to establish a close relationship among the administration, the faculty, and the athletic department. Often the impetus must originate with the coaching staff. There is a number of ways in which this can be accomplished. For example, the head coach or one of his assistants should be assigned to eat in the faculty room or the Faculty Club at least once a week. To assure a coach's desire to be open minded, he and his representatives should make it a point to share lunch with both those faculty members who are sympathetic to, and critical of, the sports program.

Several years ago we instituted a program at Stanford in which we invite four or five professors to join the squad for breakfast and during the taping and dressing period on game day and then follow us through the entire game. This includes viewing the game from the sidelines, spending at least a quarter in the press box, observing halftime procedures, and attending the press conference after the game. We also have included faculty and administrators on most of our road trips. From the positive responses, and requests to be included on the guest list, we know that this procedure is successful and enhances our program in the eyes of the academicians. Many of them attend several practices prior to the games to which they are invited to familiarize themselves with our plans for the upcoming game.

Similarly, post-game gatherings on Monday aid in getting members of the academic community sold on the sports program. For example, we initiated at Utah State a program to show films to the faculty of our previous week's game. The first year, about twenty persons attended; four years later, we averaged an audience of over two hundred persons.

A coach also must be available at all times to represent his program to the student body. He should be ready to make speeches at rallies, appear before smaller student clubs and living groups, and generally be a spokesman for his program.

Few coaches have to be told that the alumni closely react to their school's fortunes and failures on the football field. In colleges, particularly, the alumni often control the purse-strings and the professional future of the coaches. Our best advice is to organize the alumni to the degree that they too become a vital part of the football program. In effect, they can be the coach's most valuable representatives in the communities in which they live. Through the athletic department, it is wise to form booster clubs throughout the state or regionally. In the case of high schools, local Dad's clubs and women's auxiliaries are effective. They should be encouraged to stage dinners, barbecues, golf tournaments, or film showings—anything that will promote the school's program. These activities must be noted on the coach's calendar, and he or one of his representatives should attend. The alumni in most instances are sold on their alma mater; now it is the coach's job to sell them on him, his team, and his program. This pays off not only in interest, but in alerting coaches to prospective athletes, increased attendance at games, and a genuine concern for the goals of both the athletic department and the university. In this era of campus discontent, the easiest commodity to sell is sports, so the best use of it should be made.

In discussing the news media, it must be pointed out that a coach should develop a natural public relations touch. He should be readily available at all times. He must be cordial, tactful, have a good sense of news value, and be ready to offer information regarding his practice sessions, team statistics, starting line-ups, and the injury status of his personnel. We are the first to admit that it isn't always easy for a coach to be patient and virtuous regarding the treatment of the press. But remember the axiom: "The only way you can argue with a newspaper is to start a publication of your own." However, in most cases, newspaper, radio, and television sports personalities can be dealt with through courtesy, by supplying information, and by including them in game planning and preparation that will not jeopardize your upcoming contest. Probably the best advice is to treat the news media with honesty and candor. Once they catch you off base, there is no going back. For a number of years, we have conducted a pre-season clinic for the sportswriters and broadcasters in the area. We explain our basic offensive formations and defensive alignments, and any other pertinent information that will aid them in interpreting and communicating our games to their readers and listeners. This is a courtesy to the media, but it also provides some insurance that they will be able to explain to the public a little better just what we are trying to accomplish on the field and in our program.

Beyond the boundaries of the school, it is the duty of the coach to make himself available to the citizens of the community in which the institution is located. This is particularly important for a new coach. A natural start is to ask a friend to sponsor your membership in a luncheon or civic club. This will round out the coach's total exposure to the school and town community, and through this will come understanding and respect for the entire program. If a coach succeeds in getting *everyone* involved in his program, he will have developed a sense of loyalty and responsibility to himself, his staff, the school, and the team.

The members of the town and faculty who become sold on the coach's philosophy, his players, his school, and his program will be his best salesmen. Institutions usually are located in or near communities that take pride in their achievements and in being recognized. Coaches should make their community feel a definite part of the athletic program. In return, he should be available to participate in programs that will make the community a better place in which to live. The success of this two-fold effort will be evident in the stadium or bleachers on Friday night or Saturday afternoon.

Because of the emphasis that we place on campus and community relations, we recommend highly that students preparing for the coaching profession include in their curriculum a sound course in public speaking. Coaches must be able to present themselves in an easy, confident, and knowledgeable manner.

Whether or not this course of study has been included in his preparation for a career, the present or prospective coach should consider taking classes similar to the Dale Carnegie or PACE (Personal and Corporate Effectiveness) course on human relations. It will assist him in his everyday involvement with his players and associates and improve his self-image and his ability to speak publicly. It will also help him to clarify goals—his own and his team's—and to make the most of his potential.

Wherever a coach appears, whether as a speaker or as a non-participating guest, he must remember that he is on public display as a representative of the institution for which he works. Further, his actions, words, and deeds represent the entire profession. Therefore, he must conduct himself in such a manner that he maintains the principles, the integrity, and the dignity of his institution, his players, his colleagues, and the profession. It is only through such conduct that the profession can earn and maintain its rightful place in our educational program and make its full contribution to the American way of life. The conduct and character of a coach must be consistent and clearly delineated. His character and personality must clearly communicate the reality of his nature. This cannot be accomplished solely through the communication of speech, but in the coach's mannerisms and his entire character. And this character must not be adopted or adapted from another person or any other model; it must be his own; *he must be himself.* The coach must be eager for professional growth, through associations with other coaches, through attendance at clinics, and through reading all available professional literature.

When he appears in public, the coach must present an appearance that will enhance himself and all of those connected with the sport. One of the prime outlets for displaying his high-level professionalism is the content and manner in which he conducts himself on the speaker's platform.

Speeches

It is the wise coach who develops a unique and interesting speaking style. He must realize that his audience may be a small Parent Teachers Association, religious group, a booster club, the annual squad dinner, an alumni organization, a civic club, or a clinic attended by his colleagues.

We remember full well our apprehensions and mistakes in our first speaking engagements, and we here share with the prospective or inexperienced coach some of the techniques we have devised.

Our information, coupled with the public speaking training that is offered many physical education majors in college, should afford inexperienced speakers with at least a semblance of confidence — the key to effective public speaking.

The most important aspect of public speaking is to be oneself. Leave the levity to Don Rickles or some other accomplished comedian. We do not suggest that there is no room for humor; however, it must fit into the personality of the coach and into the program that he is promoting. The sincere speaker who has a message is the most well received. We believe that a speech not only can be informational but motivational as well; it can, and should, have meaning for both student and adult groups who are looking to the coach for leadership. Additionally, many of the quotations cited by the speaker also can be printed on cards and posted in the squad locker and training room. Both speeches and written messages can reflect what has been learned by the coach in his experience as a student-participant and as a coach. He must share this information with those who are seeking guidance.

Many great technicians on the football field have failed miserably at the banquet table. Public speaking is not as difficult as it may appear. A critical self-analysis is half of the battle, and diligent practice will do the rest in establishing confidence.

The speaker's task is to accomplish more than merely uttering a few trite phrases. He must have a specific message and deliver it in a warm and sincere manner. The speaker may possess the world's greatest message, but it will die a lingering death if the audience does not accept him.

Similar to going into a game, preparation is all important. It is not enough to jot down a few ideas and "fly from the seat of your pants." This usually will result in a disjointed, meaningless speech that will convey nothing but a series of anecdotes. Good speeches always are prepared well beforehand, and they carry a message for the particular audience.

Here are some suggested guidelines:

1. *Know* your audience and *what* they expect from you.
2. Use note cards; *do not* memorize or read your speeches.
3. Try to establish a relationship with the audience so they will consider you *one* of them.
4. The introduction to the speech should:
   a. Establish a desirable rapport between you and the audience.
   b. Arouse interest in what you have to say by showing how it applies to the interests and needs of the audience.
   c. Set forth and clarify the basic ideas which are to be discussed.
5. The discussion period of the speech should accomplish these goals:

a. It should deal with the details of the subject that the introduction said it would.

b. It should develop each of these phases with details that are specific and within the listeners' experiences.

c. It should use transitional means to illustrate the relationship and sequence of ideas.

6. The speaker is the most vital element in the whole scheme. If he appears bored, the audience will reflect that emotion; conversely, if the speaker is enthusiastic and is vitally interested in his subject area, the audience will be caught up in what he has to say.

7. Look at the audience and talk with them. Do not deliver your speech to the back of the room or out of the window.

8. Tell the truth, even if it hurts. Don't be afraid to admit your mistakes; however temper your mistakes with judicious mention of where you and your program have been successful.

9. Be sure to speak in the English tongue – don't become wrapped up in football terminology to the point the non-oriented will be lost and unable to follow your message.

10. Say something nice about the opposition that your team played last year. Offer no alibis.

11. Build up your team; players must receive recognition, and if parents and friends are in the audience, all the better.

12. Don't try to cover too much material. It is better to say a little well than to say a lot poorly or in a shallow manner.

13. Assemble speech notes in outline form and write them on a three-by-five card. This will prevent memorization and result in a natural delivery and positive audience response.

Most importantly, do not stray from the reason you were asked to speak: the speaker owes it to his hosts to give the audience the benefit of his years of experience and knowledge and to sincerely present a message that relates what the coaching profession means to both the staff, the players, and to the community.

Speakers before high school athletes, particularly, should be wary of relating stories involving football personalities of yesteryear – yesteryear for high school players is only about two years ago. Nothing is so meaningless and foreign to a high school student than being forced to listen to the exploits of a college football hero of even a couple of years past. In the first place, that college hero may never have been heard of by a boy who was in elementary or junior high school at the time; secondly, the hero now may be an "old timer" and a "has been" who, in the minds of youngsters, must be ready for a senior citizens home even though in reality he is only twenty-six years old. The young athletes are playing *now*; they want to hear about what is going on *now*.

Although we mentioned earlier that a coach who is not oriented toward comedic expression should realize his limitations, a certain amount of light humor will place the audience at ease. It also can be used effectively throughout the speech as periodic punctuation points for relief from the more serious discussion.

There are several expressions of humor that can be used to break the ice, and one of the best techniques is for the speaker initially to make himself the butt of a joke. For example, he might recite the story of a boy who told his father that he was out for the football team. At the end of the day, the father asked the youngster how he performed.

"Dad," the boy replied, "they discovered I couldn't block, I couldn't tackle, and I couldn't pass. All I could do was make a lot of noise and yell, so they made a coach out of me."

Or a coach could comment on his experiences as a player:

"Our line was so good that day, that even our own backfield couldn't get through it."

Addressing an alumni group that always is interested in spectator interest, the speaker is reminded of his own alma mater:

"I can remember when the crowds at our games were so lousy that if someone called to find out what time the game started, I asked them just what time they would like to have it begin."

Then again, the new coach in the community might be speaking before a civic club and remind the members that his predecessor failed to win any of ten games. "This will never happen to me," he promises; "I'm only going to schedule nine games."

Speeches—regardless of the audience—must be comprised of a recipe of sound information, intelligent commentary on today's football and the modern athlete; it should contain the added spice of humor. However, most speaking engagements can be an outlet for inspirational messages, particularly if the audience is composed of high school and college athletes. These are the messages referred to earlier that can serve a dual purpose of being posted in the training and dressing rooms. Although some pseudo-sophisticated athletes may brand them as passé, appropriate quotations strike the target.

Consider these:

"Confidence, like disease, is contagious."

"Success is nothing but a good idea coupled with hard work."

"A champion wants to be a champion, believes he can be a champion, works like a champion, and becomes a champion."

"Play hard but fair. Don't get kicked out of the game. You can't make any tackles sitting on the bench."

"You will play on Friday (or Saturday) the way you practice during the week."

"A quiet thinking team before the game is a loud happy team after the game."

Serious notes also should be introduced to indicate the sincerity of purpose of the coaches and the players. We believe that these particular messages are appropriate in speaking before squad banquets or father-and-son get-togethers.

We mentioned earlier that the Stanford coaches and squad members offer silent prayer and the Lord's Prayer prior to taking the field on game day. The following Athlete's Prayer would be appropriate for such an occasion or at the conclusion of a speech, something that would give the audience serious pause:

> Dear Lord, in this battle that goes on through life,
> I ask but a field that is fair.
> A chance to compete with all in the strife,
> and courage to strive and to dare.
> And if I should win, let it be by the code,
> With my faith and my honor held high.
> And if I should lose,
> Let me stand by the road and cheer as the winner goes by.

5

Levels of Teaching

It is essential that a prospective or practicing coach has the ability to make a self evaluation to determine the appropriate level at which he wishes to coach. He should examine himself thoroughly regarding the enjoyment he receives from the many facets represented in the coaching profession. If he enjoys pure teaching, perhaps he would be happier and better off at the junior or senior high school level. If he enjoys building programs, he will progress from one level to another according to his success. In all cases, he should determine what the word "success" means to *him* as a guideline. He should establish goals that are realistic and then set out to achieve them, ready to work as enthusiastically and as long as is necessary to get the job done.

Goal-setting is one of the most important considerations that must be made early in a coach's career, or while he is training to be a coach. It is necessary to engage in some self-analysis to determine the level at which a person wishes to coach, his ambitions for additional responsibilities, and just exactly what he personally wants to achieve in the profession. Once the guidelines are established, it is not difficult to set the smaller goals that ultimately lead to the major goals.

We realize that it is extremely difficult for a college student to foresee the future and to make definite long-term goals. It is obvious that it is much easier to get to the end of the road if a person knows the path beforehand. Discussions with coaches who can serve as counselors, plus the constant introspection and self-analysis, should assist the coaching aspirant in the setting of long-term goals. Self-analysis and evaluation must be practiced by the coach who is in his first few years of the profession. He must (1) recognize present abilities; (2) determine progress; and (3) make future plans.

Whether we are considering the prospective or present coach, there are countless opportunities in the profession that are available to the deserving person who sets his goals. It is not enough to be mad with ambition to the point that one becomes blind to the importance of experience. Doing a satisfactory job at all levels will provide the opportunity for advancement. There is a fixed number of desirable major institutions at the collegiate level; whereas, there are many, many more outstanding coaches coming into the profession each year. This makes the profession extremely competitive, which in turn, requires superior qualifications and constant self-improvement and self-evaluation for a coach to enjoy a successful career. However, we do not wish to discourage the beginning coach; we merely want him to keep open to all available avenues. For example, there is a need for qualified coaches wherever there is organized competition among junior high schools, secondary schools, prep schools, colleges, and sports clubs. This is the time for self-evaluation: many men prefer to remain at the junior or senior high school level because these comprise the formative years for young men. Impressionable youths at these age levels have a willingness and enthusiasm for learning, and in many instances more pure teaching can take place at this point in their education. Additionally, if the learning and improvement of skills can be achieved at this age level, the carryover into later life is immeasurable. Too many persons believe that building a total program can be realized only at the college or university level. However, a very refined program can be built in junior high school, Little League, Pop Warner League, or in high school if the merits of the program are presented in an attractive and acceptable manner.

In evaluating one's goals and available positions in the profession, the nature of the profession must be considered – the attractive as well as the unattractive features. Although instructing athletes undoubtedly will occupy a large part of the coach's time, many jobs that are available in the field are not solely in the realm of coaching. Most coaches at the junior and senior high school levels must additionally teach physical education classes or academic courses, or both, in addition to spending many hours preparing teams for interschool competition. It is only when coaches reach the college level or become head coach of a large secondary school that their activities normally are confined solely to coaching. Qualifying for a position of this type, however, usually means a coach must compile a respectable record and maintain it; otherwise, he may again be required to divide his time between the classroom and the field as he did on the way up the ladder.

However, regardless of the level a coach chooses, or the amount of time he is alloted for his athletic duties, it must be remembered that football – or any other sport – is merely part of a young man's total education. A coach is part of the faculty; sports are part of the institution's total program.

Once again, we note that the coach, particularly the beginning coach, must be willing to be flexible in all of his endeavors—not solely in football considerations. He must constantly re-evaluate himself, perhaps revise his setting of goals, and be flexible within the school in which he coaches and/or teaches.

Although, my ambition since I was a youngster was someday to be a head coach at a college or university, I recognized that it would be necessary to set smaller goals and remain flexible while I worked toward my long-range goal. A self-evaluation indicated that a variety of experiences would be necessary to become properly qualified to achieve my long-range goal. When I completed my college education, therefore, I concluded that five years of high school experience would be both necessary and sufficient. This period of time was broken down into two years as an assistant coach and three years as head coach. It was at this point that I decided that it would be important to be in a college position, preferably at the four-year level. A step of three years in a junior college might have been desirable; however, if a person ultimately wants to coach at a four-year school, he should attempt to get there as soon as possible after an initial five years of experience. I wish to emphasize, however, that it is important to be a head coach at the high school level in order to experience trial and error in the process of making final decisions. Somewhere along the line, a man just has to be the boss prior to being thrown into a major college position. These are the guidelines that worked so very well for me; but they easily could be adjusted for each individual depending upon the person and his available experiences. Valuable experience can also be gained by being a head freshman coach in college as well as serving as a graduate assistant for one of the many successful programs that are available.

Frequently, coaches who are aware of my background ask my advice regarding the type of education that they should obtain. Because coaching involves the teaching of physical skills, a physical education major in college is advisable. This provides the student with the option of entering the discipline of teaching in either the academic or activity areas. The minor field of a physical education major can be varied. Although personal interest should be the major criterion, your studies should include courses broad enough to give the prospective coach a wide base of understanding and knowledge.

It is our recommendation in this era of the "new coach" that, if at all possible, a student obtain a master's degree either while in college or during the first few Summers of his first coaching job. Most colleges require this degree before a candidate is considered for a position. There are a number of programs available in which a student can obtain both a general secondary credential and a master's degree by carrying a slightly greater or longer study program. It is well worth it, because not everyone is willing, nor has the opportunity, to give up Summer vacations while teaching to attend school to obtain the advanced degree.

There are many institutions that are renowned for their physical education curriculum. For the dedicated personality, this may not be as important as the type of collegiate athletic program and the personnel who direct it. However, we believe that most athletes choose their schools on the basis of their self-image of their participation in the future athletic program and/or their relationship with the coach. Many athletes hope to be able to participate at the professional level after graduation, and this affects their choice. Others wish to stay at their alma mater as an assistant coach, while still others want to strike out on their own. The choice is a singularly individual one. However, notwithstanding all of the variables in the coaching profession, this above all stands true: If a young coach has a burning ambition to get to the top of his profession, he must be willing to make all types of sacrifices. Coaches do not have an eight-to-five job, five days a week, regardless of the level at which they coach. A coach's willingness to spend many long hours improving his own coaching knowledge and performing the countless details which surround his task more often than not spell the difference between mediocrity and success.

A coaching candidate for a position in a higher level also must recognize the age-old adage of "being in the right place at the right time." This, of course, is not always predictable. However, this circumstance makes it even more imperative that young coaches attend clinics, conferences, league meetings, and other professional gatherings where he will become known and where he will have an opportunity to become acquainted with his coaching colleagues. Many a chance meeting has led to a step up the ladder.

6

Coach-Player Relationship

"Relevancy" has been a much overworked word in the past few years on campuses across the nation. However, there is nothing more relevant than athletics because they are experiences unto themselves. Athletes are shown every day that *real* experiences aren't always in the future, an accusation that constantly is hurled at the purely academic community. *Real* experiences in sports unfold during every practice and during every game.

In reviewing twenty years of coaching experience, we are aware that today's athletes are much more involved in a variety of activities than ever before. They have many and diverse interests which, in turn, have to be considered as a coach sets his long-term goals for each individual in relation to his total program. Not too long ago, an athlete spent all of his spare time in athletics and did not have the myriad of outside interests. However, now they are more aware of current events, social changes, politics, and school policies as they affect not only their own institution but other schools, agencies, and groups of people. Today's athlete considers sports but one part of his total life. Coaches now are competing with a multitude of desires, idealistic causes, fads, and attractive distractions. Many of these were unknown or went without notice a few years ago, but they are very real now. A player takes pride in being respected as a student and an *aware person* as well as an athlete.

One very personal and heartwarming experience will explain the values to today's athlete:

Following the Rose Bowl game, I had the pleasure of going on over to the Hula Bowl and working with the North team in a victory over the South 45-32. Three members of the Ohio State team, Rex Kern, John Brockington, and Jim Stillwagon were members of our North squad. I was tremendously impressed with these three young men because there were no sour grapes regarding their loss to Stanford in the Rose Bowl. There was nothing but a great feeling of respect on the part of these three individuals with our three participants on the same team, Bob Moore, John Sande, and Jim Plunkett. In fact, I can't think of six finer young men to be found anywhere; they reflect truly great examples of the values produced through intercollegiate athletics.

Normally during the week, the practice sessions were all scheduled for the mornings. However, on Thursday the morning was set aside for a Pearl Harbor cruise which was over at approximately 2 o'clock in the afternoon. We had set our practice schedule for 3 o'clock, and as I was entering the Honolulu Stadium locker room one of the team managers handed me a clipping from the morning paper. There was a 13-year-old boy in one of the local hospitals who was suffering from a terminal illness, and his one request was to see a real live football player from the mainland. I was quite taken with the article and passed it along to Jim Plunkett. Jim indicated he would be very happy to see the boy that evening and take some of the other players with him.

We boarded our bus and headed for McKinley High School, the site of our practice sessions. As we hit the field, I realized that there was one member of our squad missing. It was Rex Kern, the Ohio State quarterback. He showed up at the practice about eighteen minutes late, and when I asked him what had happened, he indicated that he had a stop to make at a local hospital. Rex had seen the article in the paper that morning and did not need any prompting as to what was expected of him. He had already been to the hospital to see the boy. This outstanding young man possesses the great human qualities that we would love to have in our own sons. He is truly a credit to intercollegiate football and to the University that he represents.

This is but one example of the reason today's coach must be aware of outside interests, however admirable they may be, and structure his emphasis on motivation accordingly.

Other types of players tend to want to know the reasons they are asked to perform certain tasks in order to enhance their position on the squad. Blind devotion to a common cause and the authoritative approach by the coach in achieving results is history. Open communication in the recognition of an athlete's needs and the clarification of his problems — real or imagined — are more evident and more essential in solving than ever before.

In an essay written by Dr. Wesley K. Ruff of the Stanford Physical Education Department, it is pointed out that perhaps education, child-rearing practices, affluence, and financial security all have contributed to the development of a new college student. The modern student, he says, arrives at college with an attitude of evaluation and inquiry that is unprecedented in America or anywhere else. "In an atmosphere of social reconstruction such as we are currently experiencing, it should not come as a surprise to anyone that decision making procedures, administrative arrangements, facility priorities, program priorities, goals, and personnel might be subject to attack in the form of criticism. It is my opinion, that most personal assaults are actually symbolic attacks against the 'system.'"

It is against this backdrop that Dr. Ruff sees the role of the coach as that of counselor, teacher, and administrator. As a counselor, he may help the athlete with a myriad of problems. The problems may be solved by the coach through his observation of the athlete's form, style, or attitude—athletic or in his personal conduct.

With these inter-relationships between coach and player, a mutual respect develops very rapidly. For the individual player—as sophisticated as he may be—he is stripped of all forms of worldliness when he is faced with extreme adversity in such an emotional game as football. He must possess "controlled emotion" in order to perform disciplined and intelligent reactions to constantly changing situations. He must learn to react efficiently and immediately in this violent game of man-to-man contact. In my realm of experience, the whole issue was epitomized by the late General Douglas MacArthur when I heard him speak before the American Football Coaches Association a few years ago:

He spoke of the very backbone of our American soldier as possessing "courage, stamina, and coordinated efficiency." These same characteristics must be brought out in teaching the football players the vital requisites in this sport of physical violence. The player must learn to react properly under extreme pressure in "this way of life" and it is one of the most valuable lessons that we coaches can impart to him during his formative years. In order to teach this concept, and many others of philosophical and technical nature, it is the responsibility of the coach to provide the appropriate motivation. Honesty, fairness, consistency, and open communication have to be the trademarks in coaching today's athlete. These should be the guidelines for assuming the role of coach.

For the past several years at Stanford, it has been our practice for the head coach to interview every member of the squad who turned out for Spring practice. Special interview times are allotted for each player, and our conversation generally follows the line of discussion that the athlete wishes to explore. Generally, of course, it relates to football; however, it can, and does, run the gamut of everything from girlfriend problems, to courses of study, to Summer jobs, to student participation in political campaigns.

We schedule these interviews for several reasons:

In the first place, Spring practice is demanding and generally the least fulfilling part of the football program. There is no game to play on Saturday; there is little or no newspaper coverage; there is no student interest; little of the satisfaction exists that is all part of the Autumn activity. It is at this time that the player's morale is at its lowest ebb. It is at this time that he may doubt his own capabilities because of limited opportunities to demonstrate his skills under game pressure and conditions; it is now that he may have financial worries because of lack of Summer jobs for youths. It is now that he may be concerned about his standing in relation to the rest of the squad.

It is during these sessions that we assume another role in the coaching profession, that of counselor. Today's counselor is in his most precarious and difficult position because of the so-called "generation gap." Add to this the emotional and physical highs and lows that are experienced by athletes, and the job becomes even more difficult. We have found, for example, that many athletes find it extremely painful to choose between committing themselves to football and dividing their talents among several outlets. The coach then has the problem of deciding whether to follow through with guidance or counseling. It is an individual matter that is sensitive, and sometimes it is best to refrain from interfering with the player's struggles other than to act as a listener. Everyone has his private dignity, and coaches should respect those of the athlete. Coaches never should become so involved in such activities as clinics, public relations, recruiting, staff organization, and speaking engagements that they forget to reserve enough time for getting to *know* their players.

Today's coach also is confronted with young people who wish to try various styles of life, to test traditional beliefs and values, and they often rebel against the "establishment" while advocating what they believe to be new or inventive.

Now, more than ever, we coaches must re-evaluate ourselves and our programs. We must take another look at our goals, our general and specific philosophies, our ethics, and our relationships with our players.

The coach must assess realistically what he wants to accomplish, and then expect realistically whether his athletes will work toward that goal. In our program, we believe in setting a level of expectancy, a level based on performance, not potential. It is our responsibility to aid the athlete to set a sufficiently high level of self-expectancy that, under normal conditions, he will gain significantly from our program and from our individual efforts. We believe that if self-expectancy is fulfilled on the field, it will be demonstrated in academic, social, and community pursuits.

Of course, there always is the athlete who feels infringed upon, that he is being "exploited," that he is not playing his fair share of the game, or that he will never have the opportunity to show his capabilities under game conditions. The only really effective manner in which to cope with these problems is for a coach to be scrupulously honest and fair. A coach must talk with his second-string players, pointing out to them their playing strengths and weaknesses, and encouraging them in their efforts to improve. The confidence of a substitute player can be broken if he is ignored or unduly criticized. Criticism should be made in keeping with the potential abilities of the player involved. If the players know this, they more often than not will welcome constructive criticism. It is the coach's job to assess the player's abilities and areas that need improvement and then channel them in a manner that will benefit the entire team. An athlete's enthusiasm for learning and succeeding begins when he sees the relationship between the coaches' efforts and concern for him and his own growing self-confidence and ability. His enthusiasm will progress as he fully understands his coach's faith and confidence in him as an individual and realizes that the game is the final fulfillment of success for both the team and himself.

We believe that, in great measure, our ability to understand and communicate with our players is enhanced through the interview sessions that follow Spring practice. The head coach constantly evaluates all players, in terms of their on-the-field performance both mentally and physically. Assistant coaches also conduct player conferences and make up evaluations which they record and submit to the head coach. Prior to the individual interviews with the players, the head coach reviews both his and the assistants' evaluations and uses them as background information to more intelligently discuss each athlete's position in relation to the team and the entire program.

Player evaluations

Following are some sample evaluations by assistant coaches responsible for specific offensive and defensive positions. Each is done in a different format but might offer suggestions for coaching individual players.

Offensive line

We give a resume of each of these players in several different areas and also try to list the players in the order of what we feel their potential for next Fall will be. First of all, we will rate each player in terms of the following attributes that we think are important to an offensive lineman:

1. Size Potential: This will include a boy's weight for reporting back in the Fall.
2. Athlete: This will include our evaluation of him as an overall athlete which includes his ability to run and to control the use of his body.

3. Attitude: This will include his coachability as well as whether or not he is what we would term a "winner."

4. Foot mover: This is a boy's ability to move his feet and perform the various techniques that are required of an offensive lineman. This is one of the most important attributes of an offensive lineman and is an important area.

5. Striker: The boy will be evaluated on his ability to strike a blow, not only in his drive blocking but in his pass protection.

6. Strength: This is overall strength, but most important to the offensive lineman is his leg strength and ability to perform the techniques that are required.

7. Speed: This is a boy's overall speed as related to the offensive line.

We also rate each offensive lineman in the five basic techniques that are required:

1. Pass protector; 2. Drive blocker; 3. Puller; 4. His ability to block on the run, which we are now well aware is one of the most important attributes of an offensive lineman; 5. Rate him in terms of his second effort.

Comments also can be made in the following areas to aid in preparations for the coming season: get-off, quickness, leg drive, endurance, balance, ability, follow-through, explosion, strength rather than bulk, wide base, sustain, hands, conditioning, mental toughness, and injury factor.

Following are typical individual player resumes:

Player #1

Size Potential:	220–225
Athlete:	fair
Attitude:	excellent
Foot Mover:	fair
Striker:	fair
Strength:	good
Speed:	fair

He is the kind of football player who gives 100 percent to each and every day. He gets the most out of his ability and therefore can always be counted on to give his best. I think he will be a fine football player again next year, and he should constantly work on his strength and quickness to better perform.

Pass Protector:	good
Drive Blocker:	fair
Puller:	fair
Blocking on the Run:	fair
Second Effort:	excellent

He needs to work mostly on his ability to block on the move and strike when he is either off-balance or just engages someone when he is not expecting it. He has to also work on his drive block in terms of rolling over his front knee so that he can get a little bit better strength at the point of impact. He is an excellent follow-through man, but sometimes he takes away from his original drive block by not using more of his innate strength.

Player #2

Size Potential:	200–225
Athlete:	excellent
Attitude:	fair
Foot Mover:	excellent
Striker:	good
Strength:	good
Speed:	good

I rated him a little down on attitude only because of the fact that he is a very emotional football player and needs to be handled very much as an individual. He will easily get down on himself, and we must at all times make him believe that he is a very important part of our football program. I feel that he put a little too much emphasis on weight this Spring and I think it detracted a little bit from his overall play. He should trim down just a very few pounds but should be made to realize that his strength and speed should increase proportionally as he works on it. He could be a great football player before he graduates and because of the fact that he is a slow learner he is one of the offensive lineman that we should not move to another position unless it is completely necessary.

Pass Protector:	good
Drive Blocker:	good
Puller:	good
Blocking on the Run:	good
Second Effort:	good

As you can see, he is pretty good as a football player in all areas. He will become a truly great one as he gets more experienced and continues to grow in the confidence that he has in himself. As I mentioned, this is going to be an important thing in coaching him and it is something that we must always be aware of. He does have great potential in all areas and it is going to be up to us to get it out of him.

Player #3

Size Potential:	218–223
Athlete:	excellent
Attitude:	fair
Foot Mover:	good
Striker:	fair
Strength:	fair
Speed:	good

He had a very disappointing Spring for several reasons. First of all, he felt that he was down in his weight, and this detracted from performing some of his techniques. This is a questionable attitude, but it nevertheless affected him as a football player. For this reason, I think that he should put on some weight but should at all times be assured that he can not afford to lose any of his speed and quickness. He is still a little bit hard to coach and must be made to realize that he is going to be one of the leaders of our football program and that he has to act as a football player rather than react as an individual. There is no doubt in my mind that he will have another great year next year, and it is important that he makes up his mind how good he wants to be and then does it.

Pass Protector:	good
Drive Blocker:	fair
Puller:	good
Blocking on the Run:	fair
Second Effort:	poor

He has had so much success so fast that he sometimes forgets that there's more to being a total football player than he has mastered already. I think it is going to be important for him to realize that even though some people have been talking about him as an All-American he is certainly a long way away from that and possibly is only the sixth or seventh best offensive lineman that we have at the present time. This is a sensitive area, but I think that coming from you that you can motivate him and make him realize what successes lie ahead.

Player #4

Size Potential:	227–232
Athlete:	good
Attitude:	good
Foot Mover:	fair

Striker:	good
Strength:	fair
Speed:	fair

He is a very underrated football player, and probably is one of the most consistent offensive lineman that we have. His quickness is definitely his major drawback and he should work at all times in his ability to handle his body and perform the many techniques that are asked of him. I do feel that in playing football this is very, very important to him, and he probably has one of the finest attitudes of anyone in our football program.

Pass Protector:	fair
Drive Blocker:	good
Puller:	fair
Blocking on the Run:	good
Second Effort:	excellent

He could possibly be potentially the weakest athlete on our starting line although I think it would take a good man to beat him out. I mention this only because with getting his extra year of eligibility back maybe there is a chance that we would move one of our other starters over to battle him for this starting position. I do feel that he should be complimented and given every bit of confidence that we have in him and made to realize that he has potential, not only as a college player but as a pro player as well. For this reason, I think that he should work at all times on his quickness and speed, and I don't think that in terms of techniques that there is much that he has to worry about that he won't get from us. He should be told to play handball and basketball all Summer and get his weight up a little bit more and improve his strength so that he can get the most out of what he has.

Offensive backfield

Following is a sample resume of offensive backfield evaluations, which include Spring evaluation, strengths, weaknesses, improved areas, and recommendations:

Player #1

Spring Evaluation: Football is not the only thing in his life. His varied talents allow him to succeed in many things. This Spring he was very receptive and respectful toward me. His effort was as good as any senior out there. Didn't have to make all those practices due to a class conflict, yet he came out everyday. Did everything average; never graded poorly on a scrimmage film, yet never really did anything outstanding. He left the field a better player because of his mental attitude to get what he could out of Spring ball.

Strengths: No question about his athletic ability. Rated 3 in top 22. Is highly respected by teammates and a top pro prospect. Has extremely fine hands; I rate him a receiver first. He fundamentally catches the ball better than anyone on the squad; is an ideal example of watching the ball all the way into the hands. Next, I rate him as a blocker; has great form, usually does not miss because of his wide base. Good pop and seems to enjoy blocking. I rated him a ball carrier third. This is because he just hasn't turned on yet; maybe he never will. I feel he is not a great running back due to Stanford's emphasis on the pass. His best position might be at fullback. He hits plays such as 38-12-16 exceptionally well. When he wants to be, he can be the best there is.

Weaknesses: He needs a lot of work vs. one-on-one with defense. He does not break a lot of tackles in the open field; this is one area he could be better in. His running ability with the ball is something to be desired. We need to concentrate on fewer fumbles. Also needs some work on quick starts. If he has any one major weakness, it would be regarding his desire to be the best running back on the coast. I don't think that this is one of his goals. He also should be more violent with the ball.

Improved areas: Faking and blocking. Seems to take pride in the little things. Got some work at fullback and is capable of running there. Impressed with his leadership ability and the respect others have for him.

Needs for the Fall: This Summer he needs to find a way to come back in the Fall to be the best. Is a winner and needs to be reminded of his tremendous influence on the team. They look to him for leadership; he should be aware of this. His frame of mind will determine his success. Has the tools, is coachable, and contributes a great deal. Exemplifies a Stanford football player. His best season should be ahead of him. Needs to report in top shape to prevent injury from keeping him down.

Recommendations:

    Invite back in Fall, possibly to be a captain.

    Challenge him to be the best out there.

    Stress his leadership ability and how he should set an example.

    Encourage him to set goals for himself on the field.

    Stress the need to work on little things to become better.

Player #2

He went through the motions this Spring. Performance was impaired by mental attitude and he left the field worse than when he came. However, final scrimmage was best effort. The conference session with him was extremely important for future understanding. He indicated that he plans on his best year ever, though he realizes his shortcomings and will make an attempt to be at his best in the Fall. My whole emphasis was to make him a better player when he was not carrying the ball; we laid the foundation and now must build on it. He is an individual on and off the field; he can get the job done when he wants to and this is what we must strive for. Rated 15 in top 22.

Strengths: A lot of ability when carrying the ball; strong and quick; does not have great feet but has great body lean and runs with a wide base. Tools include fine hands for receptions and good initial contact when blocking. I rate him as a runner first, receiver second, and blocker third.

Weaknesses: Poor second efforts when not carrying the ball; faking; following through with blocks, etc. Admits to not being disciplined and needs work on this area. Major weakness is what he does when not carrying the ball. Has the tools but must get him to perform. During the Rose Bowl he took pride in some of those areas; let's hope it carries over.

Improved Areas: Running game; improved his agility and basic running ability. Good work on faking emphasis and blocking. Improved in these areas when his mind was with us. Also improved his get-off somewhat.

Needs for the Fall: To report back in the best shape ever; has never had a good early season due to his poor conditioning status. Must run more than ever this Summer. Workout emphasis should be placed on getting his legs in shape. Also needs to work on catching the football. Mental attitude is important; needs to return ready to play the best football of his career.

Recommendations:

> Invite him back only to be a great player, not an average one.
> Challenge him to have his best season.
> As a senior, provide leadership by example.
> Report back in best physical condition ever.
> Set a goal to become a complete football player.

Player #3

A knee injury forced him out just as he was beginning to come around. He was overcoming a poor mental attitude which he picked up last season and during the off season. He has been used to so much success that it has been a difficult adjustment for him.

Strengths: He believes he has the ability to play. He is a hard-nosed kid with a lot of determination. Runs the ball with great power and good leg drive. He blocks well and takes pride in being a "tough" back. Rate him as a short yardage runner first, blocker second, receiver third.

Weaknesses: Does not have great acceleration; is a former tailback and takes a lot of steps. Has a tendency to run sideways instead of flying into a hole. Runs in the same place for valuable time.

Improved Areas: Get-off and blocking. Before being injured, his attitude had completely changed for the best.

Recommendations:

A good rehabilitation program this Summer is essential. I recommend that you invite him back only if his knee is completely sound.

Tight ends and receivers

Player #1

A completely new attitude in him this Spring resulted in the answer to our tight end problems. There is no doubt in my mind that we can win with him, and we should be close to last year's strength in this position. He has great feel for defeating underneath coverages and gets himself open better in these areas than other T.E's we have had. His speed has improved but is still just adequate to get deep. The fact that he does have excellent feet and a fine pair of hands will give us a real pass threat in him. His inadequacies come more in the short yardage situations as a blocker. He is not real strong and must work this Summer to build himself up to about 210 lbs. I will work on this area and assist him with the best job to help this weight problem. He has a fine attitude and desire to be a fine player. Because he is so coachable, I believe he will finish the season as a very fine tight end. Final scrimmage score was +65 based on 61 plays. His performance was as fine an individual effort as I have seen since coaching the Stanford receivers.

Player #2

I definitely feel he is our starter at one outside position. I was disappointed in his final scrimmage because it was not the complete effort I expect from him. He is not a fast learner and did make some assignment mistakes working at split end and flanker. His overall quickness is his biggest asset; consequently, he is an excellent one-one receiver. The biggest difference between him and . . . is his feel at beating underneath coverages, which will get better. I feel he should be our swing receiver and must learn both, rather than having the assignment variations. Excellent attitude; gives us a real run threat with the ball. Is a winner but must be consistent. Score: +14 72 plays

Player #3

The most natural receiver I have ever coached. He is extremely fluent and can disguise his speed better than any of the receivers. Does not force me to coach his moves as he has good feel for setting up a defender one-one and can accelerate to the ball very well. I was amazed at his progress in one week. He takes to coaching and retains things quite well. Probably the most important factor is that he wants to be a receiver. Hands are good and he will be a fine receiver by the first game. Probably the best overall blocker of the group. Needs exposure and can help us win.

Quarterbacks

Player #1

Should be our starting QB but did not show he was ready to take over this Spring. He has never been a great practice player; down deep I feel the game atmosphere in the Fall will bring the best out in him. He has gotten too analytical about the game when it comes to the individual personalities of his teammates. He must concern himself more with technical football and learn all he can before we open our season next September. The leadership will come through his natural competitive personality if he "lets it go," but he must become more knowledgeable of defenses and our plays to attack these defenses. He needs continuous throwing between now and next Fall as his greatest weakness is the deep pass. Repetition with as many receivers as we have on campus this Summer is a must for him. He should know his receivers' moves much better than he does right now. Weight is not a problem, but a Summer strengthening program could help overcome some of the minor injuries he is plagued with during the year. Definitely has the qualities to help us go all the way.

Player #2

Still uncertain as to his potential. One of those guys who has a fine touch to go along with his size. Has improved tremendously since joining us, and I feel this is the maturity that can reach outstanding potential. He gets better each day and has an uncanny knack for leading a squad. Things don't seem to upset him, and he is able to adjust as he is placed under fire. I feel he is a much better passer than we think he is. Again, because he has not reached maturity and has some bad habits, he gets careless in his drop and release at times. Needs continuous correction until it becomes automatic. As a ball handler he showed the greatest improvement and was nearly flawless in this area in our last scrimmage on Saturday. Could be our starter if he returns ready to play and goes ahead with the progress he has shown. Having him in the game gives me a certain feeling of real confidence. Very coachable; should never be embarrassed by a coach for his performance until he is more established at the position. Still does not realize how good he can be. Eligibility status should be discussed. Score: +47 61 plays

Defensive down linemen

Player #1

As he has done in all previous practices, worked hard for personal and squad improvement. Though his time spent was not very much, it was profitable. He is now in a position to be a leader and should dedicate himself to being an excellent example, especially since he will be in the vicinity this pre-season. Would like to see him report at about 250; think he could carry this amount. He should strive to include in his Summer program as many individual sports activities as possible to improve his total athletic ability. His goal should be to play well in every game, which would assure him of squad and personal success.

Player #2

Failed to take total advantage of the opportunity Spring practice provides. Though he performed well in his last scrimmage, it should be remembered with whom he was matched. He must report with an attitude that he is not satisfied with taking up where he left off last Fall. He must work hard and dedicate himself to be better in 1971. He should report at about 240. Certainly does not have a position guaranteed.

Linebackers

Player #1

I thought he had a good Spring even though he didn't participate too much. He was bigger and moved well, but I think he should try for 225 in the Fall. He understands football so much better now and can be a real leader in his position. His block protection is his only weakness, and we improved this some. He undoubtedly will be named captain; I have the same feelings about this as before, especially with a worrier like him. I think it affects his play and distracts from his interests.

Player #2

A good, solid football player and an outstanding person. I would not be afraid to start him at any one of the three backers, but I don't think he can play outside without lots of practice time. His best position is Mike. His strength is feel and pass coverage. His weaknesses are block .protection and ability to stay on his feet. This would be a concern if he played the outside. He is smart and a great team man. His weight should be about 210 which he might not make.

Player #3

Was not encouraged this Spring with his athletic ability which was to be his strength. Lacks quickness and burst, and doesn't get to ball. Didn't hit real well, but this was due to his sore shoulder some. Does not look to be a backer. He works hard and wants to do right; we should be sure not to discourage him with a move. I think he can play as a starter somewhere, though maybe not this Fall. This is a tough problem, and I'm sure you can handle it right.

4 deep

Player #1

He should play at 185-190, no more. Has a tendency to have big hips and thighs. Has ability to be a great defensive back but must concentrate more and work on his catching the ball. I feel he could be the leader of the defensive backs, not only in his play, but also in holler and in direction. A real pleasure to work with. Is a winner.

Player #2

Can be a starter at free safety or at right half. The problem is to find another starter at the other position. My feeling is that the halfback is more important but a good safety is also valuable. He has no faults, and I believe he could play any defensive position. Could be a leader of the defense along with . . . . Has no weight problem and hasn't missed a practice. Great to work with. Is a winner.

Player #3

No weight problem if he stays at 200 to play defensive back. Might be a tight end or linebacker. Good hitter and tackler most of the time. Got a slow start in Spring ball but progressed nicely. Last scrimmage was his best except for two missed tackles. He can back up the starter at strong safety. Might also be a reserve as tight end. Good agility but not good acceleration in coverage when beaten.

Player #4

Has been the biggest surprise this Spring. Is a good, fluid athlete who can run, is a good hitter and tackler, and can backup the starters at strong or free safety right now. Should improve knowledge of game and should do this with experience every week. Needs just general agility and conditioning this Summer.

Attitudes and values

In addition to individual evaluation, we must apply ourselves to other values that can make or break a football team.

Each high school and college coach has his code of conduct and rules of discipline. We demand that our players respect every coaching decision relating to practice and games. We attempt to instill sufficient pride in each athlete that he will be a responsible individual and take care of himself off the field.

One method to achieve this is to develop a proper attitude toward a learning experience. Attitude is the prime ingredient in creating motivation. If a coach creates an atmosphere of proper attitudes, then this will replace any prearranged rules or other major forms of discipline. It is vital for the coach to create in the minds of his players an attitude that they should want to get better. They must assume the role of a sponge and soak up the knowledge that a coach can impart. A willingness to follow instruction to the letter and to work countless hours to achieve proper technique will establish the desired pride in performance. Again, the responsibility of creating this atmosphere lies with the coach of today's athlete.

Although more authoritarian coaches may disagree, we believe that this two-pronged approach of discipline and pride works. One example may suffice:

Prior to the 1971 Rose Bowl game with Ohio State University, our practice strategy called for the tightest and most exacting preparation ever. We followed that program for the first several days. Early curfew hours were enforced, early breakfast was required, and we conducted highly disciplined twice-a-day practice schedules. We were determined to be ready. However, we soon realized that we were not progressing on schedule, either physically or mentally.

A representative group of our athletes asked for a meeting with me and made several requests: could the curfew hour be extended one hour; could they eat breakfast at a time of their choice during a two-hour morning period; and could they use automobiles furnished by the Tournament of Roses Committee in order to visit friends and relatives in the immediate area during the evenings. After discussing all aspects of the importance of preparation and play of the Rose Bowl game and my personal responsibility to have the team ready, I agreed to their requests with this order: the players would maintain previously established training habits, and there would be no compromise during the twice-a-day practice sessions. Leisure time could be adjusted to their satisfaction. However, the field time must be totally controlled by the coaches.

Following this conference and open communication, we experienced an immediate change in the morale of the squad, and we coaches were able to accomplish our goals in an environment of enthusiasm and dedication. The sportswriters referred to our squad as "the swingers," but we are convinced that our flexibility paid off without our sacrificing any of the required discipline. We further believe we enhanced coach-player respect. Without compromising our basic standards, the players in return paid the price by dedicated endeavor.

I believe this is a prime example of an athlete rising best to a challenge in a competitive atmosphere marked by a shared responsibility, conviction, and goal between player and coach.

Notwithstanding the fact that a coach and players create a shared responsibility, it nonetheless is necessary to choose an athlete who is a recognized leader to guide the squad during the game. This brings us to the point of the team captain, the man the squad looks to for leadership.

To be selected by the squad as a team captain should be one of the more cherished responsibilities of a football player. Getting the right type of leadership and having a go-between with the coach and athletes should enable a coach to receive the proper pulse of the squad at all times. As we look back on our coaching experience, a close parallel can be drawn between the successful teams and the type of captains that the squad selected. These should not be the popular individuals on the squad, but should be the young men who observe and command respect from their teammates. Many visits should be planned with the team captains, and they should feel free to come to the coach with any problems relating to the total squad morale or an individual who may feel he is being treated unfairly. Leadership should come as a natural response and should not be forced with the squad. Allow the team leaders to have meetings with the squad members because they can convey the proper attitudes desirable in the total makeup of the team. On the field leadership is vital when the going gets tought in a ball game. Sometimes a word in the huddle, a word of encouragement in a tight situation, or assessing the pulse of the squad prior to the contest can become invaluable as far as team success is concerned.

If a player can go on the field free of all problems or hang-ups, as the expression goes, he will perform with much more proficiency. Recognize these problems, whether they be grades, girlfriends, financial, or perhaps player or coach misunderstandings. Try to resolve them to the player's satisfaction. Any form of misunderstanding usually can be traced back to a lack of communication.

There have been many books written in the area of motivation, so we do not want to get into this too deeply. However, it is necessary for a coach to determine what really motivates his individual players. Can it be because of fear of failure? Is it because of material gain later on by participating in professional football? Is it merely to satisfy his own ego? Whatever the case may be, in order to get the athlete to want to get better every day, success plays a big part in the individual motivation. We have often thought that success is easily measured in sports that involve a stop watch, throwing the ball in a basket, or getting a base hit. One-on-one blocking is an emotional situation; therefore, it is difficult to assess day-to-day improvement. The good field teacher is quick to encourage his players by pointing out this improvement. Open communication after practice regarding daily improvement will help to motivate the athlete to want to get back on the field the next day.

It must be pointed out that a coach should always be aware never to play an athlete because he has great potential. The physically endowed boy is the one that should be on the field, but only if he is performing properly. Performance is the key, not what you think he might do because of his physical attributes. In rating total performance, each and every play must be taken into consideration. It is not enough in modern football to make one great play and then rest on your laurels for the next four or five. It is the consistent performer who should be on the field at all times. Of course this too, is the mark of a great coach when he can get top performance from the physically endowed player. This is when he will begin to have great teams.

We are great believers in the self-image concept, and attempt at all times to capture this area. We believe that an athlete tends to daydream about his performance in a stadium jammed with 90,000 people, the score tied, and only a few minutes left on the clock, with the outcome deciding the conference championship. At this point, what does he see himself doing? Where does he see himself participating? Does he see himself winning the game by catching a pass, recovering a fumble, blocking a punt, throwing a pass, making the key block in a successful run, or does he see himself carrying the ball over for the score. This will determine what position he undoubtedly feels that he can play at the college level. More often than not, he is right in this analysis of his possible position, and we attempt to take advantage of this self-image. Every Spring we allow our players to pick the position that they wish to play. Only on rare instances will we have to make position changes and do so only when we can move a boy up toward the first team or to perhaps improve the overall efficiency of the squad.

We hope that every player has a self-image of himself as an All-American. This would add direction as he set his goals regarding participation in the sophomore, junior, and senior years. The adage "To think big will be to act big," or "we are what we think we are" is certainly correct here. Sometimes, in our post-Spring practice meetings with the athletes, we have noticed that they have a rather low self-image. They only see themselves as participants on the squad, rather than necessarily contributing to win. We must help to reshape this type of self-image so realistic goals can be established for participation.

All of our staff are very goal-oriented in all areas of our total program. We set goals prior to every Spring practice, Fall season, and prior to each separate ball game. At the same time, we attempt to get our players to set goals that are realistic and attainable regarding their participation and ultimate individual success. These individual goals can be enhanced or modified by parental pressure and the player's own peer group. It is hoped that a player will set a high standard and then be willing to sacrifice and pay the price to make this a realistic and attainable goal.

A squad of young men with the common goal of top participation in a top conference should be held uppermost at all times. This will allow for team pride or an attitude that the team's success is the ultimate first before any special individual attainments. This also will affect the player's responses to adhering to appearance standards or a high level of observance of proper training habits. Though it is obviously the concept of team first and individual second, it goes without saying that all participants oftentimes reassess what they are getting out of it from a certain standpoint. Learning to work toward common goals can be extremely helpful as the individuals assess the investment of time they are making by their participation.

In interviewing athletes over the years, they have pointed out consistently that there are four things that they believe will enhance a coach's ability to gain the respect of his squad members.

1. The competence of the coach himself and, of course, of his staff; that is, competence in knowledge of the sport, flexibility in teaching methods, and competence in handling the individuals themselves.

2. To treat all members of the squad as individuals, not as robots all fitting into the same mold. Recognition here of individual differences in their levels of ability, dedication, preparedness, and in methods of motivation will increase a coach's effectiveness.
3. To create a sense of pride in belonging to the team. This is a broad area but will result in a desire to get better and help to motivate a total squad attitude toward being successful.
4. To set down certain precepts of discipline; though, for the most part, this should center in the area of participation on the field. We believe in setting rules, but would much rather attempt to create an attitude within the individual, so the rules would act merely as a guideline. At the high school level, we believe a coach should use a stronger hand in developing proper training habits. A coach should appeal to the player's pride and recognition that it just doesn't appear to be good common sense to build for a Saturday's game with a rigorous training schedule and then tear everything down that has been gained by improper training habits on a Saturday night following the game.

A coach should be ready to make adjustments or compromises off the field but must, at all times, adhere to his own standards on the field. These adjustments off the field can be flexible concerning curfew, personal appearance, recognition of class or study responsibilities, or anything else that might put a boy in conflict with the total program. However, on the field, establish set standards and be consistent at all times. Punctuality is probably the most important. Also, in order to maintain the proper level of discipline, such things as keeping the chin straps buttoned at all times, jogging to and from the practice field, never sitting down on the practice field, hustling to the center of the field on the long whistle, addressing the coaches with the proper respect, are good examples of maintaining field discipline. Let the players know what you expect and they will respond, particularly when they understand that you always have their best interests at heart.

A coach's responsibilities are many. However, it has been our experience that players are looking for four primary qualities we explained. The methods of reaching these goals depend on the level of coaching. Youngsters playing in Little League or Pop Warner competition often are looking for a coach with the ability to relate to them in the form of a father-image. They often feel the need for recognition by their peers, their parents, or the coach. They feel the need to succeed by *doing*. But, just as important, they want to enjoy the game. Therefore, it is the responsibility of the coach to combine the teaching of the rudiments of the game while allowing the youngsters enough rein to have fun. Because the boy participates voluntarily is an indication that he already has been motivated to some extent. The coach must take advantage of the youngster's need for activity in order to stimulate the learning of techniques.

Athletes in high school require a stronger hand than those at lower levels. Some of the reasons are obvious: one or two coaches have to handle up to forty or fifty boys at one time, and a more ordered discipline is required. As was mentioned previously, high school students also turn out for the squad for different reasons. Whatever the reason, the coach must recognize it and treat each individual in a manner that will produce his fullest potential.

In working with high school athletes, we have found one common quality that they look for in a coach: *fairness.* They want rules to be set down for them at the beginning of the season, and they want the coach to make them follow those rules to the letter. It is emphasized by the high school athletes that they respect a coach who will talk freely and informally with them in his office; however, that same coach must be the master of the football field and give no quarter in regard to his schedule or quality of practice.

It is at the high school level that attitudes most easily can be formed. The coach must convince his players that his way is right. He accomplishes this by the manner in which he conducts practice, the businesslike manner in which he handles his staff and his players, and the way he communicates with them. A coach at any level cannot be concerned with coaching only the players that he believes will play the major portion of the games. Each boy who turns out for practice deserves to be coached.

The reserve players occupy a unique and useful place in the varsity scheme. They are mainly youngsters who lack the strength and experience to serve on a higher unit but who are capable enough and promising enough to stay with the varsity squad. Because of their unique position, instilling and maintaining a proper attitude in them is as important as it is for the first-stringer. Their attitudes can be the strongest back-up morale for the varsity, or conversely, they can undermine the entire program. I believe that the best technique a coach can employ is to find something good in each player and encourage him to improve on that quality. Once a basis of confidence is established, the player will respond to teaching techniques and be motivated to excel in other areas of the game. The coach must instill confidence in the player that he has something to *contribute* to the team. A coach must convince the player that he should not give up on himself, and he must help him to build confidence as he learns each new technique or assignment. As these traits build, his attitude will improve and his competitiveness will increase. Competitive spirit can be a habit developed by persistence. Coaches at all levels should set goals for their players regardless of the type of opposition facing them, and these goals will become so firmly established through habitual training that they will become part of the player himself.

The player who is still learning must have an opportunity of succeeding if motivation and proper attitude are to continue. However, a coach should set high standards but continually encourage and remind the participants that they are improving. Generally, a player should be matched against another of somewhat equal size and ability. If he is overpowered easily by his opponent consistently, he might acquire a defeatist attitude. Therefore, he should occasionally be given the opportunity to experience success.

Reward and punishment are obvious and frequently used devices in developing attitudes and motivation. However, the practical and psychological responsibilities of the coach require him to know which players respond to punishment, to reward, or to firm but understanding words of encouragement. Punishment addressed inappropriately or to the athlete who cannot absorb it emotionally results in a detrimental effect on subsequent learning and performance. In no instance should a player be intimidated or shamed in front of his teammates. It is a human trait to "blow off steam," but more often than not a private conversation with an athlete will do the job better.

It must be realized, above all else, that an athlete's attitude generally has its beginning in his first sports activity. Therefore, the coach must aid him in establishing a mental conception or image of his own goals and the goals set up by his coach. This is where attitude starts.

7

Staff

The size of a coaching staff varies with the size of the school and the level of the institution. In some instances, it will vary according to the degree of importance the school places on athletics. The staffs in junior high schools, high schools, and colleges range from one to eight or ten men.

Most young men who graduate from college begin their careers as assistant coaches, generally at the high school level. Whether he joins a two-man staff or a multiple-member staff, he becomes a member of the official family of his particular sport. As a family, the group must work together in harmony, respecting each other, giving of themselves, and directing all of their efforts toward a common goal of success for the head coach, the team, and the program. There are few "one-man bands" left in the coaching profession.

Coaching competence, regardless of the field assignment, naturally is a prerequisite. Of equal importance in the assistant's personal characteristics is loyalty, a quality that must be reflected in on-the-field teaching and off-the-field relationships with interested members of the community. We do not mean to imply that a head coach is looking for a "yes" man; there is a time and place for an assistant to voice his opinions and that is in the staff meeting room. Complete discussions, and yes, often disputes, take place behind the closed doors of a football coaching staff meeting room. The loyal staff, however, always is united when the coach makes his final decision.

In addition to coaching competence and loyalty, an assistant coach must exhibit aggressiveness, initiative, attention to detail, intelligence, and a desire to advance in the profession. All of the attributes that a coach looks for in one of his players also are required of his assistants.

In most high schools, a head coach does not have control over the selection of the assistants with whom he will work. In many instances, he will inherit the assistants who were on the previous staff. Therefore, it is extremely important for the head coach to study very carefully the strengths and weaknesses of the people assigned to him. In assessing the merits of his staff, a coach immediately will see all levels of experience and interest in coaching. In some cases, he will find himself associated with an assistant who covets the head coaching job for himself. It is a challenge to the head coach to work with this type of person in a very positive manner. It is at this stage that coaching the coaches is a big part of the total preparation. All staff members must be motivated, and a head coach must realize that getting the most out of people is the essence of good management. To accomplish this, he must analyze their strengths and weaknesses by *spending time* with them. Involve them in football discussions; find out how important it is for them to achieve success with your team and in the profession. Determine what will motivate them for a top effort on the field.

Assistant coaches should be given responsibilities in detail, and they must know what is expected as a result of their teaching. If they are fairly competent, allow them to figure out their own methods of getting results. If they aren't, then the head coach must continually coach them before they can be expected to coach the squad members.

One of the worst mistakes a coach can make is to continually watch an assistant to be certain that he is coaching properly. The head coach should be able to delegate a teaching responsibility and then allow the assistant coaches to take over without the need for constant surveillance. This atmosphere also will enhance the efficiency of the head coach. The ability of the head coach to get the most out of his staff will determine the ultimate success of his program. If the head coach sets the pace for his assistants, they will respond accordingly.

However, it is a two-way street. A head coach must *command,* not *demand,* desired attributes in his assistants through his own characteristics and personal relations with his subordinates. Every staff member must be given fair and equitable treatment. The blame for defeats must never be shifted to the assistants, even though it may be obvious that one is responsible. Show a willingness to support an assistant when he feels ready to apply for a head coaching position for which he is qualified. Make every effort to obtain the best possible salaries and fringe benefits to make living easier for the assistants and their families. Try to know and understand not only your coaches but also their families. It is particularly effective to have an interview with both the coach and his wife, to understand their goals and the compatibility of their goals to yours.

Even after a compatible professional and personal relationship is established with the assistants, a head coach must be prepared to take up the slack in needed areas. For example, if a strong line coach is on the staff, but there is only adequate help in other areas, the head coach must then become the backfield coach. A high school staff composed of three or four men usually includes one or two who have had some solid experience both as a player and a coach. The others will be merely filling up the staff while their major interest lies in the academic areas that they teach as part of their school assignment. In an instance such as this, it is up to the head coach to sell himself to them and observe all of the rules of human relationship that will result in getting the most out of them. Make them feel that they are a definite part of your program and give them responsibility when it is determined that they can handle it.

A high school coach who is short-handed on his coaching staff might be able to enlist some volunteer help from members of the community. There may be one or two former college players who will welcome the opportunity to help a few afternoons a week, on Saturdays, or in pre-season practice. Many times qualified coaches from Pop Warner or Little Leagues can make a contribution to the program.

When a coach assumes the head position in a new school, he should develop all the possible new ideas and adjustments to the current program and not make change just for the sake of change. He should spend a great deal of time surveying the general attitude of the players, the staff, and the administration. A word of caution: do not be too quick to judge on past records. A new coach should survey the fields, equipment, and training room area so he can make some definite decisions that will point toward establishing a winning attitude. He often will find that this is probably his best opportunity to make improvements in field equipment, training and locker rooms. It also could be an opportune time to add a staff member or two. This also is the appropriate time to meet with the administration and outline a program of positive ideas. The coach must show a willingness to accept certain responsibilities to the institution in which he works. The same loyalty that he seeks from his assistants must be given to the administration and the school. The coach who has prepared himself for the field of education may be asked to assume his share of committee responsibilities in the solving of school problems and issues. Coaches at the high school level, particularly, may expect to be asked to serve on committees concerned with social affairs, public relations, counseling and guidance, student activities, curriculum, admissions, and orientation. These areas not only are parts of the coach's responsibility to the institution; they will provide him invaluable experience and background for a lifetime career in the total educational process.

At the beginning of pre-season training, the two most important meetings for the head coach in a new position are in meeting with the squad for the first time and the first staff session. Prepare for these diligently. Break down every single element you want to get across to them in order to create favorable first impressions. The staff should be approached in a businesslike manner, and certain standards should be set for their conduct both in the meeting room, on the field, and off the field. Communicate freely and try to reach the point that everyone is looking at the program through the same set of eyes. If this can be accomplished, it will not be necessary to establish a lot of rules and regulations and it will go a long way toward developing a winning attitude.

In selecting a style of play, I believe that in many instances a coach follows the system of his college coach. However, as is mentioned frequently in this text, the personnel should be examined very carefully before deciding on the system of play that will be used. In addition, he should examine what has been successful or what has failed at the institution. The head coach must examine his own personality. As much as he may admire a Bear Bryant, an Ara Parseghian, or a John McKay, and want to emulate their coaching styles, the head coach must be practical and realize that it just doesn't work. A coach must teach according to his own personality, or the squad and staff will quickly see through the false facade.

Begin with a positive attitude and be ready to work twenty-five hours out of every twenty-four if it is necessary to get the job done satisfactorily. Be result-oriented with both the staff and players rather than constantly task-oriented. You are now in a position of top management, and your success will lie in your ability to get things done through the people with whom you work.

8

Role of the Coach's Wife

(Editor's note: The following remarks relating to the role of the coach's wife were written by Mrs. John Ralston.)

Although my observations and responses admittedly are biased, I am convinced that there are few professions in which a wife can either be of greater help or of greater hindrance than in the coaching profession. I have been fortunate, indeed, to have been a coach's wife for twenty years. I have shared professional and personal victories; I have shared professional and personal defeats. However, it all has been worth the journey. My experiences may apply to coaches' wives specifically; they may apply only generally. However, I believe that the attitude and philosophy with which a coach's wife approaches her role will in many ways aid and complement his success.

Your peace of mind and empathy in most instances will give him needed strength and understanding in a profession that consists of a myriad of factors, all of which evolve around emotion.

Hopefully, young coaches and their wives who read this book will profit from what I have learned by experience through the years, and that it will be profitable to you and your husband or your future husband. This certainly is not to infer that my way is best nor always feasible for you, but perhaps one or two of the ideas or lessons that I have found to be successful can be utilized by you to make your life in coaching a bit smoother and happier.

My husband frequently has said he would have been wiser to have interviewed the wife of a prospective staff member instead of the coach himself. He strongly feels that the distaff side can, and does, wield a great deal of influence on the coaching husband. Hopefully she will be a good influence, but it's not always the case, I'm sorry to say. An optimistic, helpful woman can be invaluable in this highly emotional way of life, and a negative, selfish person can spell total disaster. Stop and think for a moment: how many coaches do you know who have left the profession because of their wives being unable to cope with the overall situation? I'd really hate to feel that I was responsible for my husband giving up something he loves so dearly and to which he has dedicated himself so completely throughout the years. There is always room for improvement in everyone, including myself. Even now, I find myself neglecting to do some of the things I have been advocating for so many years that coaches' wives should do to make the road to success a bit easier.

If given the opportunity to go back fifteen years or so, with the knowledge that I possess today, I feel I would be a far more understanding person. I would strive to be a much better listener and so much more empathetic — not sympathetic. I wouldn't get nearly so bogged down in my own little world, and I would do more for my husband just to show him I truly care. All men need that strength that comes through love, whether or not they will admit it verbally.

John and I are great believers in every one, of any age, setting goals for himself. Without goals where does one head, what direction does one take, and where does one eventually care to end up? Just what is your goal?

Goals are personal things. Most goals are yours, and yours alone, because there are no two people in the world with absolutely the same wishes and desires. I do not contend that one cannot share goals with a spouse or another member of the family. This is done, but usually these are the big, big goals you both dream of together.

Goal setting should happen early and consistently throughout every marriage. Set as many goals as you wish but make sure they are attainable to a reasonable degree. Some might be a bit harder to realize or take a lot longer to reach, but don't despair; this is all part of the game. Make an affirmation that you *shall* attain these goals, write them down if it makes them more believable for you personally, but actually picture yourself having reached the end result of your dream. This works! I have proof beyond a doubt that you can make it work if you sincerely believe in and physically work toward the desired result.

Goals can and should be used in all areas of life. One personal goal my husband and I set for ourselves six years ago was to travel in Europe before our children graduated from high school. To do this on a coaching salary is almost unheard of, as most of you know by now. It was a pretty wild dream at best, but we worked hard together and never once felt this could not be done. I'm from a farm in Nampa, Idaho, and John is from a very small town in northern Michigan, so a trip to Europe was just about the last thing either one of us dreamed we'd ever be able to do. But . . . last Summer all five Ralstons toured Europe, Great Britain, and Ireland. In June of this year our twin daughters, Sherry and Terry graduated from high school; thus our 'wild dream' or attainable goal, however you choose to call it, was reached. It can be done!

The example just quoted was family and personal; but without our firm belief in goals, I sincerely doubt if our dream of the Rose Bowl would ever have transpired. Hogwash! you say. Well perhaps so, but I doubt if you'll ever convince John and me that our goal setting didn't play an important part in Stanford's trip to Pasadena in January 1971.

So very many years ago, while dating John, I attended my first Rose Bowl game. The University of California was playing there under Coach Lynn Waldorf and John was on that team. That was the first time I knew he aspired to coach that particular football game someday. He already was working on his goal even at that early date. About seven years later, after climbing the coaching ladder step by step, first as an assistant high school coach under Rod Franz at Mt. Diablo High School in Concord, California, on to head high school coach at San Lorenzo High School, then to freshman coach at University of California at Berkeley to assistant varsity coach under Pete Elliott, John returned to the Rose Bowl as an assistant coach. That wasn't good enough. He had to be the "boss." He realized he needed far more preparation to do that, so he set out to obtain it. Apparently I, too, was readying myself for the role I later was to play as 'Mrs. Head Coach.' I did encourage him in each advancement, both by being willing to move often and take a salary cut at times. This is so important . . . flexibility! As you probably know by now, no two days are the same in coaching and we, as wives, must be very willing to bend and move quite rapidly. To prove how strongly we felt about being ready to move quickly with no financial ties, we didn't buy a home until we had been married for ten years. I don't advocate everyone doing this, but it did work well for us. We always felt a home would slow us down if professional advancement presented itself unexpectedly. Looking back I feel now we must have appeared to be very transient to our employers. I regret this impression because we have always been extremely happy at every school where John has coached.

After four enjoyable years at Utah State University in Logan, Utah, John could finally see the first chance of his dream coming true. He was hired at Stanford University. It was mandatory to John that he be employed by a school that is eligible to play in the Rose Bowl; secondly, we had to win the conference championship to be invited to compete there. It happened, but not without millions of people helping us along the way. John's sphere of influence must have permeated the whole coaching staff here at Stanford, wives included. No one can be as dedicated and enthusiastic as he was without it rubbing off. Everyone had the same dream, and it was just a matter of time until this goal was reached.

Goals do work, and I urge you to try their effectiveness. Affirm to yourself that you already have beaten your biggest rival or that your husband has been offered the job he has been longing for.

Monetary goals certainly are acceptable. A new position often results in a more lucrative salary, thus enabling one to buy that new home or automobile, take that long-desired vacation, or even go back to school. As Browning said: "Goals should be within your reach, but not within your grasp." Set the big goals, and then see how quickly the smaller goals are reached along the way. Speaking of salaries, the coach's first salary is somewhat of a shock. Some coaches' wives may have had the equivalent of a coach's yearly salary just for spending money during their last year in college. Don't worry; I went through the same thing, and I learned many good lessons. I learned, for example, at least ninety different hamburger dishes, and I'm pretty good with hot dogs too! I also learned all there is to know about housework, child care, gardening, and decorating on a shoestring because we couldn't afford professional help then. Don't be afraid to be thrifty or frugal. These values will remain with you forever. If it is any comfort, the salary does improve as time goes by; just be patient and your turn will come.

Continue to grow as an individual. This, I think, is vitally important to your husband's success. It doesn't matter what school you graduated from. Putting it bluntly, and I shall, it really doesn't matter *what* you did ten, five, or even two years ago. What are you doing now to further your education? A great deal of this education comes by growing and maturing as an adult person, just in meeting people, raising a family, and in coping with everyday life situations. On the other hand, that can only go so far until one realizes that "Fair Hubby" has surpassed you in many educational and social situations. Opportunities for self-improvement are boundless, particularly in an academic community. For example, I have audited courses in creative writing at Stanford, learned to play an adequate game of bridge when John was coaching at the high school level, taken a course in golf at Utah State University; I also have taken the Carnegie courses in public speaking and human relations while at Stanford. Helping John meant public speaking lessons for myself, thus enabling me to face an audience with relaxed self-assurance and poise, better prepared for a hurried impromptu talk or a well organized dissertation. These are just to show you areas in which I sought additional instruction. Although I took these courses for my own pleasure, each one made me a better helpmate for my husband in his position.

I believe that if a wife's education ceases when she graduates from school, she is being unfair to herself, her husband, and her family. I graduated from nursing school before John and I were married, and I still work occasionally just to keep abreast of medicine and modern nursing trends.

Part of my recommendation to keep one's hand in education is prompted by my feeling of responsibility to become more well-rounded than the average housewife because of the many types of persons with whom we associate. Our ordinary daily routine forces us into situations many women never experience during their entire lifetimes. No matter what level of coaching your husband is engaged in, you still must deal proficiently with students, faculty, alumni, civic leaders, parents, and your next door neighbor. I believe we owe it to our husbands to proudly represent him. It is extremely easy to become stagnant and watch the world go by. However, you married a coach for better or for worse, so it is important to keep up with him in his professional and personal pursuits.

Frequently situations do arise when one can be of valuable assistance to "Sir Spouse". I remember so vividly a short time ago, after that fabulous game played by the New York Jets in the third annual Super Bowl Game in Miami, Florida. The community of Crockett, California, planned a great testimonial dinner for one of their outstanding native sons, Jim Turner. Now, all you "Football Buffs" will remember that Jim kicked those three field goals in that contest enabling the Jets to end up the World's Football Champions for that season. Jim is a great friend of ours, having played four years of collegiate football for John while he was coaching at Utah State University in Logan, Utah. So it would seem fitting to have the "Ol' Coach" attend the banquet to say a few words in Jim's behalf. The only trouble was, John had been committed to do the very same thing for the new San Francisco 49er, Gene Washington, on the same night in Long Beach, California. No dates could be altered to fit John's busy schedule. He felt very bad that he couldn't be in two places at once. Just guess what happened? You're right! He very generously offered his wife as a substitute. And what is even worse—they accepted! Off I drove in a blinding rainstorm, about 100 miles each way. I represented my husband and spoke on Jim's collegiate football experiences. John's audience that night was twice the size of mine, but we decided after he got home that we had spoken to about 1,200 persons in one evening between the two of us. There are many opportunities to help out if you care to. Always be prepared and willing and you will be called on often.

How involved should a wife become in her husband's work? This question is frequently asked of me by younger coaches' wives. In the actual coaching of football, I say very emphatically "stay out," "off limits," or anything else that qualifies as a great big "no"! My husband avidly shares this viewpoint, the reasons being: (a) one can't tell the coach how to coach his football team; (b) one can't say whether your favorite alumnus or friend was right or wrong in criticizing the last crucial call your husband may have made when we lost a close, or even not so close, ball game; (c) one can avoid a heated argument at the supermarket Monday morning if one can truthfully say "I really don't know that much about the

game so I couldn't say for sure if we should have punted or not";
(d) one is less likely to get caught by the press with a stupid quote
one wishes could be revoked later. If the press thinks ahead of time
you're a real dummy about football, they don't waste time asking
anything except "is your husband at home, Mrs. Ralston." I have a
very basic knowledge of the game and so far that has proved sufficient and "safe." I highly recommend it.

In smaller communities, a coach's wife is expected to participate
in community affairs. I realize babies and small children limit
activities, but there always are group baby sitting accommodations
that can solve that problem. You might have to take your turn, but
that will further involve you in the community and its feminine
members. Adjusting to a small town was no problem to me because
I was raised in a small rural community. However, I can see where
wives from a cosmopolitan city might have a slight adjustment
to make. It could be a traumatic situation to transfer oneself from
being the girlfriend of the college football hero in June to just another housewife in a town of 10,000 persons a few months later.
Instead of 80,000 football fans in the stadium, the local high school
might draw a gate of a few hundred. After a busy campus community life, with all the cultural outlets and recreational facilities
there or in a nearby city, it can be a real shock to end up at Blue
Valley High School, the state's leading farm town. You probably
have three choices: (1) go home to mother; (2) stay and make life
miserable until your husband gets out of coaching or moves; or
(3) look at all of the positive aspects of your life and begin building
from there. We've been in just this situation, and it turned out to
be some of the best years that we've had in our marriage and in
coaching. There are good, interesting, and well educated people
in every community. One very quick way to break the ice is to become involved in community affairs. It is an aid to your husband to
be represented "downtown" when he has so little time to get overly
involved in civic affairs. It is equally important to become a participant in school affairs such as the P.T.A., the women's faculty
club, mothers' clubs, and any other such organizations where you
probably will be both "Mr. and Mrs. Coach" ninety percent of the
time. More often than not, the coaching husband will be traveling
or reviewing game films on Sundays. Even though the coach is
unable to attend church, people appreciate seeing his family attend occasionally and taking part in the activities. In John's case
he is well represented. His wife and son Larry sing in the church
choir, so if we are ever absent, there is no way to hide.

I firmly believe that all coaches, regardless of their professed
religions, realize they cannot do their jobs alone. They very often
seek help from a "Higher Being," whether it be in a church pew on
Sunday morning, or in the dressing room just prior to an athletic
contest. I personally think it is most important to see a whole family

together in church. Try it out if you haven't already; it is one of the greatest morale builders in the world.

Entertaining constitutes one of the major activities a coach's wife becomes involved in. This useful job was inherited the day you married a coach. The clue to giving a successful party reminds me of a comment may by Coach Lynn Waldorf many years ago: "The difference between a good speech and a bad speech is approximately 1,000 speeches."

I feel the same way concerning giving parties. One learns new and useful entertaining tips each time guests are in one's home. Again, relaxation in entertaining comes through experience and good preparation. These two areas are inseparable; one gains through the other. A relaxed hostess is an extremely well prepared hostess. Good preparation is gained primarily through a lot of experience, so obviously one must jump right in and get one's feet wet.

Don't hesitate to entertain because of the physical appearance of your home. The most important element in entertaining is the warmth and sincerity with which one shares herself. The home, food, beverage, and service are secondary. We have been extremely fortunate to entertain some very outstanding and well-known persons from all walks of life. I consider this one of the important "fringe benefits" of coaching. Our home is just average middle class, at best; but to this day, we have never hesitated to invite anyone to visit regardless of his station in life.

Some of the most enjoyable entertaining that I have known was when John coached at San Lorenzo High School in California. We'd have the entire team over for dinner on Thursday nights prior to the Friday games. We just couldn't afford to feed forty or fifty boys each week, so the players' mothers often would furnish some of the food. I never quite knew what we'd end up eating, but nobody was left hungry and it did more to cement a football team than anything we ever did.

When we were at Utah, we served ice cream, and I still can see that group of players getting off the rented bus and absolutely engulfing our home. We had some pretty good ice cream "scoopers." Everyone had to help because after dishing out the first five gallons of ice cream, players such as Merline Olsen, Clark Miller, and Tommy Larscheid needed help on the second five gallons. Even their strong arms got weary.

The Stanford team stays in a nearby motel the night before the game, so frequently the team comes on Thursday night. I prepare cider, donuts, and gallons and gallons of milk. It's great fun to entertain the players at all levels of coaching. It requires very little time or effort, and doesn't cost a great deal compared to the value received. This is a perfect time to invite some of those good fans downtown to "foot the bill" for the donuts, ice cream, or whatever else you wish to serve. You'll find that many of them are delighted to help out, and are happy to be told what they can do to help—especially if told by a cute little coach's wife who "really needs help." Put some of your feminine talents to work and see what happens. It's a great way to get a team and community "pulling together." Surprise your husband sometime and insist he have the team over. You'll enjoy it just as much as the boys. And your husband will be so pleased—believe me!

My husband always has been extremely fond and loyal to his home and family. He feels a healthy home atmosphere with only our family present is something the players miss. Their visits to our home relax them, dispel tensions, and gives them an opportunity to see that the Old Coach is really human after all—he lives in a house, eats at a table, and sleeps in a bed just like any other normal human being. Sometimes he becomes a figurehead during the seasons and possibly displays seemingly inhuman qualities in the stress of day-to-day practice or during an emotional Saturday afternoon game. We attempt to remedy this by inviting the boys into our home under very relaxed conditions.

A coach and his wife must deal with the alumni—especially at the collegiate level. They come in all sizes, shapes and kinds; they are good, bad, and in-between. Rarely, however, do we have to deal with an unpleasant person or situation. Fortunately we are in a fun occupation and people generally treat it accordingly. Entertaining at this level is quite diversified, particularly after a game.

It is an individual preference between you and your husband. Discuss it early in your coaching career and decide what is best for your personalities and budget. After you have set a precedent, people automatically expect it to be this way. Granted, your methods will fluctuate occasionally, especially with a change in positions or schools; but it has always been my desire to do exactly as my husband wishes after the games. After all, this is his day; let him enjoy it as best he can. He works all year long to show the public what he has accomplished on only ten Saturday afternoons. After the game I strongly feel it is my goal and responsibility to provide an emotional outlet to satisfy his needs, whatever they may be at this particular time. Anything else on entertaining that I relate is personal. I can't tell you what is the best in your situation, just in mine. You have to decide what to do and how to do it.

We entertain quite frequently when John is in town, especially during the season. We have an open house for just about anyone and everyone after every home game. We started doing this a few years ago and we entertain anywhere from fifty to three-hundred and fifty people after each game. John doesn't care to go out publicly after the games, so this method has served us well. All of our staff and their wives are here to help entertain if the crowd gets overly large or loud. One might question the figure of three-hundred and fifty people—it's quite true, after a few of the games. For example, after the Big Game (California), USC, or UCLA, the crowd can grow quite large. Everyone does not come at once, but I do remember so clearly after the Big Game in 1965 when a friend of ours who also is a well-known East Bay restauranteur, an ex-teammate of John's and a good University of California alumnus came to our house in his chartered bus — not alone, but with forty or fifty of his friends. I had been forewarned and 'Boots' earlier in the day had sent over loads of delicious food from his restaurant for the buffet table. Strangers and all mingled together to celebrate Stanford's victory over the University of California that day. Our children at that time were very young and the bus driver was kind enough to take them and some of their little friends for a ride on that great big bus all by themselves. They shall never forget that ride . . . What a thrill!! 'Boots' Bus' still arrives after most Big Games.

At these after-game get togethers, I have found it easier for me to serve, for lack of a better name, what I call a "Finger Buffet." Fortunately we are blessed with three exceedingly helpful children and through the years they have helped me prepare a buffet table that would add to the enjoyment of a cocktail party, suffice for a dinner if need be, or tide over a hungry fan until he goes elsewhere for another engagement. Serving food in this manner solves many problems. It provides an opportunity for the hostess to circulate among the guests and not be a slave to the kitchen, as all the work is done ahead of time. I can't stress strongly enough the importance of preliminary preparation, especially when one does not know the exact number of guests, and I rarely do. A finger buffet is just exactly that! Guests can handle everything with their fingers. Silverware and china are not used at all. Be sure to provide lots of napkins, placed in strategic spots, always available for slightly drippy canapes. This is a simple thing to do, but it saves hours of hard work and expense in cleaning a favorite piece of furniture or a freshly shampooed carpet. It also saves embarrassment for the guests if they can clean a slight spill by themselves and not have to call the hostess every time there is a small accident. Serving hors d'oeuvres in this manner allows one to use paper plates and napkins and frees one to spend more time arranging flowers and candles to create a festive mood. It also makes the guests feel at home and comfortable, regardless of the game's outcome.

Teamwork is the name of the game . . . not only on the actual football field but in every area of the coaching profession, from the least significant to the most important task that requires attention. It is mandatory that each of us be able to work willingly and well with all the other wives in our department and especially in our husbands' own individual sport. This is a valuable attribute to perfect early in a coaching career; without this optimistic willingness, it's a lost cause as far as your husband's success is concerned.

Here at Stanford University, we feel that we have one of the best, if not the best, coaching staffs in the country. Everyone bends over backward to be helpful. It's truly great to know one has such capable people to call on at a minute's notice, and they have yet to let us down no matter what the request might be—large, small or in between. Can your superiors or associates truthfully say that about you? I surely hope so; if not, perhaps that is a small area on which you can work and remedy, thus helping your husband become the highly successful coach he desires to be.

Oftentimes we get together for staff potlucks just for ourselves or for other people we wish to entertain in our home. As a staff works together, one soon finds out who does what well.

Usually, we have used potlucks as a method of entertaining. They're the least expensive way to entertain and often end up being one of the most enjoyable. Nobody minds bringing something. Beverages, as well as food, are brought to a potluck. Organize it and do the calling and you're on your way. I think, as the wife of the head coach, that it's a great precedent to set early in one's career. Subsequently, any or all of your assistant coaches won't feel shy about having a potluck at their homes to defray the cost of doing it by themselves on a limited budget.

There is no set time or occasion to have a potluck. We've had potlucks for farewell parties, hello parties, entertaining parents and athletes, cocktail parties, picnics, and about anything you can name.

"People who live in glass houses shouldn't throw stones"!! This is an old old cliché; I don't even know its origin, but I do know it is very applicable to our immediate situation in coaching. Your husband is in the public eye the majority of the time and you are very often there right along with him. This being the situation, many things each of you does and says is of interest to the general public. As a "semi-celebrity" your husband is often times on display. We as coaching families must be extremely careful of our appearance, words, and actions so we present the best image of our profession to the public in general.

All too quickly a derogatory statement you might have uttered, possibly in jest, makes the rounds and soon ends up as something you definitely would not like to be associated with at any time. We as wives have to be doubly cautious because of so many petty jealousies . . . words and statements grow to such vast proportions before one can even realize what is happening. Weigh and measure very thoroughly any statement that might have even the slightest tinge of controversy or derision. One may suffer unending misery for a comment made by you unthinkingly in a weak moment. A favorite quotation of mine is extremely applicable in these situations. I think of it often and will share it with you.

> The Moving Finger writes; and, having writ,
> Moves on: nor all your Piety nor Wit
> shall lure it back to cancel half a Line,
> Nor all your Tears wash out a Word of it.
> from the Rubaiyat of Omar Khayyam, verse 71

No matter what we say or do, it cannot be erased in any way . . . it might be amended or later corrected but it can never, never be eradicated completely. You did it or said it and even tears cannot nullify what has been done. If only we could see what we are saying or doing before, instead of afterward when it is too late for tears. It's a good lesson for all coaches' wives, I think.

Coaching may be looked upon as a "glamour profession" by some people. But you and I as coaches' wives, know it takes many long, hard hours of work and dedication to accomplish set goals. Many hours away from home and family are spent by an aspiring young coach. Sadly enough, it really doesn't improve much as success is attained; as a matter of fact, this year was supposedly one of the most successful for the Ralstons and it was, on paper. What with a conference championship, a Heisman Trophy winner in Jim Plunkett and a victory over the tremendously successful Ohio State football team in the coveted Rose Bowl, one would think they've "got it made." This was a hard year—difficult from the standpoint that John was away from home six days and nights of every week instead of a usual four. This is really where one must show some stamina and real dedication as a coach's wife. He needs you now like he's never needed you before. I just can't tell you the truth of that old statement, "It's lonely at the top."

Provide the strength he needs, raise the children, entertain the guests, travel all over the country, and listen when he needs a "sounding board" or a friendly companion. You shall be richly rewarded someday. Always remember your husband's successes are your successes—also, you're in on all or most all of his failures.

Over the years I wonder what we'd have done without a constant sense of humor. Dealing with so many different people of all ages, and situations of all types, a sense of humor is "vehemently vital." Temper edges would, could, and did wear extremely thin under stress and strain.

Laughing at totally impossible situations is the only salvation at times. Use laughter often, it's a perfect remedy for numerous situations and I highly recommend it. Again I think of a quotation I enjoy in reference to the lighter or brighter side of life. "Two men looked out from Prison Bars, one saw the mud and one saw the stars." Think about it!

How well do you listen? I mean especially to your husband. You might be flattered to know, if you don't already, that you are the only person in the whole world a coach can confide in at times. It must be reassuring for you to know that you alone are the one person who knows all of his inner thoughts when many fans and newspapermen are clamoring for any little tidbit of information. Since you are in this unique position—listen well and cherish his confidences. If you are chosen as a "sounding block," react accordingly and don't betray this rare gift he has given you.

I have always cherished personal friendships as the greatest assets one is allowed to possess. When you find such a friend, nourish that relationship tenderly. I've had such a confidante through the years. Sue has six lovely children, cares for a beautiful home, and is just brimming with talent and personality. She is always busy and active and I have yet to stop for a cup of coffee but what she doesn't drop everything and listen. She is a small person with the biggest shoulders, I know—I've leaned on them often. Never once have I told her something in confidence that doesn't remain just exactly that—a confidence. She and her husband Dick have been through more heartache and happiness with us than anyone. Always cherish these confidences and friendships and never, never betray them.

I feel I would be remiss if I did not mention my feeling about raising children in this highly emotional business. I don't know about your families, but I can tell you John has no greater fans at his games than his own youngsters. One San Jose newspaper writer, Dan Hruby, said in his column after our University of Washington game last year that he witnessed a scene in the little green dressing room at the open end of our stadium that he'd never seen before and never will forget. Anyone in the room couldn't help but be moved. Standing in the center of a litter strewn dressing room, dirty with after game furnishings stood the Ralston family alone, all five of us clinging to each other in a very tearful, happy embrace. We had just won that coveted honor to appear in the Rose Bowl Game—a dream we had been working toward for 20 years. Anyone in coaching can partially understand the depth of emotion we felt. Although it may be difficult for anyone outside the profession to understand, it was the deepest degree of happiness anyone could possibly attain. The highest emotional peak of five lives had culminated right at that very time. Needless to say, that was one of the ecstacies reaped from this sometimes slightly unpredictable profession.

Our children are, and always have been, a very integral part of our coaching life. It is a lonely, fatherless existence for them the majority of the time. It is especially hard for a son when he is expected to be the "Big Athlete" on campus. Little do they know he really digs the piano and the a cappella choir! He will be likened to his father unmercifully. All his life he hears, "Well, well, are you going to grow up and be a big football player like your Dad was?" I must admit—that statement really got to me after about 15 years, I boil everytime I hear it. It's a fallacy of the American public, categorizing people.

Another statement or question that drives me right up the wall in a big hurry is the statement: "Now that football season is over, what is your husband going to do?" Even as I write it I get a bit annoyed—I shouldn't, because how many people in the world know what goes into the life of a football coach—not too many, I guess.

If your husband is as dedicated as mine, accept the title and role of "football widow" and treat it gracefully. Your schedules probably are similar to mine, but I'll share ours with you just for comparison. Starting with the end of August, John moves in with the team that has assembled early for "two-a-day practices" in the Fall before our first game. He does just exactly that—moves in! He sleeps there every night and eats all three meals with his boys. When the season actually starts he arrives home about ten or eleven p.m. each day but never eats a meal with us, Saturday and Sundays inclusive. His first meal with us is usually Thanksgiving. If he can manage it, he spends that weekend at home with us before he starts off recruiting and speaking at banquets all over the country. This continues until Christmas and he gets to eat at home that day, if we aren't in a Bowl game or an All-Star game of some kinds. Out of the eight years at Stanford we have been home at Christmas just three days. The others were spent away from home when John coached the East-West Game, Hula Bowl, or the Rose Bowl. The National Convention is held in January and a very concentrated recruiting period follows. John eats dinner at home about one out of every five days. Then it is usually too late for the children to join us. After that, Spring Practice is held in April and May. And this year he coached the All-American Game in Lubbock, Texas, in June. He spends the rest of the Summer conducting and attending football clinics, speaking to service and alumni groups, and then he finishes recruiting and goes into another football season.

I go with John to recruit athletes occasionally. This is very special for me. This is a personal thing with all coaches—how much a wife should enter into recruiting. I quite enjoy meeting the athletes and their families. It makes the game far more interesting and personal for me if I know the families involved. Another reason I think I'm invited to go recruiting with John is either to drive home while he sleeps or else to keep him awake while he is driving. I hate to admit it, but I have a feeling that is the main reason I get to go so often, supposedly to help recruit!

One has to actually live this life to really appreciate how good or bad it can be. We have a fun definition of the coaching profession —"One day you're drinking wine at Ciros and the very next day you could be stomping the grapes in Fresno." I enjoy a quote made by Mrs. Pat Nixon recently saying, "Life in politics has drawn us together while it has kept us apart." I think that is a fine explanation of our life in coaching. It has been well worth the journey. The years I have been a coach's wife have been the most exciting and rewarding any person could ever experience. I am truly grateful to have been allowed to live this life and to share with my husband and family the honor and glory, the sorrow and heartache. The agony and ecstasy are nothing compared with the rich, full life we've shared as a very close coaching family. Hopefully, each of you will share similar experiences in your lives and emerge as richer and wiser persons. Good Luck to each of you and if I can leave but one thought with you in closing to make your way a bit easier — acknowledge an old favorite saying of John's, "and with all thy getting, get understanding."

9

Practice Tips

The foundation of a successful football team usually is laid during Spring training. It is a time for the introduction of new defenses, new pass patterns, new formations, plus any new ideas relating to individual techniques.

Most college and universities are limited regarding the number of days they may practice, and high schools usually are allowed ten days at the most, with no pads of any kind allowed. As a consequence, the coach must accomplish the most he can in a short period of time in order to set the stage for the coming Autumn season.

First, only the coach knows exactly where he is at this point in time. He has his basic knowledge and experience; what remains now is for him to implement them into play, for better or for worse. Second, he and his staff must use their abilities to *evaluate* their personnel and the staff's technical football knowledge to realize the greatest success. If this is done, the coach will be ready to attack the regular season with the best possible chance of success.

Because we have had innumerable inquiries from beginning coaches regarding a high school ten-day practice plan, we will review several elements that must be part of the sessions as well as the coaches' relationship with the players:

Tradition

The school's football tradition must be evaluated and analyzed. Has it been a winner or a loser? Determine exactly how this particular tradition will affect the upcoming season.

Football attitude

This includes the attitude that prevails among the student body, the surrounding community, the players, the other coaches in the athletic department, and the administration. These elements are important because the football program must fit into the school. The first-year coach must understand it and realize that his success will depend largely upon his ability to mold his particular program within the atmosphere of the school and the community. Many coaches make wholesale changes just for the sake of change. We believe strongly that this is the wrong approach. Make the changes that are necessary for a successful program; however, one should not overlook those elements that have been successful in the past. The coach must prove to his colleagues and the community that he is developing a sound program. With that approach, we believe they will want to join the new coach and do what they can to help. Sooner than he thinks, they will be on his bandwagon.

Personnel

One of the most important factors involved in a coach's first Spring practice is the preliminary information he can obtain regarding his personnel. A primary problem is that Spring practices coincide with other sports activities. Although it is important that players participate in Spring drills, this is a sensitive area and a coach must recognize the existence of other sports programs. A coach can place a player in conflict if he insists that he participate in Spring practice at the expense of another sport. Nevertheless, a coach can accomplish a lot of preliminary work on his total personnel assessment even though they all aren't engaged in Spring training. He can discuss personnel with other coaches in the athletic department as well as other members of the faculty who are familiar with the players as individuals. It would be advantageous for the new coach to talk with his predecessor to obtain his opinions. An important aspect is to look for the performer, not the player with potential. We will examine this further as we discuss the practice plan.

A new coach also looks for players who will win for him next year. One of the most important elements in football is to establish a sound base; but it also is important to prove to the players that there is a new or continuing winning attitude with which to identify. Some of the attributes that should be present in personnel are pride, intensity, aggressiveness, leadership, character, and intelligence. Sound preliminary screening relative to these attributes is important in future planning.

It is important — particularly in high school — to observe football players who are engaged in other sports. A coach can obtain a good idea of the players' athletic potential as well as obtain an insight into some of the competitors he will coach in football.

The new coach should determine whether there are any films from previous years so he can ascertain what has been done in terms of offense and defense. More recent films are needed to evaluate the abilities of personnel who still are in school. The grading sheet which is illustrated is important to use while viewing a film.

INDIVIDUAL POSITION GRADE SHEET

Name: _____ Position: _____

PLAY	GRADE	COMMENT	PLAY	GRADE	COMMENT

TOTAL SCORE: _____

TOTAL PLAYS GRADED: _____

Evaluate each individual who will be an integral part of the squad next year. A separate sheet should be filled out for each player. The grades should be given purely on a plus, 0, and minus basis because it is not known what has been asked of the player, and it is difficult to rate him in specific areas such as techniques or assignments. The main purpose of the grading sheet is to have a worksheet during coach-player discussions prior to, or after, Spring practice. The coach and players each will obtain a better mutual insight.

A coach must be conscious at all times of the types of players he is looking for. We are questioned at clinics all over the country concerning position requirements. At Stanford we do not have specific position requirements in terms of left tackle, right tackle, and other individual spots. However, we do believe that athletes are categorized basically into three distinct areas: skilled, non-skilled, and specialist. We break down our positions both offensively and defensively in terms of skilled and nonskilled positions, the latter being the player who plays nonspecialized positions. Once a coach has an idea of the talents for which he is searching, he must keep the evaluations of these talents and abilities uppermost in his mind when approaching his practice plan. Let us review some important guidelines for the new coach:

1. Sell yourself and your program.
2. Don't try to do or be something or someone you aren't.
3. Evaluate your experience and knowledge and couple it with any staff suggestions and background to determine the proper starting point.
4. Establish a program and determine what off-the-field elements will affect success, then introduce them to the program.
5. Present a first-class program, something everyone will want to be associated with. Most of us in the coaching profession are selfish and very competitive, and we would like to believe that everyone wants to play football. This isn't always the case. A coach's program will attract the type of players and attitudes that are required to be a part of that program.
6. The squad must become acquainted with the coach as an individual and with the basic ingredients of his program. It is important that a coach set aside some time to get together with the players in a relaxed, informal atmosphere. Players want to be involved, and the more that they can see the coach as a human being and an individual who wants the best for them, the more receptive they will be.
7. Approach the squad with these two goals: (a), the coach is to be evaluated on his ability to impart his knowledge. He can attend many clinics and gather a multitude of

information, but if he cannot impart this knowledge to the squad, he will not be a coach; (b) a coach can claim that title only if he does a job of allowing his players to come as closely as possible to reaching their potential. A coach must constantly work on the attitude of the team and the individuals. And their attitude begins with a reflection of the coach's attitude.

Ten-day practice

After establishing guidelines, it is time to outline the ten-day no-pad workout. We break it down into eight distinct areas which should be thoroughly examined prior to the setting of the practice schedule:

1. Calisthenics
2. Evaluation of the individual
3. Teaching of the football position
4. Agility drills
5. Position, fundamentals, and skills (very general)
6. Teaching of assignments (basic)
7. Execution (teamwork)
8. Conditioning

Ten-day spring practice format (one-and-one-half hour practice)

	Time	Activity
Calisthenics	5 minutes	Stretching; neck
Individual	10 minutes	Sprints; special skills (throw, catch, strength)
Football position	10 minutes	Quarter eagle; wave
Agility	15 minutes	Selected drills
Position skills	20 minutes	Blocking; tackling
Assignments	10 minutes	Rotation learning
Execution	15 minutes	Team execution (get off, pursuit)
Conditioning	5 minutes	Relays

Calisthenics

The new coach should emphasize the calisthenic portion of his Spring practice plan. These drills should incorporate stretching exercises to avoid pulls, as well as to warm up the athlete to prepare him for practice. The stretching exercises, as well as other related exercises, should be thought out not only for preparation for practice but also to give the player an idea of what to work on during the Summer months. Players who have tight muscles and have trouble warming up should be given special attention by a trainer or other competent person.

Calisthenics especially are beneficial for the contribution to morale and team unity. This particularly is important in two-platoon football and sometimes provides the only opportunity for the entire squad to be together. We think it is a good idea for the head coach or one of his assistants to lead the calisthenics because it contributes to an overall team feeling.

Even though the high school Spring practice program will not include actual contact, we strongly suggest incorporating neck exercises into this time block. Because a coach constantly is fighting time in a ten-day program, he should devote only enough time to calisthenics as he feels is important.

Evaluation of the individual

The first area is to teach and to test the individual players. Opinions in all areas of evaluation will give a coach a clear appraisal of the squad potential as well as to provide an opportunity to determine a system of play.

There is a definite trend to time athletes at all levels in the forty-yard dash. We believe this is sound because players like to compete against the clock. There always should be provisions for timing players individually as well as by position. Individual winners and the ten fastest players on the squad should be singled out. We have begun to utilize ten yard sprints to test get-off and initial speed. There are basic drills that will provide an idea of the players' basic abilities in agility and related quickness. A detailed drill analysis is noted in the drill book; the basic wave drill, along with some sort of slalom shuttle run and other running activities, can be used to determine agility.

Players should be weighed and measured to determine their size potential. This also aids in giving instructions to players regarding their reporting weights in the Fall.

Strength is important, but it must be coupled with explosion if an athlete is to reach his potential. (This is discussed in detail in another chapter.) If an athlete is too bulky, he will not be able to move well. We evaluate through the use of pullups, pushups, clean and jerk, bench press, and other similar methods.

It is important for a player to know the requirements for endurance. This is an area in which the self-image comes into play because some athletes do not have endurance; therefore, it must be proved to them that they can go one-hundred percent all of the time and still be fresh in the fourth quarter. Endurance is an important prerequisite for today's athlete, especially when he must play both ways. He must be in shape to out-condition his opponent in the fourth quarter. Endurance emphasis can be accomplished by clocking the players in the mile run so he can work on his own during the Summer and test his improvement when he reports in the Fall.

Conditioning is an element that concerns a person's own pride and the sacrifice he puts into football. The player can learn from habits formed during Spring practice, however, and he will know what will be expected of him in the Fall. We do not necessarily advocate a lot of conditioning in the Spring; we believe its priority may be dependent upon what was required under the previous coach's regime.

Reaction time is a fundamental whose value is not always recognized by many coaches. For us, it has become a very important facet of our total program. Although there are many drills for teaching reaction time, the most important one is having one player react to another in a specific skill. A coach cannot have a successful offense unless the players react to the starting count and get off with the ball. The defensive players must react equally well to the offense in terms of offensive movement, formations, actions they see, and responsibilities.

The importance of the quarterback in a football program is becoming more evident every day. Consequently, any player who thinks he might be able to play the position should be given the opportunity to show his talents. Running and passing drills, all of which are illustrated in the drill book, can be set up to test the abilities of prospective signal callers. A coach should emerge from Spring practice with a very definite opinion of his quarterback's abilities and then formulate his offense accordingly.

Special skills such as passing, catching, kicking, running, and more detailed fundamental abilities should be other targets to point toward during Spring drills.

In summing up the individual and coaching goals in the Spring, the evaluation sheet (pp. 76–77) should be helpful. Each player should be evaluated by each coach during the course of the Spring practice so the head coach has a definite opinion concerning his specific abilities. This may appear to be a lot of work, but the first Spring practice is so important to a beginning coach that he must try every means at his disposal to get a successful program off the ground.

Football position

It is our strong belief that each football program should have its unique trademark as well as being known for something. A beginning coach should sell the Football Position or "bent knee" position to his squad and convince his players that ultimate success will be based on the individual player's abilities to learn to bend

PLAYER EVALUATION SHEET

Name _____ Class_____ Date _____

_____ _____ _____ _____ _____
Offensive position   Defensive position   Height   Weight   School

Films -- Opponent   _____

Jersey color & number   _____

Instructions: Rate player by circling appropriate number:
1. Outstanding 2. Above Average 3. Average 4. Below Average
5. Poor

Rate Everyone:
Quickness   1-2-3-4-5   Size Potential   1-2-3-4-5
Agility   1-2-3-4-5   Durability   1-2-3-4-5
Balance   1-2-3-4-5   Speed   1-2-3-4-5
Strength   1-2-3-4-5   Aggressiveness   1-2-3-4-5
Explosion   1-2-3-4-5   Intensity   1-2-3-4-5
Reaction Time   1-2-3-4-5

If Possible:
Intelligence   1-2-3-4-5
Leadership   1-2-3-4-5
Character   1-2-3-4-5
Pride   1-2-3-4-5

Instructions: Using the same values as above, rate the player for
the abilities listed for his individual position category:

OFFENSE

ENDS		INTERIOR LINEMEN	
Blocking	1-2-3-4-5	Pass blocking	1-2-3-4-5
Avoiding being held up	1-2-3-4-5	In line	1-2-3-4-5
Faking	1-2-3-4-5	Pulling	1-2-3-4-5
Receiving short	1-2-3-4-5	Trap	1-2-3-4-5
Receiving long	1-2-3-4-5	Downfield	1-2-3-4-5
Receiving in crowd	1-2-3-4-5		
Ball carrying ability	1-2-3-4-5		

RUNNING BACKS

Elusive open field runner	1-2-3-4-5
Power runner	1-2-3-4-5
Outside runner	1-2-3-4-5
Inside runner	1-2-3-4-5
Leg drive to break tackles	1-2-3-4-5
Blocking for run	1-2-3-4-5
Ability to catch ball	1-2-3-4-5
Pass protection blocking	1-2-3-4-5

QUARTERBACKS

Quickness in setting up to pass	1-2-3-4-5
Quickness of delivery	1-2-3-4-5
Throw short	1-2-3-4-5
Throw long	1-2-3-4-5
Ability to locate secondary receiver	1-2-3-4-5
Ability to avoid rush	1-2-3-4-5
Ability to throw off balance	1-2-3-4-5
Play calling ability	1-2-3-4-5

DEFENSE

LINEMEN

Strength & ability to defeat

a. 1-on-1 block	1-2-3-4-5
b. double team block	1-2-3-4-5
c. trap block	1-2-3-4-5
d. rush passer	1-2-3-4-5
Recognition	1-2-3-4-5
Lateral movement	1-2-3-4-5
Pursuit	1-2-3-4-5
Tackling	1-2-3-4-5

LINEBACKERS

Ability to key & diagnose	1-2-3-4-5
Use of hands and arms	1-2-3-4-5
Lateral movement	1-2-3-4-5
Pursuit	1-2-3-4-5
Tackling	1-2-3-4-5
Pass coverage ability	1-2-3-4-5
Ability to catch ball	1-2-3-4-5

Note: On defensive ends who do not meet our size requirements, grade as linebackers if possible

BACKS

Ability to key & diagnose	1-2-3-4-5
Pursuit	1-2-3-4-5
Tackling	1-2-3-4-5
Coverage	
a. zone	1-2-3-4-5
b. man to man	1-2-3-4-5
Fight for ball	1-2-3-4-5
Range of coverage	1-2-3-4-5
Ability to catch ball	1-2-3-4-5

SPECIALTIES

Pass	1-2-3-4-5
Punt	1-2-3-4-5
Kick off	1-2-3-4-5
P. A. T. & F. G.	1-2-3-4-5
Punt & kick return	1-2-3-4-5
Punt snap	1-2-3-4-5

Position Player is best suited for: Offense _____   Defense _____

Using our rating system, WINNER, WON'T GET YOU BEAT, WILL GET YOU BEAT, LOSER -- How would you rate him?

_____

Other information: _____

_____

_____

his knees and perform in this position. It is applicable to both offensive and defensive positions, and therefore the incorporated drills will be used by all players. The amount of time spent in this area each day probably will decrease during the ten days, but the coach should allow the necessary time for emphasis and establishment of a sound base during the opening sessions. A player constantly should be reminded that a balanced coiled position is the key to playing football. One must be balanced to hit, and when a player hits, he must uncoil so he is doing the hitting. Most players want to hit, but it has been our experience that very few have the necessary know-how. Teach the football position and impress upon the player how he will be able to improve the control of his body action. The player must be able to balance and control himself before he can control his opponent. Show the player, and prove to him, that he can improve his quickness and accuracy as well as develop reactions and recovery. The proper emphasis will definitely improve the mobility of the players to move in all directions.

The two most important drills to emphasize the football position are the quarter eagle drill and the wave drill.

The quarter eagle drill

The quarter eagle, bent knee position, is what makes a team win or lose. It is impossible to move laterally or forward unless the knees are bent. You must work to improve movement to a point where you can move like a shortstop. The important aspects of the bent knee position are (1) toes forward; (2) knees bent; (3) heels on the ground; (4) tail down; and (5) feet shoulder-width apart.

For the quarter eagle drill, we like to work in groups of two:

¼ TURNS ON "HIT" COMMAND

COACH

For the half turn drill, emphasize quick choppy turns, and work the feet:

The wave drill

This drill is a very important tool in evaluating the progress in the teaching of the football position. We generally line up the players in two or three lines facing the coach, who administers the drill. We also suggest that a player executing the drill is much more effective than the coach who merely stands and indicates one direction or another. The drill begins by a direction indication by the administering coach or player. The athletes run in the direction indicated, watching either the ball or the other player. On a change of direction, they should plant their outside foot, drop their tail, and push off in the other direction with a cross-over step. A coach constantly should evaluate the body position of the participants and stress the importance of body lean as well as proper body balance. The ability to change direction probably is one of the most important qualities of a football player and an educated coach soon will discover the abilities his athletes have in this area. The following is our set-up for the wave drill as well as our "Z" drill which is a more competitive wave drill.

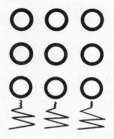

COACH SIGNALS DIRECTION WITH BALL OR HAND (OR BETTER, PLAYER LEADS BY HIS OWN MOVEMENT)

For the "Z" drill, players face each other. As offensive player moves defensive player mirrors his movements, touching the lines from side to side in a five-yard square.

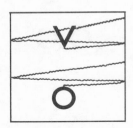

Agility and quickness drills

Agility and quickness are not necessarily natural to the average athlete. They are abilities that can be taught, learned, and built upon. Speed is natural, but a player's quickness can be improved and his agility can be improved every week. Quickness can be inspired by coaches. We believe that a coach can sell the fact that a player can do a job quicker than he did the last time.

In selecting agility and quickness drills, a coach should give careful thought to each drill and exactly what he is trying to evaluate by its structure. A drill without purpose and without proper evaluation is of no value. The following is our drill theory, which will serve as a guideline for the beginning coach.

    1. Selection of a drill—purpose
        a. Know the purpose; what are you going to try to teach?
        b. Is it going to be a reaction drill, a conditioning drill, or a quickness drill?
        c. It is important to let the kids know.
    2. Create a game situation
        a. Is this a real thing? Will it happen in a game?
    3. Repetition
        a. To develop a reaction, repeat something many times in order to develop a reflex.
        b. Repetition builds confidence, self discipline and perfection.
    4. Reactions
        a. A drill must have more than one reaction.
        b. Include second, third, and fourth reactions.
    5. Movement
        a. Include a lot of running in a drill.
        b. Movement is vital in the improvement of quickness and agility.

6. Drills must be competitive
    a. Players must compete against something.
    b. Have a stop watch on them—this helps emphasize speed and quickness.
7. Have a variety of drills
    a. Players have a concentration span and you must be aware of it. It is shorter in high school than in college.
    b. Don't "drag-out" your drills.

Following are some suggested basic agility and quickness drills to incorporate for the entire squad:
    1. Quickness, like a bolt of lightning or a snake's tongue is what we are working toward.
    2. Crowther Sled Drill: Hit-Hit-Roll-Attack!

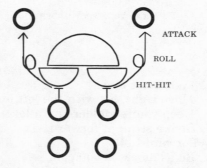

    a. Hit-Hit, then roll and attack something. Can use a bag.
    b. Build a foundation for this.
    c. Show the players how far they can move in six seconds.
    3. Crowther Sled Drill: Hit-Tackle

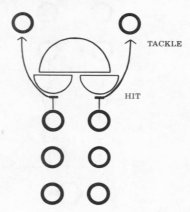

4. When working on the sled, keep your feet up under you.
5. It's good to pick up an object because you must use leverage and football is a game of leverage.
6. Seven Man Sled Drill: Hit-Butt and Roll Drill

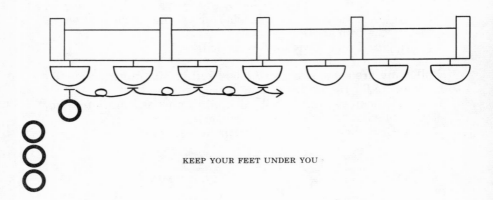

KEEP YOUR FEET UNDER YOU

   a. Pads don't give.
   b. Move right, hit with the left forearm.
   c. Keep your shoulders parallel.
   d. Strike straight forward.
7. Two Forward Rolls
   a. Be as quick as you can.
   b. Work the feet three or four steps.

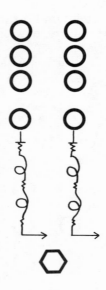

8. One Forward Roll and Fumble Recovery
   a. Dive for the football.

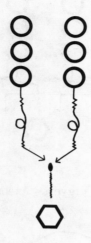

9. Combination Drill
   a. Forward roll, then either wave, recover fumble or belly dive.

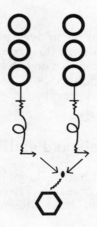

10. Crab Drill
    a. Emphasize keeping the feet up under you.
    b. Move your body.

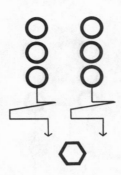

11. Monkey Roll
    a. Use three players — execute a figure eight.

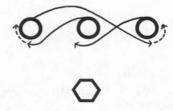

    b. Backs do this with a ball in their arm.
    c. This is used primarily for offensive and defensive backs.
12. Bag Agility Drill
    a. Keep your shoulders parallel to the line — knock the bags down, then recover a fumble.

Agility can be compared to a dog chasing a stick. If you fake the throw, he goes and gets right back. This is the same as it is in football. You have to be able to recover in a quick manner.

Position fundamentals and skills

Fundamentals and individual techniques are necessary if a player is to reach his fullest potential. These fundamentals should be taught enthusiastically at least fifteen to twenty minutes every day, and a coach should be constantly aware of incorporating the basic fundamentals into his entire practice plan. Our suggestion is that in a ten-day Spring practice format that the coach spend as much time in this area as possible. The football team will build much quicker with a sound fundamental base rather than with an emphasis on a lot of different plays, terminology, and execution.

There are basic position fundamentals and skills that are unique to each offensive and defensive position, and a coach should devote a lot of time and research into the areas that will be stressed for each position. The following is a sample of some of these fundamental skills, and a coach constantly should be evaluating the individual's improvement in these areas. Many of these skills can be practiced by the players during the Summer months, and if a player is deficient in a particular area he should have a special program outlined for him to assure success in the Fall.

Offense — Line:
1. Strike
2. Set-up
3. Block on move
4. Pulling courses and techniques

Quarterbacks:
1. Drop
2. Throw
3. Exchange

Receivers:
1. Catch
2. Patterns
3. Block
4. Tight end release

Backs:
1. Back to hole quicker
2. Violent, effective running
3. Confidence in blocking
4. Faking
5. Fumble concentration
6. Scoring — outside thirty yard line

Defense — Down Four:
1. Tackling
2. One-on-one reaction (total)
3. Proper pass rush lanes
4. Improve go and slant techniques
5. Improve pass rush versus area blocking

Linebackers:
1. Tackling
2. Block protection (strike)
3. Pass drop — area
4. Don't over-pursue
5. Rush techniques

Four — Deep:
1. Pass drop
2. Playing the ball
3. Tackling
4. Man coverage
5. Zone coverage
6. Five under
7. Disguise secondary
8. Block protection

Assignments

Assignment learning should be incorporated into the Spring practice plan so players will have a jump on learning in the Fall. A coach should teach the basis of his offense or defense and not try to become too complicated. It is far better to have a fundamental technique carry over than the learning of assignments. A coach should initiate his terminology in its simplest form and establish the basis of his offensive and defensive systems. We suggest the following rotation learning system that has been very effective for us in mastery of our offensive assignments. Dummies or even target jerseys can be used to portray odd or even defenses as well as three and four-deep secondaries, and the teams can rotate through and check assignments. Defensively we utilize our squares which are outlined on the field to simulate an offensive alignment. Defenses can be checked out versus these squares to be sure that the basic learning is being initiated.

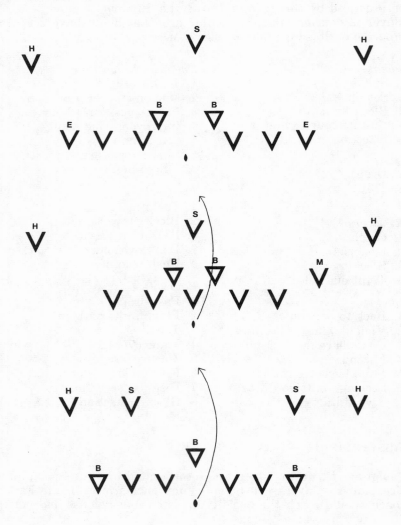

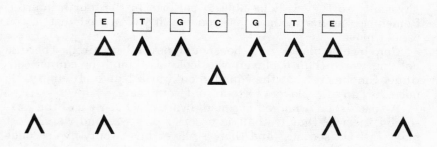

Execution

Team execution is an area that a coach also should evaluate very thoroughly in the Spring. We find that most coaches work on the team aspect and consequently neglect the individual. We do not advocate a lot of team time when practice days are limited, but we do feel that it definitely has its place. A coach should work on the plays that require a lot of execution and timing and use this opportunity to experiment with new ideas both offensively and defensively. Team work can be done versus air or by use of light bags or shields without pads. Execution can become very important if a beginning coach is attempting to evaluate certain personnel and their abilities to perform a specific type of offensive maneuver. Once again, we emphasize that Spring practice is for the individual, and the coach should spend only the amount of team time that he considers necessary. Team get-off and pursuit emphasis will have a lot of carry over for the Fall.

Conditioning

In structuring the amount of conditioning that is necessary in a coach's first Spring practice, he must consider the past performance of his team. If physical conditioning was a definite weakness, he of course should stress this area to a greater degree. Normally there is not a lot of extra time during the Spring; therefore, a coach should get as much running accomplished during the actual practice session. At the same time, he should constantly stress the demands placed on the players in the Fall and impress upon them that their conditioning base will be built during the Summer months.

We still believe a team can out-condition people, and the players should be well aware of its importance. We constantly should push our athletes to higher levels and demand more and more of them physically so they will be able to perform in the fourth quarter. Remember: no matter how fast you are, if you are exhausted, you cannot move.

Convince a player that he should never look tired. There is nothing worse than a player who looks as though he cannot continue. Emphasize that the squad should look lean and hungry. Do not allow any fat players to represent your team.

A coach'should make his squad aware of what we call the "six-second theory," that football is a series of six-second wars. Most plays last six seconds, and then a player has twenty-five seconds to recover and to get ready to go to war again for six-seconds. You can sell your players that they must be able to go all out for these six-second periods, and if they do that, you will be building a base for a successful football program. In evaluating our drills, we tell a player that any reaction or agility drill that lasts over six seconds is a conditioning drill.

Hopefully, a coach will not have to spend a lot of practice time on conditioning but will make an effort to impress upon a player the importance that he must carry out a successful program on his own.

Utilization of relays and/or other competitive running drills will achieve the desired conditioning much faster than routine running exercises with no purpose.

Summer letters

During the summer, we have used various forms of communication to keep in touch with our squad. We formerly sent up to ten letters each Summer to keep them informed regarding our progress and to relate some details concerning the season. However, we now send five specific letters, and they have been sufficient and effective. Following is a breakdown of our Summer letters:

Letter #1   June 18
               General information – reporting weight
Letter #2   July 1
               General information – expectations in Fall
Letter #3   July 15
               General information
                    a. Workout schedule (first) – Dickey
                    b. Offensive and Defensive terminology sheets – White & Gambold
Letter #4   July 30
               Specific invitation to early reporting group
                    a. Workout schedule (second) – Dickey
                    b. Specific Offensive and Defensive assignment information – Staff
Letter #5   August 12
               General information – final reminders

SUMMER LETTER #1

DEPARTMENT OF PHYSICAL EDUCATION AND ATHLETICS

STANFORD UNIVERSITY
STANFORD. CALIFORNIA 94305

June 8

Dear Varsity Squad Member:

This is the first of a summer letter series that will number some four or five and will be spaced evenly throughout the balance of the vacation period. These letters will convey both football information as well as reminders on the progress of your summer conditioning. Digest all of the information so that you will be taking the first step on the road to the conference championship. From time to time, we will be sending return post cards, which you should fill out and send back to us immediately.

We hope that you **are firmly** established on your summer job and are enjoying the break from studies. We want the summer to be an enjoyable one, and yet at no time should you allow yourself to get out of shape. However, as we talked about prior to your leaving the campus, gear your workouts both physically and mentally to peak on or about August 20th.

Your workouts should always stress quickness and endurance. These two objectives must be attained prior to your reporting back to the campus. Guidelines on the proper conditioning program will be sent to you in the subsequent letters.

If weight is a problem, lose it right now . . . don't wait! Your weight should not exceed _____ lbs.

Our staff sends along their best wishes for a most enjoyable summer to you and yours. Should any problems arise at any time, get in touch with me here at the Athletic Department.

Sincerely yours,

John Ralston
Head Football Coach
Stanford University

DEPARTMENT OF PHYSICAL EDUCATION AND ATHLETICS

STANFORD UNIVERSITY
STANFORD, CALIFORNIA 94305

July 1

Dear Varsity Squad Member:

Reflecting back somewhat on the 1969 season, I personally felt a great confident attitude among our squad members every time they went on the field.   This comes from a squad characterized by solid, dedicated performance with tremendous pursuit of purpose toward a common goal.   In a sense we turned the corner two years ago and from that time forward we are geared to nothing but winning performances.   When we assemble in the fall, we all want to build on a confident, successful attitude that in turn   makes for a team feeling that victory will be ours, in each of our eleven games.

There is no easy way to build this type of an attitude.   The only way is one of hard work and meticulous preparation.   We must make every minute count when we reassemble in the fall, as our first hurdle is a big one.   The University of Arkansas plays outstanding football and in their opening game of last year they swarmed all over Oklahoma State from the opening whistle, and did not let up throughout the sixty minutes.   This is the type of team that they have.   They are extremely quick, extremely dedicated, and are made up of good solid athletes.   Our staff has been hard at work studying all of their games of last year, and we will have several films on hand when we assemble in the fall to study.

Every year at this time I list the following six items, as I believe they are the key to winning football.   I realize with the veteran players that you have read this information over and over, and yet with new players it is often good to use these as reminders.   Check them over thoroughly and ask yourself in all sincerity just how you rate on each item.

    1.   Your liking to hit harder than the man opposite you.

    2.   Your willingness to work harder in practice in order to execute better the fundamentals of tackling, blocking and running.

3. Your knowledge and understanding of football and your assignments both on offense and defense.

4. Your condition. Be in better condition than your opponent. Remember you can never be in as good a condition as the other team . . . you are either in better shape or worse shape.

5. Your willingness to push yourself when you are tired. This is the true test of you as a man.

6. You must think in terms of the team, as well as yourself, at all times. This is vital if we are to have the proper discipline and morale, which, in turn, is vital in a winning organization.

In your next letter, we will send you some terminology information as well as your first detailed workout schedule. We assume at the present time that you are gradually working yourself back in shape, and of course at the same time, enjoying your vacation period. Remember, if weight is a problem, lose it now so that you won't have the problem during the month of August.

Also, if you have a problem with the 36 unit progress rule, be sure that your incompletes are made up now . . . don't wait!!! Coach Christiansen will be in touch with you, and is perfectly willing to help you out, but in most cases you know exactly what must be done. Again, I urge you, do not procrastinate, but get this responsibility out of the way at the earliest possible date.

I can't wait to get started this fall, and I hope that you share this enthusiasm. Continue to enjoy your summer, and if any problems arise, call me collect at 415-321-2300, ext. 4512. If I am not on the campus, be sure that you get in touch with one of our coaches, as they will all be here during the summer.

Sincerely yours,

John Ralston
Head Football Coach
Stanford University

DEPARTMENT OF PHYSICAL EDUCATION AND ATHLETICS

STANFORD UNIVERSITY

STANFORD, CALIFORNIA 94305

July 15

Dear Varsity Squad Member:

I just returned from Lubbock, Texas, where I participated in the Coaches All-America Game with the West Squad. Unfortunately, we were on the short end of a 34-27 game, which I am sure you were able to see on television. Bubba Brown and Don Parish played a big part in the ball game, which was witnessed by a record 42,000 people.

The big topic of discussion the entire time I was in the Southwest was the opening football game with the University of Arkansas. We had two fine players on our squad from Arkansas, Rod Brand and Cliff Powell. If these two athletes were any indication of the type of football players they have at Arkansas, you can rest assured they will be a formidable opponent.

It was a great experience in this truly collegiate football country and it serves to focus attention on the upcoming season. We are about at the midway point in our summer break, and I am sure you are like all the rest of us in casting an anxious eye toward the 1970 campaign.

You will notice that we have enclosed some information, both on your summer workouts as well as terminology information. We will be adding some more technical information in your next letter that will be sent on or about August 1st. Be sure to digest this information thoroughly, as you will be tested on it when you report back.

The running and workout schedule should be followed closely and we will be sending additional information in your next letter. As I stated to you previously, gear your workouts to peak around August 22nd when we will be reporting back. Continue to enjoy your summer, and if any of our coaches can be of service to you, please be sure to give us a call.

Sincerely,

John Ralston
Head Football Coach
Stanford University

SUMMER LETTER #4

DEPARTMENT OF PHYSICAL EDUCATION AND ATHLETICS

STANFORD UNIVERSITY
STANFORD, CALIFORNIA 94305

July 30

Dear Varisty Squad Member:

In observing the date on this letter, I can't help but get a chill
when I think that before another month rolls around we will be well
on our way to total preparation for the 1970 season. Our staff cannot wait to begin and I trust that you, too, share this enthusiasm.
1970 will be the Year of the Indians, and a conference championship
is our goal. The momentum we gained last year must be continued
from the outset of our practice sessions. The confidence that we
achieved in winning the last six games must be carried right into
the Arkansas opener.

Our staff has been working diligently throughout the summer in preparation for the fall. The offensive coaches have completed their
individual notebooks, and are mailing them to you separately. These
must accompany you when you return to the campus. The defensive
coaches are still involved in several decisions, but are assembling
the same type of notebook that will be ready when you report on
August 22nd.

Consider this as your formal invitation to join the Stanford Varsity
for early practice on August 22nd. If an emergency should arise
that would prevent you from complying with this schedule, please
get in touch with me immediately by phone. Make it a collect call
to 415-321-2300, ext. 4512.

Enclosed please find a return post card that should be filled out
and mailed immediately. Do this as soon as you finish reading
this letter.

We would like you to report here sometime Saturday afternoon,
August 22nd. Check into Toyon Hall between the hours of 3:30 PM
and 5:30 PM. You will be asked to deposit $1.00 when you re-
ceive your room key. This will be refunded later in September
when you check out. Have your own blankets when you arrive
and your linen will be issued by the attendant. At 6:00 PM we
will have our Welcome Back Dinner. We will not have a curfew
on this first evening together.

Our schedule for Sunday, August 23rd, is still being adjusted. However, this is a rough schedule at the present time:
    8:00   AM   Everyone up
    8:30   AM   Breakfast

9:00 to 10:00	AM	Church services for those desirous of attending
10:15	AM	Squad meeting in Toyon Hall
11:00	AM	Demonstration of Exer-genie stretching exercises
12:15	PM	Lunch
1:00 to 1:45	PM	Equipment issue by positions with your coaches. Proper fitting will take place at this time.
2:00	PM	On field-Picture Day with writers and photographers
4:00	PM	Offensive and defensive meetings in rooms to be assigned
6:00	PM	Dinner
7:00	PM	Optional meetings if needed
11:00	PM	Lights out

Monday morning, August 24, will be as follows:

7:00	AM	Everyone up
7:30	AM	Breakfast
8:00 to 10:00	AM	Physical examinations for offensive group. The offensive group will be on the field at this time.
12:15	PM	Lunch

We will then swing into our regular program that afternoon. Our first three days will be no-pad workouts and we will move into our regular two-a-day pad practices on Thursday, August 27th.

Coach Randy Cardin, Coach Dave Currey, Coach Bill Moultrie and myself will be living in Toyon Hall all through the early practice sessions.

Personal automobiles will be parked at the Toyon Hall parking lot from 7:00 AM until after dinner each practice day. Use of personal automobiles during the day must be authorized by the coaching staff.

Watch your meals from now on. Do not eat between meals and try to eat balanced protein food. Get your feet toughened so that blisters will not be a problem. Report at or under the weight we requested at the outset of our summer letters. REMEMBER, QUICKNESS AND ENDURANCE ARE VITAL!!!

Again, we want to urge you of the importance of bringing all written material back with you when you report. Be in top physical shape on August 22nd.

One more letter will be forthcoming. Let's get mentally and physically geared for 1970.

Sincerely,

John Ralston
Head Football Coach
Stanford University

RUNNING WORKOUT SEQUENCE
#1

1. Warm up: Jog an 880, which is one half a mile.

2. Carry out your agility program that was sent to you in your last letter, don't forget to stretch and <u>warm up well</u>. This should include:

    a. Jumping jack or side straddle hop

    b. Trunk rotator

    c. Wind mill - toe toucher

    d. Alternate toe toucher and belly slapper

    e. Hurdlers exercise - stretch fully both legs

    f. Belly roll - arch back - hands behind the back

    g. 10 bridges - front and back

    h. Stretch outside and inside of ankles

    i. Elbows between the knees while in squat position - push out with elbows--push in with knees - alternate

    j. High step for 10 yards--(Run lifting knees as high as possible--emphasis on the leg lift, not speed)

    k. Bear walk - 40 yards

    l. Carioca - Cross field twice over and back

    m. Run backwards - cross field over and back--repeat with angle run crossing over one way, then the other alternately.

3. Run **five** laps around a football field, running the sidelines and walking the turns. When running the sidelines, start out at a slow pace and gradually pick it up until you reach 80 to 90 percent effort.

4. Execute 50 sit-ups and three sets of 20 push-ups, resting three minutes in between each set. If this does not tax you, increase the repetitions in each set.

5. Warm down - jog an 880, one half mile; sprint the last 50 yards.

DEPARTMENT OF PHYSICAL EDUCATION AND ATHLETICS

STANFORD UNIVERSITY
STANFORD, CALIFORNIA 94305

August 12

Dear Varsity Squad Member:

This will be your final letter prior to your reporting a week from Saturday, August 22. Everything is in readiness and our entire coaching staff is chomping at the bit ready for the first practice sessions.

Gear up your workouts to the maximum in this final ten day period so that you will be razor sharp to start our drills. We have less time than ever to prepare for an opening game and must be set to move rapidly into the technical aspects of the game.

Everyone of us has a tremendous responsibility to each other. All of us are integral parts of a total machine. At no time can we let down and fail to give 110% on the road to success.

Be ready! Get keyed! Wow! <u>The time is now!</u> See you in a week,

Sincerely yours,

John Ralston
Head Football Coach
Stanford University

RUNNING WORKOUT SEQUENCE
#2

1. Warm up by running an 880.

2. Carry out your agility program that was sent to you previously.
   <u>Warm up well</u> .... this should include

   a. Jumping jack or side straddle hop

   b. Trunk rotator

   c. Wind mill - toe toucher

   d. Alternate toe toucher and belly slapper

   e. Hurdlers exercise - stretch fully both legs

   f. Belly roll - arch back - hands behind the back

   g. 10 bridges - front and back

   h. Stretch outside and inside of ankles

   i. Elbows between the knees while in squat position -
      push out with elbows--push in with knees -
      alternate

   j. High step for 10 yards--(Run lifting knees as high
      as possible--emphasis on the leg lift, not speed)

   k. Bear walk - 40 yards

   l. Carioca - Cross field twice over and back

   m. Run backwards - cross field over and back--repeat
      with angle run crossing over one way, then the
      other alternately.

3. Run twenty 50 yard sprints. Run these by starting slow and
   gradually pick up your pace so that you are going full speed at
   40 yards. Finish the last 10 yards of each sprint at full speed.
   Run each one of the 50s on a one minute interval. This means
   that if it takes you seven seconds to run the 50, you will be
   taking a 53 second rest before the next 50 yard sprint. As you
   gain the necessary endurance, decrease the interval time and
   work toward a goal of one 50 yard sprint per every 30 seconds.

4. Execute two sets of 50 sit-ups and three sets of 20 push-ups.
   Do the sit-ups between each set of push-ups.

5. Warm down by jogging an 880. Sprint the last 100 yards.
   Really push yourself in this endeavor.

We have found Summer letters to be very advantageous, and we encourage beginning coaches to incorporate them in their programs if they seem to be appropriate. A coach must sense the attitude of his players regarding letters; if he believes the players are receptive and can profit from them, they should be used. Players and coaches at the high school level generally live in the same community, so letters may not be necessary. However, it might be important to have periodic get-togethers, and players might be encouraged to engage in informal workouts.

The well-organized coach can lay important groundwork during the Summer that will aid in creating the desired team attitude when practice begins. It is during this time that the coach has the opportunity to communicate with the squad specific offensive and defensive information, weight programs, and his football philosophy. One word of caution: most players who elect to play football are excited about the coming season; a coach therefore must guard against overdoing a good thing to the point that the players are tired of too much preparation before actual practice begins.

A useful tool is a postcard for players' responses. It also serves as a method of evaluating the players' attitude.

SUMMER POSTCARD

I.   I am running my mile
     ( ) Five times around a football field
     ( ) Four times around a quarter-mile track
     ( ) Other (specify) _____

II. Are you able to have weights available to follow
     the weight-lifting program?   ( ) Yes   (   ) No

III. Did you check out canvas shoes before leaving
     for the summer?   ( ) Yes   (   ) No

IV. Did you check out football shoes before leaving
     for the summer?   (   ) Yes   (   ) No

     Signed _____

The Summer letters have been used by us in our program in the past along with the accompanying enclosures which stress our philosophy of football along with pertinent information regarding conditioning.

Preceding each set of instructions is a message emphasizing the importance of carrying out the suggestions. The first three letters discuss conditioning and it is emphasized that a regular running program should be followed, together with general conditioning tips, workouts, and weight procedures. The fourth letter sets forth the elements necessary for becoming a champion; the fifth one discusses the general philosophy of football and the player's worth to his team; and finally, a letter is included which offers news notes concerning squad members and the qualities of a great collegiate football player.

The attitudes that make a great football player should be instilled in the players during the entire year and particularly should be emphasized during Spring drills and in Summer letters. Following are some sample attitude and conditioning memoranda designed to encourage mental and physical excellence.

CONDITIONING

I. You must return in good physical condition
   A. To decrease possibility of injury
   B. To decrease fatigue and muscle soreness during first two weeks of practice
      1. You concentrate better while learning when you are not tired and stiff
      2. You operate better physically when you are not tired and stiff
   C. To have the movement and strength needed for football

II. Method of attaining good physical condition
   A. Continue with the exercises and running outlined in the previous conditioning letter. (Do abdominal curls with hands clasped on top of head.)
   B. Add two exercises that should be done six days a week, preferably before going to bed
      1. Gripper
        a. Position: hands gripping any round object like a floor lamp or chair leg
        b. Execution: take a deep breath, squeeze with fingers, thumbs, and palms. After about 5 or 6 seconds, let your breath out slowly, then breathe as normally as possible until end of exercise, which is about 10 seconds from beginning.
      2. Ski Exercise
        a. Position: take a "sitting position" with your back and back of head resting against a wall, upper legs parallel to floor, feet directly under knees, and arms at sides.
        b. Execution: remain in this position for two minutes.
   C. Add ten fifty-yard sprints three days a week. (Continue to run mile one day a week. You must be able to run a 6-minute mile by the first of September.)

PLEASE BRING THIS AND THE OTHER CONDITIONING FORM WITH YOU WHEN YOU RETURN.

PHYSICAL CONDITIONING PROGRAM

I. Purpose
   A. Develop explosive strength
   B. Develop body to leathery toughness
   C. Develop endurance

II. Methods
   A. Proper sleep habits
      1. Between 8 and 9 hours sleep every night
      2. Get sleep at about same time every night
   B. Proper diet habits
      1. Do not overeat
      2. Eat foods that you know are good for you, such as: milk, cheese, eggs, meat, fruit, vegetables, soup, fruit and vegetable juices, whole wheat bread, etc.
      3. Prepare food properly by having it broiled, baked, or boiled
      4. Do not eat foods that you know are bad for you, such as: soft drinks, candy, pastries, fried and greasy food, spiced food, etc.
   C. Avoid harmful stimulants
      1. Tobacco
      2. Alcoholic beverages
   D. Proper physical exercise for those who have access to weights
      1. Exercises
         a. Weight exercises--3 days a week
            1) Warm up
            2) High pull
            3) Stand-up press
            4) Heel raise
            5) Sitting raise
            6) Bench press
         b. Additional exercises--3 days a week
            1) Abdominal curls
            2) Neck exercise
         c. Mile run--1 day a week
      2. Exercise instructions
         a. Warm up
            1) Stretch groins and hamstrings
            2) Side straddle hops (50)
            3) Clean bar from floor to chest rest position, press to arm extended position over head, lower to chest rest position, lower to floor. Repeat, without stopping, for 10 repetitions. Use between 100 and 125 lbs.

b. High pull exercise
1) Position: crouch, feet shoulder width apart, toes well under bar with ankles touching bar. Hands on bar slightly wider than shoulder width apart, palms toward you. Knees bent, shoulders higher than hips. <u>Eyes remain on object such as ceiling light or point where ceiling and wall meet, throughout entire exercise.</u>
2) Execution: extend legs and back <u>simultaneously,</u> pulling the bar to shoulder height, coming up on toes at end of pull, lower bar to floor. Take hands off bar and come to standing position before doing another repetition. Repeat, without stopping, for 5 repetitions. Do 3 sets.

c. Stand-up press exercise
1) Position: same as for high pull exercise
2) Execution: clean weight to chest rest position, press to arm extended position overhead, lower to chest rest position. Repeat, without stopping, for 5 repetitions. Do 3 sets.

d. Heel raise exercise
1) Position: normal erect stance, feet shoulder width apart, knees slightly bent, with balls of feet on a two-inch support. Bar in neck rest position.
2) Execution: lift bar and body weight, by raising heels off the floor as high as possible, while transferring your weight toward your big toes, hesitate for a second, lower heels to floor. Repeat, without stopping, for 10 repetitions. Do 3 sets.
(This exercise can be done close to a wall to help maintain balance by touching wall with your forehead.)

e. Sitting raise exercise
1) Position: normal erect stance, feet shoulder width apart, feet flat on floor, and toes pointed straight ahead. Bar in neck rest position.
2) Execution: lower body into a sitting position by touching a chair or bench to determine "sitting position," keep heels on floor, rise to erect position. Repeat, without stopping, for 10 repetitions. Do 3 sets.

    f.   Bench press exercise
        1)   Position: lying on bench face up, bar at chest rest position, with palms away from you. Vary grip from shoulder width to a wider grip.
        2)   Execution: press bar to arm extended position over chest, lower to chest position. Repeat, without stopping, for 5 repetitions. Do 3 sets.
    g.   Abdominal curls--3 days a week, other than weight exercise days
        1)   Position: lying on back, knees forming right angle, feet on ground, hands clasped behind head.
        2)   Execution: bring head and shoulders up in curling motion and touch one leg with opposite elbow, return to original position, then curl up touching other leg with other elbow. (This would be 2 repetitions.) Do 50, until you can do 50 without stopping, then do as many as you can without stopping until you are able to do 100. Use a soft surface so your tail bone will not be irritated.
    h.   Neck exercise--3 days a week, other than weight exercise days
        1)   Position: hands and knees on ground. Partner straddles you placing his hands first on back of your head, second clasping hands on forehead, third placing hands on left side of head, and fourth placing hands on right side of head.
        2)   Execution: attempt to move your head in the direction of your partner's hands for six seconds in each of the four directions, while partner keeps head from moving.
    i.   Mile run--1 day a week, other than weight exercise days
        1)   Run in canvas shoes
        2)   Run 4 laps around a quarter-mile track, or 5 laps around a football field including end zones.
        3)   Make your objective a 6-minute mile
3.   General rules for 6 weight exercises
    a.   This routine should be done 3 days a week with 1 or 2 days off between workouts
    b.   Do all exercises in an explosive manner.

    c.   Rest no more than 2 minutes between sets, and no more than 3 minutes between exercises

    d.   Stop on the fifth or tenth repetition each time even though you can do more

    e.   Do first set of each exercise with 25 to 50 lbs. less than maximum weight which is used for the other 2 sets

    f.   Start with 100 lbs. as maximum weight for each exercise

    g.   Increase your maximum weight (which will become different for each exercise) each day you exercise, if possible

    h.   You should be increasing your maximum weight to the point where you are not always able to do the prescribed number of repetitions

E. Proper physical exercise for those who do not have access to weights

    1. Exercises

        a. Isometric exercises--6 days a week

           1) Warm up

           2) Middle pull

           3) Stand-up press

           4) Heel raise

           5) Leg press

        b. Additional exercises--3 days a week

           1) Abdominal curls

           2) Neck exercise

        c. Mile run--1 day a week

    2. Exercise instructions

        a. Warm up

           1) Stretch groins and hamstrings

           2) Side straddle hops (50)

           3) Six-count burpees (which includes push up) (20)

        b. Middle pull exercise

           1) Position: normal erect stance, feet shoulder width apart, heels off the ground, knees slightly bent. Hands shoulder width apart, palms toward you, on bar, rail, or any immovable object about waist high

           2) Execution: take a deep breath, pull straight up on immovable object, thinking in terms of pulling it out of the ground. After about 5 or 6 seconds, let your breath out slowly, then breathe as normally as possible until end of exercise, which is about 10 seconds from beginning.

c. Stand-up press exercise
  1) Position: standing in doorway, normal erect stance, feet shoulder width apart. Hands shoulder width apart, overhead, on door frame, elbows bent.
  2) Execution: take a deep breath, tighten your legs and rear, press straight up on door frame, thinking in terms of "lifting the house." After 5 or 6 seconds, let your breath out slowly, then breathe as normally as possible until end of exercise, which is about 10 seconds from beginning. (Stand on boards to adjust height if necessary.)

d. Heel raise exercise
  1) Position: standing in doorway, normal erect stance, feet shoulder width apart, heels off the floor, knees slightly bent. Hands overhead on door frame.
  2) Execution: take a deep breath, mentally lock your arms in a static position as much as possible, push straight up with your toes, feet, ankles, and lower legs, thinking in terms of "lifting the house." After 5 or 6 seconds, let your breath out slowly, then breathe as normally as possible until end of exercise, which is about 10 seconds from beginning.

e. Leg press exercise
  1) Position: sitting position in doorway, back against one side of door frame, feet against other side of door frame, knees bent.
  2) Execution: take a deep breath, press hard against the door frame, thinking in terms of straightening your legs. After 5 or 6 seconds, let your breath out slowly, then breathe as normally as possible until end of exercise, which is about 10 seconds from beginning. (Use a cushion or pillow between your back and door frame.)

f. Abdominal curls (see instructions above)

g. Neck exercise (see instructions above)

h. Mile run (see instructions above)

PRE-SEASON CONDITIONING PROGRAM

I.   GENERAL
    A. Workout 4 times a week during the rest of July.
    B. In August, workouts should be 5 times a week.
    C. Calisthenic exercises should be done at a <u>quick tempo</u>. Otherwise you get little value from them.
    D. At <u>first</u>, do not <u>push</u> hard on the springing part. Get muscles used to the stress moderately. You destroy more than you build if you pull a muscle before you are ready for the hard work.
    E. Your total workout will last 45 minutes to an hour.

II.   THE WORKOUT
    A. 5 minutes of stretching exercises: This will protect you against muscle pulls.
    B. 15 minutes: Calisthenic exercises.

	1st Week Jul. 18-24	2nd Week Jul. 25-31	3rd Week Aug. 1-7	4th Week Aug. 8-14	5th Week Aug. 15-21	6th Week Aug. 22-28
Pushups	2 sets of of 8	2 sets of 10	3 sets of 8	3 sets of 10	3 sets of 10	3 sets of 12
Sit-ups	2 sets of 10	2 sets of 12	3 sets of 10	3 sets of 12	3 sets of 15	3 sets of 18
Pullups-Chin	2 sets of 5	2 sets of 6	2 sets of 7	3 sets of 5	3 sets of 6	3 sets of 7
(Burpees) Squat Thrusts	2 sets of 10	2 sets of 12	2 sets of 15	3 sets of 11	3 sets of 12	3 sets of 14
Jumping Jacks	2 sets of 10	2 sets of 12	3 sets of 10	3 sets of 12	3 sets of 15	3 sets of 18

    C. 5 minutes: Repeat stretching exercises:
    D. 10 minutes: sprints:
        1st Week: 3 of 25 yds.   4th Week: 8 of 30 yds.
        2nd Week: 6 of 25 yds.   5th Week: 10 of 30 yds.
        3rd Week: 7 of 30 yds.   6th Week: 12 of 30 yds.

    E. The Derby: 10 to 15 minutes.

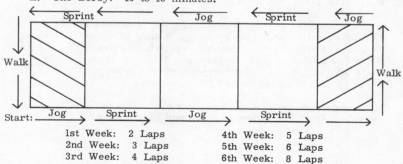

        1st Week: 2 Laps   4th Week: 5 Laps
        2nd Week: 3 Laps   5th Week: 6 Laps
        3rd Week: 4 Laps   6th Week: 8 Laps

"DO NOT BE SORRY ON SOME AUTUMN SATURDAY AFTERNOON FOR WHAT YOU DIDN'T DO THIS SUMMER"

AN APPROACH TO FOOTBALL

The main purpose for participation in football is based on the participant having FUN. We sincerely believe that it is more FUN to win and at the same time believe that the player who has the courage and determination to prepare himself to be a winner will derive a considerable amount of personal, worthwhile advantage from participating in the game of football.

Preparation to WIN is a vital part of the approach to the football program.

A winning attitude and the development of a tremendous WILL TO WIN must be a vital part of the thinking of all coaches and players.

There are three qualities which a player must develop in order to gain a spot on a winner:

1. He must contribute constructively to team morale.

2. He must have the courage and determination to get himself in BETTER physical condition than his opponent.

3. He must concentrate--minimize mistakes.

Football is a physical game, and the contact element of the game must be thoroughly enjoyed (not just tolerated) by the player. Football is a courage sport which is to be played with intense abandon. You must be determined to dominate your opponent in the man to man part of the game. You must take a real delight in playing the game with all the hardness and intensity with which the game is meant to be played. The name of the game is KNOCK.

Football also is a mental game, and those who play must have a belief in themselves, their teammates, and the institution. If you believe there is anyone on your schedule you can't beat, do not insult your school by representing it.

Losing should be bitterly disappointing but in no way should your disappointment be shown by brooding, making of excuses, deriding your opponent, show of ill temper, or lack of poise. Coaches and players should show their distaste for defeat by beginning immediately after a loss to make every effort to win the next game. No defeat is ever final unless the loser despairs.

The greatest measure of a player's worth to his team is found in the effect which his actions and attitude have on team morale.

There is no more spectacular, more inspiring, and more enjoyable sports event for a player than participating in a championship or bowl game. The road there, however, is made of many blocks, tackles, and wind sprints. If you want to be a champion, you must be a sound fundamental football player. Only condition, concentration, hard work and responsiveness to coaching will get you there.

We believe in the dignity of <u>every</u> player on the squad. The sixth stringer is just as important a person as is the first stringer. This does not mean that equal technical attention will always be given to the sixth and first string. It is part of being a man to learn how to "ride the bench" if there are people of greater ability playing. All players who display the courage, attitude and self-lessness necessary to contribute to the team's success will receive the respect of coaches and players.

The player who puts out second effort <u>all the time</u> is the only one who can become a champion. A great football player is:

ALWAYS PURSUING

ALWAYS GANG TACKLING

ALWAYS COMING ON

"A WINNER NEVER QUITS--A QUITTER NEVER WINS!"

PHILOSOPHY OF FOOTBALL

There are two functions which our football program should serve in order to benefit those people participating in the sport:

1. It should be fun
2. It should contribute in a most worthwhile manner to the education of the participants.

Winning football certainly contributes greatly to the amount of enjoyment that a participant derives from the game. The player who learns how to prepare himself sufficiently to win in this highly competitive sport has learned much in terms of group unity, self discipline, courage, and application of effort.

For these reasons, preparation to WIN is a vital part of the approach to the football program at Stanford University.

A winning attitude and a tremendous WILL to WIN must be a vital part of the thinking of all coaches and players.

It is essential that our squad be better conditioned than the opponents. This is one advantage that can be gained completely through determination.

The dignity of the individual player is to be preserved. The fifth stringer is as important a person as is the first stringer. This does not mean that equal technical attention need be given to the fifth and first string. It is part of being a man to learn how to "ride the bench" if there are people of greater ability playing. All players who display the courage, attitude, and selflessness necessary to contribute to the team's success should receive the respect of coaches and players.

The effect of a player's actions and attitude upon team morale is the greatest measure of his worth to the team. The coaches need not hesitate in taking necessary measures to deal with actions which adversely affect team morale. In extreme cases, it might be necessary to dismiss a player from the squad.

One of the truly important aspects in developing a WILL to WIN is found in how one reacts to a setback. Coaches and players while constantly seeking to minimize the errors which cause defeat must be ready to bounce back from defeat with greater determination. Immediate preparation to win the next one should be the pattern followed.

Losing should be bitterly disappointing but\in no way should our disappointment be shown by brooding, making of excuses, or show of ill temper or lack of poise. The way coaches and players should show their distaste for defeat is by beginning immediately to make every effort to win the next game. No defeat is ever final unless the loser despairs.

The physical aspect of the game must be thoroughly understood and enjoyed by the player. It is a courage sport which is to be played with intense abandon. The player must be determined to <u>dominate</u> his opponent in the man to man part of the game. The player must be convinced of the value in second effort.

This is a contact sport and the player will not enjoy it unless he takes real delight in playing with <u>all</u> the hardness and intensity with which the game is meant to be played.

He must take real delight in performing <u>all</u> the fundamentals of the game--blocking, tackling, <u>and running</u>. He must want to be "in" on every play. When the going gets tough, he must get tougher. No department of play must be unimportant but <u>defense</u> must be the most important. On defense, he can best show what kind of a football player he is by:

> Always pursuing
> Always gang tackling
> Always coming on.

THE NAME OF THE GAME IS --- KNOCK!

THE QUALITIES OF A GREAT
FOOTBALL PLAYER

1. HE HAS A BURNING DESIRE TO WIN!

2. He is in school first and foremost to gain an education.   As
    a result, he never cuts classes without a pressing reason.
    He prepares his work accurately and on time.   He has regular
    study habits.   He has the courage to push himself to the limit
    of his scholastic abilities.

3. He prepares himself physically and is in top condition the year
    round.

4. He is a team player and glories in a team victory.

5. He is bitterly disappointed by defeat, but he reacts to defeat
    by more determined effort and resolve, not by a childish
    display of temper or by an unsportsmanlike series of excuses.

6. He loves to run, tackle, and block--football's three most
    fundamental actions.

7. He learns his assignments thoroughly.

8. In a game he DOMINATES HIS OPPONENT.   The great football
    player is more relentless, better conditioned, more confident,
    retains greater poise, and takes better advantage of the breaks
    than the man against whom he is playing.

9. He never quits, never admits defeat, and plays every play as
    if it is the crucial one of the game.

10. He works on his weaknesses.

11. He is intent to come off the field every day a better player
    than he was when he went onto the field.

12. He is willing to make sacrifices involving limited social
    activity and adherence to training regulations.

13. He strives for a better position on his squad.

14. He hustles all the time.

15. HE HAS A BURNING DESIRE TO WIN!

ARE YOU A GREAT FOOTBALL PLAYER?

HOW A CHAMPION CONDUCTS HIMSELF

1. Be courteous to officials--it is an indication of poise.
2. When you are penalized, run to your huddle spot with no quibbling or grousing. Show that you came to play, not to talk--it is an indication of poise.
3. Always run on and off the field when involved in a substitution situation--it is an indication of poise.
4. Keep your chin off your chest after you have made an error. We all know it was not committed by you on purpose.
5. If a teammate makes an error encourage him; do not ride him.
6. Do not be a "tough guy" after the whistle, but show tremendous mental toughness every second that the ball is in play.
7. Turn down doing the things which will keep you from being a champion, even though you may be subject to criticism for not "going along with the crowd." This takes guts sometimes. Show that you have got the necessary stuff.
8. Remember that what you do on and off the field reflects on your teammates. Be a credit to your teammates, your parents, and your school.
9. At half time and at the end of the game sprint to the locker room. Do not hang around waiting for coeds and photographers.
10. Make up your mind that you will beat every opponent you play; team for team and man for man. Determine to dominate your opponent, but FIRST, do the necessary things to prepare yourself to dominate him.
11. Never think about how tired you are! If you know you have done a better job of conditioning yourself than your opponent has, think about how tired he is.
12. ALWAYS PURSUE! ALWAYS GANG TACKLE! ALWAYS BE COMING ON!
13. ALWAYS RETAIN POISE.
14. Delete from your dictionary the words "easy," "can't," and "soft." If you have really got the stuff try drawing a line through the word "AUTOMOBILE" also.
15. Make your goal line stand hold up!
16. Get off the ground! Run back to the huddle!
17. Do all these things at all times, but especially at those times when the tide is going against you.

BE A CHAMPION ON AND OFF THE FIELD!

Reporting day

After using various gauges to determine the physical condition of our squad members when they report in the Fall, we have arrived at this method as the most effective:

A mile run, timing of three forty-yard dashes, number of situps that can be done in ninety seconds, and a determination if they can perform up to fifty pushups and ten pullups. With these requirements, an important measure can be made regarding just how badly a player wants to play the game; if he can make the necessary sacrifices during the Summer to perform well in these exercises, he is ready to begin the Fall training program. We have found that most of the players in the skilled positions can run a mile in under five minutes and thirty seconds; the nonskilled or other position players run it under six minutes fifteen seconds. Running a mile, with the endurance it requires, often is a mental as well as a physical test. There is considerable literature that discusses running and the aerobic system, and coaches should be familiar with it. It always helps if players believe they are in better condition than their opponents, and it ultimately will contribute to their endurance and success as the season progresses.

Our primary advice in this regard is to discourage coaches from becoming so obsessed with rigorous tests that their initial teaching efforts suffer. The emphasis that is placed on early practice will continue in peaking a team for its first game. Therefore, the tests should have meaning and be a bridge to the teaching of techniques that are required under the emotional stress of a game such as football.

The Stanford coaches send to players a considerable amount of offensive and defensive information during the Summer, and we therefore have the opportunity to test their memories during our first no-pad workouts. We have used both the oral and written methods. Both have been very effective in determining exactly what they have retained. The offensive players are given several written questions, and they are asked to draw a play and fill in their assignments. The defensive players are asked to fill in their assignments and responsibilities; we also require them to list on a separate sheet of paper some of the different terminology that has been sent to them and to identify by sight the different formations we anticipate playing against in the Fall.

We also ask individual players to present the information orally to his fellow players, and we find that it is one of the most effective ways to test their knowledge. It is extremely rewarding to hear a player explain his assignment and the reasons for it. It also opens one's eyes regarding the amount of thought that some players give to their assignments and responsibilities. Many of their thoughts are incorporated by the coaches in their teaching techniques. This technique of oral presentation also results in team respect and admiration.

The mental testing of players is important because both offenses and defenses are becoming so sophisticated and detailed that a good base must be established to be sure that they understand exactly what the coach is attempting to accomplish. If the players are not able to understand or the explanation is too complicated, then the teaching technique should be geared to the slowest learner. There is no place for mental mistakes in football because we know that there will be more than enough technical and physical mistakes. It will be a long season if mental mistakes are not eliminated.

Following are samples of some of the written tests we have given our players both offensively and defensively.

OFFENSIVE TEST

1.   Name this formation and number all backs and linemen.

---

2.   Name this formation and number all backs and linemen.

3. Name these formations.
   a.

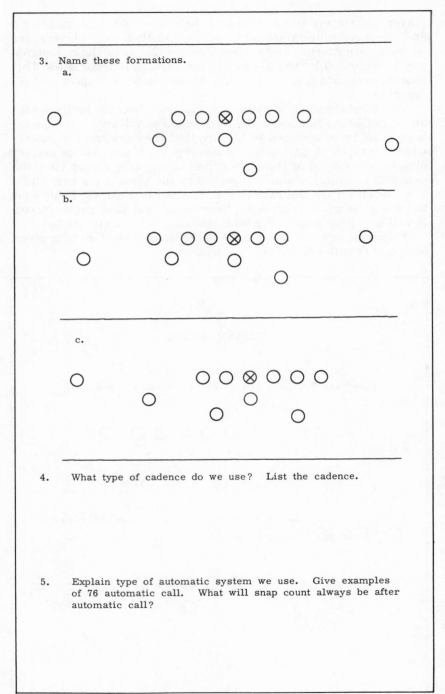

   b.

   c.

4. What type of cadence do we use? List the cadence.

5. Explain type of automatic system we use. Give examples of 76 automatic call. What will snap count always be after automatic call?

6. Blacken your position in the huddle and list all others.

Ball

7. How do we designate point of attack?

8. On this formation draw arrow, back, and linemen to show point of attack.

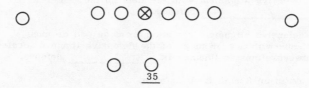

35

9. Match column A with column B and name a play in each series.

Match			Play	
_____	A.	70	_____	1. Method of holding defense to better utilize a particular pass.
_____	B.	60	_____	2. Quick passes.
_____	C.	90	_____	3. Planned check-off short passes behind line of scrimmage from dropback.
_____	D.	Draw	_____	4. QB pass action strong after taken run fake.
_____	E.	Screen	_____	5. Dropback passes.
_____	F.	Roll Out	_____	6. QB pass action strong or weak with no run fake.
_____	G.	Bootleg	_____	7. Pass action by QB away from backfield action utilizing a better fake than in bootleg.

_____ H. Sprint   _____   8. 5 man go patterns.

_____ I. Running Play_____   9. Late hitting runs
          Fake Passes   off of our dropback action.

_____ J. Waggle   _____   10. Pass action of QB
                              away from action of the backfield.

10. List as many of running plays as you can in their proper
     position above formation drawing.

    ○   ○ ○ ⊗ ○ ○ ○   ○
               ○

11. A defensive alignment with the man on the center is a
     _____ defense.

12. A defensive alignment variation from an odd or even
     defense with one or more of the defensive linemen located
     between offensive linemen is _____ defense.

13. Draw in an 8 man front defense.

    ○   ○ ○ ⊗ ○ ○ ○   ○
               ○
            ○   ○

14. Defensive alignment which employs a defensive back or LB
     in a tight position on a wide receiver is called a _____.

15. Defensive alignment used with time running out or in long
     yardage situations and characterized by few rushers and
     numerous secondary coverages is a _____.

16. When a defensive linebacker aligns on our tight end and a
     down lineman is outside we refer to this as an _____
     alignment.

17. Any defensive charge other than a normal charge is called a
     _____.

18. A defensive stunt involving one or more linebackers is called
    a _____.

19. Draw a Pro 4-3 defense.

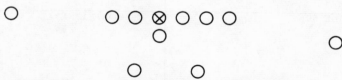

20. Draw a 60 (splits) defense.

21. We have a list of team objectives and goals which we will
    discuss. List your own personal goals and objectives you
    have set for the 1970 season.

OFFENSIVE ASSIGNMENTS TEST

1 -
2 -
3 -
4 -
5 -
6 -
7 -
8 -
QB -
FB -
HB -
FLK -

44

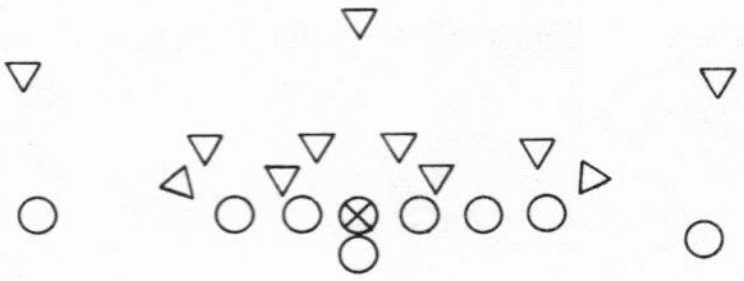

50

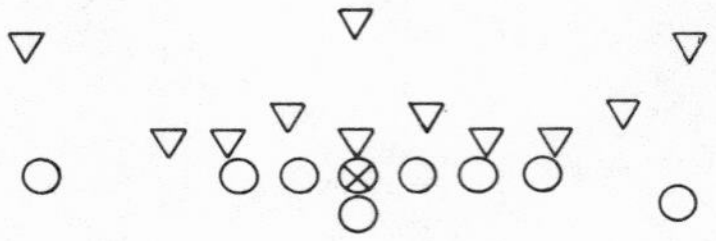

43

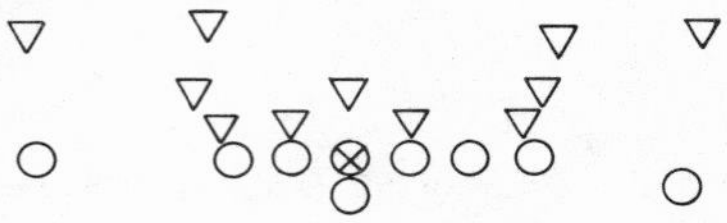

SPLIT 60

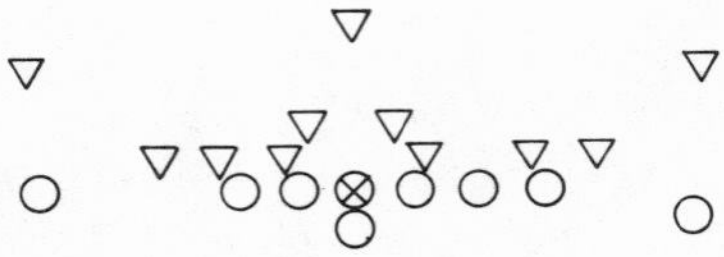

61

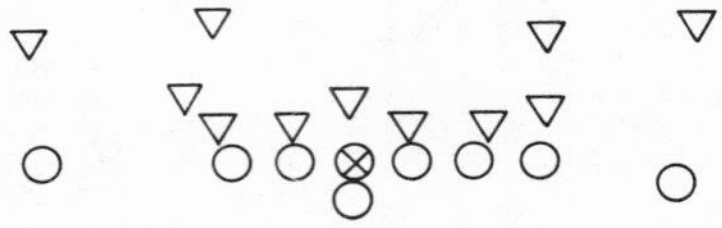

WIDE 60

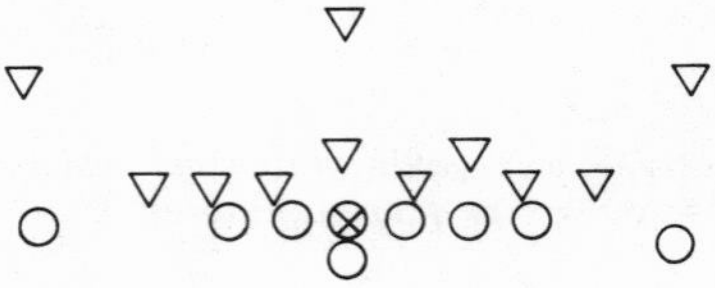

65 GOAL LINE

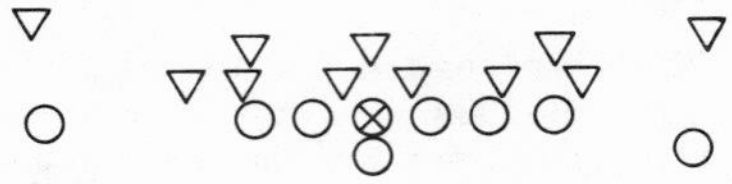

DEFENSIVE ASSIGNMENTS TEST

Left T

Left G

Right G

Right T

Strike

Mike

Whip

```
DEFENSIVE TEST

Defense: _____

| Position | Align | Run Responsibility | Pass Responsibility |
|----------|-------|--------------------|---------------------|
| Strike   |       |                    |                     |
| Mike     |       |                    |                     |
| Whip     |       |                    |                     |

Note coaching points -
```

Offensive and defensive season notebooks

When our players return to campus in the Fall, we issue them a
small spiral notebook for them to keep. After a mental test, they
index the notebook and then review our entire offense and defense as
it is introduced. It is the responsibility of each player to keep up his
notebook and to record the pertinent coaching points and emphases
that his coach places on particular plays or maneuvers. The coaches
check the notebooks periodically, and they often profit from the
players' insights. The accompanying sample index indicates the
areas that we stress.

INDEX--FOOTBALL NOTEBOOK

The notebooks are important to a player only if the coach stresses their importance to him. If a coach quizzes his team periodically, either on individual papers or on the blackboard, he will find that many careless mistakes will be eliminated.

Fall practice preparation

When the football coaching staff assembles during the last days of August or the first of September, it is necessary that overall season planning be wrapped up. The staff at this time must have studied all charts, movies, and statistics from the previous season, most particularly those compiled during Spring training.

The organized and well informed head coach gives considerable preliminary thought to the outlines of his Fall practice plans prior to calling staff or group meetings. Following some general comments, we will outline in detail later in the chapter some Fall practice hints that have been advantageous to our program.

First, it follows that if two teams are equal in ability going into a game, the difference might be in which team gets the most out of its practice sessions during the week. This does not necessarily mean having the squad engage in a lot of hitting, scrimmaging, or full team work throughout the week. It might be possible that the best way to get the most out of practices is *not* to practice at all. Remember the old axiom: the reason a team practices in the first place is to get better. If the coach feels that the players are not improving, then he should give them a day off. They may be getting stale; they may be getting bored. Motivation is virtually impossible to instill under these conditions. If a team is playing its biggest rival or is facing a championship game, the players' adrenalin will be running high all through the week. When this occurs, the team will leave the ball game on the practice field if a lot of heavy hitting or scrimmaging is required. Under these circumstances, it is better to back off on the amount of practice that is required of the squad. This will allow the players to get ready mentally and do their heavy hitting during the game. A coach should survey his opponents for the season and plan on heavy hitting before the easier ball games and ease up on the amount of scrimmaging as he approaches the tougher games. In all cases, a coach must be highly organized and know exactly what he wants to accomplish prior to the actual practice sessions.

Second, practice variations are vital. Different approaches to practice should be studied so the routine boredom does not set in. For example, on certain days it might be advantageous to meet in the locker room and run to the practice field together. On other days, call for special early groups or have chalk talks prior to the start of practice. When the team hits the field, the start of practice should be varied. This can be accomplished by having group calisthenics, team calisthenics, and a running program which can be done by positions or by teams; if a coach is stressing heavy conditioning, practice should begin with interval running sessions to tire the team initially prior to practice. Whatever is done, practice should be varied even for the mere sake of variation.

Third, set a tempo and attempt to maintain it throughout the practice session. Water breaks now are highly recommended in the middle of the practice period; however, a coach must be cautious that he does not lose tempo following the break. Five minutes should be allowed for the break, and the team then should be required to pick up the practice schedule and tempo immediately.

Fourth, we believe that high school players must play the actual game a lot more than is necessary at the college level. More complete scrimmages must be scheduled for the beginning player so he can experience the total "feel" more than he does during breakdown drill work. Confidence for the individual, which can be instilled during a practice session, is vital for top game performance.

Fifth, it is the responsibility of the coach to keep everyone involved and on the move during each practice session. Coaches often want to teach only their top players at the expense of training the lesser squad members. However, we owe it to ourselves and to the participants to coach everyone who is in a uniform. If a coach feels he must concentrate on his top players or teams, then he should spend time with the remaining players either before or after practice. *Each player must believe that he is a better performer after every practice session.*

Sixth, and of paramount importance, is the time schedule. Punctuality is the key and cannot be violated. A team must be both on and off the field at a predetermined time to maintain good morale. If practice is set between the hours of 4 p.m. and 6 p.m., this does not mean it is from 4 p.m. to 6:15 p.m. If a coach is consistent regarding the time the team is dismissed, then he always can demand that the players report for practice on time. This precise scheduling also aids the efficiency of the assistant coaches in the time allotments for their individual drills. Assign the time allotment to a manager, and instruct him to give a five-minute warning prior to each time allotment break. Nothing can kill morale on a football team more rapidly than by breaking down the time schedule on the field.

Seventh, a coach must set certain specific discipline standards that he wants to maintain at all times during practices or game situations. These will vary; however, these are some examples: don't allow players to sit down on the practice field; chin straps must be buttoned throughout the entire practice except perhaps during the water break; shirt-tails in at all times; run full-speed from one drill to another; jog to and from the practice field; players must properly address all of their coaches either by the titles "Mr." or "Coach"; and maintain a clean locker room, one in which the team can take pride. There are numerous other standards which might be included. Perhaps some coaches want to enforce only a few. But whatever they are, the enforcement must be consistent in maintaining a top standard of morale and performance. Whatever standards are required, punctuality is the *one* that must be included. If a player is late to practice, he should be punished so he will be on time at the next practice; in all fairness to the rest of the squad, one or more players cannot be allowed to be late.

Eighth — and this is a *must* — practice that which will be used in a game. This may appear to be very obvious; however, it must be emphasized. Often, we coaches tend to set a complete running and pass game and will practice each one of the component parts equally in time. This is very impractical if there are certain plays that will not be used in the upcoming game. We believe very strongly in coaches calling the plays during a game; by this measure, they will be aware of the plays that should be practiced. If the coach is calling a good number of pass plays, then those are the plays that should be practiced. The same holds true, of course, if a preponderance of running plays is to be called.

We have a number of specific suggestions that are products of the many years of organizing our Fall practice. Some of these guidelines may be of assistance in practice or organization and provoke a good deal of preliminary thinking that is necessary prior to the all-important few days before the initial game. It will be seen in the illustrations and outlines that follow that we make up a tentative practice schedule that will result in the most effective use of our time. There are certain drills that we go through every day: calisthenics, neck exercises, and movement in agility drills. These should be included in every practice until they either are mastered or no longer serve their purposes. The team get-off period, which includes the full team defensive pursuit, is all-important. We attempt to structure our practice so each coach will work on basic player skills each day. These include the ability to strike, to block on the move, to pursue, to tackle, to perform the exchanges, the quarterback's basic drop and throw, and drills to improve the receivers' hands. We then provide for individual and group technique teaching periods during which both offensive and defensive coaches can work on techniques specifically related to the plays and/or defenses that are being introduced. These periods are extremely important because the players should be mastering the individual skills and techniques that are related to the plays, thus ensuring more efficient performance. It is important to have the field areas numbered so the individual coaches and players may move rapidly from one drill to another.

We move from the individual drills to group or half-line or smaller team drills and begin to build on the plays and/or defenses that we are introducing. These are followed by team situation scrimmages, which can be either live or full speed and apply to game conditions both offensively and defensively. Included are obvious down and other situations that will occur during the normal course of a game. From there, we make the transition to team scrimmages, all-out, move-the-ball scrimmages that can be full-speed with or without tackling. If certain standards of pursuit and full-speed blocking are required, it isn't always necessary to run the risk of injuries through tackling and pile-ups.

A kicking period should be included in each day's practice in order to produce regular improvement. Equally important is a full-speed pass-rush period, something we often use as a wind up to practice. It illustrates the progress that is being made by both offense and defense and gives the coach a ready check-point.

An outline such as this is advisable because it provides the head coach a ready reference in discussing practice plans with his assistants. It also gives them a preliminary idea of methods to organize their own teaching progressions and to set their own individual practice schedules and time allotments.

Also included in this chapter are charts with suggestions for preliminary practice organization. The first is a weekly practice organization technique that we have used for our offense to obtain a long-range view of exactly which fundamental drills we plan to use. It also indicates which technique drills will be added in specific areas of running and pass offense, the kicking game, and conditioning.

Early Fall no-pad workouts have been introduced to the member schools of the Pacific-8 Conference, and it usually amounts to at least three days of no-pad conditioning and teaching. It gives the coaches an opportunity to test the players' physical condition, as well as a chance for them to learn assignments when there is not the pressure of pads and full contact. This no-pad period has worked out so well for us that we would continue it regardless of any possible change in the conference rule. Practice organization for this period is also included in this chapter.

The first week or ten days of practice must be extremely well organized because time does not allow for experimentation. A coach must accomplish each day the tasks he sets for himself, the staff, and the team. He cannot afford to get behind in introducing new plays and/or polishing up the team's execution in individual techniques.

Here is a sample practice outline:

3:45 – 4:00	Specialty period
4:00 – 4:10	Calisthenics. Vary the types
4:10 – 4:25	Basic period. Movement and agility
4:25 – 4:45	Group drills
4:45 – 5:10	Combination drills
5:10 – 5:25	Kicking game
5:25 – 5:55	Team work. List all plays and defenses that you are going to work on. (More detailed practice scheduling will follow)

FALL PRACTICE OUTLINE

I. Tentative practice outline
    A. 4 minutes calisthenics
    B. 4 minutes neck
    C. 7 minutes agility, movement/quickness drills
    D. 5 minutes team get off, cadence, automatics
    E. 15 minutes basic technique period
    F. 15-20 minute periods individual and group technique teaching related to plays or defenses being introduced to team drills to be emphasized
        1. If 41 sweep is the play then each position should have the necessary breakdown drills to master the fundamentals required against all defensive possibilities
            a. 2 & 3 angle drill
                4 & 6 pulls
                5 drive
                7 pull seal
            b. These drills can be learning drills, or competitive drills, depending on the emphasis.
    G. 20 minute team drill periods.
        1. Full team or 1/2 line, middle 6 vs. defense shields or line
        2. Sweep drill
            a. All necessary positions vs. all defenses to eliminate mistakes of execution and indecision.
    H. Team "situation scrimmages"
        1. Live or full speed reactions
        2. Provide game situations for team offense poise and polish
            a. 40 yards and in
            b. 3rd down situations
            c. Short yardages and goal line
            d. Field situations
            e. Clock situations
            f. Score situations
    I. Team scrimmages
        1. All out "move the ball"
        2. Controlled, repeat plays
    J. Kicking periods
        1. Punt protection and coverage
        2. PAT & FG
        3. Kick off return
            a. These techniques can be done individually or as a team
    K. Pass rush periods

WEEKLY PRACTICE ORGANIZATION

MONDAY	TUESDAY	WEDNESDAY	THURSDAY
I. Fundamental Drills	I. Fundamental Drills	I. Fundamental Drills	I. Fundamental Drills
_____	_____	_____	_____
_____	_____	_____	_____
II. Running Offense	II. Running Offense	II. Running Offense	II. Running Offense
_____	_____	_____	_____
_____	_____	_____	_____
_____	_____	_____	_____
III. Pass Offense	III. Pass Offense	III. Pass Offense	III. Pass Offense
_____	_____	_____	_____
_____	_____	_____	_____
_____	_____	_____	_____
IV. Kicking Game	IV. Kicking Game	IV. Kicking Game	IV. Kicking Game
_____	_____	_____	_____
V. Conditioning Game	V. Conditioning Game	V. Conditioning Game	V. Conditioning Game
_____	_____	_____	_____

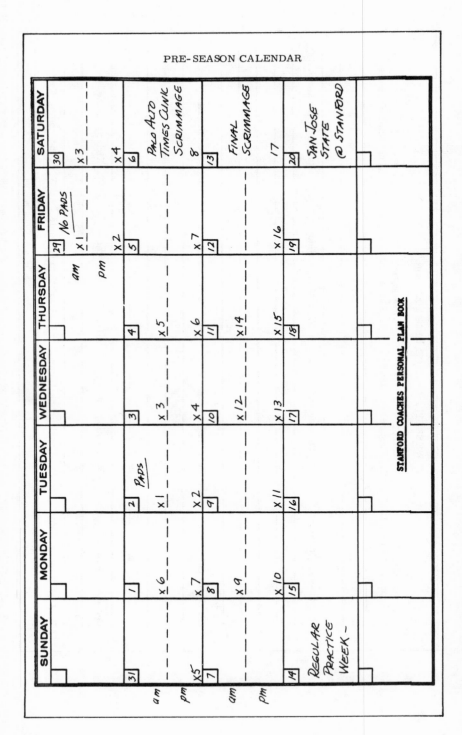

STANFORD COACHES PERSONAL PLAN BOOK

	SUNDAY	MONDAY	TUESDAY	WEDNESDAY	THURSDAY	FRIDAY	SATURDAY
am pm						No Pads 29 x 1	30 x 3
am pm	31 X5 7	1 x 6	2 Pads x 1	3 x 3	4 x 5	5 x 2	6 Palo Alto Times Clinic Scrimmage
		8 x 7	9 X 2	10 X 4	11 X 6	12 x 7	8
am pm	14	8 x 9	9 X 11	10 x 12	11 x 14	12 x 7	13 Final Scrimmage
	Regular Practice Week –	15 X 10	16 X 11	17 X 13	18 X 15	19 x 16	17
							20 San Jose State @ Stanford

SUGGESTED FALL OBJECTIVES AND POINTS OF EMPHASIS

Offense

Objectives
1. Running Game Attitude
2. Execution + Understanding
3. 2nd QB
4. Punters Consistency
5. Inside 25 offense
6. Goal-line variety
7. F.G. Protection
8. Coverage after pass
9. Man patterns

1. 70 Pass prot.
2. 41 Sweep
3. 37
4. 43 Trap
5. 34 CTR.
6. 90
7. 49 Pass
8. 16 Trap
9. 41 Boot
10. 13
11. 45 CTR
12. 60
13. 15 Draw
14. 45 Draw
15. HB Quick Screen Short
16. F.B Screen Strong
17. Q 37
18. 70 Delays
19. 59 option
20. 35
21. 51 option
22. 51 Roll
23. 44 Trap (Tackle)

Ball in play
1. Huddle
2. Spacing
3. Numbering
4. Formations
5. Cadence
6. Automatics

Defense

Objectives
1. Minimize errors - Create + entire understanding
2. Pass rush
3. Pass defense
4. Linebacker depth
5. Goal-line Confidence
6. F.G. or P.A.T. Rush
7. Punt receivers
8. Hold opposition to under 2 TDs

1. 44 - 34
2. 31 - Even -
3. 65 Slam
4. 65 dog
5. Over - 44
6. Under -44
7. 65 Pinch -
8. Indian
9. Goal line

Kicking

Offense
1. Punt Protection and Coverage
2. P.A.T. Protection
3. F.G. + Coverage
4. K.O. Return
5. Onside Protection
6. Tight Punt + Coverage
7. Play from P.A.T. or F.G.
8. Play from Punt formation
9. Take a safety

Defense
1. Punt Return
2. Punt Rush
3. Punt Hold-up or Unsure
4. P.A.T. + F.G. Rush
5. K.O. Coverage
6. Onside K.O Coverage
7. K.O. from 20
8. Quick kick return

OFFENSIVE PRACTICE ORGANIZATION

		Fri. Aug. 29	Sat. Aug. 30	Sun. Aug. 31	Mon. Sep. 1	Tue. Sep. 2	Wed. Sep. 3	Thur. Sep. 4	Fri. Sep. 5
A.M.									
15	Warm Up	70 41 Sweep / 16 Trap	13-47 Spread Punt, 51-59 Option		44 Trap (36T) / 51 Reverse / 49 Toss / Sneak	70's / Trap	Screen / 13-47	41 Boot / 22	
15	Ind.	Technique teaching	Technique teaching		Technique teaching	Technique teaching	Technique teaching	Technique teaching	Technique teaching
15	Gp. #1	Technique teaching	Technique teaching		Technique teaching	5 on 4 Drill	Dive Drill	22 Drill, 70 / 21 Sweep, 25 Draw	
15	Gp. #2	7 on 7	7 on 7		Trap Drill 44T, 36T, 16T	7 on 7	7 on 7	7 on 7	7 on 7
15	Team #1	Polish	13-47, 51-59 Option plays		Polish / 51 Reverse / 51 Roll / 51-59 Option / 49 Toss / 13-47-41 Bootleg	Pass rush Drill	Screen drill (1/2 line) / Pass rush	41 Boot / 51 Roll / 41 Sweep	
	Team #2	Conditioning Huddle break/ Get-off	Conditioning Spread, punt & cover		Conditioning Kick off return				
P.M.									
15	Warm Up	15-45 Draw Screens	51 Roll / 41 Bootleg	PAT-F.G. 90's, 22, 37, 21 sweep	Goal line & short yardage Jump & Wedge	Sweep / Draw	51-59 Option / 51 Roll	37, 90, / 44 Trap	Goal line / Short yardage
15	Ind.	Technique teaching	Technique teaching	Technique teaching	Teach Goal line & short yardage	Technique teaching	Technique teaching	Technique teaching	Technique teaching
15	Gp. #1	Technique teaching	Technique teaching	Technique teaching	Short yardage drill	Skeleton sweep drill	Option drill (1/2 line)	Perimeter, Option, Sweep	51-59 Jump, Sweep sneak, Wedge drills
15	Gp #2	13-47 drill / 51-59 drill	13-47 drill / 51-59 drill	7 on 7	7 on 7	7 on 7	7 on 7	7 on 7	7 on 7
15	Team #1	Draw-70 drill	51 Roll / 41 Bootleg	22, 37, 90	Goal line / Short yardage	Draw drill	Middle 6-Trap Draw-13-47	Middle Six 37-22-44T	Pass Rush
	Team #2	Screens Polish	Draw/70 Screens	Polish Trap-Sweep 51-59 Option 70's PAT & FG	Polish all plays All kicking	Polish drill 70-Trap-Sweep Draw	Pass Rush 70 Screen 51 Roll	Pass Rush 90-70 Bootleg	Polish (all plays)

WEEKLY PRACTICE CALENDAR

August 31	September 1	September 2	September 3	September 4	September 5	September 6
A.M. -- 59 Sweep No A.M. Meeting 9:15- Early Gr. 9:30-11:20 Prac. 9:30-Cal. 9:35-M. &Q. 9:45-B. Drills 10:00-Team 10:05-B. &S. 10:20-I B Tech 10:35-II 59 Sw. Tech. 10:50-III Team 59 Sw. & Drill 11:05-IV Same Finish w/ huddle & break to LOS 11:20-IN	A.M. -- 22-23 Blast 8:25-8:45 Meeting 9:30- Early Gr. 9:45-11:30-Prac. 9:45-Cal. 9:50-M. &Q. 10:00-B. Drills 10:15-Team 10:20-B. &S. 10:35-I 22&23 Blast Tech. 10:50-II Team 22-23 Bl. & Drill 11:05-III 59 Roll Dr. 11:20-IV 59 Sw. Dr. 11:30-IN	A.M. No A.M. Meeting 9:15- Early Gr. 9:30-11:20- Prac. 9:30-Cal. 9:35-M. &Q. 9:45-B. Drills 10:00-Team 10:05-B. &S. 10:20-I 59 Sw. Drill 10:35-II 59 Roll Stop Drill 10:50-III 33, 22-23 Bl. Drill 11:05-IV 59 Roll 57 Stop Dr. 11:20-IN	A.M. No A.M. Practice	A.M. -- 39 Option Screen 8:25-8:45-Meeting 9:30-Cal 9:35-M. &Q. 9:45-B. Drills 10:00-Team 10:05-B. &S. 10:20-I 39 Opt. 10:35-II Team 39 Opt. & Screen & Drill 10:50-III Same 11:05-IV 59 Roll 57 Stop Dr. 11:20-IN	A.M. -- 51 Sweep, Kicking 8:25-8:45- Meet (Poss. no Pads) 9:30-Cal. 9:35-M. &Q. 9:45-B. Drills 10:00-Team 10:05-B. &S. 10:20-I 51 Sweep Tech 10:40-II 51 Sw. & Dr. -33 11:00-III Same, Finish w/ PAT&FG & Cover, if pos.) 11:15-IN	A.M. -- Draw at 3 8:25-8:45-Meet 9:15-9:30-Early Group 9:30-11:20-Prac. 9:30-Cal. 9:35-M. &Q. 9:45-B. Drills 10:00-Team 10:05-B. &S. 10:20-I Draw at 3 Tech. 10:35-II Team Dr. at 3 & Dr. - 59 Roll 10:50-III 59 Sw. Dr. 59 Roll- 36T 11:05-IV Screen & 22 Roll 11:20-IN
P.M. -- 59 Roll 2:30-3:00-Meet 4:00-6:00-Prac. 4:00-Cal. 4:05-M. &Q. 4:15-B. Drills 4:30-Team 4:35-B. &S. 4:50-I 59 Roll Tech 5:05-II Team 59 Roll & Dr. 5:20-III Same 5:40-IV 59 Sweep Drill 6:00-IN	P.M. --57 Stop, 33 Kicking-Punt Prot. 2:30-3:00-Meet 4:00-6:00-Prac. 4:00-Cal. 4:05-M. &Q. 4:15-B. Drills 4:30-Team 4:35-B. &S. 4:50-I 57 Stop & 33 Tech 5:05-II Team 57 Stop & 33 Drill 5:20-III 22-33 Bl. Drill 5:35-IV 59 Roll 57 Stop Dr. 5:50-V Punt Prot. & Tm, Get-off 6:00-IN	P.M. -- 22 Roll 2:30-3:00-Meet. 3:45-5:30-Prac. 3:45-Cal. 3:50-M. &Q. 4:00-B. Drills 4:15-Team 4:20-B. &S. 4:35-I 22 Roll Tech, 4:50-II Team 22 Roll & Dr. 5:05-III 59 Sw Dr -59 Roll Dr 5:20-IV Kicking Punt Cov. 5:30-IN 7:00-7:25- Night Pass Group	P.M. -- 44 Trap-- 47 Dive 2:00-2:30-Meet 3:30-5:30-Prac. 3:30-Cal. 3:35-M. &Q. 3:45-B. Drills 4:00-Team 4:05-B. &S. 4:20-I 44T & 47D Tech. 4:35-II Team 44T & 47D & Dr. 4:50-III Same 5:10-IV Team - Work Huddle & Break 59 Sw., 22-23 Bl, 59 Roll 5:30-IN	P.M. No. P.M. Meeting 3:30-5:30-Prac. 3:30-Cal. 3:35-M. &Q. 3:45-B. Drills 4:00-Team 4:05-B. &S. 4:20-I Screen & Op. Dr. 4:35-II 44T & 47D Drill 4:50-III 57 St. - 59 Roll Dr.- 5:10-Team Work Huddle-33,57 St., 22 Roll, Punt & Cover 5:30-IN 7:00-7:25-Night Pass Group	P.M. -- 99-36 Trap 2:30-3:30-Meet. 3:45-5:30-Prac. 3:45-Cal. 3:50-M. &Q. 4:00-B. Drills 4:15-Team 4:20-B. &S. 4:35-I 99 & 36T Tech. 4:55-II Team 99 & 36 & Drill 5:15-III Same 5:30 IN. Finish w/ Punt Prot. & Cover 7:00-7:25-Night Pass Group	P.M. 2:30-3:00-Prac. (Team Review) 4:00-6:00-Prac. 4:00-Cal. 4:05-M. &Q. 4:15-B. Drills 4:30-Team 4:35-B. &S. 4:50-I 33, 22-23 Blast Dr. 5:05-II 39 Opt. 44T-47D Drill 5:20-III 51 Sw. 36T 5:40-IV-99-57 Stop- Draw Dr. 6:00-IN

131

A coach must be creative in the last five minutes of practice. Players must want to come back tomorrow, and they should feel that they have made some progress.

In review, the practice schedule is only an illustration of the necessity of having a plan for everything. Top executives, whether in education, business, or government, cannot function in top efficiency without a sound plan. Sound planning should include learning experiences that are similar to those that will confront the athlete under game conditions. Sound planning does not mean that a coach should become locked into a routine. He must be creative, but the creativity must be analyzed, practiced, and tested before attempting to make it operational. It must not be the result of a hastily-instituted whim to reshape a losing streak or merely a change for the sake of change.

The organized coach must have a pre-season calendar similar to the preceding indicating practice days as well as introduction of plays, defenses, and kicking information. This calendar should occupy a place on a convenient blackboard in the meeting room so it can be filled in for all coaches to see.

Season objectives and other points of emphasis should also be in clear view for easy reference.

Practice plans

Stanford has employed numerous practice formats, and the following illustrates their evolution during the past several years. We began by posting every practice plan; although it is preferred by some coaches, it was not effective for us. The Stanford coaches came to the conclusion that the players evaluated the practice plan in every detail. As a consequence, we felt they saved themselves for the drill that required an all-out effort. The latter is important, of course, but total effort in all areas is important. Therefore, we have evolved to a plan wherein each individual coach takes his specific practice schedule to the field, and the head coach maintains the full and complete plan. He then administers the details that involve the entire squad. The outlines show our first type of practice plan which included both offense and defense on the same sheet of paper, with a very detailed explanation of exactly what we planned to accomplish. The small boxes indicate field position, and each coach was responsible to know the location of his position and to be there with his equipment and ready to proceed.

The practice plan on page 134 is specifically for offense because we prepared both offensive and defensive practice plans. These included an area in the north end corner for field designation and position.

The practice outline on page 135, currently used by our coaches, is divided into the types of periods that will be used each day. It

DAILY PRACTICE CALENDAR

Third Day-2nd Practice

4:15   Early Group-C's LongSnap-Punters-PAT men - FB's
4:30   Calisthenics-John
4:35   Team Rhythm Drill
      (5) Rhythm Start
      (5) 7 man sled
4:45   Offensive Group Work

4-5-6-7-Mac	3&2-Dutch	Backs-Bob
59 Sweep	(10) Release	Plays-Sheehan
(10) 37 opt.--	2 on 1	
39 opt.		
2-3-4-5-6-7		
(10) 42-41-Mills & Bks.		

5:05   Combination Group Work

3-7 Mac & Dutch	Back's & 8's-Bob
(10) Drop Back	Pass Offense vs.
Pass Prot.	Pass Defense
Aggressive P.P.	
(10)4&6 3-5-7	
Trap Pull Seal	
Turn-up Check Seal	

5:25   Combination Team Work

White 2-3-4-5-6-7+All Backs	8's-1 QB
Vs B&R-P&P-B&R	Mack-Bob John
Middle Six Drill Rod-Mike	(10) Patterns
	(10) Join 3 D

5:45   Kicking Game
      White 2-8-HB's&FB's
      Mac-Dutch-Bob
5:55   Form Teams
      White A&B Vs. Red C
      Teach 42 & 22 No Shields Review
6:10   Team
      Pass Scrimmage
      4-3-2 on plays
6:25   Running
6:30   IN

Early Group-Punt Receivers

4:15   Early Group-Punt Receivers
4:30   Calisthenics-John
4:35   Team Rhythm Drill
      (5) 7 man sled
      (5) Recognition
4:45   Defensive Group Work

P&P-B&R-Rod	E's-Dick	M&M-Mike	3 Deep-Bill
(10) Skate	(10) Skate	(10) Goal-line	(10) Goal line
(10) Front 4	(10) Revol Rotation	(10) Basic-- Resp.	(10) 3 Deep Inter.

5:05   Combination Group Work

P&P-B&R-Rod	E's-M&M-3 Deep-Bill-Bob
(10) Goal line	Pass Defense vs. Pass
Charge	Offense--Mike-Dick
(10) O.C.--	
H.U. 2 on 1	

5:25   Combination Team Work

B&R-P&P-M&M-Rod	E's-Dick	3 Deep
Middle Six-Mike	64 Chg	(10) Rotation
Drill	Goal line--	(10) Vs. Routes
	charge	
	Basic Run-- Resp.	

5:45   Kicking Game

Red B&R-P&P-E's-M&M	Receivers	Punters-1 Center
Rod-Mike-Dick	Bill-John	

5:55   Form Teams
      Red A&B Vs. White C
      All Calls-Goal line
6:10   Team
      Pass Def. Scrimmage
      4-3-2 on Plays
6:25   Running
6:30   IN

affords each coach the opportunity to do some preliminary planning the night before he gets the actual time breakdown. As we mentioned, this has been most successful; however, keeping faith with our philosophy, it is subject to change as another plan appears to be more effective.

The completed practice plan on pages 136–37, is the actual form given to the head coach for his administration of practice.

PRACTICE SCHEDULE

	3	4
	2	5
10	1	6
9	8	7

\# _____ Date _____ A. M. _____ P. M. _____

Calisthenics: Team__ Group__ Drill to be Filmed
                                Circled

Per	Time	Area	Time	White	Vermeil	Hampton	De Sylvia	Ralston
Specialty								
Agility								

PRACTICE SCHEDULE

#_____ Date_____ AM_____ PM_____ Uniform: Pads_____ Shorts_____

Pre-Practice: Specialty_____ Skill_____ Meetings_____ Strength_____

Time	Area	White	Dickey	Theder	Currey	Time	Area	Gambold	Christiansen	McCartney
		Warm up: (Cal. Neck)								
		Individual:								
		Group #1:								
		Group #2:								
		Team #1:								
		Team #2:								
		Conditioning:								
		Opportunity:								

TIME-AREA PRACTICE SCHEDULE

TIME AREA	WHITE	PRACTICE SCHEDULE CHRISTIANSEN QB, FB, HB	THEDER	DATE	A.M. GAMBOLD	P.M. PEASLEY LB	UNIFORM PADS McCARTNEY	SHORTS DESYLVIA
TIME	1-3-7		2-8-x		4-deep		Down 4	
10:15	Warmup	Cal. & necks						
10:22	Agility	Hi knee crossovers	Stretch hi knee		Cals. neck Pass drop	Wave z-drill Run move. recoil bd.	Hands & toes quick feet Seven man reactor	
10:30	Quick feet crowther drive, duck walk, 1/4 eagle	Stance start	Route running, net drills shoulder catch					
10:45	Drive prog. Up/back black shld.	Running 4 blking 41 sweep 37	All patterns		2 yds 6 yds cuts	Reactor sled	Teach--read	
11:00	Set up prog. Set up mirror tandem 2-drive	Backs pass routes wide flare flat far	Block check stalk align		Line angle ball	Pass drop	Teach--quick	
11:15	G/C sweep fold drive T/drive pull-seal	70 pass offense with ends HB & FB with White	With Chris. all passes		Basic explanation (cover squares)		Option-responsibility 44	
11:30	Speed, punt and coverage				Punt hold up-- go get it outside			
11:38	Team starts & running		37 sweep		(20-yards in) Straight away curves			

136

2:50	Pre-practice:	SPECIALTY SKILL		MEETINGS	STRENGTH		
3:00	Group cal. hi knee 4-pt carioca	Coil & neck stretching high knee	Group cal. neck stretch high knee	Back 8-yard touch wave pass drop	Cals. neck hi knee wave	Bag reaction triple hit	Cal & neck agil: shuffle angle, shadow
3:15	2 groups drive prog. set-up progr.	Stance & slants ball handling	Net drills carioca passing shld. passing pass routes	Wave over bags, eye opener, blk prot., light bags, B. P.	Stance, starts, recoil board	Ball reaction deep middle	Jump technique pattern recog.
3:30	3 grps. draw/screen tech. 1 on 1	Strip draw-screen	1-1 vs. def. backs	Review base	Review base smoo (sled)	Review base	1 on 1 vs. Roger
3:45	Sweep/ trap drill	Sweep/ trap drill	Punt return	Punt ret'n.	Punt return	Punt return	Punt return
4:00	Draw/70 drill	Draw/70 drill	Draw/70's	Teach over	Teach over	Teach over group	Teach over
4:15	Screen drill Polish 70 Draw/screen 70 sweep trap	Polish all; sweep 70, draw, sweep	Polish screen 70's draw sweep	Over spaces	Over team	Over team	Spaces over
4:30	Team lineup grass drill	Grass drill		20-yard spaces	Team		Team

Assigning of specialists, game week schedule, late classes

It is important for the head coach to assign members of his staff to be in charge of various areas of specialization. If a head coach has a limited number of assistants, then he must bridge the gap. Whatever the case may be, a coach must determine the most important areas and practice them in an early group or after practice. Assistants should be placed in charge of research, techniques, and coaching areas such as the long snap, the punter, place kickers and

---

DAILY STAFF PRACTICE RESPONSIBILITIES

Coach Ralston:

1. Practice tempo - overall
2. Practice plan - general outline
3. Medical co-ordination
   a. Red Cross personnel
   b. Water break
4. Time designations on field
5. Assign areas and coordination (at least 1 hour prior to start of practice)

All Coaches:

1. Punctuality vital - assign laps for delinquents and administer.
2. All players in your group in full uniform including hip pads - send back if not.
3. Hustle to practice and after practice when on fields.
4. Button chin straps and shirt tails in.
5. No lying on ground.
6. Straight lines in calisthenics.
7. No water after practice.
8. Sprint to center on long whistle (including coaches).
9. Acknowledge water break (allow players to loosen helmets).
10. Acknowledge Red Cross shirts and limits of individual.
11. Be sure your personnel have proper shirts.

Specific Coordinators: Constant Awareness (make recommendations to John)

1. Mike White: Consistency
2. Jack Christiansen: Punctuality
3. Roger Theder: Hustle on & off
4. Bob Gambold: Morale
5. Ed Peasley: Physical condition
6. Max McCartney: Tempo
7. Terry DeSylvia: Player insight

---

holders, punt and kickoff receivers, and offensive specialists such as the quarterback and receivers. A coach commits a grave error if he neglects these specialists. They will win or lose ball games, according to the manner in which a coach teaches and emphasizes the team's need for them.

ASSIGNMENT SHEET

Specialists, Early Group, or Late Group Work

1. Centers--long snap, Mike White
2. Punters --Bob Gambold
3. Place kickers and holders--Ed Peasley
4. Punt or kickoff receivers--Max McCartney
5. Quarterbacks--Jack Christiansen
6. Pass receiving group--Roger Theder

The head coach's weekly checklist should be followed for complete preparation prior to each game—the following is our schedule from Sunday to Saturday game day:

WEEK'S SCHEDULE

SUNDAY	MONDAY	TUESDAY	WEDNESDAY	THURSDAY	FRIDAY
Film study	Defense--best six runs, four passes of opponent	Practice plan	Practice plan	Practice plan	QB meeting
General evaluation	Offense--test new plays	Film study - opponents	Goal line scrimmage--offense & defense	Finalize the kicking game-set drills	Signal caller meeting
Examine results in light of goals	Double-check kicking	Set base offense	Short yardage, offense & defense	Speedie-two minute offense	No workout if home game; short workout if away
Dinner--coach's report on game	Practice plan	Play cards-key sheet defense	Prevent situations offensive and defensive	Final game plan. Tendencies of opponent	
Squad film study	QB review session, calls	Offensive sequence	All phases of kicking	Clean meeting room	
Staff meeting Mental approach to week.	Bring along personnel who didn't play	Situation scrimmage	Game automatics	Set suit-up and travel list. Post during practice	SATURDAY Pay Day! Preparation Meets Opportunity
Scout report oral to staff	Offense and defense film studies	Finalize preparation teams	Film own offense & defense		
Discuss own personnel	Scout report to squad in evening	Interchange of game plans--defensive & offensive coaches	Finalize defense		
Base offense	Set preparation teams	Group concentration	Write-up defenses		
Defense beginning	Use same color jerseys as will in game	Game plans to squad	Team concentration		

139

Day-to-day evaluation

In our experience as coaches, we have been exposed to almost all types of coaching methods related to which players should be on the first team from day-to-day and the manner of getting the most out of the players. It is our guess that each individual coach must express himself according to his own standards and set the rules for personnel advancement. When we were with Coach Pete Elliott at the University of California, he moved players up and down depending upon their day-to-day performances. This, of course, has substantial merit because it places a premium on consistent performance in practice. The player also knows that he is being evaluated individually each day, that he must maintain the coach's standards. He realizes that every day he must do his best to perform better than the other players competing for his position or he would lose his job.

We followed this technique for many years; however, we then realized that the personalities of several different assistant coaches were involved, and it was impossible to be consistent. Each coach could be consistent according to his own personality and standards, but the head coach could not possibly oversee six or seven different assistants.

Therefore, we instituted a policy of considering the individual involved rather than one of setting up arbitrary rules. We have standardized our personnel evaluations on the performance of our players over the long haul and according to the confidence we have in them. We believe that it is the responsibility of every coach to get the full potential from his players, and therefore, he should treat each one of his players as an individual in order to help him reach his full potential as an athlete on the football field.

Some players require the confidence of staying on the first team and of experiencing improvement. They generally are aware that their position is not threatened, and it would be ludicrous to juggle them up and down to keep them off balance. Others, however, need a psychological jolt, and seeing their names on a second team roster might give them the jolt they need and have a positive effect on their performances.

The dominating factor in coaching is to see improvement; if an individual player is handled correctly and an attempt is made to understand him, his performance on the field will improve with proper technical coaching.

The following are our offensive and defensive personnel cards which we post every day. We know that every player wishes to see his name on the board, and we want him to know that we are doing some evaluating each and every day. He knows that if he is letting down himself and the team, then his name will appear in the appropriate place for everyone to see.

Split End	7 $-\frac{26}{12}$	6 $\frac{24}{0}$	5 $-\frac{6}{2}$	4 $-\frac{5}{22}$	3 $-\frac{4}{24}$	2 $-\frac{2}{24}$
Alvarado ^{49}	Seymour	Lightsey	Searle	Beinhard	Sharp	Moore
Helms	Meyers $-\frac{5}{18}$	Saibel $-\frac{5}{24}$	Tubb $-\frac{3}{24}$	Blown $-\frac{4}{19}$	Zeisler $-\frac{4}{28}$	Pasa -9
Tamplis $-\frac{2}{6}/13$	Shollick $-\frac{3}{18}$	Reinhard	Shorlen $-\frac{3}{23}$	Fair $-\frac{3}{24}$	Carr $-\frac{6}{15}$	Nemic $-\frac{11}{31}$
	Kuppers		Hoftienne		Coleman $-\frac{7}{22}$	Delang
Cross $-7/15$					Doe	Burke

	QB	HB $-\frac{24}{3}$	FB $-\frac{18}{4}$	Flkr
15-0	Plunkett	Brown	Williams	Washington $-\frac{5}{23}$
23-4	Bunce	T.Brown $\frac{26-2}{}$	Plostma $\frac{27-4}{}$	Vatske $-\frac{8}{33}$
24-0	Fujikawa $\frac{13-0}{}$	Dorsey $\frac{4-3}{}$	Shockley $\frac{12-3}{}$	Stubblefield $-3/5$
	Goedel	Marnagan $\frac{4-0}{}$	Howey	Koehn
	Blaymaier	Kawasta $\frac{4-1}{}$		

141

DEFENSIVE PERSONNEL CHART

LANCE
2S(-3) MOORE
_____ KILLEFER
9(-6) WATERS
22(-11) HALL

SPEED
3(-23) MCCLURE
_____ LAZETICH
1C(-24) BUTLER
_____ VIRGA

CAT
11(-9) GROSSI
31(-17) GRAVES
2S(-15) SMILEY
_____ SATRE
_____ GLAD

QUICK
2S(-4) TIPTON
_____ ALEXANDER
3(-3) ADAMS
10(-11) HCRRCRO

RIP
23(-2) JONES
8(-8) GODDERZ
3(-1) CROSBY

MOVER
20(-7) BROWN
34(-14) SCHULTZ
8(-3) LODATO

STRIKE
23(+3) PARISH
32(-15) PLATT
_____ CLAUSEN
9(-5)

WHIP
PRESTON 2 3(-3)
HOROWITZ 3 2(-3)
BROOKS 9(-2)

LEFT HALFBACK
_____ MOORE
_____ PORTER
4(0) PARISH
4(0) GOODMAN

SAFETY
1S(-5) RINKER
96(-3) SQUERI
4(-3) TIETGS

RIGHT HALFBACK
2C(-6) KLOOS
11(-8) HOLLIDAY
_____ SCOTT
5(-2) VUCINICH

Key sheets and situation charts

We have found it advantageous to have a key sheet for effective teaching methods during teaching and/or testing periods. It is a breakdown of the particular play and/or defenses that we stress at a specific time, and it allows the various coaches to concentrate on exactly what their individual players are accomplishing. We believe that most good coaches do an excellent job of teaching fundamental skills and in evaluating films, but the weakest area is in the individual teaching in a group or team situation. It is somewhat similar to watching television: it is natural to follow the ball; however, the efforts of one individual performer are hard to determine. Because of this, a key sheet or situation chart is very important

KEY SHEET

OFFENSE

No.	Situations	Play	Defense	Comments
1	1-10	51 Roll #4	40	FB quick
2	2-5	49 Toss	60 U	Watch crack course
3	3-1	37	40 Pinch	T block
4	1-10	51 option	40	Check QB Resp.
5	2-10	16 Trap	4-5-2	Check Draw Resp.
6	3-10	74 maximum	60 Blitz	Check RB, FB, Block
7	1-10	94	44	Max Cover
8	2-4	FB screen short	40	Check HB clear
9	3-7	60	4-5-2	TE must get open
10	1-10	17 Draw	44	FB lead block

DEFENSE

No.	Situation	Defense	Play	Comments
1	1-10 (Run)	31	21 Sweep	Check Contain
2	2-6 (Run)	44	23 Blast	Cover support
3	3-3 (Run)	44 Pinch	37	LB'r Course
4	1-10 (Pass)	Even	22 Roll	Check Contain
5	2-2 (Run)	Odd	Strong option	Check FB Resp.
6	3-9 (Pass)	Even Dog 4	QB draw	Draw Resp.
7	1-10 (Run)	65 Man	41 Boot-leg	Secondary key
8	2-10 (Pass)	45	Strong screen	LB'er Support
9	3-10 (Pass)	Even	Flanker curl	Underneath relationship
10	3-12 (Pass)	Odd	TE delay	Lb'er Depth, field coverage

because it forces the coaches to zero in on the point of attack or on a certain technique that requires improvement.

When using these particular aids, it is important that the drill be more in a teaching tempo and in a controlled atmosphere so the coach can make corrections or repeat the play if desired. Curious things happen to players when they get in a group or team situation. Sometimes the most obvious and important teaching point will be forgotten when there is the added factor of emotion or pressure to which a player must adjust. A coach must be detailed in this at all times, and he should use any kind of assistance to be sure he is concentrating on the individual and helping him to improve on fundamentals while putting together a full team and execution situation. There are obvious situations to cover, such as stopping the clock, performing the two-minute offense, as well as coming into and going out of the goal line. The successful coach concentrates on these areas and involves his players in the understanding of decisions relating to these elements.

SITUATION CHART

10 Yd Line Coming Out

1. 1/10 37
2. 2/7 34 Ctr.
3. 3/2 41 Full

25 Yd Line Coming Out

1. 1/10 92
2. 2/10 HB Quick Screen
3. 3/7 60

40 Yd Line Coming Out

1. 1/10 74
2. 2/2 79
3. 3/2 51 Roll #4

50 Yd Line

1. 1/10 98
2. 2/12 17 Draw
3. 3/4 22 Roll

40 Yd Line Going In

1. 1/10 41 Boot #3
2. 2/8 16 Trap
3. 3/5 49 Toss

30 Yd Line Going In

1. 1/10 45 Ctr.
2. 2/12 FB Screen Short
3. 3/14 74 Max.

20 Yd Line Going In

1. 1/10 16 Trap
2. 2/1 Special
3. 3/1 Sneak at 4

10 Yd Line -- In

1. 1/10 51 Opt.
2. 2/10 43 Draw
3. 3/7 60 short

4 Yd Line -- In

1. 1/4 41 Full
2. 2/2 22 Jump
3. 3/2 33 Wedge
4. 4/1 Sneak at 6

Game day

Now is the time to earn your money. There was a misconception at one time that the hay was in the barn about the middle of the week before a game, and that there was not too much that could be done from there on in. We do not subscribe to this philosophy and feel that the decisions that are made during the game will give a football squad the edge. Organization prior to, and during the game, is the key.

Game day begins the night before during pre-preparation. It is advantageous to have the squad meet together informally, go to a movie, have dinner — or as we did at one time in high school — just get together at someone's home for hamburgers or hotdogs. At Stanford, we vary the Friday night routine from week to week, although it usually consists of dinner and a movie together. Following the movie, we have a dish of ice cream, and get the team to bed by 11 p.m.

On the day of the game, our squad arises at 8:45 a.m., with a 9:30 pre-game meal prior to a 1:30 p.m. starting time. Eating four hours prior to the game allows the correct amount of time to digest food and to get ready mentally for a top effort. Following the pre-game meal, we have some group meetings with the coaches, and I speak to the squad briefly before we proceed to the dressing room. This is about as close as we get to a so-called pep talk.

Prior to our team meetings, the coaches get together for a complete substitution briefing. All coaches inform me of their exact plans for substitution, what quarter they will make changes, what they will do if a first team player is injured, which players they want to be in the game if we are ahead, and other similar details. This is an extremely detailed meeting because I, as head coach, do not want to worry about these considerations during the game.

Over the years, we have made several adjustments in an attempt to reduce the number of details for which the head coach should be responsible. In this way, I am able to perform a much better job of total game administration than if I am bogged down with a lot of routine tasks. For example, we always have done a major part of the play-calling, both offensively and defensively. At one time, I felt very strongly that this could not be delegated to an assistant coach. I have changed my mind; however, the coach in charge of calling the plays is well briefed. A great deal of staff time is spent during the two days prior to the game in going through sham games, looking at films, and discussing what to do on certain down and distance situations when the ball is on a certain part of the field.

I prefer to be involved in just four areas during the course of the game: 1) making all kicking decisions; 2) keeping track of the scoring combinations; 3) encouraging the squad; and 4) making adjustments in the game plan. Substitution, play selection, defensive calls, order on the bench, and individual player adjustments are handled by the assistants.

The night before the game, we attempt to keep the players relaxed so they will be able to get a good night's sleep. The day of the game is all business. During the pre-game meal and briefing sessions with the squad members, we insist on quiet and intense mental concentration. Even though different players get ready to play differently, they must realize the seriousness of the task ahead of them.

We move the squad to the locker room in time to give them fifty minutes to dress. This should give the players ample time to get ready to take the field and still not have to hurry. Assuming that a good share of the taping already is completed, forty to fifty minutes is sufficient time in the dressing room.

We vary the amount of pre-game warmup time depending on the day's temperature and weather conditions. Our time schedule for a 1:30 p.m. game is as follows:

12:46 – all specialists take the field for a good warmup prior to the entire squad assembling for calisthenics. This includes passers, receivers, punters, centers, place kickers, and holders. Punters must kick in both directions so the receivers can get a chance to field the ball looking in both directions.

12:58 – the entire squad is on the field for some brief stretching calisthenics given by the captains.

1:02 – players break into groups with assistant coaches for additional stretching and routine drills pertinent to their positions.

1:09 – A skeleton pass group, offense and defense, is assembled and some pass patterns are run. The offensive and defensive lines continue drilling separately and then work together on drive blocking, pass protection blocking, defensive charges, and perhaps combination stunts.

1:12 – Entire squad gets together in front of the goal posts where the first offensive team runs against the second defensive team, and the second offensive team runs against the first defensive team. Two offensive plays are run with each team.

1:14 – Squad returns to the dressing room. Players are given time to check their equipment, use the restroom, etc.

1:22 – Squad prayer led by myself. We observe a few minutes of silent prayer and then repeat the Lord's Prayer together.

1:25 – Captains return to the field.

1:28 – Entire squad takes the field.

Between 1:25 and 1:28, we remind the squad of the basic fundamentals of the game, which, if properly performed, will result in a win.

A coach should follow his game plan to the letter whenever possible. He should utilize his entire staff with one or more coaches in the press box, if there is one; otherwise, they should be seated high in the stands. The other coaches on the field should know their responsibilities and follow them to the letter. The players should conduct themselves in an orderly fashion on the bench. It even helps to have the managers mark the benches to indicate where players should sit. A coach must be able to communicate rapidly with his players during the game. When one of the teams, or individual players come off the field, he should report directly to the coach prior to checking with the trainer.

I believe in having a time for everything, and a coach should have had an opportunity in advance to mentally go over every possible situation that possibly could arise during a game. However, he still must be prepared to do his best thinking in the heat of battle. If a coach has a sudden idea during the game, he should do it. He must not place himself in the position of saying at the end of the game, "I wish I had done this or that when I thought of it." It is much easier to play hunches and eliminate the problem of second guessing.

Halftime organization can be the key to the win. Hustle the squad into the locker room. The amount of time available should be divided into three sections. If it is a fifteen-minute half, one-and-one-half minutes should be allowed both for getting off and back on the field. This breaks the remaining time into three four-minute periods. If the half is twenty-minutes long, the same intervals break the locker room time into three five-and-one-half minute periods. The locker room should have been checked very thoroughly to be sure the blackboards are in place and that the squad knows exactly where to sit.

During the first period of the halftime, the players should sit quietly in their prescribed seats, sip cold soft drinks, take care of themselves, and consult with the trainer. This gives the coaching staff an opportunity to meet outside of the locker room area to review the first half. If any adjustments are to be made in the game plan, this probably is the best time to make them. The second period of the halftime should be spent with the coaches moving freely around the locker room answering questions, bolstering morale, and starting a general briefing on the second half requirements. The third period should belong to the head coach. He should review the first half, indicate mistakes made, the advantages gained, and then he should discuss what has to be done in the second half. At this point, if the game plan is not getting the job done, he should explain the changes to the team. The coach's final words must motivate the players before they again take the field. Each coach has his own personality and method of motivating his squad members, and it remains an individual and personal matter.

We emphasize the halftime organization because it must be extremely productive in a short period of time, and the coach must believe that the team is going back on the field better prepared to play the second half.

Immediately following the game, the players should get together for some brief comments by the coach regarding the game, and he should outline what is expected of the team in getting ready for the next game. Every coach hopes to talk to a loud and boisterous group, celebrating a victory. He should allow the players to get everything out of their systems; however, he then must sober them with some words regarding what is in store for them prior to the next game. He should give them a word picture of what the locker room will look like the following week if they follow his instructions during the week of practice.

Post-season incentives

The differing financial conditions of schools often dictate how elaborate will be their post-season banquets or get-togethers. No matter how restricted the budget may be, it is likely that even the most economy-minded school can afford a hamburger feed. Getting together at the end of a season not only caps off the year, but it also sets the tempo for the future program. It affords an opportunity to pay tribute to the outstanding players and to let them know that their performances are qualities that a coach looks for. It also gives a coach a chance to include guests who are important to his program.

Stanford is fortunate to have a friend of the University in Dan Lee, the owner of a local restaurant, who is the host of our yearly banquet. Some might feel that a formal banquet in a San Francisco hotel might be more appropriate; however, Mr. Lee's loyalty through the years and the atmosphere that prevails at his restaurant have been a very important part of our post-season banquet. The guest list includes many of the persons who have assisted in our program, and their presence gives them a deeper insight into what we are attempting to accomplish and an opportunity to share in our successes.

Awards

We believe that if awards are given, they should be voted on by the team because it means much more to an athlete to be recognized by his peer group. Most valuable player and most outstanding player awards are obvious and traditional. However, we include awards such as best hitter, best student, most improved player, most inspirational athlete, the players' player, and other awards that pay tribute to the attributes we are attempting to develop. The latter awards include the outstanding scout team and preparation team player, as well as the most inspirational nonlettermen. These awards are important for morale, and the attitudes of these award winners utlimately will determine the team's success.

This is a sample of a voting card used by players for determining awards:

All-star games

I have been honored on many occasions to coach various all-star
games, including the East-West, Hula, and Coaches All-America
college contest. Although a number of mistakes were made in the
early games, I learned that there are some very important considerations and procedures to follow when coaching in this capacity.
First, it is essential to realize that the players who were asked to
play in an all-star game already had achieved success in their own
conferences and leagues, and it is important that a coach respects
their abilities and does not institute wholesale changes in their
basic fundamentals and techniques. Most players are selected for
specific positions, and therefore it is important for a coach to determine as much about the athlete as he can so he is able to take
advantage and utilize the abilities that he has available.

Probably the most important single element in coaching an all-
star game is to institute a simple system of terminology for ease
in communication and in the learning of assignments and responsibilities. Simplicity is the key, and a coach must realize that if he
has a complicated offensive and/or defensive system, the ultimate
success of the game can be affected by the abilities of all of the
players to grasp his style of play. For this reason, I have concluded
that the best manner in which to present offense is to name the
formations and plays so there is no room for error.

We eliminate our conventional color and number system in favor of the following descriptive names for both formations and plays, i.e. Pro-Right, Blunt, which is our regular 37 play from a red formation. Illustrated below is a complete all-star game offense, which easily can be learned and executed in the normal ten-day period that is alloted:

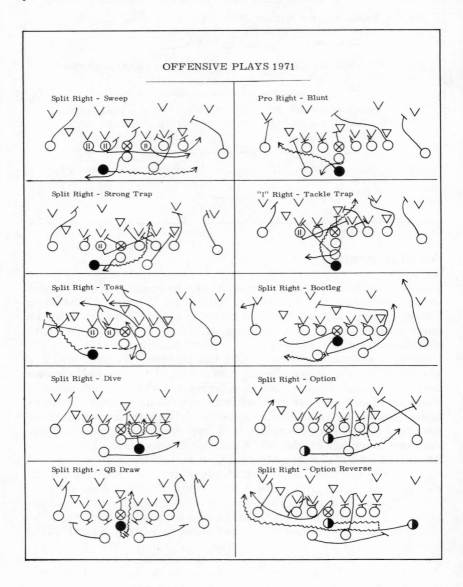

OFFENSIVE PLAYS 1971

Split Right - Sweep

Pro Right - Blunt

Split Right - Strong Trap

"I" Right - Tackle Trap

Split Right - Toss

Split Right - Bootleg

Split Right - Dive

Split Right - Option

Split Right - QB Draw

Split Right - Option Reverse

We believe strongly that the purpose of an all-star game is to allow the public to be able to see the nation's best football players in action. Therefore, both offensively and defensively there should be no aim by the coaches to fool or confuse their opponents by any type of trick or gimmick that would detract from the performance of the great athlete. It has been our experience that most all-star

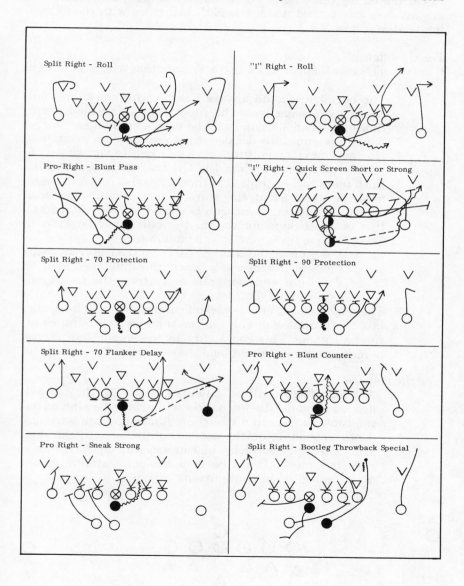

games take this into consideration and establish, prior to the game, a set of rules for the coaches and players to follow. These rules enhance and simplify the game and minimize the mental pressure on the players and make the game more enjoyable for the crowd.

Most defenses are outlined very specifically, as well as other rules related to both offense and kicking. The games in which we are involved are played under the N.C.A.A. rules with the following modifications:

For the offense
1. The two teams should use a T formation with a balanced line.
2. The backfield should always line up with not more than one man missing from the regular T. This would mean that one backfield man could be used as a flanker.
3. It has been mutually decided to not use any man in motion.
4. No movement or shifting may be used, except that two backfield men other than the QB may shift alignments.
5. Each team will be limited to three offensive sets and these must be declared at the start of our practice sessions.
6. When any kicking formation is used, that is, punt formation or place kick formation, the ball must be kicked.
7. The offensive lines may split as follows:
    a. The guards and tackles will be split 2 feet from their adjacent linemen as a maximum split.
    b. The tight end can split away from the tackle no more than 3 feet.
8. The only time an onside kickoff can be used will be in the last two minutes of the half or the last two minutes of the ball game. This could vary in the second half if one team has a 4 touchdown lead.

For the defense
1. A 4-man front shall be employed similar to the pro 4-3 defense. The middle linebacker will always be aligned on the center's nose in a two-point stance and can vary his depth depending on the down and distance. In extreme short yardage situations, he can move up on the center's nose but must always be in a two-point stance. Note: diagram for the base alignment.

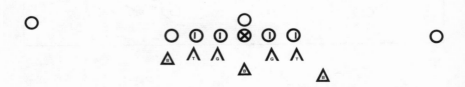

2. The guards and tackles (the pros call them tackles and ends) shall be aligned on the outside eye of the offensive linemen in a 3-point or 4-point stance. They must always be aligned in this same position. Their depth on or off the ball will depend on the down and distance situation.
3. The outside linebackers will have some flexibility if they are aligned on a split end side. Their base alignment will be off the ball outside the defensive tackle, but they are free to use a walkoff alignment or can even go out to a press position on the split end. Note: diagram below.

4. The outside linebacker on the tight end side will be aligned in a head up position on the tight end. He will always be in a 2-point stance, and is free to vary his depth dependent on down and distance.
5. Both outside linebackers are free to rush on the snap of the ball providing that the backer on the tight end side comes outside the tight end. The backer on the split end side is free to move up on the line and rush providing he does so outside the defensive tackle.
6. The middle linebacker can *never* be involved in a stunt situation.
7. The four deep will be free to align themselves any way they so desire, but cannot be involved in a stunt between the offensive linemen from tight end to short side tackle. In other words, there is no "safety blitzing."
8. If a secondary player aligns himself inside of the offensive linemen, he must be at least 5 yards from the line of scrimmage. However, on an acute short yardage situation this could vary.

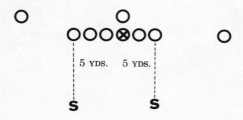

9. When the ball is inside the 5-yard line, the secondary is free to move up to a much tighter position.
10. In any kicking formation (whether it be punt or place kick) the front seven, that is, the down 4 and the 3 linebackers, are free to rush. In this situation the linebackers may take a 3-point stance.

10

Clinics

The great coach — or the coach who aspires to be great — is similar to the great academicians, lawyers, or doctors who realize that they never will reach a point where they will stop learning. Because a coach essentially is a teacher, it is incumbent upon him to stay in step with his fellow educators and enrich himself professionally. It is a responsibility that he owes to himself and to the thousands of youngsters he teaches and influences throughout his career.

Clinics mean different things to different persons. For some it is an opportunity to get together with old friends and repeat familiar stories both from their playing and coaching experiences. At the other extreme, there are those who studiously spend their time taking copious notes and try to obtain as much knowledge and innovative ideas as possible. The information may not be appropriate for their current programs; however, they file it away in their memory for possible future use. A happy medium can be reached in a coach's reasons for attending clinics, but the emphasis on a learning experience should work hand in hand with the social attractions. It is to the coaches' advantage to seek clinics that emphasize the structure of basic techniques and coaching drills. A speaker at a clinic who dwells on the higher philosophies of the game has his place if he can create some inspirational insight; however, a coach should seek a clinic that offers a balance that also includes information that he can relate meaningfully to his own players.

The word clinic generally connotes a gathering of several hundred or several thousand coaches seated in an auditorium and being subjected to a structured program. However, there is a variety of clinics on a smaller scale that oftentimes produces more of value in a personalized manner. We believe every coaching staff, whether it is one-man or ten-man, should conduct its own clinic at the beginning of every Fall season. Our staff has conducted a miniature clinic of its own for several years, and it has improved our own teaching techniques; it helps each coach to understand the teaching and reasoning behind his colleague's work. It also provides a "dry run" to prepare each coach prior to his personal teaching. The clinics become rehearsals to erase all margin of error, to generate communication, and to measure effectiveness. Constructive criticism is welcome, and we believe strongly that a much more cohesive staff is the result.

Another beneficial technique to increase individual and staff knowledge of particular football trends is to assign each coach a research responsibility. These presentations broaden the horizons of the entire staff and provide exposure to the specialized coaches. It is increasingly difficult, particularly at the college level, for an individual coach to obtain a full overview of a total football program. It most assuredly is essential in the professional progress of an assistant coach who aspires to a head coaching job. We have found the in-house clinics to be beneficial, especially when defensive coaches are given offensive research projects, and the offensive men must delve into defensive problems.

Visiting and observing practice sessions of other teams is another form of clinic. Because high school coaches do not have a lengthy Spring training period, it is advantageous for them to visit nearby college campuses and observe their programs and procedures. If there are several coaches on the same high school staff, perhaps each member could visit a different campus and observe a variety of systems and coaching techniques. After the entire staff compares notes and observations, the head coach is in a position to incorporate the best elements that are compatible with his program. We strongly recommend that as a coach evaluates his own football program, he also assesses what is being done by outstanding coaches in nearby schools. The Stanford staff has spent considerable time at the various professional camps, and they always are anxious to share with us their ideas and coaching methods. We are confident that any coach who conscientiously makes such visitations will be enriched and very probably will have a sense of reinforcement of what he already is doing. Such visits necessarily are of short duration; perhaps the time will come when coaches, like teachers, will enjoy the luxury of a year's sabbatical leave to make an intensive study of systems, programs, and methods throughout the United States. Stanford's door always is open to fellow coaches, and we are confident that a similar code of hospitality exists at most other institutions.

Of course, we realize the limitations of time and restrictions of travel that prevail in most schools. In that event, it is recommended that coaches take the lead and organize clinics in their own immediate areas. In larger cities, the clinic could be open to all high school coaches. In smaller communities, it could include coaches in junior high school through junior college levels with invitations going to coaches in the immediate surrounding area. The Stanford staff conducts a clinic at least once a year for the local high school coaches, and a general invitation is issued to any others who wish to attend. We have found that these clinics constitute a two-way street: we must organize our coaching philosophies to be easily communicated, and we gain valuable information from the high school coaches during free-wheeling discussions and question and answer periods.

Clinics should not be for the sole benefit of the high school, college, and professional coaches. High school coaches would be doing their programs and the community a service by organizing clinics for Pop Warner, Little League, and junior high school coaches in their areas. The beginning level coaches would receive invaluable advice and counsel, and the high school coach would profit by explaining his own program.

FOOTBALL CIRCUIT CLINIC, MAY 1, 1971

8 - 9 A.M.	Registration - coffee, milk, donuts
9:00-9:30	Head Coach John Ralston Topic: Practice Schedule

9:30 - 10:00	Offensive Coach - Mike White
	    Topic: Agility Drills for Linemen;
	          Board & Bag Drills

10:00 - 10:30	Quarterback & Receiver Coach - Roger Theder
	    Topic: Drills for Passers and Pass
	          Receivers

10:30 - 10:50	Defensive Coach - Bob Gambold Topic: Linebackers - Techniques and Drills
10:50 - 11:10	Defensive Line Coach - Max McCartney Topic: Pass Rush Drills
11:10 - 11:30	Defensive Back Coach - Jack Christiansen Topic: Drills in Teaching Man Coverage
11:30 - 11:50	Head Coach - John Ralston Topic: Review and Announcements
12:00 - 2:00 P.M.	Practice and Scrimmage

Our use of players as part of all of our clinics is based on our belief that on-the-field demonstrations must complement chalk-talks and lectures. They forcefully illustrate the formal segment of the clinic and afford visiting coaches an opportunity to see in action techniques that can be transmitted to their own players.

Too often, clinics are slighted or ignored because they are inconvenient, too much work to sponsor, or infringe on otherwise free time. However, the true coach—the great coach—knows that when his desire to learn ceases, his coaching effectiveness ceases.

The schedule is included in this chapter of a clinic that we offered last year, and the format could be used for any level of coaches and schools. The program began with lectures by each assistant offensive and defensive coach, followed by some general comments by the head coach. We then adjourned to our practice field and conducted a regular hour-long practice with our varsity for the sole benefit of our visitors. We had detailed the practice plan during our lectures so the coaches were aware of exactly what was going on, and they could concentrate on the area of their particular interest and needs. The practice was followed by a full-scale one-hour scrimmage. A social hour followed, and both Stanford and visiting coaches exchanged views and ideas that we believe aided everyone materially in his program.

Included with this was a practice schedule that was filled in by the attending coaches. They were able to refer to the drills as they watched an actual practice session. (This schedule is reproduced on page 137.)

Trends

One of the most exciting aspects of coaching is in examining and evaluating through clinics and other avenues the many prevalent and innovative trends in football. The game never stands still, systems and ideas constantly are changing, and different leagues and areas in the country periodically come up with different styles of football.

The coach who seeks to improve his program and himself professionally will have a fulfilling experience by keeping abreast of new ideas in football or in observing the return of an aspect of the game that long has lain dormant but still is effective. Obviously, we do not recommend that the young coach attempt to fit every new trend into his program, but for professional growth, he should read and observe the trends of today to keep up-to-date with everything that is developing in the profession. Much of this can be accomplished by regularly attending clinics. Then it becomes the coach's particular responsibility to communicate this information to his players and coaching staff. We will examine some of these trends, offer our opinions, and relate their effect on the Stanford program.

Two-platoon football

In the college ranks, some cumbersome substitution rule changes have resulted in the return to two-platoon football. It definitely is the age of specialization, and we attempt at all times to have separate offensive and defensive teams without asking any athlete to go both ways. Many of our colleagues at the college level are examining the possibility of playing talented athletes both ways; however, it is our firm belief and practice, that we should try to find twenty-two first team players rather than put the physical pressure on a player to try to go the whole way.

We realize that many coaches are beginning to find that some of the skilled positions, such as receivers and defensive backs, possibly could be interchangeable and play both ways. However, we have not examined this concept thoroughly enough and do not feel it would be applicable to our particular philosophy. We suggest that a coach examine his personnel, and attempt to play quality athletes in each position. If this is not possible, then two-way players should be identified and given a try-out. It should be realized, however, that they may be placed in a very difficult position against a team that has twenty-two players who come into the game fresh each time the ball changes hands.

The two-platoon system allows for specialization in a variety of areas. This is a great boon to football and gives many athletes a chance to play who might not otherwise have that opportunity. However, a coach must be very selective in choosing his personnel, remembering that it takes different types of courage and physical abilities to play all of the positions in football. In this instance, a coach should not close his eyes to a possible first-string athlete who may not be the classic mold of a football player.

Stopping the clock

The new college rule, which calls for stopping the clock after every first and ten, has changed the game considerably. Offenses formerly were putting the ball in play from fifty to sixty times in a game; now we often get off from eighty to ninety offensive plays. Similarly, defense units must play a good deal longer in some games; this, of course, can have an appreciable effect on the ultimate outcome of the game. In addition to allowing for more play, stopping the clock adds a new dimension to coaching because there are methods of conserving time by quick huddles, or electing not to huddle — particularly late in the half — to get plays off in a reasonably short time. Typical of other changes in football, it took us three or four years to thoroughly examine this particular idea, and we still are searching for new ways to increase our offensive output to make it more successful.

Pro influence

In many instances, college and high school coaches are reluctant to admit that the professionals who make a living and spend twelve months a year talking, thinking, and studying football can help us to any great degree. We may have shared this opinion several years ago, but one of the most important moves we have made has been to open our eyes and ears to the professional coach and player. We also find that the subject is discussed at length at high school and college clinics. The professional influence, from a technical standpoint, is obvious when one considers the number of colleges and high schools that use the professional passing game and professional defenses. When we decided to move the ball with the forward pass, we spent most of one Summer visiting professional football camps in California. The coaches and players were extremely hospitable and always anxious to help us to learn more concerning the intricacies of their game. After this experience, we wondered why it took us so long to realize the advantages they had to offer because professional coaches have spent years ironing out philosophies and techniques related to their offenses and defenses; we only regret that we did not seek their help sooner. The interested coach who lives in California can spend the month of July observing five professional teams during their practice camps. Similar camps are located in other areas of the United States. As we have cautioned throughout this book, we do not believe that an over-abundance of technical information necessarily is useful to a coach at different levels; however, the professional teams are ahead of most of us in the teaching of individual techniques. It can be a rich experience for any coach to talk with some of the great professional technicians as well as the players.

A great effect on our success have been the use of professional players to help us in coaching during Spring practice. Although we coaches tend to be somewhat self-centered and believe our knowledge is supreme, it is obvious to us that sometimes our players would rather have techniques explained to them by a professional who is making his living playing the game. The high school or college player naturally respects the professional, and the older athlete can relate his experiences in a very practical manner. He has gone through many of the same levels of learning as the student athlete, and he knows the attendant problems. Howard Mudd, an offensive guard, was the first professional player to assist us in our program on a full-time basis in Spring practice. A member of the San Francisco 49ers at the time, Mudd spent the entire Spring practice helping our offensive line coach. The effect he had was appreciable. The linemen naturally gravitated toward him and respected his advice concerning techniques and his thoughts on what makes today's athlete successful. Since that time, we have had other professionals, including John Brodie, Gene Washington, Malcolm

Snider, Len Rhode, and several others assist us during Spring drills. If for no other reason, they aided us because our players were extremely receptive, and therefore they were able to reach the athletes in areas where there might have been a communication gap with the regular staff. This arrangement can be used by coaches at all levels, and they would be in error if they did not seek the assistance of former or current players in clearing channels of communication. The goal of every program is success, and any avenue that can be utilized should be explored. The coach who uses outside personnel must, of course, indoctrinate the volunteer regarding the techniques, terminology, and system that are in use.

Defensive pursuit

We definitely are involved in the age of specialization in football, and this specialization, coupled with the increased physical abilities of the athletes who currently are playing football, has changed the entire structure of the game from the defensive standpoint. Coaches at all levels have very fine athletes playing defense, and the success of their programs depends to a great degree upon great pursuit. This trend is important from both an offensive and defensive standpoint. Offensively, we must be able to evaluate the type of pursuit an opponent uses and be able to do something to counteract it. This was such a concern with us prior to the 1971 Rose Bowl game that our first offensive play from scrimmage was a wide reverse. We faked our option play to the strong side and pitched the ball to our flanker, Eric Cross, who ran to the opposite side. Because of Ohio State's great physical abilities and the emotion of the game, it was very easy to fool them and to take advantage of their determination to make the tackle on the play that they were anticipating. We believe that there will be an added emphasis on reverses and counter actions in the next few years in an attempt to neutralize the great emphasis on pursuit. Defensively, we must guard against reverses or counter plays and constantly stress proper pursuit angles and relationships to the ball.

False key or influence football

There currently is a trend toward offenses using various types of influence or false key plays. These can be very effective, for example, against defenses that are based on reading on the move.

Arkansas opened its game against Stanford in 1970 with two plays in which they pulled their offensive tackle, causing a reaction by our defensive tackle. They then ran in right behind him without blocking the man involved. The fact that Stanford's tackle was so well schooled in his basic responsibility allowed Arkansas to make one twelve-yard gain without blocking him. The better coached the defensive personnel, the more effective this offense can be.

During the Stanford-University of California game in 1957, Joe Kapp utilized this method of influence football very successfully.

Stanford was using an Oklahoma (5-4) defense with the two inside linebackers keying the movement of the offensive guards. Cal's influence maneuver was to pull the guards to the outside, thus removing the linebackers from inside support. Kapp then would step back, look at the movement of the middle guard, and sneak on the opposite side of his movement.

Triple option and other option forms

Darrell Royal of the University of Texas, along with several other outstanding coaches, has had considerable success recently with the option approach to football. This trend relates to several other elements we have discussed because it utilizes the quick-hitting form of offense as well as the use of backs blocking the linemen to assist in picking up the various defenses that are presented to him.

The other obvious trend from the option series is that it forces defense coaches to make specific assignments and responsibilities in terms of the option particulars. For example, we believe we must assign at least two men to the fullback in the triple option, one man to the quarterback, and at least one man from the line of scrimmage to the pitch man. When a coach analyzes the factors in this perspective, he runs out of players quite quickly, and it is not hard to determine why Rex Kern of Ohio State was able to run with such freedom in the early part of the Rose Bowl game in 1971. His success forced us to change our plan and assign two men to the quarterback and one on the fullback. When we did this, their fullback, John Brockington, broke for a forty-three yard run without anyone touching him because the man assigned to him was blocked out of the play.

Stanford's best running play for the past three years, even considering Jim Plunkett's great passing abilities, has been the option play. We want to expand on this play, but it depends upon the attributes of our quarterbacks. The one serious drawback of this philosophy, obviously, is that in a third and ten situation, the quarterback must be able to perform the pass game in order to keep the drive going. If he has even a minor injury, therefore, it will impair the total success of the series. A coach must make a definitive determination concerning the team's depth before it can depend upon the option series. We have reached the conclusion that the best way is to utilize several forms of the option on a very simple basis. The triple option, the counter option, the swing option, and the belly option all present the defense with different problems. It is possible to simplify all of these maneuvers and put the basic pressure on the defense without placing too much on the quarterback.

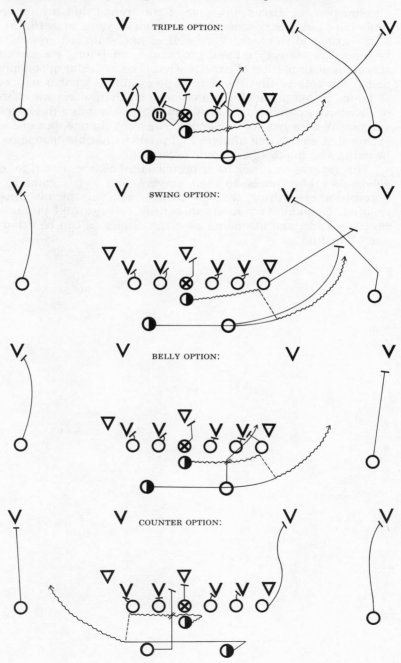

TRIPLE OPTION:

SWING OPTION:

BELLY OPTION:

COUNTER OPTION:

Keeping ahead of the trends

Our purpose in discussing some of the trends that are prevalent in football today is because it has become obvious to us that in certain sections of the country, as well as in certain conferences, they become very stereotyped and predictable; therefore, we advocate a thorough examination of exactly what the particular opponents are doing. We believe that the coach who examines what is happening to teams in his particular conference and then alters his offensive or defensive approach to stay ahead of these trends will experience success. We are not recommending constant change, but are advocating that each coach analyze and predict what his opponents will be doing and make adjustments accordingly.

This returns us to our basic premise that coaches owe it to themselves as professionals, to their players, and to the game to stay abreast of everything that is transpiring. This means constant reading, frequent visitations to nearby colleges and professional practice fields, and attending as many clinics as can be fitted into one's schedule.

11

Offense

The first real breakthrough for a coach seeking success is to be flexible enough to depart from former beliefs and habits in offensive football. We often have said that a coach must be intelligent enough to choose the type of offense or defense that will produce success against the best teams he will face; he must assume of course, that modifications must be made in terms of his personnel. Many coaches, particularly those who are new to the profession, tend to emulate the coaches and the systems under which they played in college. They are not being realistic because they often force the players to fit the system rather than fitting the particular talents of the players to a system in which they can play to their best advantage. Additionally, coaches all too often do not assess the defenses they will be facing, and they end up playing into the hands of their opponents.

A coach, therefore, must determine the strengths and weaknesses of his own team and those of his opponents, and he must assess critically his available talent.

One of the most important elements of a successful offense is to *be known for something.* Stanford historically has been known as a passing team. There have been years when Stanford has digressed from that emphasis, but four years ago we made the decision that from that point forward we must throw the ball to win. We did not make an arbitrary decision to throw the ball forty or fifty times in a game, but we knew we had to throw the ball to win — not necessarily a lot, but effectively.

It is obvious that a re-evaluation of available personnel must be made each year. Even though the talented Jim Plunkett has graduated, we will continue to base an effective offense on the pass.

We will re-evaluate our offense in terms of our present personnel to determine the type of pass actions and related plays that will be most effective, using the talents of our present players. As we discuss specific plays and/or throwing actions, we will relate some of the elements that are important in utilizing various actions and will suggest some pass offense schemes that are dependent on particular football strengths. For example, there are various types of pass offenses that depend on the strength of outside receivers, talents of tight ends, and the blocking and pass-catching abilities of offensive backs. We point out, however, that our ability to place a different emphasis in our offensive program has changed some of our offensive attitudes on moving the ball which has contributed significantly to our success. These changes have been made in accordance with our philosophy that we must determine what will win for us and then allow the necessary time to accomplish the mission. Regardless of the various types of offense, notwithstanding all of the X's and O's, the key to the offensive game boils down to an analysis of the personnel, the use of individual abilities in setting up a total attack, and intelligent analysis of the opponents in the league. Because of the ability of our quarterback during the past three years, we had a solid base from which to build. We also were blessed with a number of highly talented receivers. After analyzing our players, we selected the opponent that almost always is a "must" to defeat. In Stanford's particular case, the University of Southern California dominated the conference. Because of its traditional superiority, we built our entire program on methods of beating the Trojans. It is, and has been, the consensus of our staff that we cannot power off tackle against a team of USC's caliber and expect to win consistently. Therefore, the pass game has been the vehicle that can best offset their usual physical superiority. Coincident with the ability to pass against the top team is the necessity of keeping it off balance — again the philosophy of being known for something. To some degree, therefore, we have to throw out the down and distance tendencies and pass on the run downs and run on the pass downs. (An explanation and example of this procedure appears in another section of the text.)

Being known as a passing team immediately suggests that a team passes fully sixty percent of the time. The fallacy of this notion was illustrated vividly in the 1971 Rose Bowl game when Stanford passed only thirty times in the eighty times it had the ball. However, the point remains that opponents are "kept honest" when they face a team that is known for something. With this psychological edge, whole new offensive horizons may be exploited. Additionally, opponents must spend valuable practice time preparing for the element for which a team is "known," and the passing team can anticipate what will be done to try to stop it. In essence, the team is making the opponent play his game. Teams from Pop

Warner to collegiate ranks can become known whether it is passing, power running, field goal ability, or conservative but effective three-yards-a-down football.

Principles of offense

Down and distance football

Down and distance football is an area of offensive planning that very well could be unique to Stanford. We adopted it only after thorough and exhaustive research and development. We relate down and distance situations both to offensive play-calling and in studying our defensive plan as it relates to the trends of our opponents. From an offensive standpoint, our philosophy is that most down and distance situations occur either in what we call normal situations or obvious situations. Normal situations are first and ten, second and five to seven yards and third and three. The obvious situations are categorized into short yardage and long yardage downs. Here is our formula:

Normal	*Obvious*	
	Long	Short
1-10	1-10 plus	1-10 minus
2-5-7	2-8 plus	2-4 minus
3-3	3-4 plus	3-2 minus

After analyzing our game statistics for several years, it has become apparent that the team that can play a game and stay in the normal situations generally is successful; that is, we stay with what we call close to the down and distance and therefore eliminate or minimize the amount of times we are in obvious situations. If we are unable to perform in the normal downs and therefore face a lot of obvious situations, then we know that we have minimized our chances for success. The obvious situation makes it very easy for the defensive team to anticipate exactly what the offensive move will be. It is very apparent, for example, that in long-yardage situations the offense must pass. Conversely, in the short-yardage situation, the obvious tendency is toward the running game. Our success is based on the fact that we are willing to call plays that the defense does not anticipate, and it thereby *keeps them off balance.* A coach must realize that in these obvious situations, the defense will have a plan to combat his team's particular strengths. Because of this, we spend a great deal of practice time during the week performing our obvious situation offense. The ability to make the first down on third and one or two or third and ten is going to determine our ultimate success. We have concluded that there are several considerations that can help a team be successful in the obvious down situation: (1) It is important to utilize various formations: these formations can help to predict coverages or even possibly alignments; (2) The use of *motion* or some other maneuver provides a good opportunity to easily predict the defense and/or cause a defensive problem of which we can take advantage; (3) We also are examining very closely *maximum protection* and the possibility of one or two man receiver patterns on third down and long, or any long yardage situation. If a passing team uses the flood principle, and on third and ten continues to employ it, we feel its chances of success will be minimized because of the defensive emphasis on pass rush and related coverages.

Attacking defenses

One of the major break-throughs that our staff has made is the ability to understand and to evaluate defenses to a deeper degree. Many coaches believe they have a good understanding of defenses, but until they really dig into the basis of each and every alignment and each and every coverage, they will not have the ability to attack a defense effectively. This has become increasingly obvious to us because opponents use all types of alignments and coverages, and we must acquire a knowledge of them to formulate a more efficient attack. In our down and distance theory of football, of course, we know that in the obvious situations we will be in a better position to predict what a team is going to do defensively. In the normal situations, however, we realize that most teams really are unpredictable; therefore, we must understand their defenses and their defensive philosophy and try to communicate this to our quarterback. With our goal of keeping a team off balance, we try to make the most intelligent percentage play. With this consideration, we have examined and utilized automatic calls to a greater degree than we ever have previously. We realize that Jim Plunkett has a good feel for automatics, but we believe this is possible because of the time we spent teaching him the weaknesses of certain defenses so he could make an intelligent change at the line of scrimmage. We like to call our plays from the bench because we think we have a better knowledge of what the opponent is going to attempt to do. But we believe strongly that the well-educated and coached quarterback can perform simple automatics at the line of scrimmage, and therefore, we must examine the various defenses and try to help him. (See section on coaching the quarterback)

Here is a sample of the manner in which we break down a particular defense before the season and determine some of the areas that we anticipate might be most vulnerable.

4-3(pro) 4 deep

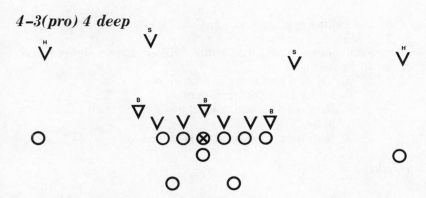

Coaching Points:
1. Determine man to man or zone coverage if possible.
2. Use even split rules. (Guard splits.)
3. Strong sweep, attack LB on TE.
4. Middle game attacking is good.
5. Defensive personnel are key to attacking this defense as MLB and outside LB are keys to strength of defense.
6. Must test containment of D.T.'s. (Pro ends.)
7. Free safety is key.
8. Attack short zones.
9. Check drop of MLB.
10. Alignment and play of strong safety is important.

44 press 3 deep

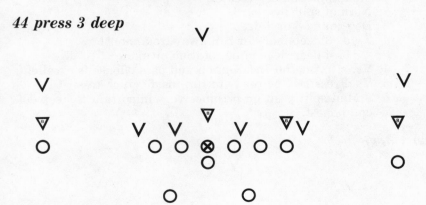

Coaching Points:
1. Even split rules. (Guard splits.)
2. Pass game concentrate more on backs and TE than wide receivers.
3. Middle trap and draw key play.
4. Attack LB on 2 man.
5. Wide receivers vs. press disregard all crack blocks and release deep.

6. Determine type of Press & Coverage.
7. 2 Man flex position.
8. Run zone pass patterns, control LB'ers strong; delays good.
9. 45 Press man:
    a. TE and Backs as key receivers.
    b. Delays to wide receivers
    c. Run man to man coverage out and then attack run area.
    d. Run man to man pass patterns.

50 (Oakie)

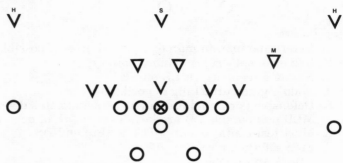

Coaching Points:
1. Maximum split by tackles.
2. Normal split by guards.
3. Determine 3 or 4 deep.
    a. 3 deep monster run away from monster.
    b. 4 deep determine rotation or man.
4. Vs. stunting 50 Def. Option and pass offense is excellent.
5. Vs. Press Def. be ready to run inside quick toss.
6. 8 Man split position becomes very important to keep def. end honest.

60 3 deep

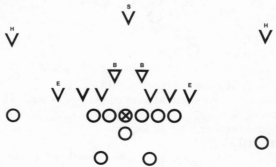

Coaching Points:
1. Maximum splits by guards.
2. Normal splits by tackles.
3. If man in 2 area is LB.
   a. Split the 2 man in certain plays.
   b. Run at LB.
   c. May change "hot receiver" key to LB on him.
4. Must be alert for End-LB combination on strong side and split side.
5. Maximum splits by wide receivers to prevent rotation.
6. If Def seldom uses 60 U and 60 Me stunts 44 Trap is excellent play (has possibility even on stunts).
7. Determine straight 3 deep or rotation.
8. Weakside run game poor vs. 60 def.
9. 60 Def. 3 deep be alert for overload rushers.
10. 2 Man and QB key inside strong LB & not LB on TE.

These alignments can be discussed in early season quarterback meetings to begin to familiarize the personnel with the relative strengths and weaknesses of the defenses that are expected during the season. When attacking specific teams that utilize these defenses, one must zero in a little further because an apparent weakness of the defense might be a strength, depending on the type of personnel that are playing in particular defensive positions. We attempt to utilize our offense, particularly the running game, to get the *best play* from the *best set* against the *defense* that we are going to face. We used to feel that we had to have a play or series of plays, and that they would be effective against anything the defense presented. We now realize that this trend is difficult to follow because running a Green Bay sweep or a base play against a split six would be a bad percentage call; therefore, it would be better to formulate a play that would be more successful. The important consideration is to examine and evaluate what the opposition is doing defensively, and do an intelligent job of attacking it without bogging down with too many assignments or too many intangible elements that the players can't possibly handle. The tendency to introduce elaborate defenses and coverages is the result of the increased use of the passing game.

Running to daylight or quick-hitting offenses

Another principle in football is in offenses that predicate their running game on running-to-daylight versus quick-hitting football. We currently are going through a transition, and there appears to be more of a trend to the quick-hitting type of offense that causes some mistake in the defensive assignments related to the ball carrier. O. J. Simpson popularized the run-to-daylight technique when he was playing at the University of Southern California, and he was almost miraculous in his ability to run wherever the defense presented a weakness. Most of us, however, do not have backs of this caliber, and we must realize that defenses are so sophisticated that they have the ability to take away a particular area; we therefor must examine methods of hitting them quickly to possibly force an error, or of attacking an immediate weakness.

Simple blocking patterns

Stanford teaches simple blocking patterns instead of line calls because defenses are extremely sophisticated and have the ability to change at the last minute or to perform many varied stunts and maneuvers. The ability to call blocks on the line of scrimmage and/or change the blocking for the best possible play can get a team into trouble and possibly cause a poor percentage play when a simple approach to blocking and getting off might be the better answer. The more varied alignments that we face, the less we feel we can pull guards; and, of course, this is something each individual coach must examine and determine as he sets up his own system.

Here are some detailed considerations that we believe should be made in formulating the Elements of a Successful Offense:

Stressing offensive goals and objectives to the team

Today's athlete has a strong desire to be *involved* in his school's program. The more that they can see the offense through the coach's eyes, the more they will be able to make it work efficiently when the chips are down.

Goals and goal-setting are very tangible elements to consider in offensive football. Stanford ranked third in offense in the country in 1969, and the players' pride in that position was related to their knowledge that they helped to make it possible. We stress goal-setting by telling our players what percentage we plan to pass and to run, and how many yards we would like to make and average over a season so they will know exactly what is expected of them.

At the start of each year, we issue to our players the important goals and objectives for the coming season. Also included are the specific results of our offense in these particular areas from the past season. We are careful not to set specific goals such as making 500 yards per game or having a sixty percent pass percentage. Rather, we discuss a realistic improvement in the areas that we feel are important to our success.

Following were the goals and objectives as we started the 1970 season:

1. Poise
2. Score inside 10
3. Key third down plays
4. Short yardage & goal line offense
5. Downfield blocking
6. Performance — second effort
7. Receiver ability to run after catch
8. Runner/back ability to run after first hit
9. Execution — Simplicity — Confidence — Individuality

		1968	1969
10.	Cut down turnovers	fumbles 22/lost 12 int. 18 (*Total 30*)	f. 27/lost 15 int. 19 (*Total 34*)
11.	Minimize bad plays (automatics)	246 yds.	276 yds.
12.	QB protection (Times sacked)	13 times	11 times
13.	Punt coverages	2.2 return ave.	50/108 ret.
14.	Kick Off return yardage	17.8 ave.	19.6 ave.
15.	T.D.'s	run — 16 pass — 18 FG — 6	run — 17 pass — 26 FG — 10
16.	Drives — position we give up ball position we get ball		
17.	1st downs	run — 92 pass — 106	run — 110 pass — 143 — 262
18.	Scoring per quarter	61/95/57/55	79/102/82/86
19.	Pass percentage	52.5	56.8
20.	Penalties		**Stanford:** 60/634 Opp.: 43/106
21.	Total yardage per game	run — 177.4 (3.4 ave.) pass — 252	run — 196 (4.3 ave.) pass — 299

22. Offense nationally — 1969 (3rd in nation)

San Diego State	531.1
Houston	513
Stanford	**495**
Ohio State	493
Texas	483

		1968	1969
23.	Scoring nationally (5th in nation)	26.8	34.9

San Diego State	46.4
Texas	44.3
Ohio State	42.6
Houston	38.6
Stanford	**34.9**

24. Pass offense nationally (3rd in nation)

San Diego State	373	per game
Florida	301.6	per game
Stanford	**299**	per game

Staff attitude

We believe that staff members on both offense and defense should build an attitude that will be easily evaluated and accepted by the squad. We have observed that many coaches tend to head off in their own specific directions; this becomes readily apparent to the team and detracts from the total receptivity of the individual players. When two coaches are going in opposite directions in their teaching or attitudes, or when one coach is reacting negatively to the head coach, it becomes very apparent to the players. It won't be too long before he loses confidence in them and starts looking right through the coaches as they teach. Coaches must talk with each other concerning their individual techniques, problems, and ideas, and the players then will develop an attitude of cohesiveness.

Keeping an opponent off balance

As we discussed in our down and distance football philosophy, we believe that it is extremely important for an offensive team to select its plays to keep the defense off balance. The basis of this is having a thorough knowledge and/or insight into what the defense is thinking. The ability to anticipate what the defense will do and then to present plays and/or situations that they do not expect is the underlying basis for success according to this philosophy. This obviously can be done by running when the opponent anticipates a pass and vice versa. This also can be accomplished by utilizing a different form of run or pass than possibly has been used before in a similar situation, either in that particular game or a previous one.

Consistent pass game

We will analyze the pass game further as we discuss different aspects of offense, but our basic philosophy of the consistent pass game is the necessity of developing a *total* pass game once that emphasis has been determined. Identical to the total offense, a coach must determine what he wants to be known for in terms of pass offense. The choice must be made: a team cannot be known both as a great dropback and rollout team. The defenses that are presented today are so sophisticated that a team must excel in a specific area so no defensive stunt or maneuver can destroy the basic offensive plan. To complement this, a team must develop different types of pass protection and/or draws and screens that relate to the basic pass action. (Pass actions and protections are discussed elsewhere in this book.)

It is paramount that a coach and his team believe that they can execute their pass game regardless of the defenses they face. The pass game should be structured so it will be successful against everything from a one-man to a ten-man rush. Our technique is to keep the pass game simple enough to give the quarterbacks, receivers and protectors enough understanding that they can cope with whatever problems they face.

A flexible run game

As we mentioned in the discussion of today's football trends, high school and college defenses are varied, sophisticated, and specialized; virtually every alignment and stunt imaginable are employed. For these reasons, we re-emphasize our philosophy of flexibility, this time in relation to the running game. The one exception that we allow is the great back who is able, because of his great abilities, to take advantage of the defense. In our particular conference, however, if a defense decides it doesn't want us to run in a particular area, we generally don't. This may sound like a very academic statement, but after the ball is centered it is very difficult to bring it back. Therefore, a team has to do the best it can with what has been called.

Most defenses and defensive alignments make some running plays function better than others; as a consequence, we place varying emphasis on the running plays that we prepare from week to week. This is a considerable departure from the philosophy we followed in the past. In those days, we approached the running game in much the same manner as we now do the pass. We ran the off-tackle play, the sweep, and the inside trap regardless of what the defense did. Now we have a better knowledge of the defensive alignment and personnel, and we attempt to coordinate our flexible running game with the passing attack that we plan to emphasize in a particular game. This results in an examination of the three or four running plays that should be successful through sufficient practice. We reach our conclusions through an analysis of the opponent's history, films, scouting, and our previous meetings.

Know your opponent

The previous discussion prompts us to point out that a coach should know his opponent and be able to attack him intelligently with both the run and the pass.

The first steps are to examine very carefully the positions of the opponents on the schedule. A chart should be made on the opponents as they appear on the upcoming schedule, listing opponents, film exchanges, last year's opponents that played a similar style as yours, offensive formations, defensive alignments, strengths and weaknesses in the opponent's personnel, and notations regarding what will be effective against them. A coach should talk with his colleagues in his conference to obtain any information regarding his opponent's strengths and weaknesses. As we have discussed throughout this book, there are certain games on the schedule that are the most important to win. If a given team must be beaten in order to win the championship and it is played early in the season, a coach must use every ethical method to learn everything possible concerning that opponent. Intelligent planning will eliminate last-minute grasping at straws.

Although we are the first to admit that we are just scratching the surface in our understanding of the complex and varied defenses, we recommend staff discussions to determine the most intelligent manner of attacking different defenses. Our defensive staff offers considerable information to the offensive coaches relative to the specific strengths and weaknesses that they see in our own defenses. Applying these observations, we feel we can set our game plan based upon the percentage weaknesses of a particular defense.

Don't beat yourself

Following this rule will aid in eliminating mistakes that can keep the play from being successful. An offense generally beats itself, and one of the most frequent offenders is the coach who overcoaches the individual and attempts to teach more details than the athletes are capable of comprehending. We constantly are amazed at the number of younger coaches who try to gather all the new ideas, plays, and actions in an attempt to innovate or fool their opponents. A coach who is confident in certain plays that are adaptable to his own personnel usually will enjoy a successful offense if he spends the time practicing and perfecting the plays to eliminate mistakes. It is a very simple formula: a coach who has twenty plays in his repertoire and practices each one-twentieth of the time would accomplish more by using five plays and spending a greater amount of time on each. We hasten to add that we do advocate introducing innovative plays if they are appropriate under the circumstances. We must point out that if we have had one glaring mistake over the years, it has been that we have not established an emphasis from year to year, stuck with it, and practiced it for the appropriate time. Calling a trick play or a stimulating maneuver by no means is a deterrent from a team's overall success. Rather, it many times complements that for which we are known.

Coordinating your offense with defensive strengths

It is advisable to evaluate the strengths of your defense in order to establish the type of offensive philosophy that you will use from year to year. If your defense is extremely strong and you have confidence in its abilities, then it naturally will have an effect on your offensive beliefs toward gambling and/or taking changes that might not otherwise be tried because of inherent defensive weaknesses.

To the casual observer, our success during the 1970 season was based solely on the success of our offensive team. From a coaching standpoint, we believe that much of our success was based on the abilities of our defense to make the big plays and to stop our opponents at the crucial times. We indicated earlier in this book that football success is based on the ability to play defense; we carefully examine these defensive strengths so we can utilize the appropriate offensive maneuvers.

As we examine the 1971 season, we are very aware of our defensive strengths, and consequently we feel that this may add a different emphasis to our play selection in the obvious down situations. For example, if we are faced with a third down and fifteen yard situation, and we feel the percentages are against our making the yardage, we very possibly might call a better percentage or safer play so we can ultimately kick the ball and allow our defense to gain the all-important vertical field advantage.

Don't forget the fundamentals and basic skills

Later in this chapter, we will discuss specifically our offensive fundamentals and discuss on-the-field coaching of those basics. But let it be said now: if a coach cannot teach basic fundamentals and execution in offensive football, he probably won't be successful. He also will fail if he spends too much time attacking defenses and theorizing about offense while neglecting basic fundamentals and execution.

We at Stanford were well aware of these concepts during our practice for the 1971 Rose Bowl game against Ohio State University. We spent the first eight days without one thought of Ohio State's defense. We determined, that after an eleven-game season, our fundamentals were well below the point they had been at the beginning of the season. It was an extremely painful admission for us, but it was obvious when we examined our films that the good old blocking, faking, drop of the quarterback, release from the line by the receivers, and other fundamentals were much inferior to our early football practices. In response to this, we returned to the starting point, emphasizing fundamental techniques. We therefore share with you our experience that there really is no excuse for a coach to allow his team to be out-fundamentaled. When players know what they are to accomplish, the coach must be certain that he has communicated to him the proper fundamental approach to all the techniques he is expected to use. We know that we have neglected these practices at times in the past, and therefore strongly intend to continually remind ourselves and our players of the importance of basic fundamental skills in the future.

Early decisions on game plans

It may be an obvious statement that early decisions should be made on game plans so a team can practice what will be used in its next outing. However, it is discouraging, and somewhat amazing, to note the number of coaches who violate this cardinal rule. Because we play Saturday games, we know we are in a difficult position if we have not decided on our passing and running game emphasis by the previous Monday at the very latest. If a coach delays until Tuesday or Wednesday to decide on his game plan, his players are cheated of the opportunity to prepare properly. Too often this delay is dictated by an overemphasis on the time spent on attacking defenses and adjusting defenses and blocking schemes to the various stunts and maneuvers the opponent might use. Another chapter will discuss practice organization and the utilization of time; however, it is sufficient to say at this point that a good deal of what a team is going to use from week to week can be decided in the Summer or in meetings when the emotional stress of a season is not a factor. As a coach examines his upcoming opponent, he probably will have a very good idea of what he is going to use offensively or defensively. When the opponent later is scouted, it will in many cases substantiate the information that already is known. This affords the intelligent and well-organized coach, who examines teams in advance, a pretty good notion of the areas he will be required to stress. With this behind him, he can formulate quickly a specific game plan to help his personnel attack strengths or weaknesses in his upcoming opponent.

Study your play-calling procedure

Based on his study and analysis of the opponent, the coach is better qualified to call the original plays for the quarterback. In addition, it takes a little pressure off the quarterback, allows him to execute better, and gives him an opportunity to evaluate the defense at the line of scrimmage. He then can take advantage of a specific situation.

Shuttling players in and out of the game is not an effective means of calling plays because it takes away the quarterback's leadership position. It also could affect his confidence because it is obvious to everyone that he is not his own boss, and some of the effectiveness of the offense is damaged. We use a very simple system of signalling plays from the sideline by one of the offensive coaches. Although this has been very effective, it still is examined each year. Because various teams have quarterbacks with differing capabilities and attitudes, it would be presumptuous of us to recommend calling every single play. If the quarterback from his position does not agree with the effectiveness of the play, for example, it is probable that he cannot execute it well. Because of our emphasis on communication as the most important single factor in coaching, it would be remiss of us to tell our quarterback that he must *always* follow our instructions. Although we do determine whether we are going to run or pass in our down and distance principle, for example, many times we merely indicate that we want some sort of pass action. We have found that the quarterback generally calls the play in which he has the most confidence; consequently he usually does a superior job because he is much more sold on the given play. This is a prime example of our belief in flexibility, and we constantly are attempting to come up with the right answers for a specific situation rather than setting up a specific pattern that might be unsuccessful from year to year.

We use these arm signals to communicate from the bench to the quarterback:

Hand on head—70 pass
Kneeling—60 pass
Turned sidewise—90 pass
Back to field—screen
Drawing movement with hand—draw
Raising one foot—bootleg
Hand on belt—51 roll
Three fingers and pass signal—pass 38
Three fingers—38
Two fingers—22
Hand on neck—41 full
Three fingers and four fingers—34 counter
One finger—13
Toss movement—toss
Four fingers and five fingers—45 counter
"T" signal with one finger—16 trap
"T" signal with four fingers—43 trap

It is a very simple system and is based on *eye contact* with the quarterback. A coach can give false signals until the quarterback sees him, or another coach can give the signals if there is concern about the opposition stealing the signals.

Automatics

Until the last year or two, our staff always was split down the middle on the relative merits of automatics. It was the age old argument of why change something if it is coached well enough to be successful? Also, we considered the ever-present negative aspect of the chance for mistakes when a play is changed. We now firmly believe that an automatic system can be beneficial at all levels.

This does not infer that an over-abundance of automatics must be called in a given game. It merely means that the quarterback must be given the necessary tools, based on his knowledge of defenses, to eliminate the bad percentage play. If attacking defenses is important and certain defenses lend themselves to certain offensive maneuvers, the quarterback must examine the defenses at the line of scrimmage. He should have the opportunity to call a simple automatic, for example, if a play designed to hit in the number two hole is jammed with three defensive men. Again, he should have the option if the opposition has a defense that would indicate a better percentage by attacking elsewhere. So long as automatics are put into the play book on the first day of practice, they can be practiced to the point that a positive attitude is created among the players. If this is done, they will become an integral part of the offensive game.

Short yardage, goal line offense

When a coach bases his offense on the pass game, he immediately places himself in a difficult position when attempting to chip out short yardage or the necessary inches to score a touchdown. This became apparent to us early in our passing program, and we were quick to evaluate and take the necessary steps to work out a plan that could be successful. We realized that no matter how much emphasis was placed on the pass game, we still had to get the ball into the end zone from the one-yard line and make those crucial third down and short yardage plays. With our philosophy of down and distance football, we believe that the defense has a pretty good idea of what we're going to do when we get into those short yardage positions. We also have a pretty good idea of what we should do; therefore, we must come up with something to enhance our chances. The single most important adaptation that has helped us is the use of a two tight end offense. We use the two tight ends with the flanker, and maintain our basic offensive alignments. Probably the most revolutionary aspect of our goal line offense is the departure from our basic lineman's stance. To cause greater emphasis on our drive blocking technique, we have initiated the use of a four-point sprinter's stance for our offensive linemen. Although this four-point stance would not be advantageous in our regular pass offense, it definitely does enable our linemen to perform their responsibilities more effectively in these particular goal line and short-yard situations. There is an added bonus in that we still are able to execute a running play fake pass or other related action passes from this stance which allows us to maintain our basic offensive philosophy of keeping a team off balance.

We are extremely proud of our goal line offensive success, and we constantly are asked what our secrets are. In a subsequent chapter, we will explain specific plays and pass actions that have contributed to our success.

Player progress and film evaluation

We have conducted a lot of research and put in considerable time to devise the best method of evaluating our offensive players after viewing our game films. Before devising our current method, we even used the old baseball percentage system, pluses and minuses, and other forms. We believe that it is most important not to create a negative attitude in a player's mind in relation to grading. It should be explained to him that it is a sound vehicle to assist him in practice the next week and to aid him to perform better in the next game. Degrading a player could destroy his morale, and in reality, it indicates that the coach did not properly prepare the athlete for the game. If the grading system is approached with a healthy attitude, the coach will be able to examine and discuss with the player his deficiences and improve his play.

We use the enclosed grading sheet and we insert each player's name in the appropriate box. The smaller boxes give us an opportunity to grade every play, and when something is done that needs improvement, we make comments in the right hand margins.

Here is our grading procedure:

We enter the number of plays that the athlete actually has played during the game. If his performance on a given play is to the satisfaction of the coach, he will receive a check mark. If we are unable to grade a play, the letter N is entered; therefore, he is not penalized. The remainder of the plays then are graded specifically with our TEAM system, which gives both the coach and the player a basis for communication regarding the player's performance as well as guidelines for improvement in the future. Although most of these grades are negative, we work very hard to use them in a constructive way to help to create a confident and positive attitude of improvement in our players.

The scoring is called our Team System. This is the way it is set up:

T — a mistake related to technique and is worth minus one point.
E — mistake related to effort and is worth minus three points.
A — an assignment mistake and is worth minus four points.
M — a mental mistake which is minus two points.
S is a super-play and is worth a plus five points. One additional grade is an L, or *loser*, for which a player receives a minus five points.

Effort is the responsibility of the players. We demand a certain

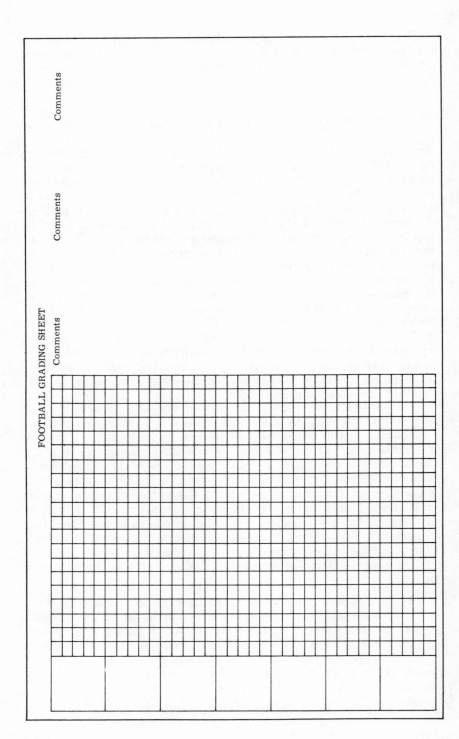

FOOTBALL GRADING SHEET

Comments

Comments

Comments

INDIVIDUAL PLAYER FILM GRADING SHEET

A. Player_____

B. Position_____

C. Opponent_____

D. Grading System:

	Point Value	
T - Technique	-1	T_1 - Drive T_3 - Block or move
E - Effort	-3	T_2 - Pass T_4 - Other
A - Assignment	-4	Prot
M - Mental	-2	
S - Super	+5	
L - Loser	-5	
N - Not Gradable	-	
✓ - OK	-	

	1	2	3	4	5	6	7	8	9	10	Comments
A	✓	✓	T_1	✓	T	✓	✓	M	S	✓	1E - (3A Poor Target)
B	✓	✓	✓	T_2	T_2	T_2	✓	✓	T_2	A	
C	✓	T_2	✓	✓	L	T_2	✓	M	✓	S	(5c - Penalty)
D											
E											
F											
G											

SCORE	TOTAL PLAYS	COMMENTS	COACHING POINTS
10 T --- -10	75	9 T were pass protection	needs tandem & mirror drill
2 E --- -6	N - 5		
1 A --- -4	+70	poor effort crossfield	must work on crossfield technique
2 M --- -4	-24		
1 S --- +5			
1 L --- -5			
-24	46		

amount of effort, and if he is not performing to capacity, we must push him harder.

Assignment mistakes are related to both the coach and the player; if we find someone making too many mistakes in a game that he is not making in practice, then we examine his abilities in relation to our program. Mental mistakes sometimes are inter-related with techniques; but we grade them down further because sometimes it is a mental mistake based on a technique, such as moving the wrong foot or not taking the proper course. The super plays and the loser plays obviously are those we want to concentrate on because they affect the program most drastically. When we find two or three super or winning plays, we pay particular tribute to the athletes involved because it not only affects their attitude but the spirit of the entire team. Super plays include a perfectly executed technique, a great effort, or an exceptional second effort. Loser plays include penalties or total lack of effort.

Two-minute offense

Too many men in the coaching profession fail to plan and prepare for the two minutes of football during which more games are won or lost than in perhaps any other period of time. We are referring to those fleeting moments when a team is backed into a corner and is trying to beat the clock either at half-time or at the end of the game.

Stanford calls it the REBA offense, and therein lies a story that inspired our development of the technique. During our pre-season practice last year, a woman named Reba who was in charge of the training table impressed us with her zip and enthusiasm. Her speed and quickness illustrated to us the kind of earnestness of purpose that we wanted to perfect in what we heretofore had called our "hurry-up" offense. It didn't take long for REBA to become immortalized as our two-minute offense.

Whether or not coaches come up with similar nicknames, the important thing is to prepare for those critical times. We admit that in the past we were guilty of failing to properly prepare for such contingencies, and they cost us football games.

Two-minute offense is considered by many coaches in the same category of the kicking game; it is something that is talked about extensively, but little practice time is devoted to it.

The key to the REBA offense is *speed.* It is essential that all players *sprint* to and from the huddle.

When selecting a pattern of play or plays to use, these rules should be followed:
1. Limit time in calling and executing.
2. Advance the ball and stop the clock.
3. Set exact procedure of communication between officials on the precise amount of time remaining and the number of times out remaining.

When the huddle cannot be utilized during the REBA offense, all plays should be called from automatics (live color). Stanford uses such words as "speedie," "jet," and "tank" to indicate the play. Speedie is a quick side-line out-of-bounds play; JET is a pass play that is used on first down. The TANK call is a run on first down. Subsequent plays will be called with the live-color automatic system depending on the results of the previous play. This is the breakdown and timing of the REBA offense:

I. Two minutes to one minute remaining
   A. Emphasis must be placed on hustle, poise, and proper execution.
   B. Do *not* call time out (unless absolutely necessary)
   C. When feasible, utilize an automatic (live color) or incorporate the jet and/or tank series (with the exception of poor field position).
   D. All plays must be off in fifteen seconds or less. Use quick cadence.
II. One minute to no time remaining
   A. Utilize times out (huddle only when clock is stopped)
   B. Understand what stops the clock
      1. First downs (clock starts after ball is marked)
      2. Out-of-bounds play
      3. Incomplete pass
      4. Penalty
      5. Measurement. May be requested anytime when ball is close to marker.
   C. Use speedie quick pass; throw out of bounds if covered.

The REBA offense requires *poise* and *confidence* and the ability of a team or individual to make the critical run or critical pass go all of the way. It is designed to successfully keep the ball moving, so we could ultimately score. Using this offense to perfection very well could turn the game around.

One of the most important elements of the two-minute offense is having the ability to properly read the clock and take intelligent advantage of the remaining times-out. We learned it the hard way.

We had a definite game plan for the 1969 game with the University of Southern California. Victory would have given Stanford the Pacific Coast title and put us in the Rose Bowl. In the final two minutes of play, we drove almost the length of the field and went ahead, 24-23. However, a breakdown in our planning led to our defeat because we had not learned to take time off the clock. We had two times-out left during the final drive, and we used one prior to the successful field goal that put us ahead. It came after a third down play that set up the field goal. As soon as the play stopped, we called time-out. If we had planned our strategy properly, we would have let the clock run and asked the official to count off twenty-four seconds of the twenty-five second allowable count between plays and then taken time out. This would have taken the clock to about thirty-eight seconds prior to our go-ahead field goal. Because of this lack of planning, however, we had kicked off after the field goal, and USC had the ball on its fifteen-yard line with fifty-five seconds to play. The Trojans were able to get off eight plays, and the final play with no time on the clock was a successful 17-yard field goal that resulted in a USC victory, 26-24. The lesson is obvious. Stanford's field goal was the final offensive play for the

Indians. Had we a plan for taking time off the clock, it would have been extremely difficult, if not impossible, for USC to have made a long drive in so short a time. It was the difference of kicking the field-goal with one minute and two seconds left in the game or with thirty-eight seconds remaining.

In summarizing the two-minute offense, we have developed a check list which, if followed, will either save or waste the clock depending on our situation. These are included:

Save the clock:

1. Hustle at all times
2. Use quarterback pre-planned option strategy
3. Down rolling punts quickly
4. Use pre-planned touchdown series
5. Punt out of bounds.
6. Request measurements when ball is close
7. Space times-out intelligently
8. Hustle to huddle after the tackle
9. Eliminate the huddle if possible
10. Use quick snap counts
11. Throw sideline or out-of-bounds passes.

Waste the clock:

1. Break the huddle slowly
2. Use long signal count
3. Unpile slowly after the tackle
4. Get back to the huddle slowly when on offense
5. Run wide but stay inbounds
6. Eliminate pass
7. Never call time out
8. Take the full alloted time to place the ball in play
9. Eliminate penalties which may stop the clock
10. Keep the ball within bounds

Terminology

Consistent with our belief in full communication between players and coaches, we advocate the establishment of a uniform, easily communicated system of terminology. The coach who can establish such a system of communication and knowledge that can be imparted to his players is on his way to being successful. It all begins with a sound terminology system. When players hear a particular term or the coach calls his attention to a specific mistake, he reacts to the terminology knowledgeably. For example, when we refer at Stanford to a base defense, an odd-defense, a four-three defense, or a five-two coverage, our entire team knows what we mean.

Stanford's offensive terminology is as follows:

Type of offense – pro

A. Utilizing a split end and flanker attack, along with wide slot and multiple receiver formations (i.e. two quick receivers, both sides or three quick receivers on one side).

Offensive numbering system

A. Interior Line
   1. Strong side tackle – #3
   2. Strong side guard – #4
   3. Center – #5
   4. Short side guard – #6
   5. Short side tackle – #7
B. Tight Ends
   1. Strong side tight end – #2
   2. Short side tight end – #8
C. Wide Receivers
   1. Split short side end – split end
   2. Split strong side back – flanker
D. Backs (Numbers designated for play clarification)
   1. Quarterback – #5
   2. Fullback (behind center) – #3
   3. Running back (or fullback) – #2; ("I Back"), #1 (behind strong side); #4 (behind short side)

Formation alignment system

A. We utilize the flip-flop system of strength with our offensive line and backs – strength is designated by a right or left call following the formation desired. The backs and split receivers line up in relation to the offensive line strength.

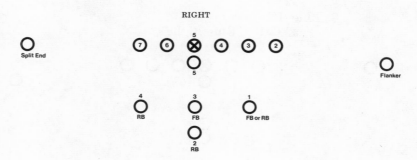

RIGHT

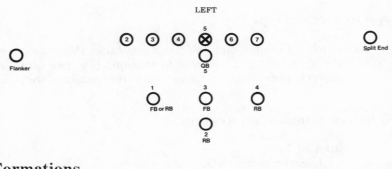

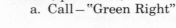

Formations

A. We indicate our formations by the use of colors (i.e. Red, Green, etc.)
   1. Green (split backs)
      a. Call – "Green Right"

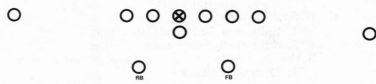

   2. Red (Pro)
      a. Call – "Red Left"

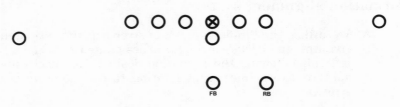

   3. Blue (I)
      a. Call – "Blue Right"

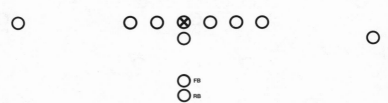

4. Purple (Double Wing)
a. Call—"Purple Left"

5. Black (Wide slot, can be Red, Green or Blue)
a. Call—"Black Right"

6. Orange (Triple Receivers)
a. Call—"Orange Right"

7. Brown (Cross Flanker)
a. Call—"Brown Left"

189

Cadence (snap counts)

A. Non-Rhythmic
1. *Set*—Down—*Hike*—*Go*
   a. Set—(Quick Count)
      (1) First of our "Get Off" commands
      (2) We come to the line of scrimmage ready to go, so after a one second pause the *set* can be utilized to start the play
      (3) *Set* can also be used to stem the backs or initiate motion
      (4) Any automatic must be called after the *set* command
   b. Down—(Separation Pause)
      (1) A term not used to initiate a play
      (2) Term used to reset the team after stemming and also gives us a separation between an automatic call and hike command
   c. Hike—(Normal Count)
      (1) Second of our "Get Off" commands
      (2) Mandatory starting count after an automatic call
   d. Go—(Long Count)
      (1) Third of our "Get Off" commands

Automatic systems

A. We utilize the "Live Color System"
1. Prior to a game a color will be designated as the "Live Color" which can be called after the *set* command to indicate a change in the original play called
2. Example: Live Color—Red (*Set*—Red 37, Down, *Hike*)
   a. Because of the "Live Color" the original play has been changed to 37
   b. When an automatic is used the snap count automatically goes to the *hike* command regardless of the original count
3. Any color called other than the live color is a false call and nothing changes

Stemming (shifting in the backfield)

A. The *set* command will initiate all shifts in the backfield

B. If the play is called on *set*, the backs must line up in the formation called
C. Running back and fullback may shift to any formation or to a cheated position to better perform their assignments
D. Normal Shifts
    1. Green to Purple
    2. Red to Green
    3. Blue to Red
    4. Green to Red
    5. Brown to Orange

Motion

A. Motion will be indicated in the huddle by the quarterback
    1. Man going in motion will be designated by QB (i.e. RB)
    2. Motion strong (to the strong side)
    3. Motion short (to the short side)
    4. Short motion (one or two step motion)
B. It is the QB's responsibility to coordinate the length of the motion with the snap count

Huddle

A. We utilize a closed huddle
B. The center forms the huddle 7 yards from the line of scrimmage
C. Stance—Everyone except QB, hands on knees looking at QB the best he can
D. The flanker and split end leave huddle as soon as they hear the play
E. Center leaves the huddle as soon as he hears the play and snap count
F. Rest of team breaks the huddle on the QB's command and sets the designated formation strength
G. Huddle:

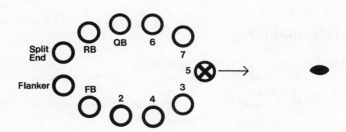

Play call procedure

    A. First call (not usually used)—Formation Variation (i.e. Over)
    B. Second call—Specific Formation (i.e. Red, Green)
    C. Third call—Formation Strength (i.e. Right or Left)
    D. Fourth call—Play being called (i.e. 37 or 74)
    E. Fifth call—Use of motion if used
    F. Sixth call—Snap count (i.e. *Hike, Set* or *Go*)
    G. Seventh call—"Ready Break" by QB, on the command break the team claps their hands, yells break and moves to the line of scrimmage

Play calling system

    A. Most of our passes are called in series (i.e. 60, 70, 90, etc.)
    B. Most of our other plays are called by designating the ball carrier at the point of attack
    C. Point of attack (a path directly over the offensive lineman called) (i.e. 37) the #3 back over the #7 lineman

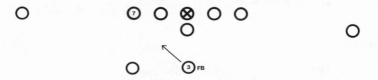

    D. Numbering of backs and point of attack—*Right Formation*

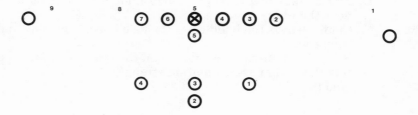

Play terminology

    A. 70 Series (Dropback pass series)
        1. (7) or first digit indicates dropback pass protection to the line
        2. Second digit (i.e. 4) indicates the routes being run by the receivers

3. 70 Series indicates swing pick—up to the FB and RB
4. In the 70 series pass routes will vary from 8—13 yards, most patterns have a designated 12 yard depth
B. 60 Series (Dropback flood series)
    1. (6) or first digit indicates dropback pass protection to the line
    2. (6) also means 5 man or total flood patterns by the receivers
    3. Second digit (i.e. 4) indicates the type of flood patterns being run
    4. Receiver routes depth is exactly as in 70 series
C. 90 Series (Quick pass series)
    1. (9) or first digit indicates quick pass blocking by the line
    2. Second digit (i.e. 6) indicates the routes run by the receivers
    3. In the 90 quick series, pass routes are run at a 4 yard depth and are thrown to the two wide receivers
D. Draw Series (late hitting runs off our dropback action)
    1. 15 Draw, 45 Draw, 35 Draw, 55 Draw
        a. The term draw indicates to the line that draw blocking is being used
        b. The first digit (1) indicates the back in the #1 position is the ball carrier
        c. The second digit (5) indicates the point of attack is the #5 hole
        d. Backs key center on an odd defense and the guard his side on an even defense
E. Screen Series (planned check off short passes behind the line of scrimmage, behind a screen set by the offensive linemen).
    1. HB screen short, FB screen strong
        a. Screen short indicates to the line that the screen is taking place on the short side; this involves the shortside guard and center
        b. (HB) indicates that the running back will be the receiver of the screen on the short side
F. Roll Out Series (QB roll out strong or short after a token run fake)
    1. 51 Roll—"Pattern 4"
        a. (1) Roll indicates to the line that we will use roll blocking to the strong side
        b. Pattern 4—indicates the routes being run by the receivers
        c. 51 Roll indicates the QB is rolling out to the strong side after faking the 41 running play

    d. In all 51 Roll patterns the split end will run a deep post pattern and flanker and tight end will run patterns at their normal dropback pattern depth

G. Bootleg Series (Pass action by the QB away from the action of the backfield)
  1. 41 Bootleg—"Pattern #3"
    a. (1) Bootleg means to line that we will use bootleg blocking on the short side away from the point of attack (1)
    b. Pattern #3 indicates the routes being run by the receivers
    c. 41 Bootleg means the QB is faking the 41 running play and bootlegging to the opposite side to throw a pass
    d. Because our bootleg pass is thrown quickly off the bootleg fake our receiver pattern depth does not have to be adjusted from their dropback depth
    e. Bootleg passes are usually thrown to our SE side

H. Sprint Series (a sprint out series performed by the QB with no running play fake)
  1. 51 Sprint—"Pattern #8", 59 Sprint—"Pattern #3"
    a. (1) sprint indicates to the line that we are using roll out blocking to the strong side
    b. Pattern #8 indicates the routes of the pass receivers
    c. 51 Sprint indicates the QB is sprinting out to the strong side to pass
    d. In our sprint series we may run various receiver pattern depths, the usual depth will be a 6 yard pattern

I. Running Play Fake Passes (the QB will make a good fake of a running play to fake and hold the defense to better utilize a particular pass pattern or receivers)
  1. Pass 37—"Pattern #7"
    a. Pass 37 indicates to the line that we are using roll out blocking on the short side
    b. Pattern #7 indicates the routes being run by the receivers
    c. Pass 37 indicates a good fake by the FB and QB before the throwing action

J. Waggle Series (Pass action by the QB away from the action of the backfield, usually utilizing a better fake than in the bootleg)
  1. 37 Waggle—"Pattern #8"

a. (7) Waggle indicates to the line that we are using roll blocking on the strong side away from the point of attack (7).
b. Pattern #8 indicates the routes being run by the receivers
c. 37 Waggle indicates a good 37 fake by the FB and QB and then a waggle action pass course by the QB to the strong side away from the point of attack
d. Because of the delayed QB action on the Waggle, receivers must deepen their designated pattern one yard
e. Waggle passes are designed to throw to the strength of our pro formation

Play terminology — running plays

A. Running back strong series
1. 41 Sweep, 41 Down Sweep, 43 Trap (Green)
    a. 41 Sweep
        (1) 1st digit (4) indicates that the running back in the #4 position is carrying the ball. The second digit (1) indicates the point of attack is the 1 area or wide to the strong side
        (2) The added word sweep indicates the type of blocking being used by the line and backs
        (3) When an additional word like down is used, it indicates an alternate form of sweep blocking
    b. 43 Trap
        (1) The numbers again indicate the ball carrier and the point of attack
        (2) The term trap indicates trap blocking by the line
2. 41 Full, 45 Counter (Red)
    a. The numbers indicate the ball carrier and the point of attack
    b. These are two complimentary plays from Red formation to get back to the strong side of our formation (to the TE)
    c. *Full* indicates the fullback is replacing the strong guard who is pulling to the strong side
    d. *Counter* indicates the play starts like a 41 Full, but ends up in the 5 hole. The fullback

runs his same path and blocks his man out. The backside guard and center will usually use a fold principal.

B. FB Short Series (Red)
    1. 37, 35, 34, Counter
        a. 1st digit (3) indicates the fullback in the #3 position behind the QB is the ball carrier
        b. The fullback attack is a complete complimentary series and the second digit will be utilized to attack the defensive alignment
        c. The second digit (7), (5), or (4) indicates the point of attack and the backfield action. The word counter alters the backfield action, and line blocking off the basic 37 action

C. Toss — Trap Series
    1. 49 Toss, 16 Trap
        a. The number indicates the ball carrier and the point of attack
        b. The added words (trap, toss) indicate the type of blocking by the line and the action of the backs

D. Dive — Option Series
    1. 13, 47, 51 Option, 59 Option
        a. These are four complimentary plays utilizing straight ahead drive blocking
        b. We will usually attack a team with the *dive* plays (13-47) and if they adjust their defenses we will follow up with the option plays (51-59) off the dive action
        c. It is important that the pitch man adjust his lineup so that he has a good relationship with the QB

E. Counter and Reverse Series
    1. 44 Tackle Trap, 51 Option Reverse
        a. These are definite change of direction plays
        b. The tackle trap is a counter off our base 37 play. The added words indicate the shortside tackle will be the trapper
        c. The option reverse is off our base 51 option play — the flanker is the ball carrier from a cheated position

F. Sneak, Jump, Wedge Series (Goal line and short yardage plays)
    1. Sneak at 4 or 6
        a. The number indicates the point of attack of the QB sneak
        b. The line will know the blocking at the point

of attack; we usually use a type of wedge or
straight ahead blocking
c. The backs will fake in the opposite direction
of the sneak
2. 23 Jump
a. Numbers indicate play and point of attack
b. The play dictates the blocking being used
c. The term *jump* indicates that the ball carrier
will use his jump technique to make short
yardage either on 3rd or 4th down or in a
goal line situation
d. It is very important that there is no penetration and that all the defenders at the point
of attack are occupied
3. 35 Wedge
a. The numbers indicate the play and point of
attack for the wedge
b. The 2nd digit (5) plus the term *wedge* indicate to the line that the apex of the wedge is
the 5 man — all other linemen block to him

Defense — terminology

A. *Odd defense:* a defensive alignment with a man on the
center, the rest of the defensive personnel can be lined
up in a variety of alignments and coverages. We usually
categorize these defenses in the 50's.
B. *Even defense:* a defensive alignment with men lined up
on the offensive guards and no man on the center, we
usually call these defenses 40 or 60. Alignments and
coverages will vary.
C. *Gap defense:* a defensive alignment variation from an
odd or even defense with one or more of the down defensive
linemen located in the gaps between offensive linemen.
D. *Combination defense:* a defensive alignment usually utilizing both the odd and even principals. Usually has a man
on the center and also a man on one of the offensive
guards. A very common combination is the Oakie-Eagle
alignment.
E. *7 Man front:* a defensive alignment with the defensive
linemen and linebackers numbering seven. They are
complimented by four defensive backs in a variety of
coverages. The "7 Man Front" can line up in a variety of
defensive alignments.
F. *8 Man front:* a defensive alignment where the defensive
linemen and linebackers number eight. They are comple-

mented by three defensive backs. The eight men can line up in a variety of defensive alignments.

G. *Pass/Run ratio:* a team's normal ratio of pass rushers to pass defenders. Normally 4-7 or 5-6. When stunts are used, this of course changes.

H. *4 Deep:* pass coverage used by defenses which employ four defensive backs in various types of coverages. May employ man-man, zone coverages, or combination coverages.

I. *3 Deep:* pass coverage used by defenses which employ three defensive backs in various types of coverages. Zone variations are characteristics of three deep teams.

J. *Man:* pass coverage in which one/all defensive back(s) or linebacker(s) is/are assigned to cover a receiver by himself.

K. *Free safety man:* pass coverage whereby three defensive backs are assigned three receivers man-man and are backed up by a safety in zone coverage.

L. *Rotate:* pass coverage which may be executed off of a 3 deep or 4 deep secondary alignment. In this coverage the outside HB will come up to cover the outside flat and the adjacent inside safety will cover the deep outside behind the jump HB.

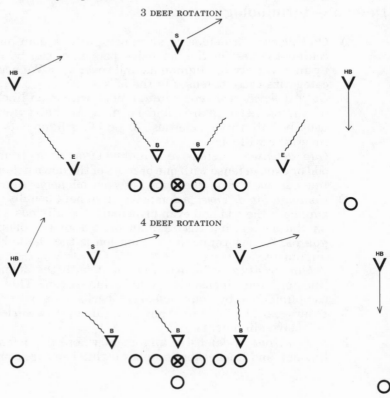

3 DEEP ROTATION

4 DEEP ROTATION

M. *Invert:* pass coverage off the four-deep secondary alignment in which the inside safety will cover the outside flat area and the halfback will back up to cover his deep outside area.

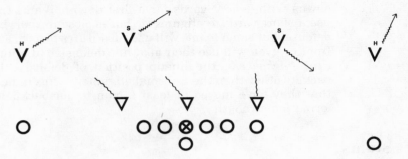

N. *Press:* defensive alignment which employs a defensive halfback or linebacker in a tight position (1-3 yards) on a wide receiver in zone or man to man coverage.

(DOUBLE PRESS: HB AND LB)

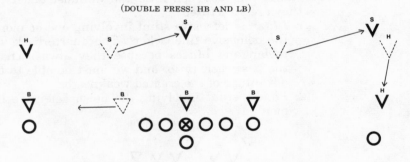

O. *Prevent:* defensive alignment used with time running out before the end of the half or game to prevent the long pass. May sometimes be used in long yardage situations. Characteristics are few rushers and numerous secondary coverage men at 10-30 yards depth.

P. *"Bastard" split:* alignment of a wide receiver at a distance of 1-3 yards from adjacent offensive linemen.

Q. *Tight split:* alignment of a wide receiver at a distance of 4-9 yards from adjacent offensive linemen.

R. *Normal split:* wide receiver alignment at 10-14 yards from adjacent offensive linemen.

S. *Eagle position:* the positioning of a defensive linebacker over our offensive tight end. This also can refer to a linebacker in the same relative position on our split side. The eagle position usually indicates a man inside our offensive tackle and also a man outside our tight end.

T. *Goal line defenses:* defensive alignments used when a defensive team faces a goal line situation (inside the 5 yard line).

U. *Short yardage defense:* defensive alignments used by defensive teams in short yardage situations (3rd and 4th downs with 1 or 2 yards for a first down). Teams try to use a short yardage alignment that is close to their basic defense, but some teams will use substitutes to form a new front or even will use their goal line defensive alignment.

V. *Plus linebackers:* the lineup position of defensive linebackers other than their normal alignment. *Plus* indicates that they have moved at least a man to our backfield or formation strength.

Stunts

A. This term is used to indicate any movement by the defense other than their basic charges. Any defensive position or positions can be involved in a stunt. Stunts may or may not change the pass/rush ratio and we must understand how they are structured.

1. *Blitz:* a defensive stunt involving one or more of the defensive linebackers. The quarterback must understand blitzes because they always change the pass/rush ratio, and we must be able to take advantage of the created weaknesses.

2. *Pinch:* stunt involving the down defensive linemen

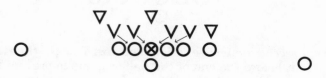

3. *Limbo:* stunt involving the cross charge of two adjacent down defensive linemen.

REVERSE
LIMBO

4-3
LIMBO

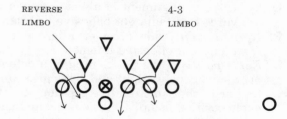

4. *M:* blitz involving the middle linebacker in a pro (4-3) defense. (M stunt may or may not involve down defensive linemen)

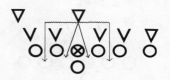

5. *S:* Blitz involving the strong side linebacker in a pro (4-3) defense

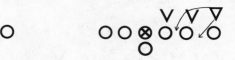

6. *W:* Blitz involving the weak side linebacker in a pro (4-3) defense

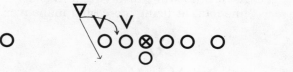

7. *Twist:* a middle blitz stunt involving the two defense guards and the middle linebacker in a pro (4-3) defense

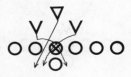

8. *U:* a blitz stunt involving the two inside linebackers and the two down defensive guards in a
split six (60) defense

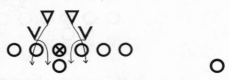

9. *Me:* a blitz stunt involving the two inside linebackers and the two defensive guards in a split
six (60) defense

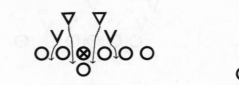

10. *Slam:* a half line or total front stunt or blitz similar to a pinch involving the down linemen and
ends or linebackers

4-3 SLAM   60 SLAM

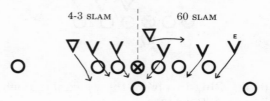

11. *X:* a blitz stunt involving a linebacker and down
lineman, utilizing a crossing maneuver.

4-3-x

50-x

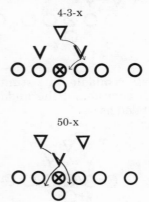

12. *Divide:* a blitz stunt used in the Oakie (50) defense to put pressure on one side of the offensive line

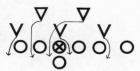

Defensive alignments

A. 60 (split six)

60 ALIGNMENT WILL BE
CALLED "SPLIT 5" WHEN
THE SHORTSIDE END IS
INVOLVED IN A FOUR DEEP
SECONDARY

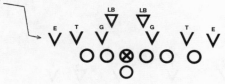

B. 50 (Oakie)

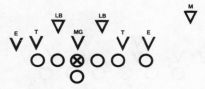

203

C. 4-3 (Pro)

D. 5-3

E. Gap

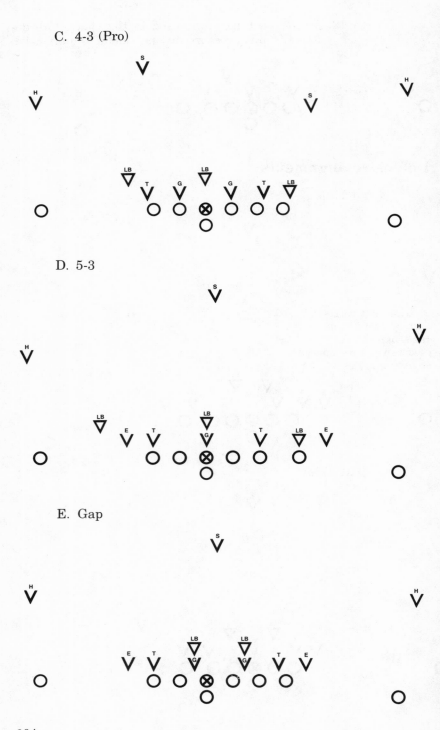

F. Eagle

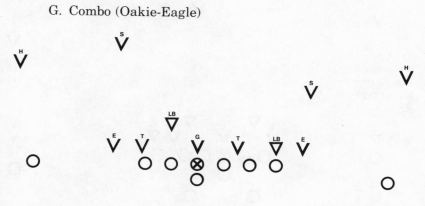

G. Combo (Oakie-Eagle)

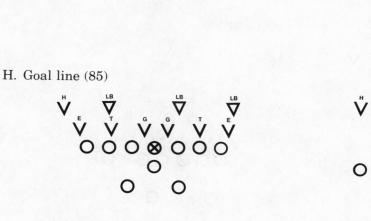

H. Goal line (85)

Special coverages

A. 4-5-2

5 UNDERNEATH
CAN BE MAN OR
ZONE COVERAGE

B. 3-5-3

5 UNDERNEATH
CAN BE MAN OR
ZONE COVERAGE

C. 4-4-3 (double press)

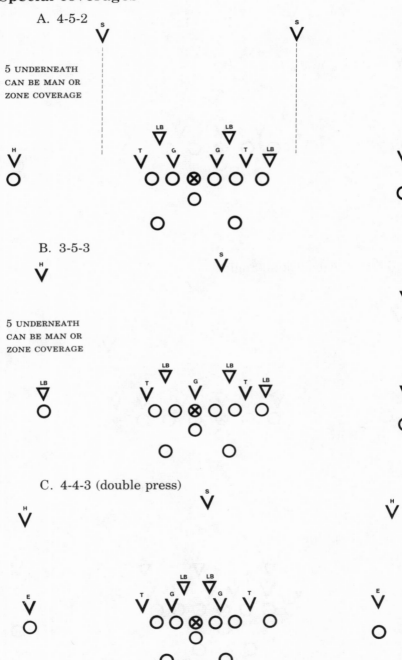

D. Prevent (usually a 4-4-3 ratio)

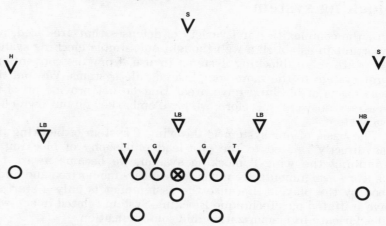

E. Pre-Rotated 4-4-3 Coverage (Secondary alignment prior
to the snap of the ball, from a 4 deep secondary)

F. Free Safety Man

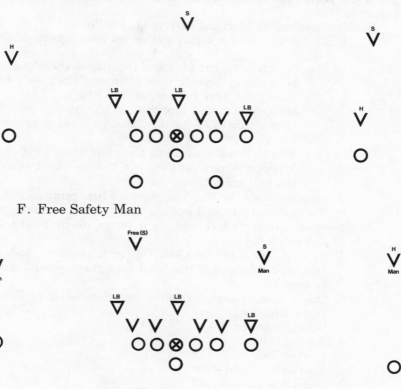

Blocking system

With the complexities and variety of defenses that are faced, it is important to establish a well thought-out, simple blocking system. There are many blocking systems in use, from the conventional count system to the more complicated rule systems. We find that these forms of blocking have areas that do not provide all of the necessary answers; therefore, we have embarked on our own offensive system.

The basis of our system is the wing-T system of blocking that was directly related to the post-lead philosophy of blocking. In examining the wing-T blocking system, we became aware that *one word* assignments are much more easily memorized and understood by the players. Because the assignment is only a start, we have initiated our Technique Blocking System related to one-word rules for ease in memorization and communication.

This system has proved extremely successful for us and has allowed us to teach the basic assignments and then effectively allow the player to understand the total play so he can perform his responsibilities.

Stanford's offensive blocking system is as follows:
1. Player is given a technique as an assignment on each play
    a. By knowing the play and technique, the player will be able to answer the offensive lineman's basic questions: who, how, what and where.
    Who: Whom do I block?
    How: How do I get to the man I am supposed to block?
    What: What do I do to the man when I get there?
    Where: Where do I engage the man and where is the ball going?
2. Stanford uses the flip/flop offensive line principle.
3. We concentrate on blocking the line of scrimmage or down lineman first and then worry about linebackers and down field.
4. In our technique blocking system, position and sustaining of blocks are the most important results we are looking for.
5. Our offensive line personnel are numbered as follows:
    Tight End — #2
    Strong Tackle — #3
    Strong Guard — #4
    Center — #5
    Shortside Guard — #6
    Shortside Tackle — #7
6. Flip-Flop Alignment
    Right 7 6 5 4 3 2

Left   2 3 4 5 6 7
7. Backs and linemen are numbered as follows:

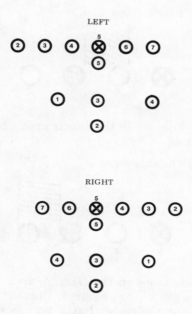

8. By the back designated, FB (#3), over the offensive line-man's line-up position (#7) (i.e. play 37), the wide plays are numbered with #1 being outside the tight ends line up position (i.e. 41 sweep), play 37.
9. Plays are called: Formation (Blue, Red, Green), Right (strength of line), Number play (i.e. 41 Sweep)
10. With each offensive play, the offensive lineman will be given a technique which will be his assignment.
11. Techniques
    a. A lineman's technique will fall into three basic areas, plus techniques that will fall into special categories such as pulls, etc.

    (1) Covered Area

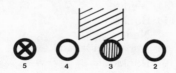

Techniques in the *covered* area—drive, set up, scramble, post, reverse, blast, cut off, cut down, influence, draw, quick.

(2) Inside Area

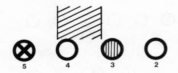

Techniques in the *Inside* area—Lead, angle, inside, cut off.

(3) Outside Area

Techniques in the *Outside* area—reach, slant, roll.
  Area/Technique Blocking System Coaching Points—Try to reach a complete knowledge so that if no one is in the technique area, the knowledge will impulse the blocker to take care of the most important threat to the play.

(4) Additional techniques
    (a) Pulls:
        Hook
        Seal
        Seal Outside
        Run a course
        Trap
    (b) Screen:
        Short
        Strong
    (c) Quick Screen:
        Short
        Strong
    (d) Near Safety
    (e) Wedge
    (f) Backers:
        Near Backer
        Across to a backer
    (g) Backside
    (h) Crossfield

Offensive line techniques – (play assignments)

STEP	TARGET	AREA	POSITION OF MAN TO BE BLOCKED

Covered area

1. Drive

MAN	PLAY	COVERED	ON OR OFF LOS

This is our basic one on one block. Points of emphasis are the proper step at the man being blocked, along with the head at the proper target. The explosion and follow-through, along with the proper wide base. The blocker must constantly be aware of keeping himself between the defensive man and the ball carrier. Emphasis on blocking high to pin the defensive man's arms. Drive the legs with short choppy steps. Try to straighten the legs of the defensive man.

2. Set up

INSIDE	INSIDE NUMBER	COVERED	ON OR OFF LOS

This is our basic pass protection block. The blocker moves his inside foot and quickly assumes his set up position. Bring hands up under chin with elbows down (this protects against pulling and turning), keep head up and look at the man's numbers. Keep feet moving. Tail is down and well under the blocker for good balance. Establish and maintain an outside foot to crotch relationship with the defensive man. With this relationship, the blocker should position himself between the defensive man and the QB's throwing position. Pop the defensive man if he challenges you, otherwise maintain your position until the ball is thrown.

Two things that cannot happen to a successful pass blocker: (1) don't let the defensive man get head up on you and (2) don't let him get his hands on you. Chapter 12 will discuss in detail our pass protection techniques.

STEP	TARGET	AREA	POSITION OF MAN
			TO BE BLOCKED

3. Post

STRAIGHT AHEAD	MIDDLE—	COVERED	ON LOS ONLY
FAVORING LEAD	SLIGHTLY		
BLOCKER	FAVORING		
	THE PLAY		

The post technique is used in our double team blocks. The post man applies an aggressive drive technique on the man in his area on the line of scrimmage. He must always consider that he will have to block the man by himself and not depend on his lead blocker. When he does feel the pressure of his lead blocker, he must try to take the man back and off the line of scrimmage rather than try to turn him and block him down the line of scrimmage.

4. Quick (Cut down)

MAN	PLAY	COVERED	ON OR OFF LOS

The Cut-Down block is used in our quick passing to cause a defensive man to react to you so that the ball can be thrown over his head. The technique is a quick violent step at the man in a somewhat exaggerated high position. As soon as the man reacts to this movement, you must immediately change your direction to cut him down at the knees or lower. As immediate follow through is important in this block so as to keep the defensive man's hands down so that he cannot keep them up and bother the passer.

5. Draw

DICTATED	PLAY	COVERED	ON LOS ONLY
BY PLAY			(DOWNFIELD)

Techniques used anywhere along the line of scrimmage on our delayed running plays. The play will usually come off some sort of pass action and will hit the prescribed hole. The offensive lineman will usually take a step or some movement to the prescribed area of attack and then block away from this particular area. We, of course, take preference to the men on the line of scrimmage and put our head between them and the point of attack. If no one threatens the area immediately, then you would continue downfield and take anyone who would be threatening to tackle the ball carrier.

6. Influence

INSIDE   PLAY   COVERED   ON LOS ONLY

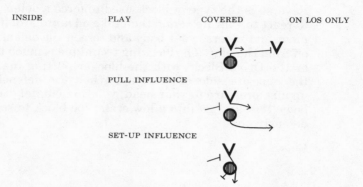

PULL INFLUENCE

SET-UP INFLUENCE

Influence technique is used on a man on the line of scrimmage to make him react to your movement and then set him up for another blocker who will probably be trapping him out from an inside out position. The offensive blocker takes a violent step to the inside causing the defensive man to react to him, and then releases off his outside foot and picks up anyone who might threaten the play. The position of the defensive man and his reaction will usually dictate the target used by the influence blocker. The pull or set-up is also an effective way to influence a defensive man.

7. Scramble

MAN   PLAY   COVERED   ON OR OFF LOS

The scramble block is a low one on one block where the blocker, for the most part, will be in a low blocking position and a good share of the time will end up in an all-four crab type block. The blocker should use the same step and target as in the drive block, but must remember to block more with his face so that he does not lose contact by having his head down too low.

8. Reverse

MAN	OPPOSITE PLAY	COVERED	ON OR OFF LOS

Reverse is the type of block used to force a defensive man to react to your head and then take advantage of his movement and reverse your body and screen the defensive man off from the play. The blocking technique is much the same as the Drive Block, with the blocker putting his head on the opposite side of the play. When the defensive man applies pressure to your head, you immediately turn your body 180° and go into a low crab type block to screen the defensive man.

9. Blast

MAN	PLAY	COVERED	ON LOS ONLY

An aggressive one on one block used on the line of scrimmage only. These blocks are used on our Blast Plays and the backs will pick up the linebackers in each case. It is important on a Blast Play to control the line of scrimmage and form a breach so that the offensive back can have a clear shot at the linebacker and therefore make for a successful play.

Inside area

1. Angle

INSIDE	PLAY	INSIDE	ON OR OFF LOS

A block in your inside area using our Drive Blocking Technique, it is important in an Angle Block to anticipate the movement of the man you are blocking. If it is a man on the line of scrimmage, you must be aware of quick penetration and must take your steps accordingly. If you are angle blocking a linebacker, you must be aware of quick flow by the linebacker, and therefore, must take the proper step in that instance as well.

2. Lead

INSIDE	PLAY	INSIDE	ON LOS ONLY

The Lead block is the other half of our double team or post-lead technique. This block is applied only on the line of scrimmage and the lead blocker must get off and get into the defensive man as quickly as possible so as to help his post blocker. As soon as the post and lead blocker both have contact with the defensive man, they should try to take him off the line of scrimmage rather than to try to turn him and move him down the line of scrimmage.

3. Inside

INSIDE	INSIDE	INSIDE	ON OR OFF LOS

A technique similar to a cut-off to protect the inside area. The technique is used in our inside trap game and therefore must be performed on or off the line of scrimmage. The blocker takes a quick inside step and is aware of the positioning of the men in the inside area. If no one is on the LOS he must be alert for a LB'er stunt or a slanting lineman. When he engages a defensive lineman or LB'er he must try to take him back and off the line of scrimmage with an inside target. If no one challenges him he can lead directly up field and help the runner.

4. Cut off

INSIDE	INSIDE	INSIDE	ON LOS (CROSSFIELD)

Cut off is a technique used when the ball is definitely away from the offensive blocker. It is initiated by a quick inside step and movement to get your head in front of any

215

defensive man who may be in your path on the line of scrimmage. If there is no man in this area, the cut off technique usually results in a crossfield or downfield blocking movement by the blocker. Cut off technique is usually a quick movement where the blocker throws his head and shoulders by the defensive man, and in effect, keeps himself between the defensive man and the ball carrier in a low scramble position.

Outside area

1. Roll

OUTSIDE	POSITION OF QB	COVERED	ANYONE WHO
		OR OUTSIDE	THREATENS AREA

Our pass protection technique is used with any type of action or sprint out pass by the backfield. The blocker immediately, on the snap of the ball, blocks any defensive man in the covered or outside area. The blocker must be ready for any type of rushing action and must be ready to either apply the good aggressive block on the rusher or or chop him down if the occasion arises. If no one threatens the area immediately, the blocker must pivot and back up toward the anticipated position of the passer and look for anyone who might be in a threatening position.

2. Reach

OUTSIDE	PLAY	OUTSIDE	ON OR OFF LOS

The Reach block is executed with a lineman outside step and shooting the head to the outside of the defensive man. This block will usually result in the scramble technique since you are giving the defensive man the benefit of telling him where you are going. This is a hard block to finish and is important for the offensive man to continue to keep his body between the defensive man and the ball carrier.

216

3. Slant

OUTSIDE   PLAY   OUTSIDE   ON OR OFF LOS

The Slant is an aggressive block applied in the outside area. The blocker uses a Drive blocking technique and must take into consideration the position of the defensive man that he is blocking. If the defensive man threatens the line of scrimmage, he must take away penetration first. If the Slat block is being applied on a linebacker he must take into consideration flow and take the proper step.

Pulls

THE PULLING TECHNIQUES FOR OFFENSIVE LINEMAN: The pulling technique for offensive linemen will be an open step in the direction of your particular pull. Each pull will dictate a little different first step and these will be explained in the individual pulling technique.

1. Hook

"4 – HOOK 2"

The offensive lineman will have a designated area to apply his hook block. This will determine his first step and also the depth he must get to apply the hook block in the particular area. In the hook block, the offensive lineman must either hook the defensive man immediately and get him on the ground by shooting his head and shoulders by the defensive man, or he must be in a position to get his head on the far hip of the defensive lineman and keep him occupied so that the offensive runner can break off of the block. The worst thing that can happen on a hook block is for the offensive lineman to throw the block too soon and not occupy the defensive man.

2. Seal

"#6 — SEAL #2"

The puller will have a designated area to seal and this will, to a great extent, determine the step he will take and also the depth of his pull. When sealing a particular area, the offensive lineman must be square to the line of scrimmage when he comes to his particular area. In a seal block the lineman is looking for anyone who is trying to come inside out through him to get to the ball carrier. If no one is in the particular area when he gets there he immediately continues upfield and becomes a crossfield blocker on anyone threatening the play.

3. Seal Outside

"#4 — SEAL OUTSIDE #7

The offensive lineman will be given a specific area to seal and the seal outside area is generally two yards outside of the designated area. For example, seal outside of 7 would be 2 yards outside of the 7 man's original line up position. The lineman, as in the regular seal block, must be in a sealing position when he hits the line of scrimmage. His shoulders should be square to the line of scrimmage and he should be looking for anyone who is approaching the ball carrier from an inside out position.

4. Run a Course

#4 — RUN A COURSE AT #1

#1 — AREA

The puller will be given a designated area, such as 1 or 9, to run a course and this will dictate his original step and also the depth of his course. Whenever an offensive lineman is running a course, he is heading for a specific area and will block anyone who threatens him, either from the inside or the outside. Our run a course technique is the same as our crossfield. You will apply a running shoulder block on any defensive man whom you run into head on, or else you will apply a cross body block at anyone who crosses your path.

5. Trap

#4 — TRAP #6

The offensive line will be given a specific area to trap and this will dictate the step that he must take to get into that area, as quickly as possible. The trapping technique is an inside out course in order to form a breach in the defense for one of our trap plays. The course is the most important thing in our traps and the blockers must be ready to trap the man; or, if he is not in a position to be trapped, he must make an intelligent decision to lead upfield and pick up someone else.

Additional techniques

1. Wedge

| INSIDE | INDICATED APEX OF WEDGE | "5 WEDGE" | ON OR OFF LOS |

Our Wedge blocking plays can be called over any specific lineman, i.e., 3,4,5,6, or 7. The designated man is the apex or front of the wedge. All adjacent linemen will fire out to the inside and put their heads in the armpit of the adjacent lineman. We will use an inside drive technique and each lineman is responsible for the inside gap between him and the next adjacent man.

219

STEP	TARGET	AREA	POSITION OF MAN TO BE BLOCKED

2. Near Safety

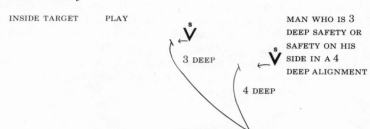

INSIDE TARGET	PLAY		MAN WHO IS 3 DEEP SAFETY OR SAFETY ON HIS SIDE IN A 4 DEEP ALIGNMENT

Technique used primarily by our tight end to block a specific man downfield. It is important to release quickly off the line of scrimmage, take the proper cut off angle, and then apply a high cross body block on the assigned man. It is important in our downfield blocking technique to apply a running shoulder block if meeting the man head on, and a cross body block if there is any angle involved between you and the defensive man.

3. Crossfield

INSIDE	PLAY	"7 CROSSFIELD"	ANY MAN WHO THREATENS THE AREA

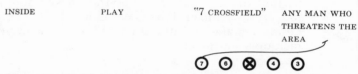

Our downfield blocking technique used by any lineman who does not have a specific assignment on the line of scrimmage. The important thing in a crossfield block is taking the proper angle in order to cut off the anticipated position of the defensive pursuit man. A crossfield technique is a running shoulder block if meeting a blocker head on. Otherwise, the blocker should use a high cross body block throwing his head and shoulders by the defensive man. It is important to throw the block at the last possible minute and to be sure to follow through and roll and keep the man occupied as long as possible.

4. Backside

INSIDE	NUMBERS		ON OR OFF LOS

Technique used by offensive lineman on play action or

roll out passes when he is on the side away from the
throwing spot. It is a zone blocking maneuver usually by
one or two lineman working together to protect the passer
from the back or "blind" side. On the snap of the ball the
backside lineman moves aggressively to the inside, and
positions himself off the near foot of the next adjacent
lineman. He should be in a position to protect the QB and
take anyone that shows. He should use his set up techniques and keep position on the defensive man. If no one
shows, his head should be on a swivel and be ready to
help someone else. The backside technique will also be
used by a roll blocker when no one threatens his area.
Remember: position is the most important factor. Know
where the QB is and also where the defense is.

5. Screen

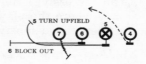

Our delayed screen blocking techniques all result after the
offensive linemen have counted 1/1000, 2/1000. Then each
of the linemen sprints in the direction the screen is being
thrown and executes one of the following techniques:

(a) *Short or Strong:* Technique used by 2 adjacent linemen, the direction will be designated strong or short.
After the required pause the lineman will sprint together one behind the other in the call direction. No
specific assignment is given except to sprint and point
to anyone who threatens the receivers or any potential
tacklers. The second man must be alert not to double
up on the same man. The blocker should use an aggressive open field block to clear the way for the runner. You must know where the receiving spot is and
where the potential defenders are.

(b) *Turn Back:* The blocker sprints 8 yards out from his
original line of scrimmage and turns back toward the
line of scrimmage to protect the intended receiver.

(c) *Block-Out:* The offensive blocker sprints 8 yards out
from his original line of position and blocks inside
out to anyone threatening the intended receiver. If
there is no one in that area, he would immediately
turn upfield and escort the ball carrier.

(d) *Turn Upfield:* The offensive blocker sprints 8 yards

out from his original line of position and turns immediately upfield and executes a crossfield block on anyone who is threatening the receiver. The target that he will use on the defensive man will be determined by the angle he is taking to the pass receiver.

6. Backer Blocks:
(a) Near Backer:

MAN   PLAY   BACKER ONLY

The technique used by an offensive lineman to block a specific backer in his immediate area. The technique used is an aggressive Drive block and the offensive lineman must know where the play is hitting and use the proper target to keep the defensive man away from the ball carrier.

(b) Across to a Backer:

INSIDE   PLAY   BACKER ONLY

A technique used to tell an offensive lineman to go across inside and block a linebacker. The block used is an aggressive drive block on the backer with the proper target depending on where the play is going. The blocker must go across very fast so that he doesn't miss the backer who steps up into the line.

7. Additional special goal line and short yardage techniques: Jump and Sneak.
Jump—Aggressive drive blocks from 4 point stance—block play called (i.e. 23 Jump).
Sneak—Aggressive drive blocks from 4 point stance—favor area called, similar to wedge (i.e. sneak at 4).

Stanford offensive formations

BLUE RIGHT

BLUE LEFT

RED RIGHT

RED LEFT

BROWN RIGHT

223

BROWN LEFT

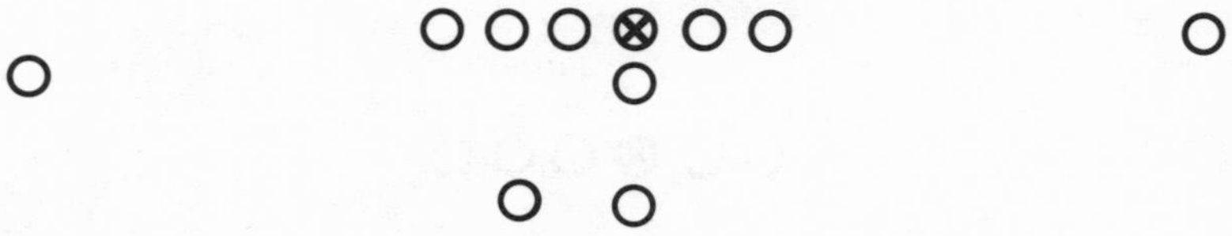

GREEN RIGHT

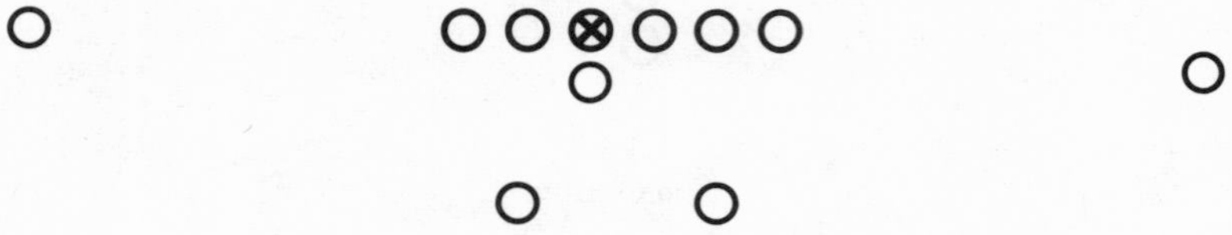

GREEN LEFT

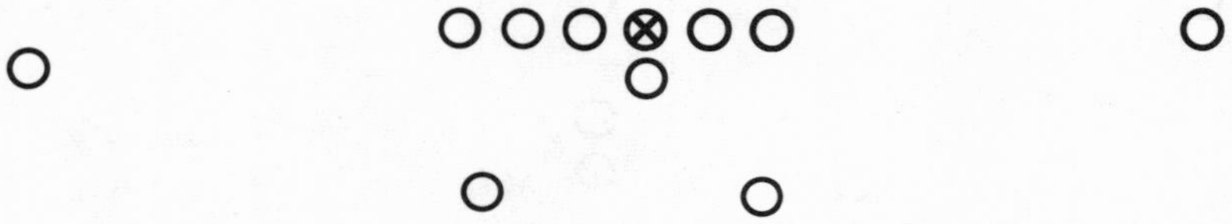

TAN RIGHT

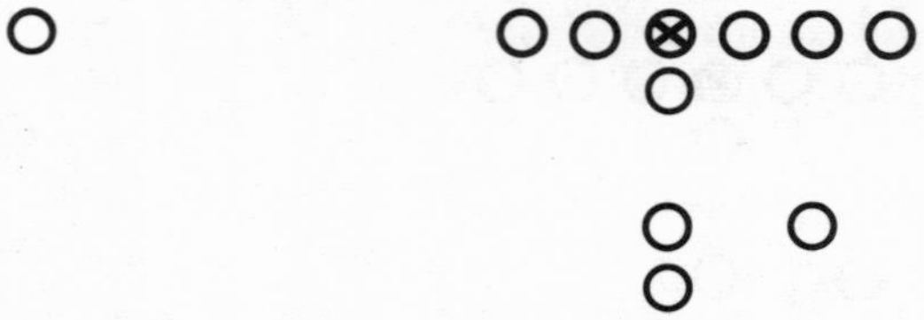

TAN LEFT

PINK RIGHT

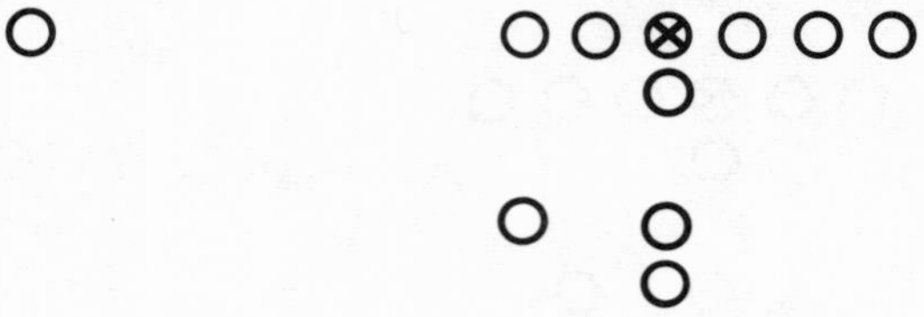

PINK LEFT

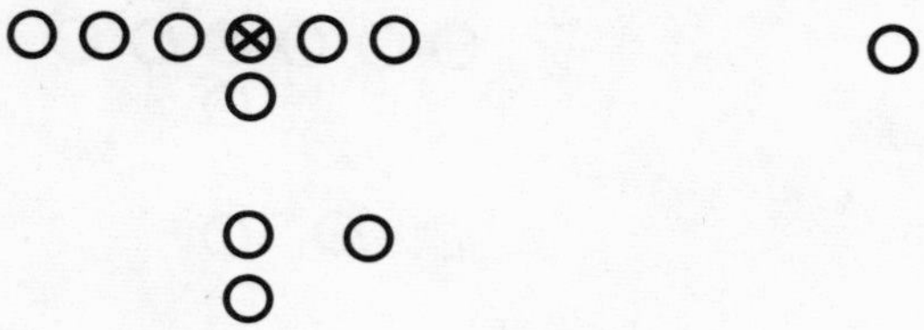

T RIGHT

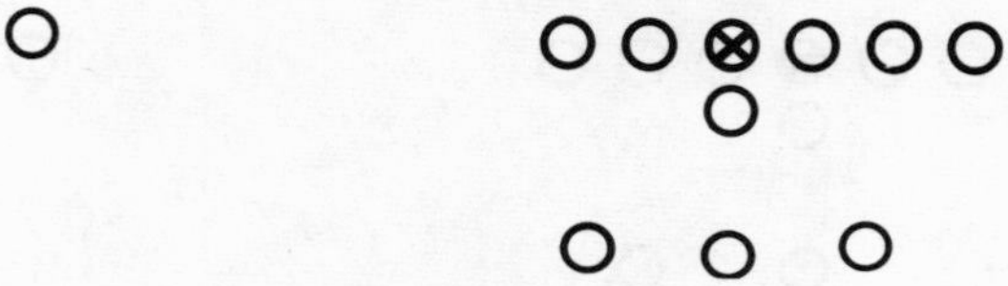

T LEFT

RED RIGHT WING

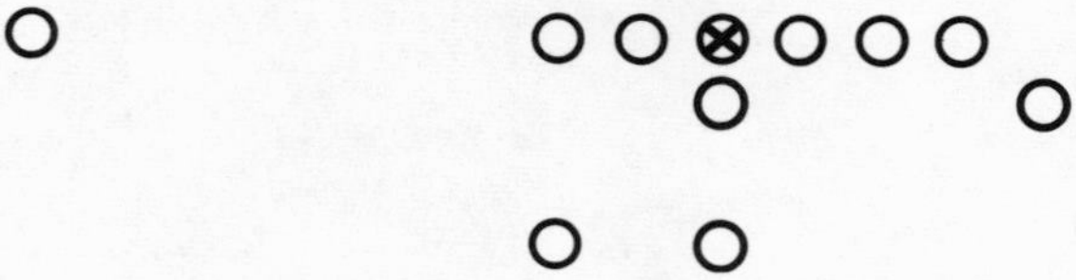

RED LEFT WING

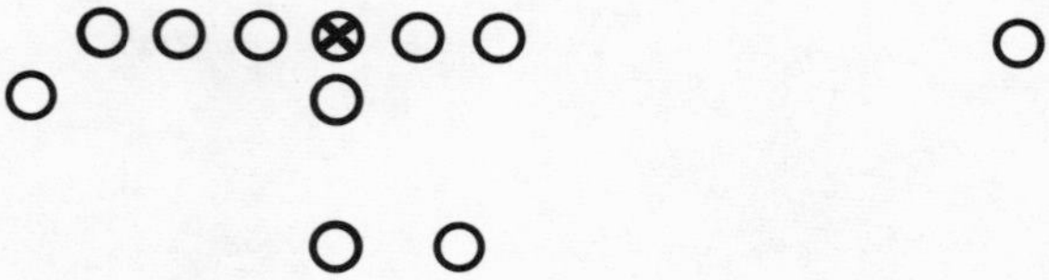

BLACK RIGHT

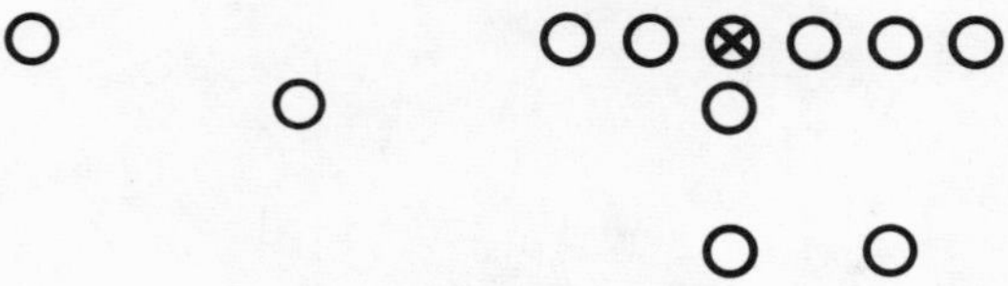

BLACK LEFT

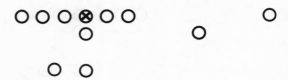

END OVER RIGHT T

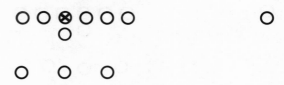

12

Passing

Although Stanford's success during the past few years has been due in large part to the passing game and we have been known primarily for that element of football, we did not enter into it without a thorough examination and analysis of our personnel and staff capabilities. We have great confidence in our abilities in this area; however, we emphasize that every coach must take a long look at his total program before deciding on *any* particular offense or defense. We return to our basic philosophy that a coach should fit his system to his personnel rather than deciding first on a system and then attempting to work in the personnel accordingly. We also recommend that, in formulating and organizing any system, a coach should proceed according to the amount of information he and his staff can impart and how much his players can absorb. We admit candidly that when we started the pass game, we made the common mistake of trying to accomplish too much at the start. We discussed the attack with many experts and tried to initiate an entire pass offense without easing into it gradually, learning thoroughly as we progressed. Consequently, after the first and second years, we began eliminating more and more plays and decided our attack would be more efficient if we executed *fewer* plays *better*. We now believe that we have most of the bugs out and have developed a complete pass offense. We also have determined what we teach best, and we devote a good share of our teaching emphasis to these strongest phases.

At the outset, we point out strongly that the pass game itself by no means is the sole answer to becoming a successful team. Knowing when to use the pass and recognizing what and how to complement various pass actions probably are more important than the actual pass action.

As we have mentioned before, we believe a coach must determine what will win for him. We realized that Stanford had to have an effective pass game in order to win in the Pacific Eight Conference.

We also want to point out to the reader that because of our effective pass game, we devote considerable attention to it in this textbook. This should not be construed to mean that we do not respect nor realize the importance of the running game. To the contrary, it has its appropriate place with the appropriate philosophy and personnel; we dwell somewhat more on the passing game simply because that is our philosophy and that is where our success has been.

When we started concentrating on the pass game, we were told that a successful passing attack must key on the strong safety. Then someone talked with Roman Gabriel, and he pointed out that he keyed on the weak safety. Someone else said he keyed somebody else, and it became apparent that we could key on a lot of people if the defense promised to do the same thing every time; but this unfortunately is not the case. We are going more to a primary-oriented system of throwing the ball, and we attempt to key the person or persons who will take away the pattern that is being called. This makes it easier for the quarterback, and probably more important, gives the receiver something to identify with and puts the pressure on him to get open.

As we move into another year and prepare for another season, we are examining our passing strengths, both in terms of the quarterback and the receivers, so we can make the most effective use of the weapons we have. Two elements have become important to us as we gain more knowledge of the passing game and as we evaluate our opponents and what the defenses are doing in trying to stop us:

1. It has become obvious to us that contain is the one weakness in defenses designed to stop the pass. Most defensive coaches will try to defense the dropback passing game with some sort of four-man contain. We realize now that although we base our pass offense on this particular action, our future success will be determined by our ability to break down the obvious weaknesses in the defensive alignments that we face. The use of the roll-out or sprint-out, as well as the predetermined flush patterns, are areas in which we are conducting a great deal of research.

2. The second area that we are examining is the important need to include in the pass game some sort of linebacker control. Having been spoiled with a person of Jim Plunkett's abilities, we now know that we must base a good share of our passing on the use of running play, fake passes, and/or some type of bootleg or counter action pass to hold or freeze the linebackers who move back and take away our short zones. We also are examining the use of the

fake draw to complement our passing actions. We feel this will have an effect not only on the linebackers but on the pass rushers as well.

Continuing in the area of general concepts, we always have believed that it is necessary to set the total program in such fashion that the top team in the schedule can be defeated. In Stanford's particular case, the University of Southern California dominated the conference for four successive years, ending in 1970. As a consequence, we built our entire program on methods of beating USC. Our staff's composite thinking is that we cannot power off tackle against a team of USC's caliber and expect to win consistently. Therefore, the pass game has been the vehicle that perhaps can best offset their physical superiority. Coincident with the ability to pass against this top team is the necessity of keeping it off balance. It follows then that, to some degree, we have to throw out the down and distance tendencies and pass on the run downs and run on the pass downs. As we view our schedule, this general structure must be constructed in such a manner that we peak ourselves on the fifth week. We believe that all coaches must examine their schedules to determine exactly when to peak their football teams for the key games.

From our experience with the pass we have learned several insights:

1. To develop a successful passing game, a coach must have quarterbacks and receivers who love to throw and catch the ball. No matter how much in-season coaching is done, the pass offense is as successful as the time and effort throwers and catchers are willing to spend perfecting execution and timing on their own. If these players attend Summer school, or live in the vicinity of each other, they must have the incentive to meet together daily to practice according to their own schedules. Rarely do youngsters have to be encouraged to play catch; it is a natural instinct held over from childhood. Unlike youngsters in European and South American countries who learn first to kick a ball, American children first are encouraged to "catch or throw the ball to Daddy." This practice continues until most youngsters therefore are willing to work at becoming proficient in both throwing and receiving.

2. The exposure of the pro game, as well as the use of specialized athletes by our substitution rules, makes the passing game the most exciting element in football today.

3. We believe a football team at any level can be built faster with the use of the pass and its related actions. As we noted earlier, if for no other reason, the players enjoy throwing and catching the ball, and it allows a coach to

take advantage of the abilities of a few skilled athletes without requiring the physical concentration the running game demands.

4. The pass and related actions are most effective against the many defenses and varied stunts that a team faces. It allows a team to work *behind* the line of scrimmage instead of forcing the action through the line.
5. With great personnel, a coach can establish a winning running attack; however, the passing game is a great equalizer against a superior physical team.
6. Passing and related actions, such as draws and screens, are the best methods of getting out of trouble or scoring when a team is behind or needs yardage in the waning moments of the first half or at the end of the game. Football is a game of third downs, and the pass is one efficient way of controlling the ball. More often than not, teams face long yardage on third down, and the pass is the most efficient way of moving the ball great distances.
7. A passing team must be willing to attack from anywhere on the field. It must be ready to throw on any down and distance situation.
8. Creating in the minds of the defensive players the importance of a pass rush will enhance the run game. Also it will reduce the amount of defensive slanting.
9. The drop back game creates more holes into which to throw the ball because of the full utilization of the field. Roll-out passing tends to limit the area because of the lateral movement of the ball and the passer.
10. Our middle receiver is vital if we utilize two wide receivers. This element is considered thoroughly in our selection of personnel for the tight end position.
11. It is not the number of times that the ball is thrown; it is the *effectiveness* of the pass game when it is employed. It also follows that sooner or later in a ball game, the football *has to be thrown*.

In evaluating our pass offense, here are some guidelines for a coach who is considering adopting a pass philosophy:

1. Utilize a formation or formations that lend themselves to both the run and the pass.
2. Spread and isolate receivers to force full field defensive deployment and coverage.
   a. Prevent hold-up or ability to divert patterns.
   b. Spread out and advance ball where defenders vacate.
   c. Utilize variations in backfield alignment to require adjustments in coverage.
3. Perfect a limited number of pass routes. Utilize flood or multiple receiver patterns whenever possible.

4. Use a flexible pass offense to get the ball to any receiver. Stress complementary patterns that clear areas and the dependence of each receiver on another.
5. Establish a sound, flexible system or systems of pass protection to give the quarterback confidence that he can get the ball off in proper time and make the successful decisions.
6. Utilize various quarterback throwing actions.
7. Understand defenses so the pass offense can be set up from week to week to take advantage of what the opponent is expected to do.
8. Make sure the ball is thrown at the proper time after the appropriate decision by the quarterback. The decision is made either at the line of scrimmage, during the drop by the quarterback, or before the ball is actually thrown.
9. Categorize passes in terms of depth of patterns: short, medium, long. Communicate to the quarterback the time factor: Short, two seconds or under release time; medium, two to two-and-a-half seconds; long, two-and-one-half to four seconds.
10. Know the pass principles on each pattern and communicate them to the quarterback and the receivers:
    a. Beat one on one coverage
    b. clear zone
    c. flood zone
    d. hold defenders

Ingredients of a successful pass offense

A. Thrower – quarterback
B. Catchers – receivers
C. Protection
D. Drills – motivation
E. Terminology – patterns
F. Types of pass actions
G. Attacking defenses
H. Practice organization and utilization
I. Game day
J. Pass game statistics – analyze success or failures.

The passer

Special emphasis must be placed in the areas of exchange, grip, drop, set-up, throwing motion and where and when to throw. Constant drill with proper technique should result in the necessary and successful development of the quarterback. (Chapter 14 discusses the quarterback in detail)

The receivers

Each receiver has a different style. It is the responsibility of the coach to recognize and to utilize these natural talents to develop each receiver's ability to get open, and, of course, to catch the ball. (Chapter Fourteen discusses receivers in detail.)

Drills and motivation

All types of drills should be studied and researched and special methods of motivation should be utilized to insure that players perform effectively. (The drill book discusses all of our drills in detail.)

Practice organization

It follows that if the pass game is the basic method of moving the ball, it is vital to spend the necessary amount of time to become proficient in the method of attack. We devote about fifty percent of each day's practice to the passing game. We have found that we must spend time every day throwing the ball versus no defense (throw versus air); throwing versus a defense that will give us the proper coverages which we will meet on the following Saturday (instructional seven on seven); throwing competitively against a skeleton linebacker and secondary defense (competitive seven on seven); and then full team pass scrimmage so we can review our entire pass game timing (pass rush drill). In this last concept of teaching the pass game, we prefer a full speed pass rush but not necessarily including tackling the quarterback.

Game day

With all of the practice time and preparation that the pass game necessitates, we believe strongly that the organization as well as adjustments during the actual game will contribute to a team's ultimate success. A team obviously starts a game with a definite plan, but will be forced to make some adjustments depending upon the opponent's emphasis. The press box procedure, as well as sideline communication, must be based on poise and confidence so no opportunities will be missed. During the progress of the game, we have found valuable information coming from the players as they experience and evaluate playing against individuals, alignments, and coverages. This player involvement should be encouraged and utilized if it is determined to be applicable.

Evaluation of the pass game

The success or failure of the pass game can be examined and evaluated in the percentage of completions, the amount of yardage per pass play called, the amount of yardage per pass play completed, the yardage after the ball is caught, the ability to control the ball with the pass game, pass protection breakdowns, interceptions, and the bad plays resulting from the passing game.

General structure

In order to better communicate the Stanford offense, our *general structure* should be noted. The diagram below identifies our numbering system:

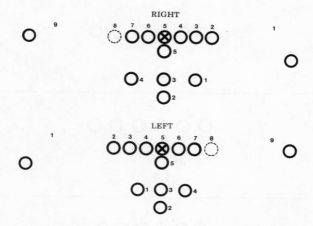

Our spacing is somewhat conventional with the line split at two feet and our fullback set at about four-and-a-half yards deep from the ball when he is at home. Our tight end is free to flex, depending on the ball, and our split end and flanker back vary their splits but primarily are from ten to twelve yards from the next adjacent lineman.

We utilize a complete flip-flop style with our personnel when we go from right to left formation. We gain efficiency by minimizing assignment teaching as well as allowing different styles of blocking versus different styles of rushing. When we flip-flop, the numbers remain the same. We do like to shift our two remaining backs from one set to the other; their movement is on our initial cadence count of "set." Our complete cadence is "set, down, hike, go." The reason we insert the word "down" is to allow us to use a live color and a change of play at the line of scrimmage. Our automatic system has been very good to us, particularly if we can read the defense prior to the snap of the ball. Jim Plunkett, our 1971 Rose Bowl quarterback, checked off at least fifteen times during that game.

The diagrams below illustrate our offensive formations which receive the appropriate color. We believe there are distinct advantages to the utilization of varied offensive formations, particularly in terms of predetermining the coverages before the ball is snapped.

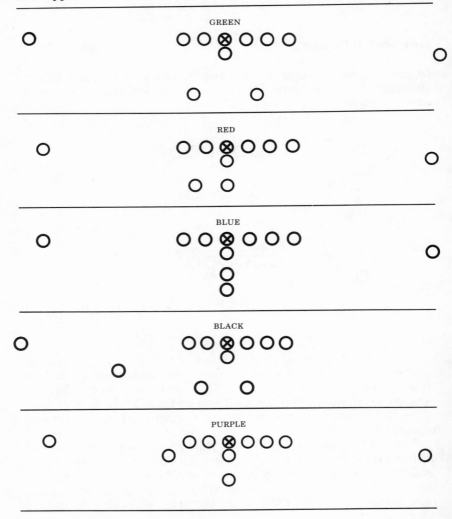

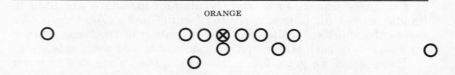

Pass protection

Although pass protection will be detailed later in this chapter a brief description will be given here. It illustrates the style of pass protection that we use against the various defensive fronts.

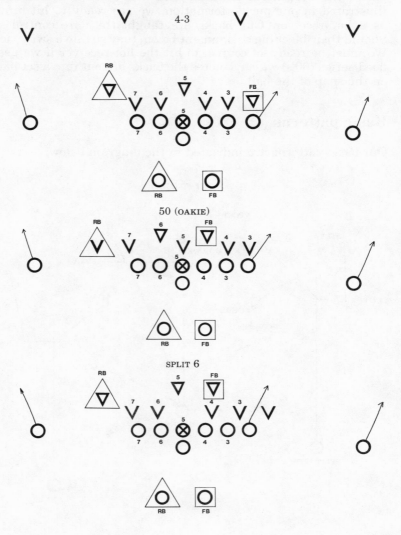

4-3

50 (OAKIE)

SPLIT 6

Our pass protection is strictly man-for-man. We are able to handle almost all blitzes with this form of protection. Our center favors the short side, allowing full utilization of the backs to pick up a four-man rush either up the middle or to the short side.

However, if we get a four-man rush to the strong side from an eight-front alignment or from the monster, then we must be ready to hit our tight end as a hot receiver. Our *hot receiver principle* of the tight end is to watch the strong linebacker as he releases into a pattern. The quarterback also watches the strong linebacker, and, if he plugs, we drop the ball to our tight end. On occasion, we use the fullback as a hot receiver if he replaces the tight end pattern. If we put our running back into a short side slot set, as illustrated in our purple formation, we are ready to hit him also as a hot receiver. Our backs are taught the flare control style. Should their blocking assignment be off, they go into a swing action. We must be ready, of course, to hit the hot receiver if we use our flood series (60's) which denotes the backs are out into a set pattern on the snap of the ball.

Basic patterns

Our basic patterns are indicated in the diagram below:

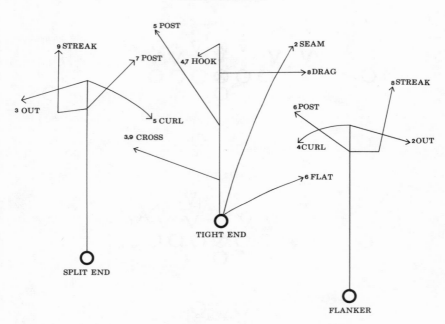

RIGHT FORMATION

The even-numbered patterns are to the strong side and our odd-numbered patterns are to the split end side. The general depth of our break is twelve yards from the line of scrimmage. If we call a running play fake pass, we call the running action and then add the pattern number. If, however, we call a particular pattern in our basic drop-back action, we merely add the pattern number as the second digit. Sixty denotes flood, seventy is our basic three-man out pattern, eighty is our fullback blocking to the short side and slow blocking our tight end, and ninety is our quick pass series.

Running back and fullback patterns

The basic pattern for both backs is the *swing*, unless otherwise designated. We supplement the backs' basic swing patterns with descriptive words to indicate an alternate route. They include flat, flare, seam, pop, fan, and screen.

We can also alter the basic routes of our tight end and split receivers by the use of descriptive words as well. They include quick-out, delay, in, flag, loop, hitch, quick post, drag and choice.

POP FLARE

FLAT

FAR

SEAM

SCREEN

SWING RB

FB

SWING

ADDITIONAL RECEIVER ROUTES

STREAK

CHOICE

FLAG

LOOP

DRAG

IN

QUICK POST

DELAY

QUICK OUT

HITCH

Attacking defenses

It will be noted in the last section of pass actions that we have many to master. It is vital to have all the components of a complete pass game in order to match the sophistication of the various opponents' defensive coverages. Over the past four years, we have run the gamut in pass offense. During Jim Plunkett's sophomore year (1968), we faced many three-deep defenses and the well executed patterns of our great outside receiver Gene Washington were sufficient to move the ball. In Plunkett's junior year, we began to throw to all five receivers with great effectiveness. We discovered that our opponents gradually were moving to four-deep defenses which we were able to read in advance. During 1970, we found our opponents utilizing the four-deep in a variety of coverages which were very disguisable. To match this defensive sophistication, we evolved into an equally offensive sophistication.

We call a lot of plays from the sideline and ask our coach, Mike White, to gain a "feel" for the coverage that he expects from down to down. To obtain this so-called "feel," we spend hours observing films of a particular team and during the week go through a number of sham games on the blackboard. Even with that preparation, much of this "feel" must be gained during the course of the game. Because of the ability of a journeyman quarterback to recognize certain conditions at the line of scrimmage, we use our automatic game to escape from any bad plays that are not recognizable from the sideline. There is no magic formula for the style of passes we call other than this general "feel." Through this process, we hope that our pass game keeps the defense off balance rather than vice versa.

As we have mentioned previously, the secret to having a successful passing game is analyzing what the defense is thinking. We analyze the opponent for:

1. Rush
2. Hold-up
3. Press (linebackers or secondary men head-on our wide receivers)
4. Coverage
   a. Zone
   b. Man
   c. Combination
5. Specific coverages
   a. Four-deep rotation (invert)
   b. Four-deep man
   c. Single or double press three-deep
   d. Three-deep zone
   e. Three-deep zone with monster
   f. Five short man or zone with two free safeties.
   g. Three-deep man

    h. Three rushers, five short man or zone, with three-deep zone coverage.

    i. Goal line coverage

We evaluate the defense in all of these areas and anticipate our offensive calls based on their tendencies. We also must remember that an adjustment in our blocking may be necessitated by a particular alignment or stunt.

In all of our basic passes, we ask our quarterback to try to recognize the respective coverages as he goes to the line. His first look is at the weak safety for his depth to try to gain knowledge of the free safety man or four across man. On the snap of the ball, he watches for the "hot receiver" and then picks up the action of the strong safety to determine man coverage or roll or invert zone. In all of our base concepts of throwing, we have a primary receiver, although any of our receivers must be set to catch the ball on any given pattern.

Another important element is attacking the six short zones. We have broken the ten to fifteen yard defensive zones into six distinct areas with a flat on both sides, a hook on both sides, and a curl on both sides. It is a good basis of communication among our staff and players, and we try to determine from week to week the short zones a particular defense will cover. Then we try to attack the one or ones that are left open by their percentage coverage. This, of course, is not always easy either; however, we find that the emphasis allows us to communicate better and to determine exactly which person can take away a particular pattern or zone, and it gives us a chance to zero in on him with our passer and receiver.

6 SHORT ZONES

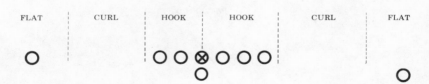

Pass actions

The elements of a total pass offense are:

    a. Drop back (70's); flood (60's)

    b. Short side flood (80's)

    c. Delays (flanker, split end, tight end, running back, or fullback)

    d. Quick pass (90's)

    e. Roll-out (51 roll, 22 roll)

    f. Sprint out (51 sprint or 59 sprint)

g. Bootleg (41 boot)
h. Running play fake passes (pass 37)
i. Short yardage passes (pass 34)
j. Quick screen short
k. Regular screen, either to the running back or fullback
l. Fullback or running back draws
m. Quarterback draw

Now to move down the list of pass actions and briefly illustrate what we attempt to do:

1. We package the drop back 70's and flood 60's to attack the underneath coverage. These actions are very effective against zone styles of underneath coverage. Note diagrams: *patterns 74, 60, 61.*

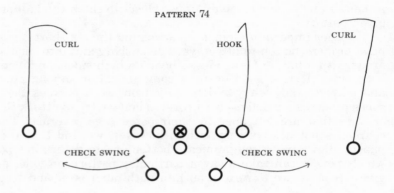

PATTERN 74

CURL HOOK CURL

CHECK SWING CHECK SWING

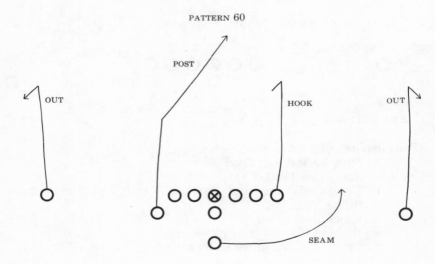

PATTERN 60

POST

OUT HOOK OUT

SEAM

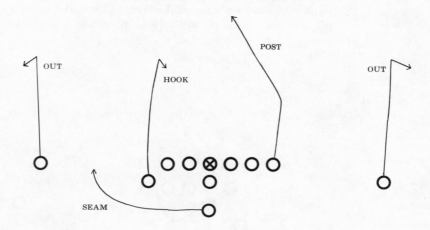

It will be noticed in our 60 patterns that we release the backs immediately, so the hot receivers are extremely important on blitzes. All receivers must be alert to receive the ball, though we like to drop the pass to the fullback to hit the seams between the underneath zone coverage. If a team is dropping off four men, it will have difficulty covering both the tight end and the fullback (60).

2. A short side flood (80's) allows us to hold our tight end and put our fullback to the short side for pass protection. This releases our running back immediately to the split end side and he is used to control underneath coverage. Note diagram: *85*

PATTERN 85

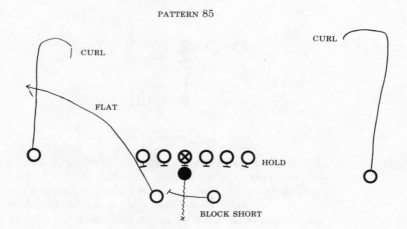

3. We like our delay pass game on obvious pass downs
   when the underneath coverage is getting out so quickly.
   Screens and draws also are effective, but we like to delay
   to all our receivers as well. Note diagram: *70 flanker
   delay*

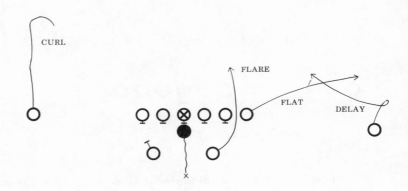

70 FLANKER DELAY

Tight-end delay: an effective delay pattern is to the
tight end. It is effective for taking advantage of deep
dropping linebackers as well as man to man coverage.

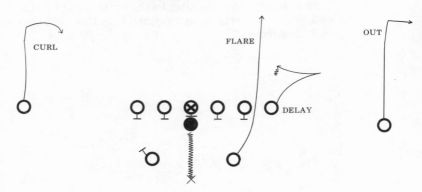

TIGHT END DELAY

4. Our quick pass is used when the coverage is off our outside receivers rather loosely. We like 92 or 93, the quick
   outs, or 96 or 97, the quick up and in patterns. Our 94 is
   merely a hitch pass to either wide receiver. Our pass protection is a cutdown technique, and we drive the fullback

and running back at the defensive ends or linebackers. On this action, we utilize a quick three-step drop and throw as rapidly as possible. Note diagram: *92*

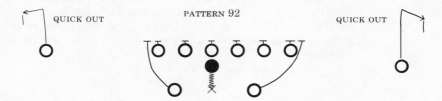

PATTERN 92

QUICK OUT   QUICK OUT

5. Rolling out allows either a good inside fake to get away from the rush or to get a sweep fake and utilize a flood. The 51 roll pattern 4, as diagrammed below, is very effective on the goal line or at any other time that we can anticipate man-for-man defense. Our primary receiver is the fullback in the flat. Note diagram: *51 roll pattern 4*

51 ROLL PATTERN 4

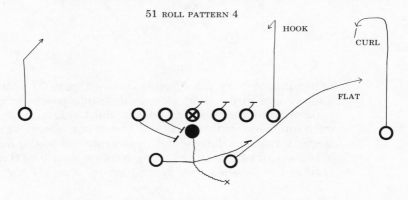

HOOK

CURL

FLAT

6. Our quick sprint outs get our passer closer to the receiver. We like to throw out-patterns (pattern 2 or 3) and can, on occasion, stop to throw to the post behind the roll zone. Note diagram: *51 sprint pattern 2*

51 SPRINT PATTERN 2

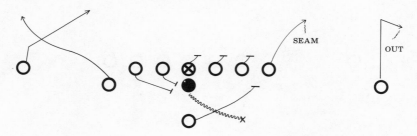

SEAM

OUT

7. Our bootleg pass is designed to get single coverage on the split end side, and we run a lot of 41 boot patterns 3 or 9. Also, against zone coverage, the crossing end can be wide open. If we anticipate man-for-man defense, we like to run 41 boot throwback to the fullback because he usually is isolated on a linebacker, and we expect to get him open deep. Note diagram: *41 boot throwback to fullback*

41 BOOT THROWBACK TO FULLBACK

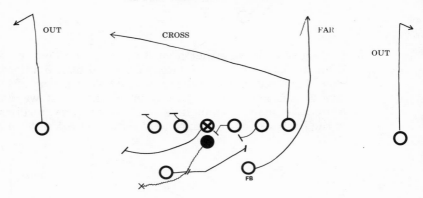

8. Our running play fake passes come off pass 37 action, and we can throw short side combination passes or can utilize maximum blocking on the short side and throw even numbered patterns back to the strong side. If we are facing a monster defense with snap rotation to the weak side, we can utilize our running back on a pattern 9 in a read of the 3 deep safety. Note diagram: *Pass 37 pattern 9 HB read*

PASS 37 PATTERN 9 HB READ

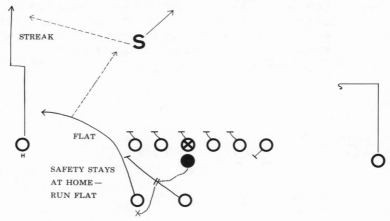

9. Our short yardage pass is 34 with the quarterback making a good ride fake to the fullback into the line before throwing a single pattern to either our flanker or to our split end. This is called pass 34 pattern 8 or 9. We like this on third down and one, or fourth down and one. Note diagram: *Pass 34 pattern 8*

PASS 34 PATTERN 8

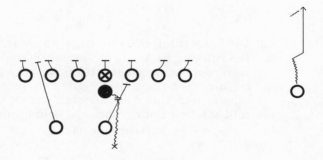

10. Our quick screen short is a great first down play. Timing is essential, and we hope to get our running back up between the crack block of our split end and the kickout block of our tackle. The quarterback drops quickly, faking a draw to the fullback, and throws immediately to a swing halfback. Note diagram: *Halfback quick screen short*

HALFBACK QUICK SCREEN SHORT

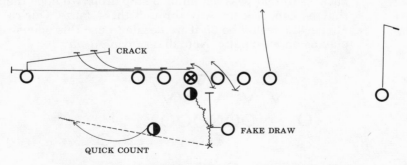

11. Our regular screens can be used on any run down or on excessive long yardage downs when the underneath coverage is moving off the ball rapidly. Note diagram: *70 halfback screen short*

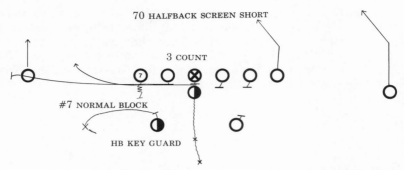

70 HALFBACK SCREEN SHORT

3 COUNT

#7 NORMAL BLOCK

HB KEY GUARD

12. We have the facility to draw to either the fullback or the running back and to vary our blocking from week to week depending on the team we play. We believe that certain backs are more gifted to draw running than others, and this can influence our decision to use our fullback or running back. Note diagram: *fullback draw*

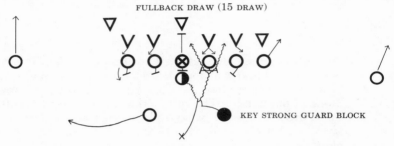

FULLBACK DRAW (15 DRAW)

KEY STRONG GUARD BLOCK

13. The quarterback draw is extremely effective against 5 underneath man or zone. In the 1971 Rose Bowl game, we found it fairly effective against the slant odd defense. We swing our backs immediately and utilize the quarterback in the 90 pass action or 3 step drop. We hope then that he can pick his way through the defense. Our call at the line would be 55 if we decide to use this offensive play as an automatic. Note diagram: *55 draw*

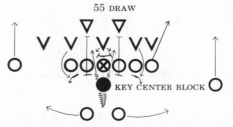

55 DRAW

KEY CENTER BLOCK

Regardless of all of the X's and O's, the key to the offensive game is to analyze the personnel and attempt to use individual ability in setting up a total pass or offensive attack. Next, analyze the opponent. If his defense can be predicted, then it will be easy to set the game plan. If his defense cannot be predicted, then perhaps it can be recognized prior to the snap of the ball. This will make it possible to get the ball to the percentage receiver. However, if the defense does a great job in disguising its coverage, then the coach must match the opponent's sophistication with his own sophistication and hope that he has the proper "feel."

Additionally, we strongly urge the coach who is interested in the pass game to be sure to evaluate the success of his throwing actions from game to game. A detailed analysis of the successes or failures of the passing actions will result in the ability to readjust or improve in the areas where work is needed. We examine every pass play individually and try to determine exactly what has caused the failure of a particular pass play. Among these areas are:

1. A bad throw
2. Poor reception
3. Poor protection
4. Bad exchange
5. Bad pattern

6. Pass thrown at wrong time
7. Poor execution
8. Good pass coverage
9. Good pass rush
10. Poor play call

Protecting the passer

We probably receive more questions from young coaches in regard to our pass protection system than any other phase of football. We are extremely proud of the success that we have had in this area, and we want to offer some insight into some of our methods. Protecting the passer in a drop-back system probably takes more study and research than any other phase related to pass offense.

Regardless of the abilities of the quarterback, his ultimate success will depend upon the confidence he has in those who protect him. The many alignments and stunts that we face in the college game pose great challenges to a protection system, and a team must practice against all anticipated problems that may arise during a game. We see all types of rushes from three-man to the more sophisticated seven and eight-man schemes. We fully realize that our opponents spend countless hours preparing to break down our system; therefore, we realize that we must spend an equal amount of time, not only on individual techniques, but on the total relationship of all the pass protection blockers.

The following information is a very detailed examination of our pass protection system, as well as the individual drills that we teach. The beginning coach who follows these ideas will find a solid base for communication as well as a perception into some of the problems facing the pass protection blockers.

Where do you start? We made a decision two years ago that we had to throw the ball to win in our conference. We made another decision that we would install the pro passing attack. It remained for us to determine how we would protect the passer against the varied defenses we face. Here's what we did: We grabbed an old set of clinic notes and looked for a system of blocking that could handle both seven and eight man front defenses. We found some ideas that the University of Alabama's coaching staff had talked about at a clinic out in California. We took this information, modified it, and this is Stanford's pass blocking system.

Its strengths are: 1) simple; 2) man blocking; 3) easy to spot breakdowns; 4) use of free men to help other blockers, or be utilized in the pass routes; 5) natural passing lanes.

8-MAN FRONT

7-MAN FRONT

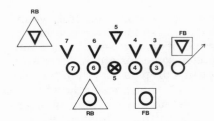

ASSIGNMENTS: BLOCKERS ARE DIVIDED INTO TWO GROUPS.

SHORT SIDE BLOCKERS (FOUR):
    CENTER #5 — AREA/MAN
    SHORT SIDE GUARD #6 — AREA/MAN
    SHORT SIDE TACKLE #7 — AREA/MAN
    RB — SHORT SIDE END (LB)

STRONG SIDE BLOCKERS (THREE):
    STRONG GUARD #4 — #1 ON LOS
    STRONG TACKLE #3 — #2 ON LOS
    FULLBACK — STRONG LB, #4 RUSHER

Teaching the individual pass protection technique

How do you measure success for the blockers in a pass blocking system? We stress three areas so that the blockers have something to shoot at in terms of goals and objectives.

    1. Number of interceptions the quarterback throws. The blockers must learn to have pride in the fact that the QB should not have to throw until he is ready. He should also not have to worry about hands in his face or balls

batted by rushing linemen. We must eliminate the bad or hurried throw by the QB.

2. Times the quarterback is flushed from the throwing spot even though the result might turn out okay. The great thing about the drop back pass is that you can draw an X on the ground and tell your line that your man will be there throwing the ball if they do their jobs.

3. Times the quarterback is thrown behind the line of scrimmage attempting to pass. We are proud of the fact that our great quarterback, Jim Plunkett, has only been thrown 20 times in two years. We are sensitive in this area that his is a protection statistic, not one to stress too much to the quarterback. Don't allow your quarterback to become so concerned about the number of losses that he throws bad balls just so the stats look good.

When teaching an individual technique we like to break it down into five distinct areas with the related drills, so that we can better communicate it to the players. 1) stance; 2) movement; 3) contact; 4) position; 5) finish.

Stance

We use a balanced 3-point stance with weight barely resting on the fingers. (A successful dropback passing game dictates a balanced stance.) We allow a pretty good stagger in the feet to help our drive block, although we realize it does hinder some techniques.

Movement

A pass blocker's success depends on his ability to move from his stance to his set-up position. We always move our inside foot first; the direction and amount of movement depends on the position of the man being blocked. We carry our fists doubled up under the chin with most of our stress on the flexed legs of the blocker and his "Center of Gravity." We set up as close to the line of scrimmage as we can so that we can force the defensive man to make his moves after we are set. If your block is on a man off the line of scrimmage, or removed a man to your outside, you must of course vary your technique somewhat. Set-up coaching points:

1) Set-up with your outside foot to the crotch of the man you are blocking. We want this inside position to force his move. 2) Keep your camera to the quarterback. (Visualize a camera up your backside; you should be constantly taking a picture of the quarterback while maintaining proper relationship to the man you are block-

ing). 3) Don't let the rusher head up on you. 4) Don't let the rusher get his hands on you. 5) "Feet and Numbers" move your feet and focus your attention on the rushers' numbers. 6) Slide to reduce distance between you and your man if he is to the outside or stunting. Keep the same relationship. 7) Keep or regain as much separation as you can from the hard charging rusher. 8) It is better to give ground, keeping position, than to over-commit and lose man immediately. 9) Know what to do if you don't have a man or if you lose your man immediately. 10) Don't lose your poise if you break down once. Analyze your opponent's technique and correct your error. 11) Know what the other men are doing . . . we must work as a unit and be able to communicate. 12) Always let the rusher make the first commitment, because over-anxiousness and aggressiveness are the biggest sins of a pass blocker. 13) Know where the throwing spot is; you are getting paid for protecting it. 14) Set-up quickly and as close to the scrimmage line as the defense allows. This will enable you to recover if a poor initial block is made. 15) If unable to get away from rusher, give ground grudgingly. Don't let rusher get into your body and force you into an upright position. Give a little ground and work your body down low again. Don't get feet close together or crossed.

Movement drills

Mirror Drill. Players work in pairs or you can rotate your linemen. Player sets up repeatedly in perfect initial relationship to the man he is blocking. One player assumes offensive stance, the other takes any defensive position the blocker might encounter. The drill can progress to a full speed drill with no contact, stressing movement, balance, and position . . . much the same as a 2-man wave drill. The drill is a great ½ speed or all out competitive pass rush drill to evaluate each individual.

FOOT POSITION

OUTSIDE FOOT TO CROTCH

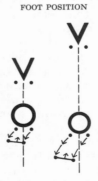

MORE DEPTH VS. LB

INSIDE FOOT STRAIGHT
BACK VS. OUTSIDE RUSHER

250

Quick Feet Drill: Administered in lines of three players at a time, in an offensive stance. On command by coach, players chop feet rapidly in set-up position with good body balance. Coach calls a somersault followed by two or three directional moves, finished with a full sprint past the coach. Good drill for overemphasis of foot movement and maintaining and regaining balance.

Contact

We find that most rushers don't want any part of actual contact with the offensive blocker, so this part of the technique takes on various forms. First of all, we have to teach the blocker 1) Patience; 2) How to use the momentum of the rusher for a successful block. How to pop the hard charging rusher under the chin, recoil, separate, and regain his position in relationship to the passer; 3) What to do about the grabbing rusher who tries to get you to lose your pass blocking balance; 4) How to cut down a hard charging rusher if all else fails, or you want to utilize an alternate technique on him; 5) How to get rid of someone's hands on your shoulders.

Contact drills

Momentum Drill: Used to teach player patience as he waits for the rusher to commit himself. Outside Rush . . . If you have established your outside foot to crotch relationship, the rusher should be forced into an outside rush if he doesn't have a pre-determined course. Let him pass "the point of no return," open your hips, stick your head on his far number, and use his momentum to run him past the throwing spot. Inside Rush . . . If you are in good inside position, the rusher will cross your face on a hard inside rush. Let him go again until he passes the "point of no return," pivot to the inside, and run him into the stack. This will be a much flatter angle than it is on the outside rush.

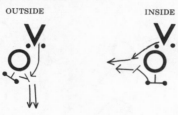

Tandem Drill: Drill used to teach the blocker balance primarily, but also pop and position. Blockers work in pairs with one man acting as the defensive man. He starts by putting his hands on the shoulders of the offensive blocker in his stance. On his own command, the blocker sets-up with the defensive man still grabbing the shoulder pads. The defensive man does everything he can to push, pull, turn, or jerk the blocker out of balance and therefore make him an ineffective pass protector. The biggest coaching point is teaching the player to squat low when pulled forward as this is the biggest problem in pass blocking. You almost have to teach him to sit down when he feels his center of gravity slipping. Incorporated also in this drill is the actual pop technique used on the hard charging rusher.

The blocker must learn the pop by a short quick extension of the legs initiated by an upward thrust of the hands aimed at the man's chin. After contact, the blocker must immediately separate, recoil, and give ground if necessary to regain his blocking position. You can also teach the blocker to ward off the grabber by a quick outward movement of the arms and hands, although that is not the purpose of this drill.

HANDS ON
SHOULDER

Cut Technique and Drill; A great alternate form of pass protection. The blocker sets-up the same way, waits for the rusher and then throws his head, shoulder, and lead arm through the rusher's far knee. After contact, it is very important that the blocker scramble on all fours to stay between the defensive man and the quarterback. We use our large shields for the drill as it is hard to practice outside of an actual scrimmage situation.

Position

We always impress upon the blocker that the most important thing in pass blocking is position. If you get set-up properly and can maintain this position, the worst thing that can happen is the man will run over the top of you, which should take two or three seconds at best. We teach this position and relationship with some basic defensive secondary drills. We also stress what to do when the rusher immediately escapes a miscalculated block.

Position drills

Line Drills: Players work in pairs two yards apart. The offensive blocker gets in his "outside foot to crotch" relationship by starting with one foot on the line. The other player straddles the line. On command, or on their own, the defensive man runs toward the blocker making any moves he can to get the blocker out of position. The blocker must keep the two yards distance while backing up and maintaining his inside position.

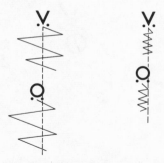

Square Drill: Same as line drill except defensive man utilizes five yard squares to make specific maneuvers. Both good drills for position, movement, and balance.

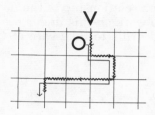

Shadow Drill: Players work in pairs much the same as in the previous drills. They face each other one yard apart. On command the defensive man moves laterally with the offensive man shadowing him. As he moves, the defensive man steps aggressively into the blocker, steps back and keeps moving. The blocker must slide, keeping position, and be ready to pop the defender.

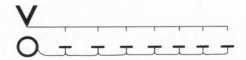

Escape Drill: Our technique of setting gives us the added advantage of being able to recover should we do a poor job of our initial block. For this reason we coach and work on an escape drill. Again, the players work in pairs with a target jersey or towel placed on the ground to represent the throwing spot. The blocker purposely misses on the line of scrimmage, pivots, and sprints to the cut off spot to get the rusher before he can close in on the passer. It has been our experience that if you take on the rusher off the line of scrimmage, then lose him, you don't have time to recover before he gets home.

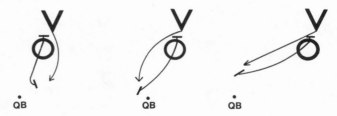

Finish

· The most neglected area in offensive line blocking is showing the player how to finish his particular block. In dropback pass protection, it is relatively easy to finish your block, because of the stationary position of the thrower. However, if the quarterback is flushed, the blocker must learn to respond to the pressure of the rusher to maintain this relationship to the new and changing position of the passer. We work on this in our position drills and often use five or six second drills to take care of the toughest possible situations.

Cover drills

The toughest phase of finishing the pass protection block is teaching the blocker to "cover" the pass after the ball is thrown. The quarterback can help by yelling cover, but he has a few other things on his mind. We try to stress it by our coverage drills, which teach the player to sense when the ball is thrown, then sprint to the receiving spot. The call ball can be incorporated in almost any of the above drills, including the following:

Four Point and Cover: Three lines doing Wave and Movement drills on all fours.

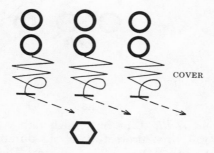

Roll and Cover: Administered in lines of three players. Movement is called the Monkey Roll. The player in the middle rolls to his left under the next player, who rolls to his right under the third player. The rolling continues until the cover call, at which time they all bounce up and sprint to the receiving spot.

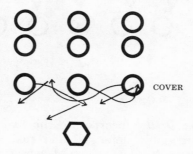

Sound and Cover: Our sound drill is a series of sharp, precise movements to our starting count. It is our feeling that it improves reaction time and consequently our ability to get off and move. We usually do our set up technique with the incorporation of the cover call.

Group and Unit Drills: Although most of your man protection work can be done individually or with the adjacent men, it is important to have three or four other drills to teach the total unit how to function. One sidelight on man pass blocking, we actually went the entire first year without ever having to.

Half Line Drill: 1/2 the line at a time against all possible defenses. The backs can also be used in their units—strong side unit (#3, #4, and FB) or short side unit (#5, #6, #7, and RB).

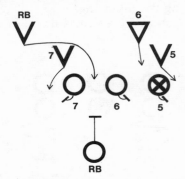

Four Second Drill: Line only, although you could incorporate the backs. Total line, protecting a big dummy stationed on the throwing spot with a ball placed on top. Defensive men can be placed anywhere and use any stunts. Use a watch and stress that we should be able to protect for four full seconds. On command let them go and see who gets to the ball first. The effect of the clock and the competitive atmosphere make it a great drill for player evaluation.

Concentration Drill: Incorporate the two blocking backs. Set up against all possible defenses, and rushes, for knowledge of assignments (men). A very important aspect is the relationship of the free men to those who might need help. If you eliminate the mental mistakes in man protection and utilize your help, it can be a great system.

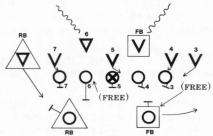

Team Pass Rush Drill: We use this team period every day in practice for at least fifteen minutes. This is a full speed team protection drill against all anticipated defenses. A passer must learn to throw behind his line, and this is the best drill we have for total team improvement and confidence.

Pass rush

Based on our experience, these are our reflections on the pass rush: First of all, it is primarily an individual thing. We don't have too much trouble with seven and eight man rushes; we do have trouble with the well coached technique or the great athlete who breaks one of our men down. (You see it on TV all the time in the pros.) It is one of the toughest things to teach at the college level. We know we have people scrambling for information, because we meet other coaches at professional camps who quiz the defensive pro coaches on pass rush techniques. Besides the individual effort, we have the most trouble with stunts involving the crossing of two adjacent linemen, or two linemen and a linebacker. We also have the obvious problem if we receive a four-man rush on our strong side.

LIMBO

REVERSE LIMBO

TWIST

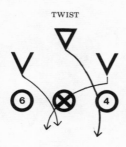

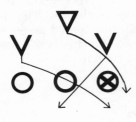

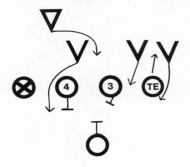

Our solution is . . . 1) adjust our pass routes and incorporate quick passes. 2) adjust our blocking pattern by using the tight end or have the center (No. 5 man) join the strong side protection, with the running back replacing him. For example:

4-STRONG BLITZ

13

Organizing and Writing Offenses

After a coach determines his best possible offensive technique blocking system, he then must develop an efficient method of writing up and presenting his offensive plays. It is imperative to be able to teach assignments quickly to avoid mistakes that might occur through lack of communication.

We continually search for the effective techniques so our players not only will be able to memorize the plays quickly, but will gain some knowledge at the same time. Learning assignments should be accomplished on the field in a competitive atmosphere. Memorization by rote is doomed to a very short lifetime. Coaches and players are missing the complete understanding of the game if the athletes do not have some insight into the play, play action, and execution.

As a learning tool, each athlete receives some assignment information during the Summer so he can begin to study and to memorize his tasks; at the same time, we include coaching points and some drawings of plays so he will understand exactly what his responsibilities are and how they are related to the particular play. For example, our offensive blocking scheme places a lot of emphasis on the finish of a particular block. It is not enough for the player to just know his assignment. He not only must know the one particular man to be blocked; he must know the direction of the play to aid him in a secondary effort according to the pattern of the action.

For this reason, we maintain as simple an offense as possible while attempting to be creative in introducing plays and the emphasis that we place in different areas.

Introduction of plays

The method, emphasis, and players' understanding of plays that are introduced will determine their success to a great degree. We introduce new plays by having the entire offensive team observe while one offensive team lines up in a prescribed formation. The offensive line faces the backs, and the receivers face the balance of the team. We set a team on defense, and the offensive players one by one give their assignments to the other members of the team. They also indicate the specific man they are expected to block in the particular defense.

We base our offense on rules; however, we realize that each coach must apply his own rules to the specific defenses he is going to face. He also must apply his rules to the maneuvers the defense can make so each man carries out an assignment even under the most difficult stunts and defenses. But whatever method is used, the player must understand what is being asked of him and also have the ability to relate to the unexpected.

Writing up offensive plays

We spend hours each week applying our blocking rules to the defenses we expect to face. Although this is of prime importance for any coach, he must be sure he does not neglect fundamentals as he proceeds further and further into the season. However, this is one of the primary reasons we place so much importance on a simple offensive plan. Under it, a team should be able to zero in on the defenses it will face, and at the same time keep its fundamentals sharp.

Following is the way that we diagrammed our offensive plays last year. Our total 1970 offense is included in the drill book with the particular write-ups we have used.

70 PROTECTION

Rules:
2. Pattern called
3. Set up #2 on LOS
4. Set up #1 on LOS
5. Set up
6. Set up
7. Set up
8. Pattern called
X Pattern called
QB Read strong LB, 5 step drop
FB Strong LB, #4 rusher, swing
RB Set up first man outside 7, swing

Coaching Points:
1. 2 man hot receiver on all patterns except 76
2. 2 man (hold call) block #3 on LOS

16 TRAP

4-3

60

Rules:
2. Near safety
3. Inside
4. Pull trap 6
5. Post, lead
6. Lead, influence
7. Near backer
8. Deep back your side
X Align
QB Reverse 8 o'clock, fake toss, hand ball to FB, drop back
FB Lead, drive for 6 area and fake block
RB Drop, cross over, fake 49 toss

Coaching Points:
1. 6 man influence may be a pull or pass pattern
2. 8 man may vary split to prevent def. end from folding under
3. 36 Trap:
   a. run with FB in normal (#3) position blue or red formations
   b. blocking same as 16 trap
   c. RB - swing shortside
   d. FB - start straight ahead, veer behind trapper (#4) guard
   e. QB - open hand ball to FB, fake drop back
4. 16 trap can be called 16 utilizing total drive blocking

Ease in learning assignments

For the convenience of the coach and the player, all of the assignments should be placed in a form for easier and quicker teaching and learning. It also provides a teaching aid during practice for the beginning coach. It is not a cardinal sin for a coach to admit that he has forgotten an assignment. It is far more important that the players understand fully the material that is being presented.

Stanford has adopted one concise format for all assignments. It aids in determining exactly what techniques a particular position should work on. With a quick glance at the sheet, for example, it is obvious that the tight end has particular blocks that he must perfect. And it is apparent that the blocks are considerably different from those of the center or guard. This technique aids the coach in setting up his practice plans and in determining exactly what emphasis he should place during each day's practice. It particularly is true in determining the emphasis for a specific season or game.

Following is the format that we use (Stanford GRID assignment sheet):

ASSIGNMENT SHEET

PLAY	2	3	4	5	6	7
41 Sweep (21 Sweep)	Angle	Angle	Pull, Hook 2	Drive Strong	Pull, Seal 2	Pull, Seal 5
33 Opt.	Drive	Drive	Drive	Drive Strong	Cut Off	Cut Off
42 (22)	Lead, Infl., Across to Backer	Drive (Post)	Drive	Drive Strong	Drive (C.O.)	Drive (C.O.)
33	Drive	Drive	Drive	Drive Strong	Drive (C.O.)	Drive (C.O.)
23 Bl.	Drive, No 3, Influence	Blast, Lead	Lead, Pull Trap 2	Drive Strong	Drive (C.O.)	Cut Off
44 Tackle Trap	Near Backer, Safety	Near Backer, Influence	Lead, Influence, Across to Backer	Post, Lead	Drive	Pull, Trap 4
36 Trap	Near Safety	Inside	Pull, Trap 6	Post, Lead	Lead, Infl., Across to B'er	Near Backer
37 Blast	Near Safety	Cut-Off	Drive (C.O.)	Drive Short	Drive	Drive
37	Near Safety	Cut-Off	Drive (C.O.)	Drive Short	Drive	Drive
39 Opt. (29 Opt.)	Near Safety	Cut-Off	Cut-Off	Drive Short	Drive	Drive
3, 4, 5, 6, Wedge	Number Called :	Man 1s Apex of Wedge - All Other Linemen Block To			Apex	
37 Draw	Near Safety	Draw Short	Draw Short	Draw Short	Draw Short	Draw
Screen Short	Set-Up, Crossfield	Set-Up Crossfield	Set-Up Crossfield	3 Count Set-Up Screen Short	3 Count Set-Up Screen Short	Set-Up
70	Pattern Called	Set-Up #2	Set-Up #1	Set-Up	Set-Up	Set-Up
80	Set-Up	Set-Up	Set-Up	Set-Up	Set-Up	Set-Up
22 Roll	Pattern Called	Roll Strong	Roll Strong	Roll Strong	Backside	Backside
90 Strong	Quick Strong	Quick Strong	Quick Strong	Quick Strong	Quick Strong	Quick Strong
90 Weak	Quick Weak	Quick Weak	Quick Weak	Quick Weak	Quick Weak	Quick Weak
36 Roll	Pattern Called	Backside	Pull, Run a Course at 9	Roll Short	Roll Short	Roll Short
Pass 37	Pattern Called	Backside	Backside	Stop Strong	Stop Strong	Roll Short

Use of offensive worksheets

We have made very effective use of mimeographed sheets of different defenses so we can quickly check the players' blocking assignments against different alignments. The following form is a sample.

OFFENSIVE WORKSHEET

Coaching Points:

Rules:
2.
3.
4.

5.
6.
7.

8.
X
FB

RB
QB

Categorizing offensive plays

We believe Stanford has a unique approach to offensive football by categorizing the phases of offense into different systems for ease in learning and communication. It has been our experience from year to year that different phases of offense require different priorities, depending on the player personnel. For this reason, it is important to categorize phases of offense and place them in logical sequence to eliminate the mistakes referred to earlier. We usually categorize only a few of our main systems so the player will obtain a better insight into our detailed planning.

The coach obtains an additional benefit from this approach because he has a better working knowledge of the different areas of emphasis as he sets up a practice plan and evaluates the success or failure of a particular play or play action.

The following blocking systems are the ones that we use the most:

1. Dropback
2. Draw
3. Roll
4. Screen
5. Sprint
6. Quick pass
7. Goal line offense, which includes jump, wedge, and sneak systems

Dropback blocking system

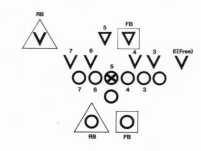

2 - PATTERN CALLED
3 - SET-UP (#2 ON LOS)
4 - SET-UP (#1 ON LOS)
5 - SET-UP
6 - SET-UP

7 - SET-UP
FB - STRONGSIDE LB, #4 RUSHER;
    FB WILL TAKE END IF STRONG LB
    DOESN'T COME
HB - SHORTSIDE END

I. Dropback system divides offensive blockers into 2 distinct units
  A. #4, #3, FB
  B. #5, #6, #7, HB
      1. #5 always blocks to shortside if no one is in covered area.
  C. Shortside unit can handle 4 man rushes.
  D. Strongside is out numbered when faced with 4 man rushes.

264

Solution:
  1. Hot receiver, QB−TE #2 Quick Pass on strong LB'er key
  2. Hold TE (#2) in to block 4th rusher.
  3. Predetermined blocking where #5 joins strongside unit and HB takes his man.

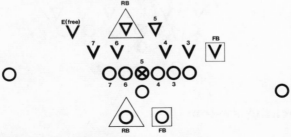

E. Additional (Basic) Protection Rules
  1. We can also *slide* the shortside if we feel there is sufficient reason (i.e., protect your HB)

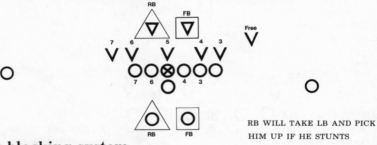

RB WILL TAKE LB AND PICK
HIM UP IF HE STUNTS

Draw blocking system

I. Draw can be called over any man; other blockers know they must (create) perform their draw technique to protect the area called.
  A. Draw at 5 (i.e. 55 Draw)
    1. #5 back (QB) at the 5 hole

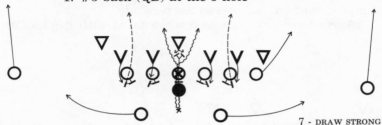

2 - NEAR SAFETY
3 - DRAW SHORT
4 - DRAW SHORT
5 - DRAW
6 - DRAW STRONG

7 - DRAW STRONG
HB - SWING PATTERN
FB - SWING PATTERN
QB - BALL CARRIER
SE - RUN CURL, BLOCK
FLKR - RUN CURL, BLOCK

B. Additional draw rules
   1. Against heavy stunting teams, you can use hot receiver principle and also be ready to assign the back not carrying the ball to a linebacker.

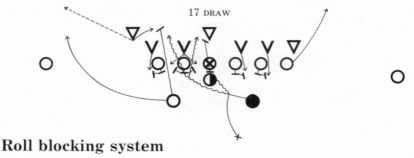

17 DRAW

Roll blocking system

I. Roll will be called either strong or short by using 1, 2, 3 or 7, 8, 9 following the type of backfield action — i.e., 51 roll, 22 roll (strong rolls), 59 roll (shortside roll).

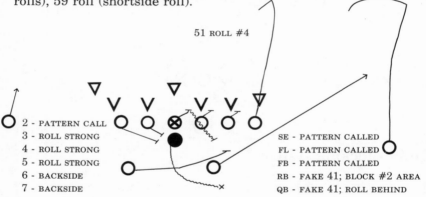

51 ROLL #4

2 - PATTERN CALL
3 - ROLL STRONG
4 - ROLL STRONG
5 - ROLL STRONG
6 - BACKSIDE
7 - BACKSIDE

SE - PATTERN CALLED
FL - PATTERN CALLED
FB - PATTERN CALLED
RB - FAKE 41; BLOCK #2 AREA
QB - FAKE 41; ROLL BEHIND

II. Roll technique is a solid drive block with good balance and position. If no one threatens, the blocker slides toward the throwing spot protecting from his area to the backside.
   A. Switch blocks are good when faced with gap situations.

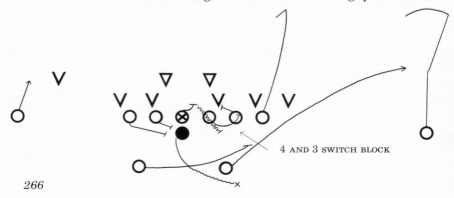

4 AND 3 SWITCH BLOCK

266

III. Backside technique is a zone blocking maneuver by the side away from the throwing spot.

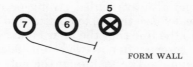

FORM WALL

    A. On snap of ball, #6 moves to a spot off the #5 man's foot and takes anyone that shows. #7 takes a relationship to #6 to protect the passer from the backside.

IV. Additional Roll blocking rules

    A. You can build in roll-out plays where backs will fake and take over linemen's assignments. When this is done, you can pull the lineman or double up on outstanding players, etc.

Screen blocking systems

Quick-screen blocking

We have the facility to call a quick-screen, either strong or short, depending upon the type of backfield action that we are utilizing. Quick-screen blocking indicates to the line that we will form a screen comprised of the offensive tackle, guard, and center to the side where the screen pass will be thrown. The quick-screen technique is a quick set up by the line and an immediate release in the direction called. The off-side guard and tackle pass-block for two good counts, release and sprint across field to assist the receiver. Our primary receiver in our quick screen is our running back, either strong or short.

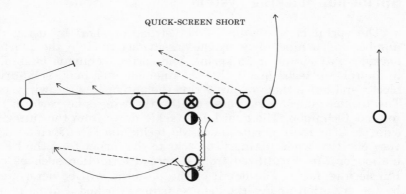

QUICK-SCREEN SHORT

Delayed-screen blocking

Delayed screens also are called strong or short, depending upon the area of the defense that is to be attacked. Delayed screen blocking indicates to the line that the guard and center on the side called will form the screen after a two-count delay, using their normal blocking techniques. The tackle on the side of the screen will perform his normal pass protection, giving ground slightly to allow the screen to release underneath his block.

The off-side guard and tackle perform their normal blocking responsibilities and release downfield only when they are sure the ball has been safely thrown. We utilize the fullback screen short or strong, as well as the halfback screen short or strong.

FULLBACK SCREEN SHORT

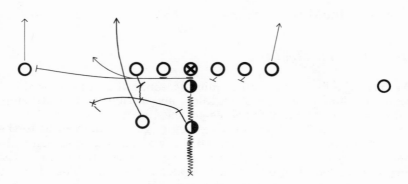

Sprint-out blocking system

The sprint can be called either strong or short by using the number one or nine following the passing action 50 by the quarterback, i.e., 51 sprint or 59 sprint. The sprint technique is similar to the roll-out technique in that the linemen must make solid-drive blocks and finish them by protecting the anticipated throwing spot. The tackle, guard, and center on the throwing side perform the roll-out technique. The guard and tackle away from the throwing side perform their normal backside technique. The sprint-out is very effective when taking two backs to the corner from the I Formation or can be utilized from a spread formation such as our Purple alignment. The depth of the patterns will be determined by the situation and/or the defense being attacked. Normally our routes are at an eight yard depth.

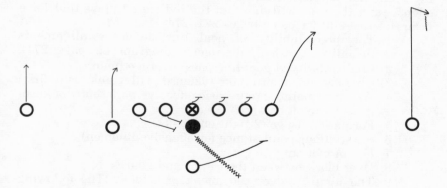

The quick-pass series

Our 90, or quick pass series, indicates to the line an alternate form of pass protection. We have examined several individual techniques and have become aware that what works for one player will not necessarily work for another. The secret of the quick-blocking technique is to get the hands of the rushers down when the ball is being thrown. The quarterback uses a three-step drop and throws quick patterns to his outside receivers. The most commonly used patterns are the quick-out, quick-post, and the hitch. The fullback and running back are very important to the protection, and they must attack the outside rushers on the line of scrimmage.

PATTERN 94

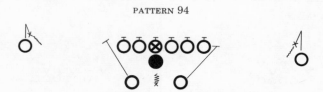

Both outside receivers run the same pattern. In this case, it is the hitch. The QB will evaluate the coverage and throw to the best percentage receiver.

Goal line offense

We mentioned earlier the importance of having a successful goal line offense. We have developed a total goal line offensive system for both the run and the pass. One of the important aspects of a goal line offense is the emphasis that is placed on it by the coaching staff. Let us examine further the important aspects of this offense, and then we will diagram the individual plays that have been so successful for us on pages 271–274.

1. The predictability of goal line defensive alignments (usually eight-five alignment—diagram on page 271).
2. Predictability of goal line pass coverage (man)
3. Obvious down situation (defense will think, run first)
4. We must maintain our basic offensive philosophy of keeping a team off balance
5. Formation usage (2 tight ends, slot)
6. Stance (four point stance for offensive linemen)
7. Use of motion
8. Over-block between the center and guards
9. The jump, wedge, and sneak principles. (The following diagram illustrates these principles)

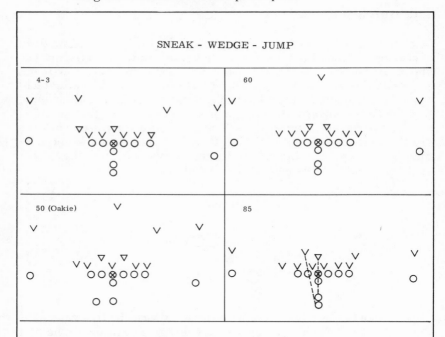

SNEAK - WEDGE - JUMP

1. Sneak: QB or 5 back carries ball over prescribed lineman, i.e., sneak at 6. Linemen all drive block with knowledge of QB route. Sneak at 6 backs run 23 jump. Sneak at 4 backs run 37.

2. Wedge: Back called over prescribed hole. Linemen at called hole becomes apex of wedge blocking. All other linemen block to apex.

3. Jump: Designated back carries ball over prescribed linemen. Back must use jump technique in executing play. Linemen block play called. Play called--23 jump.

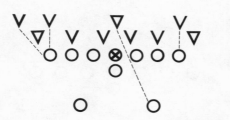

Goal line offense — runs:

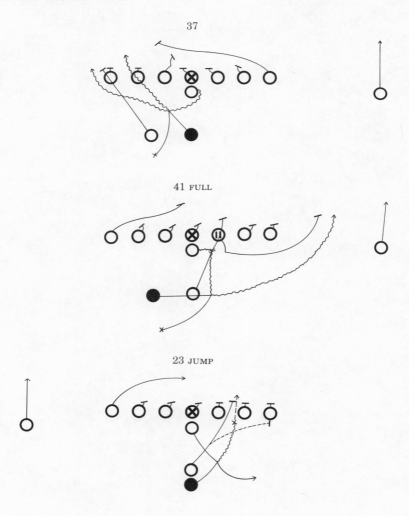

37

41 FULL

23 JUMP

51 OPTION

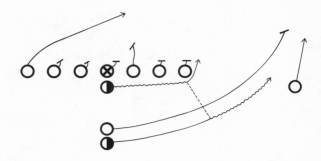

34 COUNTER

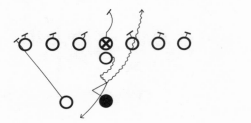

SNEAK AT 4

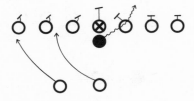

SNEAK AT 6

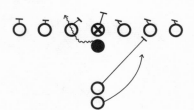

Goal line offense — passes:

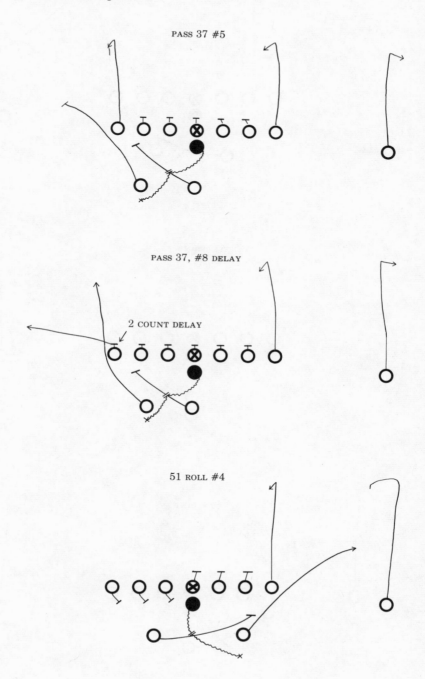

PASS 37 #5

PASS 37, #8 DELAY

2 COUNT DELAY

51 ROLL #4

51 ROLL #6

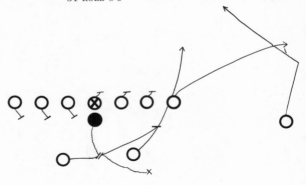

51 SPRINT #2

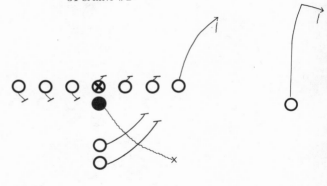

59 SPRINT #3

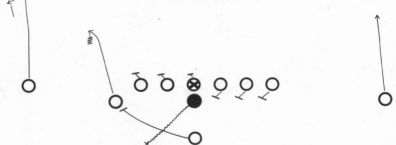

14

Position Fundamentals

The following is a discussion of the individual football player and some of the fundamentals of each position. Specific drills for each position are included in the accompanying drill book.

Line fundamentals

Center stance

Center must be able to step out with either foot. Should be a balanced stance with his feet even, toes pointed straight ahead, knees fairly wide, head up, back straight, and the tail even with the shoulders. The weight of the body is carried both on the ball itself and the balls of the feet. The ball will be with the laces up. The left hand of the center will carry all of the forward weight and should be placed on the left half of the ball, the base of the thumb at the back end of the laces, *right hand between the thumb and the index finger should be placed at the top end of the laces, but rolled around under the ball slightly. The center must learn to step as he is bringing up the ball.* Also the center must learn to lift the ball, rather than swing it back. Your left hand will leave the ball as you bring it up with the right hand. Do it quickly and solidly with a natural bend of the elbow in lifting the ball. Keep your wrist rigid. Keep right hand on the ball until you feel impact. Be sure of the starting count; you will be instructed to snap the ball on the sound. Be able to step to assignment, and you will be expected to do as good a job of blocking as any other man on the line.

Guards, tackles stance

Your feet should be about shoulder width, with the toes pointed straight ahead. You may drop either foot back slightly, so that the toe aligns with the instep of your other foot; it might even possibly be toe to heel. Your knees should be fairly wide and aligned directly over the feet. Your tail will be level with your shoulders. Your hand will be down directly under the shoulder and will correspond with the particular foot that you have back. In order to roll the necessary weight forward on your hand, extend it slightly away from you a couple of inches. Always have your head and eyes up. The amount of weight that you have on your hand will vary with the particular assignment and defense that you are confronted with. Your heels will be slightly off the ground, and the weight of your body will be carried on the balls of the feet as well as the hand. Feel that you are able to step out with either foot, as this is vitally necessary in proper blocking technique. When you are in your final stance you will notice that you have a coiled lever at the ankle, one at the knee, and one at the waist. As you fire out to make contact with your opponent, learn to uncoil these levers with maximum extension and power. Keep the levers coiled tightly and then learn to fire out on the command or starting count. Tight ends will take a stance with the inside foot back, toe to heel stagger.

Pulling linemen technique

All linemen should learn to pull properly. The method that we use for pulling is the lead step technique. You must learn not to tip off any pulling action. Pick up the near foot in the direction that you intend to go and try to gain six inches on the first step. Point this toe in the proper direction that you intend to take. Push off with your hand that is on the ground and pull back sharply your near elbow and shoulder to the direction that you intend to go. Two coaching points we use are: 1) Put your elbow in your back pocket; 2) Throw your weight over the lead foot. At the same time, throw your off arm and shoulder across your body. This maneuver will tend to pull you around sharply and get you headed in the proper direction. Be sure to stay low and drive hard as you clear your particular position. Stay low and balanced so that you can hit hard on your assignment.

Fold technique

Again, it is important never to tip off your intentions; in other words, always maintain the same offensive stance. Stay square to the line of scrimmage as your teammate next to you fires at the man over you. Raise up slightly and step with your near foot in the proper direction, making sure to keep the toe pointed straight ahead; swing your head over his tail. You will always be headed straight upfield, but making a slight adjustment upward and outward prior to your firing out. Once your teammate has cleared you, fire out by getting maximum drive off the foot that you originally stepped with. Stay low and be ready to make contact at any time; you must be able to block in or out. We must learn to execute our Fold Technique with maximum efficiency if we are to take advantage of inside defensive alignments and responsibilities.

Backfield fundamentals

Stance, start, ball handling, faking, blocking, and ball carrying of quarterback

The quarterback places his right hand under the center so that the natural break of the hand and arm rests against the curve of the center's hips. The fingers are definitely spread and slightly cupped and the angle of the hand is almost a forty-five degree angle to the right. Third knuckle of the middle finger applies upward pressure at the tip of the spine. The left hand is placed palm away, fingers spread and pointed toward the ground, the two thumbs touching so that the first knuckle of the right thumb fits into the groove of the left thumb and then aligns with the front knuckle. Therefore, the left hand is ahead of the right hand. The two hands in proper position form a cup, into which the ball is driven by the center. The QB stance is with one foot slightly ahead of the other in approximately toe and heel position, with the weight on the balls of the feet. The feet are spread about the width of the shoulders, with the knees slightly flexed. The position should be one of comfort and relaxation, with the back straight and the head up. Variation in height of the center would force the QB to adjust the bend of his knees. The center and QB must, of course, work as a team, helping each other where one has a more difficult assignment than the other. A little extra pressure is always applied by the QB on the snap count, which helps the center feel secure in that the QB hands will be with him on his charge.

Stance of remaining backs

1. *The Running Back:* The spread of the feet is about that of the shoulder width on a toe and heel alignment. This can vary a few inches, depending on the position that feels most comfortable to the boy. The toes are turned out slightly so that most of the weight is on the inside of the

feet. The hand on the side of the back foot is down, with the tips of the first two fingers touching the ground. The weight is forward sufficiently to stay on the balls of the feet, with very little actual weight on the fingers. Both the so-called right and left stances are used depending on alignment in the 1 or 4 positions (Red or Brown). The weight is distributed evenly between the feet, with the constant word of caution to avoid too much weight on one foot or the other. The heels are slightly off the ground so that there is no weight on them. The bend at the knee is approximately that of a right angle. The free arm rests across the knee, touching the knee at a point about the wrist and should be relaxed. The angle of the back is slightly up, with a definite emphasis on the face high. They are in this stance only the first second or two; therefore the feet, calves and thighs should be tensed for the start.

2. *The Fullback:* The stance of the fullback differs from the running back in that we prefer a balanced stance rather than staggered. This means that the feet should be even in alignment thus throwing off any directional tip offs. In most instances the right hand will be down with the left wrist across the left thigh. Disguise the amount of weight placed on the right finger tips depending on the direction of the start (lateral start-light pressure; forward start-heavy pressure). The head should be up at all times with eyes straight ahead.

Start

Generally speaking, for the purpose of teaching the stance and start, there are three directions a back goes; namely, right or left, straight ahead, or an angle of right or left. Having assumed the actual position from which he can best execute the direction of his move, the first action of the start is off the back foot, which we call the impulse foot. For example, if he is going at a forty-five degree angle to his left he would naturally, under these principles, assume a right stance and the drive or impulse foot would be the right one. That foot is also referred to as the "back foot." The first action is to drive his body in the proper direction with a pivoting action if necessary and in all cases amounts to a full step on the first action. For all right and left work, a sharp pivoting action is used and the first step is always a full cross over using the leg including the foot all the way out. When the movement starts, the back foot drives the weight quickly into position for full and powerful action of the front leg; the front leg in all starts is the one that produces near full speed on the second step as possible. The hips do not raise on the first step and the angle of the back should remain about the same. The arms, shoulders and hips are definitely made a part of the starting action much the same as a good dash man starts in track. If a back has several yards to go before the likelihood of meeting opposition, he comes up to his best position for maximum speed running.

Ball handling

The technique of ball exchange between QB and ball carrier is based on the theory that the ball carrier must use his eyes for other things than the ball. Therefore, a QB has the burden of properly placing the ball in the pocket. All of our plays have what we call a ball receiving spot and the ball carrier should go through that spot before veering or breaking in one direction or another. As stated above, he uses his arms to facilitate his fast start and doesn't assume a ball receiving position until that spot is reached. The ball receiving position or pocket is made simply by raising the near arm on the side of the QB to a point where the elbow is above the eyes. This near arm will have a right angle bend at the elbow and the forearm and wrist will be parallel to the ground. The fingers on this near arm should be spread and slightly cupped. The far arm from the QB will be placed palm up across the stomach of the ball receiver. The elbow should be approximately three inches away from the body. The ball will be placed by the QB on the far hip of ball receiver. As the ball is placed in the pocket, the near arm and hand are used to help place it properly and firmly in position and to further secure it. We do not encourage shifting the ball until the back is definitely out of the so-called "intense" area (three yards on either side of line.)

Faking

The faking done by the QB and the remaining backs cannot be overemphasized. We have always felt that the best faking is done when the QB and remaining backs are operating as low as possible and the running back does a tremendous job of driving and slashing as he hits the line of scrimmage. As you well know, football is a game of courage, it is a game of stamina, and without a doubt it takes more courage, stamina, and morale to make a great fake and let your teammate score than it does to cross the goal line yourself. The most important factor in the other backs making yardage outside is the faking done by the HB or FB hitting inside. *If we are to become a great team, you as a backfield performer must become a great faker.*

The QB faking will be done either with the ball or by use of an open hand fake. In either case, and wherever possible, try to follow your fake with your head and eyes. Always stay as low as possible. We will have plays in our offense that are completely dependent on you as a QB to do an excellent job of faking in order to make these plays successful.

For the remaining, or running backs, the important points in becoming a great faker are these: 1. Hit as close to the QB as you possibly can. 2. Fake through the proper hole or past the proper ball receiving point. 3. Grasp your arm as if you were carrying the ball. 4. Fight through any opposition at the line of scrimmage and continue your fake as if you had the ball until you are tackled. 5. *The fake area is from the line of scrimmage five yards downfield.* Remember the longer you carry out your fake, the longer the defense will be in doubt. All plays look the same to the defense until the backs show them where the ball is. Techniques: Bottom hand grasps elbow nearest QB and drop shoulder nearest the side of the hole.

Backfield blocking

A football team cannot perform at full efficiency unless all eleven offensive men are top blockers. This means that *every* back *must* master this fundamental. The blocks made by backs are made more difficult in that the backs are usually moving at top speed and the target is either set or moving too. The key is timing and the ability to "coil" or "dip" in motion so that you may explode into your target. The follow-through is vital and the longer contact can be made, the more effective the block will be. There is no easy way to learn to block. Remember that "the only difference between a good blocker and a bad blocker is about 10,000 blocks." The running backs block on the blunt and roll; the fullbacks block on sweeps, rolls, and the 41 full; and the flanker's stalk blocks and cracks are vital. We must master these through repetition in the early sessions prior to the opener.

The running back and fullback must also learn to pass protect on our dropback series. Getting inside position on the charging linemen will aid the block. With proper timing the head is thrown "across the bow" and the defender is driven past the pocket. Again the "coil" or "dip" is vital and the timing on the extension must be mastered.

The flanker back *must* master the stalk block. Sprint off the line and directly at the defensive back for approximately 6 yards. This should drive him backwards. As he recovers, come to balance and look him right in the eye. Mirror him. Stay up and in front of the defensive HB (Do not extend or go to the ground). Do not allow him to come by you into a support position. The success of the block will be in how long you can maintain contact.

Ball carrying

The outstanding characteristics of each ball carrier may differ. One may have a lot of speed, one may be shifty, while a third may be solid on his feet and possess a great deal of power. Every ball carrier must take advantage of his natural talent and practice diligently to become as versatile as possible. No matter what the particular style of any ball carrier may be, the most important thing for any ball carrier is *not to fumble the ball*. Good habits, careful handling and proper technique will prevent fumbles. If you carry the ball properly and are determined to hang on, *you will never lose the ball*. We constantly stress the ability of the great back to break tackles, especially the first man who gets a hand on him. In other words, make your own first block.

Always move straight toward the opponent's goal, and move as fast as you can, unless there is a definite reason for doing otherwise. Some of the reasons for doing this may be as follows: 1. To get to the hole. 2. To outflank an opponent. 3. To make better use of certain blockers. 4. To dodge an opponent. 5. To time out the play. *You must realize where you are and where you have to go to succeed.* In most cases when you are the ball carrier, you should be concerned only with scoring a touchdown on the play. The basic differences between ordinary ball carriers and great ball carriers is one of mental attitude. Ordinary men will try to make a gain and are satisfied with a run of 5 yards; great ball carriers are dissatisfied whenever they fail to score and are *always going for the goal line*. You have not succeeded completely when carrying the ball unless you do score, unless for occasional tactical situations.

These tactical situations may develop when a first down is more important than a touchdown. For example: You may have third down and two to go on your own forty yard line; here you should make the supreme effort to get the two yards (after you have used that, you can gamble on trying to go all the way).

Use good judgment always. To do this you must be aware of the tactical situations. Remember—as a ball carrier—*get to that first down stripe—get to the goal line—WHEN YOU HAVE POSSESSION OF THE BALL YOU HAVE THE GAME IN YOUR HANDS.*

Receivers

Each receiver has a different style, and it is the job of the coach to utilize these natural talents to develop the catcher's ability to get into the open. He also must have a unique type of courage. He needs confidence because he has to be *convinced* he is going to catch the ball. We mentioned earlier in this chapter that the quarterbacks and receivers must spend sufficient time together so they know each other's thoughts and moves as well as their very own. We break down receiver's techniques into stance, alignment, release from the line of scrimmage, patterns, what to do after catching the ball and the importance of downfield blocking.

We also stress the importance of the receivers learning to catch the bad pass.

In all of our drills against a zone defense, we require our receivers to sprint off the line full speed, thus driving the deep coverage back, so the linebackers and underneath coverage men are forced to be responsible for a larger area.

In man-for-man coverage, the receivers must angle in or out, weave, or use a change of pace in order to get a favorable position on the defender. We instruct our receivers to get a head-on position on an opponent and turn him with an influence to the opposite side of his final move.

As we pointed out in the discussion of analyzing quarterbacks, coaches should be aware of certain shortcomings in receivers. A catcher must be able to run under full control if he is going to be in charge of his cuts. Other detrimental points include:

1. Failure to run correct patterns and to adjust to coverage.
2. Failure to "look the pass" into his hands, or taking his eyes off the ball.
3. Failure to disguise a pass thrown off a running fake.
4. Loafing when he is not the primary receiver. He must always work to help set up other patterns.
5. Failure to fight for the ball and use of his body.
6. Failure to analyze the defensive man that will cover him on a particular maneuver.

The selection and proper use of pass offense drills go a long way toward achieving success. In addition to the drills mentioned earlier, we know that we must improve individual patterns versus the varied man defenses we are facing; we advocate basically timed pass patterns; and we have pass trees for the flanker, split ends, and tight end. We supplement these with additional called routes for the fullback and halfback as well as the other three receivers.

There are five essential points to look for in a receiver:

1. Speed: This is the one ingredient that is born in a receiver. If a coach can discover a boy in a gym class or in the track program who has great speed, he has the starting point for developing an outstanding receiver. From that starting point, quickness of feet must be developed. An outstanding receiver must have the quickness to come off the line, stop, and break to the inside or outside. A coach will find that some receivers do not have outstanding overall speed, but they will be able to get deep just because they have quick, short moves to fake out a defensive back.

2. "Touch" or "hands:" This is a quality that sometimes is never possible to develop in an athlete. The natural basketball or baseball player who has this fine touch will go up in a crowd to catch the ball; he will get his hands on it if it is anywhere near him. We emphasize the use of the body, a technique that will be discussed later.
3. Size: If a coach is fortunate, he may have an outstanding receiver who is well over six feet tall who also has speed and touch. However, we know this isn't always the case. Stanford has had some superb flankers who were in the range of 5 feet 10 inches tall. Consequently, we don't feel that it is absolutely necessary that a wide receiver has size; however, we do look for good size in the tight end.
4. Toughness: The kind of toughness we are talking about is the athlete who will play 10 games a season and do the job in each of the games. He is the one who will catch the ball in a crowd, take the shots that are part of the wide receiver's job, and still not be injury prone.
5. Blocking ability: A high school receiver doesn't necessarily have to possess this characteristic. If he has the other four qualities, they will aid him in becoming coachable to learn blocking.

There are five essential coaching points that must be learned by the receiver:
1. Stance: We are firm believers in using the three-point stance in coming off the line out of a three-point position. Three years ago, we allowed the receiver to use an upright stance, a two-point whenever he felt like he might get a man out in a press position, or if he thought he could look over a defense much better from that vantage point. However, we now believe that it is best to get the receiver out of that stance as quickly as possible; to accomplish this, he has to be in a three-point stance. We also spent a great deal of time studying films and defenses and feel that the receiver can come out of a three-point stance and know on that second or third step what kind of coverage he's going to get. In this stance, he lines up in a three-point with the outside foot back. It is always the outside foot back, simply because we feel that it is much more comfortable for the player to have the outside foot back and the head hanging naturally, with a better view of the ball. The reverse stance is awkward primarily because of the position of the head.
2. Alignment: This depends upon the type of quarterback who is being used. We line up our receiver or flanker from eight to fifteen yards, but normally we don't tighten him down at all. Our split end may be from a tight two or three

yard split all the way out to twelve yards because of his blocking assignments. Much is determined by the strength of the quarterback's arm. We determine this by lining up the quarterback on one hash mark with the receiver on another. The receiver runs an out pattern, and we determine just how quickly the quarterback can throw the ball out to him. With a strong-armed quarterback such as Jim Plunkett, our split or alignment distance might have been farther than the average receiver, either in high school or college. One of the key points is knowing the field position. If the wide receiver is near the sideline with little operating room, then he never should become aligned so wide or so short that he places himself at a disadvantage with the defensive back. Because he knows he has sideline help, the defensive back can move inside if the receiver lines up too far out before going into a breaking pattern.

3. Release: This probably is the most important phase in our training of the receiver. We previously discussed great speed, but now we are talking about an explosion off the line of scrimmage followed by a drive upfield with a slight outside release. The defensive back should be made to react, and the receiver should make it happen. An outside release is essential. The receiver must come off quickly with an outside angle to widen the defensive back, and in turn, to open a larger area in which to run the pattern. On about the fifth or sixth step the receiver should try to come back more to a head up position on the defensive back. The defensive back should be forced into a position where the receiver can go inside or outside depending on his called pattern, thus beating the defender.

If the defensive man comes out in a press position, lining up right on the wide receiver, he should come off either outside or inside and then widen to beat the man and then go right into his assigned pattern. This causes some necessary adjustments. For example, a receiver who normally would be a primary no longer may be in that position.

The technique used in release also depends upon whether it is man-for-man or zone coverage. If it is man-for-man, more individual adjustments must be made. If it is a zone defense, the most important element is for the receiver to go as deep as he can as quickly as possible. Speed is of the essence in this maneuver. The defensive man must be made to think he's facing a deep pattern wide; this makes him go deeper and the receiver can back off the pattern. A receiver has the deep responsibility in a zone, and he must think in those terms.

4. Receiving the ball: The primary emphasis here is the use of the body to aid in catching the ball. The hands are used, but they should be underneath the ball with the elbows inside. With this technique, any ball that is thrown from eye level downward will be caught with the body even if it means jumping from the ground. This technique also results in screening the defensive back from the ball. The body aids in absorbing the shock of the ball as well as the shock of the tackler. We teach our receivers to bend the shoulders inward slightly and form an inside pocket. We work with a number of drills involving a high thrown ball where the receiver will get his hands up with his thumbs down and catch the ball with his hands. The receiver should not reach out too far. Too many passes are dropped in this manner compared with the technique of getting the body in front of the ball.

5. Depth: Our starting point in depth is 12 yards. This varies with different types of actions, but the basic starting point for a wide receiver is go to that depth on all the patterns and then either come back to 10 or go deep off the 12 yard depth. The tight end's starting point normally is to go 12 yards and to run all of his patterns off that depth. There is one rule of thumb: The depth that a tight end will go may vary; if he has a 12-yard depth pattern called and gets bumped by a defensive player at the line, he will be slower getting to his assigned position. Then he must cut it to ten or nine yards and run it at that point. The ball and the timing must be correlated. If the tight end is held up and gets there later, he might shorten his depth. Stanford uses four or five basic patterns so our depths vary. We run a four-yard pattern on our quick series; we go to eight yards when we're running our quarterback sprint series; we go to 12 yards when we're running our play action whether it is a bootleg or roll-out pattern. The drop-back depth is at 12 yards, so this is the point at which we start all of our patterns.

The Stanford receiver terminology is illustrated below, followed by sample pass patterns:

Receiver terminology

Curl:	Pass pattern in which receiver widens defensive man and then turns back inside at 12 yards.
Crack Block:	Block used by wide receiver on sweep or toss.
Delay:	Type of pass pattern employed in which receiver simulates a block or camouflaged pattern before running actual pattern.

Drag:	Pass pattern run by TE in which he makes sideline cut after breaking 12 yards downfield.
Flag:	Deep pass pattern in which receiver makes outside break for end zone flag when reaching 12 yard depth. Also referred to as seam pattern.
Flex:	Maneuver employed by TE to move 2-4 yards wider than initial line-up.
Hot Receiver:	Term used to designate TE as automatic quick receiver when strongside LB blitzes on a passing situation.
Invert:	Defensive secondary coverage in which inside safety or mover covers the flat area on flow or call and outside HB covers deep 1/3.
Jump Technique:	Type of defensive move employed in a rotation coverage where outside HB moves up to bump wide receiver and not let him outside.
Loop:	Pattern run like curl except receiver turns outside instead of inside.
Man Cover:	Defensive coverage employed when defensive man is assigned an offensive man wherever his pattern takes him.
Near Back:	Closest defensive back to designated receiver.
Near Safety:	Defensive back who aligns himself inside of outside HB's.
Perimeter:	Defensive people responsible for pass coverage.
Pick:	Offensive receiver technique employed to bump or screen a defensive man from his coverage.
Plateau:	Area of reference used to designate blocking areas for wide receivers.
Post:	Pass pattern in which receiver runs downfield 12 yards and makes inside break for goal post.
Press:	Type of defensive perimeter coverage whereby a defensive man moves out and plays tight on a wide receiver.
Read:	Reference made to receiver observation of defensive movement.
Release:	Movement made by receiver as he explodes from the line of scrimmage.
Rotation:	Defensive secondary coverage in which inside safety or mover covers deep outside 1/3 and HB comes up to jump receiver.
Sideline:	Pass pattern where receiver widens defensive man, then makes outside break for sideline at 12 yards angling back to 10 yards. Also referred to as OUT pattern.
Slant:	Pass pattern whereby receiver makes inside break for post on third step.

Split
Position: A line-up employed by wide receivers.

Stalk: Type of block used by wide receivers to screen defensive back from ball carrier.

Streak: Deepest pass pattern employed in going for long TD. The streak can come off our basic out or curl fake.

Tight
Position: Line up by wide receivers closer to offensive lineman than 10 yards.

Zone: Defensive coverage whereby the defensive perimeter covers an area rather than a man.

Pass patterns

Out (sideline)

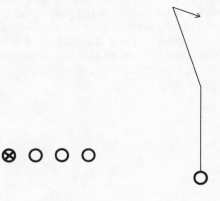

1. Explode off the ball for an outside position on defensive man.
2. Gather at 9-10 yards, come under control by slightly shortening the stride, the weight should be slightly back over the body and the shoulders are back. The last step should be the shortest and break is made at 12 yard depth.
3. Very important to snap the head toward the QB immediately as the break is made! Catch the ball about 10 yards deep.
4. Ball should be about belt high and in front of receiver.
5. Whenever a defensive man moves into a press position, the sideline pattern is automatically changed to a curl pattern as we feel the press takes the sideline pattern away from us.
6. If the defensive back should jump the receiver, we release inside and execute the sideline route behind him.
7. Split enough so that you have room for the out break.

Curl

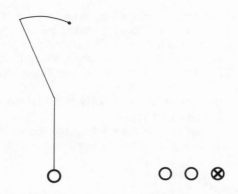

1. Explode off of the ball for an outside position.
2. Gather at 9-10 yards, plant the outside foot at 12 yards, snap the head inside and look for the ball.
3. If receiver does not see the ball as he looks he slides away from the man who can take the pass away.
4. Split should be maximum distance.

Post

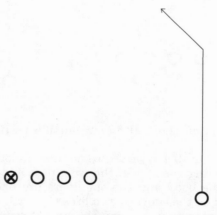

1. Probably the most difficult pass to execute as well as the most dangerous.
2. The post pattern is the most often called "automatic" by our QB's. When we find one-on-one coverage we will automatic to the inside post pattern at the line of scrimmage.
3. Exaggerated outside release is used to widen defensive man. At twelve yards we plant the outside foot and drive to the inside at an angle for the goal post.
4. Receiver must look immediately as he makes his break as we try to throw the ball quickly.

Streak

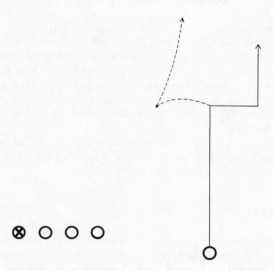

1. Explode off the line as if running the sideline pattern. Make an outside move to bring the defensive back up. Plant the outside foot and drive straight upfield.
2. Do not allow defensive back to knock the receiver off balance as upfield break is made.
3. Do not look immediately as the upfield break is made, but sprint for the TD and then look for the ball!
4. If defensive back jumps receiver, we release inside and streak past the defensive man. Receiver must now widen as he executes streak course.
5. Ball is thrown over inside shoulder, but should never pull the receiver inside.
6. QB is coached to throw the ball whenever the receiver is even with or slightly behind the defensive back.
7. Split is very important as the maximum split will not allow the secondary to rotate and still cover this pattern.

Quick patterns (90's)

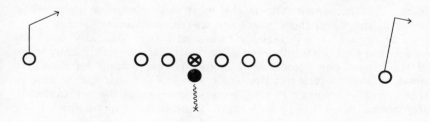

1. We use two quick routes—the quick out and the quick post.
2. Ball should be caught at 5 yard depth.
3. On the quick out we drive off the up foot and cross to the outside on the third step, cross over on the fourth step and catch the ball as we reach our fourth or fifth step.
4. Snap the head immediately as the third step is made!
5. The quick post is executed the same, but we now drive to the inside on the third step, and snap the head inside immediately.
6. We try to square the shoulders to the QB as we break inside to use our body to catch the ball and also give the QB a better target to throw to.

The quarterback

To successfully build a passing attack around a dropback quarterback, a thrower first must have a strong arm and quick feet. He must have the ability to dropback quickly, set with his feet closely together, plant his rear foot, and be able to throw the ball from hashmark to the far side line. He must be coached diligently and intelligently in the exchange, the grip, drop, set, throwing motion, and the exact spot at which he must throw. Questions that must be answered for the quarterback include: 1) The timing of the throw (either immediately on the break or more delayed when clearing a zone and beating the underneath defenders); 2) How to throw—either drilling the ball or throwing it soft; and 3) What to do in case he runs into trouble—throw to the lay off man, "eat" the ball or throw it away. Constant drill with proper techniques should result in the satisfactory development of the quarterback in these areas. *Constant* is the key word; none of these elements is mastered easily.

The quarterback must be thoroughly schooled and must understand who his top receiver is and which receiver runs the best patterns such as hooks and streaks. He must know which patterns have the best percentage of completions and whether the long or short passes are more dependable. He also must be so well acquainted with his receivers that he knows their speed so his throw will have the appropriate lead, and he has to know the exact moment that they will make their cuts. In relation to his runners, the quarterback must recognize who is the most dependable on delays and screens, and when those plays and the draw will be effective.

The area of a quarterback's responsibility naturally does not begin and end with offensive play. He must have full knowledge of the entire pass game as it is related to various defenses. He must be able to pick out the weak areas of defense and be able to throw to the receiver in that zone regardless of the original call. He accomplishes this by looking over the defense as he approaches the line of scrimmage; after analyzing the weak point, he must throw to the high percentage area. When a primary receiver is designated, the quarterback must know which defender can take away the pass or which one will be defending a particular area. In essence, the quarterback must be able to "read" the defense during his drop, so he can throw to the high percentage area.

Coaching points

When a coach evaluates a quarterback, it is imperative to determine the negative habits that must be corrected. These include the player who is a "pumper" — he winds up to throw; the quarterback who has poor use of his feet; no follow-through or failing to step in the direction of the throw. As we mentioned before, the quarterback must know when to throw hard, soft, high, or low. In this regard, he also must be able to lead the receiver and hit the receiving spot. This, of course, means throwing at the proper moment. A coach must be certain that the quarterback is using his protection to the fullest advantage. The best passer in the game is not effective if he does not drop correctly or if he fails to stay behind his blockers.

Quarterback evaluation

It is very obvious that probably the most important single player in your program is the quarterback. It is important, therefore, that every means is being utilized to effectively coach him and insure his continued improvement. We strongly suggest that the effective coach utilizes a procedure to allow every pass that a quarterback throws in practice to be charted. A manager should be assigned this duty and tally the results after each practice. On page 292 is a sample of our quarterback recording sheet and it has proved very effective for us. The obvious advantages are to evaluate the progress of your quarterback and pass offense as well as to gain valuable insight into the abilities of the top receivers.

Game plans

The offensive coaching staff and the quarterback comprise a team that mutually shares the responsibility of formulating our offensive game plan. It is the coaches' responsibility to thoroughly analyze and understand the upcoming opponent and to be able to communicate this knowledge to our quarterback. It then becomes the responsibility of the quarterback to understand the game plan and be ready to take the leadership role in the actual game situation. In our philosophy, we believe that this preparation gives the quarterback the necessary insight to make any necessary changes during the game by the use of our automatic system. As in all offenses, the quarterback shares the burden of success or failure depending upon the team's success. We make it very clear to our quarterback

PASS OFFENSE RECORDING SHEET				DATE	
Quarterback	Situation	Pattern	Result	Receiver	Special Note
1.	A. Sk. Sc. G.		C. Inc. Int. R. D.		
2.	A. Sk. Sc. G.		C. Inc. Int. R. D.		
3.	A. Sk. Sc. G.		C. Inc. Int. R. D.		
4.	A. Sk. Sc. G.		C. Inc. Int. R. D.		
5.	A. Sk. Sc. G.		C. Inc. Int. R. D.		
6.	A. Sk. Sc. G.		C. Inc. Int. R. D.		
7.	A. Sk. Sc. G.		C. Inc. Int. R. D.		
8.	A. Sk. Sc. G.		C. Inc. Int. R. D.		
9.	A. Sk. Sc. G.		C. Inc. Int. R. D.		
10.	A. Sk. Sc. G.		C. Inc. Int. R. D.		
11.	A. Sk. Sc. G.		C. Inc. Int. R. D.		
12.	A. Sk. Sc. G.		C. Inc. Int. R. D.		
13.	A. Sk. Sc. G.		C. Inc. Int. R. D.		
14.	A. Sk. Sc. G.		C. Inc. Int. R. D.		
15.	A. Sk. Sc. G.		C. Inc. Int. R. D.		
16.	A. Sk. Sc. G.		C. Inc. Int. R. D.		
17.	A. Sk. Sc. G.		C. Inc. Int. R. D.		
18.	A. Sk. Sc. G.		C. Inc. Int. R. D.		
19.	A. Sk. Sc. G.		C. Inc. Int. R. D.		
20.	A. Sk. Sc. G.		C. Inc. Int. R. D.		

QB's Name	PA/PC	PI/PD	QB's Name	PA/PC	PI/PD	Rec.	PC	PD	Rec.	PC	PD

that the most important task is to move the team and get the ball across the goal line.

Quarterback meetings

The head coach and the quarterbacks should go over every phase of the scouting report for the approaching game. The opponent's defensive weaknesses against rushing plays will be noted. The coach also will be able to outline the pass plays in his system which will be most likely to pay off against the opposition. He may put his finger on the other team's weakest pass defense man so the quarterback can send his best receiver against him in a clutch situation. This session will give the quarterback an opportunity to learn which defensive men to avoid and which linemen will spoil particular plays. The coach and his quarterback should note and discuss dangerous pass zones. Certain teams have smart pass defenders who are seldom caught off guard on passes in their zones. Others can be exploited. The scouting report must be shared with all of the team; it is of no significance unless it is shared with the player who can use it to its greatest advantage on the playing field — the quarterback. We have two or three quarterback meetings each week which include our entire offensive staff and Coach Ralston. The first one is generally on Tuesday and lasts for one-half hour. Its purpose is to present the quarterback with the defense we expect from the upcoming opponent. We try to get him to draw the defense himself and tell us what he feels the strengths and weaknesses are. We then try to emphasize for him exactly what their philosophy of down and distance football is, the defenses he can expect in different situations, and what he should be looking for as he approaches the line of scrimmage. On Wednesday we generally have another half-hour meeting where we talk about the plays we feel are the best to call on a particular situation and also expose him to the automatics we feel he should be using.

On Thursday we usually have another quarterback meeting during which we go over a mock game with the quarterback. Usually this is done with the film of the upcoming opponent. We generally call a play for him and then put on the film and have him evaluate whether or not it is a good play in that situation and if he should check off to an alternate method. We find that the use of the film, even if it is only for a very short time, has a tremendous effect on the quarterback as he evaluates what is happening on defense. If there is something that the defense is tipping off that would allow for a better percentage play, then we find that he becomes conditioned to make these decisions. We are always talking to the quarterback about the bad percentage play. We are convinced that our knowledge of down and distance offense and the utilization of what teams will do in obvious situations get the percentage on our side for successful plays. We are constantly in contact with the quarterback in this regard. On Friday we sometimes meet with the quarterback, although we generally feel that the job is done by this time. On Saturday Coach Ralston generally sits with the quarterback a few minutes after the pre-game meal to review any last minute details. Then Coach White will generally review our sideline signal system.

The use of game plans and quarterback ready sheets are important in preparation. We have indicated earlier that, when possible, we feel we are in a better position to call a good share of our offensive plays. We think our knowledge of the opponents we are going to play gives the coaches a better insight into exactly what actual plays should be called in specific situations. Most of these decisions are made during the week. We spend a good deal of time and preparation as an offensive coaching staff in determining exactly which plays should be used at which times during the particular game. We have used a lot of forms of ready sheets and offensive game plans. The following are what we have boiled it down to: We do feel that the automatic system is probably the biggest thing that previously was foreign to the basis of our teaching. Because we do make most of the offensive calls, we now feel that the well-informed, well-coached quarterback can make the intelligent automatic calls; therefore, we spend most of the time with the quarterbacks in our quarterback meetings teaching the automatics. We point out what to look for in a particular defense that would make one play better than another or make one play the type we must eliminate all together.

Our offensive game plan format appears on pages 295–97. We break down our running into the following areas with the plays in parentheses designated as secondary plays. We also break down our pass offense under the various throwing actions and indicate any special patterns for the particular game. Don't forget: Half the time the quarterback is on the sideline. Don't waste this time. Use it to formulate an intelligent evaluation within your original game plan while he is on the bench.

We also list our offensive plays by formation and provide for the player drawings of the opponent's defensive alignments and coverages.

On page 298 is the coaches' field ready chart. After the game plan has been formulated, the coach or coaches on the field or in the press box draw the form to assist them in calling our offense in the appropriate down and distance situations. The chart is divided into normal downs, long downs, short downs, goal line and short yardage situations, and two-minute offense. The defenses that a team has used also are indicated under the appropriate down and distance for easy reference. The plays then are categorized in both running and pass offense with comments where applicable.

OFFENSIVE GAME PLAN FORMAT

PRIMARY RUN OFFENSE:

OUTSIDE	OFF. TACKLE	INSIDE	SPECIALS
41 Sweep	37	15 Draw	51 Option Reverse
21 Sweep	43 Trap	45 Draw	Keep
(51 Option)	(47)	34 Ctr.	41 Sweep Pass
(59 Option)	(13)	45 Counter	
		(44 T. T.)	
		(16 Trap)	

PRIMARY PASS OFFENSE:

60	70	PURPLE	DELAY	90
	74 (In)	60 Switch	72 Split End	92
	74 (TE Choice)	74	70 Flanker	93
	78	74 (HB Choice)		94
	75	76 (FB Flat & Up)		95
	76 (TE Flat)	Bruin Special		

P. 37	41 BOOT	51 ROLL	FB SCREEN STRONG
			HB SCREEN SHORT
#5, #9	#3, #9	#2	41 SWEEP PASS
#4, #2 Delay		#4	
#6		#8	

GOAL LINE & SHORT YARDAGE:

RUNS: 37	Sneak (4 or 6)	51 ROLL
59 Option		
34 Ctr.		#2, #4, #6
22 Jump		#8 (S. Y.)
21 Sweep		
		P. 37
		8 Delay #9
		#5

Formations: Green, Purple, Blue, Red, Tight

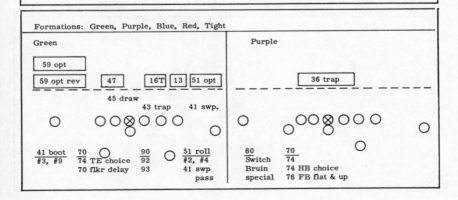

295

Blue

| 15 draw | 36 trap |

21 swp

○　　○○⊗○○○

　　　　　　　　　○

HB screen
short　　　○　74
　　　　　　○

Red

| 44 T. T. |

15 draw

　　　37　45 ctr　34 ctr

○　　○○⊗○○○

　　　　　○

　　　　　　　　　　　　FB screen
　　　　　　　　　　　　strong　　○

P 37　　　○　○　70
#6, #4　　　　　　72　SE delay
2 delay　　　　　　78, 75
#5, #9　　　　　　76　TE flat

Tight (goal line and short yardage)

Sneak (4 or 6)

59 opt　　37　　34 ctr　　22 J.　　21 swp

　　○　○　○⊗○　○　○

　　　　　　　○

　　　　　　　　　　　　　　○

P 37　　　○　　　○　　51 roll
8 delay　　　　　　　　　#2, #4, #6
#5, #9　　　　　　　　　#8 (short ydg)

UCLA Defenses and Pass Coverages

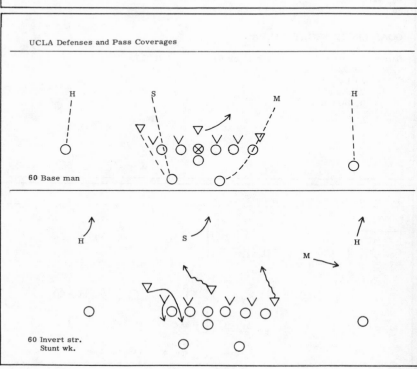

60 Base man

60 Invert str.
Stunt wk.

296

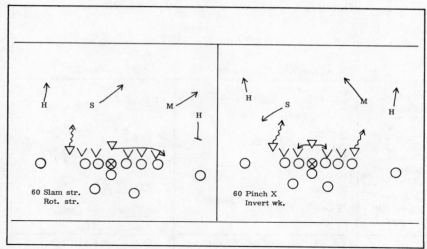

60 Slam str.
Rot. str.

60 Pinch X
Invert wk.

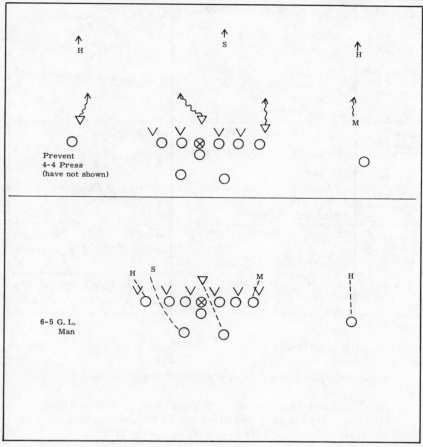

Prevent
4-4 Press
(have not shown)

6-5 G. L.
Man

FIELD READY CHART

	RUNNING OFFENSE	PASS OFFENSE
NORMAL DOWNS 1-10 2-5-8 3-4 60 BASE ZONE 60 3 DEEP MAN Outside U. me 60 3 DEEP MAN Inside 60 FREE MAN 45 MAN	Purple 34 CTR 37 Possible 51 OPT 59 OPT #45 CTR - 49 TOSS - (16 TRAP) {41 SWP {43 TRAP 15 Draw (Set-up S.S. Screen) 45 Draw -	59 SPRINT — #3 (QUICK) #7 P 37 *#5 (Check #2 Delay) *#4 41 BOOT — #3 (Set-up #9) Check F.B & T.E. 70 — 74 (In) *78 72-73 * HB QUICK SCREEN SHORT. * 51 OPT REV PASS
LONG DOWNS 1-10+ 2-8+ 3-4+ 60 BASE ZONE 60 FREE MAN 45 MAN	Call 55 IF A LOT OF 45 MAN- Purple 36 TRAP - 34 CTR. #45 CTR - 16 TRAP - A LOT OF 45 MAN - 51-59 OPT A LOT OF PASS - 41 SWP LB'er MAN - 43 TRAP	60 — SWITCH DELAY - 70 - FLANKER 71 - T.E. 70 - #74 (IN) 72-73 * HB QUICK SCREEN SHORT
SHORT DOWNS 1-10 - 2-4- 3-2-1 6-2 TIGHT 60 3 DEEP MAN (-me 60 " Inside 60 BASE ZONE	37 34 CTR. 22 JUMP SNEAK (4 or 6) 21 SWEEP 59 OPTION * check TOSS - w/ KADZIEL	KADZIEL - 41 BOOT #3 51 ROLL - #6 #4 #2 #8 (S.Y.) R 37 8 DELAY #5
GOAL LINE & (SGL) SHORT YARDAGE	41 FULL SNEAK 4 OR 6 37 23 JUMP	51 ROLL #4 #6 P 37 #5 #8 DELAY
2 MINUTE 60 BASE ZONE	16 TRAP 51 OPTION 34 CTR	74 (IN), QUICK SCREEN, DELAY 59 SPRINT - 36 TRAP, 60

Post game analysis

We can't emphasize enough the importance of post game analysis:

    a. You have to come out of a game learning something.

    b. You need a rule with which to measure your own performance. How? Have a post game chart.

c. Fill out a blank situation chart with what you actually did; then compare it with the original.

d. Ask yourself why, then answer!

Calling your plays

Our play calling procedure has already been outlined. Whether you call the plays yourself or school the quarterback to call them, don't lose sight of the component parts of the tactical situation, which are all interrelated. In order of importance, they are:

1. Score
   a. Generally, play conservatively when ahead.
   b. Take some chances when behind. They should be related to time left in the ball game, field position, and how much scoring is needed.
   c. Don't take unnecessary chances when the score is tied. A tie is better than a loss. If you are six points ahead, another score is needed. If you are eight points ahead, let your opponents make the mistakes. Remember, the *value* of a field goal! (They will almost always be called from the bench.)
   d. *Do not* wait until the time situation is desperate before opening up your attack when behind.

2. Time
   a. Always know the quarter and the time remaining. Don't take unnecessary chances right before the half. *The game doesn't have to be won at halftime.*
   b. Get maximum use of time with clock running out.
   c. How To Stop The Clock
      (1) Score a touchdown.
      (2) Get ball out of bounds.
      (3) Call a timeout.
      (4) Incomplete pass.
      (5) Be aware of timeouts remaining.

Remind your backs to get out of bounds. All passes should be complete or incomplete. Eating the ball will use up the clock.
ABOVE ALL: *Don't throw the interception!* Don't get panicky and try to win the game with a desperate play. The plays that have been successful during the game will continue to do well for you.

   d. How To Consume Time
      (1) Use almost all of your twenty-five seconds in calling the play.
      (2) Stay with ground game—remind backs to unpile slowly.
      (3) Do not run out of bounds or pass.
   (See section on two-minute offense.)

3. Weather
   a. Use kicking game to advantage with strong wind. With the wind, as a quarter nears the end, punt before changing goals, even if it might mean kicking on second or third down. A kick with the wind might be worth 10 or 20 yards, or more. If the wind is against you, late in the quarter, it is possible to hang on until the end of the quarter and kick with the wind.
4. Personnel
   a. Know the capabilities of your teammates. Short yardage men – outside runners – good pass receivers – best blockers. You must also be cognizant of the defensive personnel that is weak or injured and direct your attack accordingly. Don't run incoming substitutes immediately. Allow them to become accustomed to the "heat of battle" before allowing them to carry the ball. *Be sure* to check these substitutes to find out whether they are bringing any specific information into the ball game.
5. Field Position and Down and Distance

You and your teammates have invested a lot of work, time and sweat into your preparation for those ten two-hour contests on Saturday afternoon. One of the ways to avoid disaster during these games is to never miss an "Obvious Call." The "Obvious Call" would be the one in which you have no alternative percentage wise. These calls will comprise more than fifty percent of your decisions in a ball game. Among the many variables present in a game, the decision of whether to run, pass or kick will be constant. Your field position chart and your down and distance guides will help to alleviate your decisions somewhat. You must first become familiar with the three and four down areas in regard to the vertical field position of the ball. Our field position chart is on page 302.

   a. Your *critical zone* is from your own goal line to your own five yard line. *You must move the ball out of this area!* Your first consideration would be to punt. You will need to move the ball out to the three yard line in order to punt. If there are seconds remaining in the quarter, and you would gain a distinct wind advantage by the quarter change, it would be wise to run out the clock provided you would still have two downs to punt.
   b. Your *danger zone* is from your own five yard line to your own twenty yard line. Your first consideration here would be to move into the next zone. Run plays with maximum security and little ball handling. Again your only concern is to make a first down to get another chance to move into the next zone. You may use your quick kick on second or third down to take advantage of the surprise element and

to gain better field position. If your down requirement on third down is five or more yards, *Punt.*

c. *Your First Down Zone* is from your own twenty yard line to your own forty yard line. In this area you are attempting to get a first down so that you may move the ball out into the next zone to have better punting position. You should be grinding it out with your basic ground gainers whose complements you may use in the next zone.

d. Your *Free Wheeling Zone* would be from your own forty-yard line to your opponent's forty yard line. In this area you will have your entire attack at your disposal, and you should capitalize on the complements of the plays set up in the previous zone. You are in a three down area, and your field position is an excellent one to force your opponents by a punt to operate in their own territory. Your general guide to run or pass would be your down requirement (this would be the average number of yards needed per play to gain a first down). If in this area your down requirement is *less* than four yards, use a running play. If it is four yards, use what has been your strongest and most consistent gainer (run or pass) or some type of option or roll out pass. If your down requirement is *more* than four yards, this will indicate a pass situation. Occasionally, a pass on first down is a good call. Another good time to use a pass on first down would be immediately following a break such as an intercepted pass, recovered fumble, blocked punt, etc. Anytime that you need *two yards or less* per play on *first* or *second* down, consider this a waste down. This situation is excellent for long gainers, drop back passes, and your counter or complementary plays that help keep your basic ground gainers strong. *Remember* that the best time to run your screen or draw is in the obvious passing situation. If your rush has been internally, use a draw. If it has been from the outside, run a screen.

e. Your four down area or your *MUST ZONE* begins from your opponents thirty-five yard line to the ten-yard line. Up to this point, you have been attempting to gain better field position. You must now think in terms of controlling the ball! Your basic down requirement is 2.5 yards and you must *punch* it out. *You must not* give up the ball in this area. This opportunity to penetrate your opponent's vital zone will arise only 2 or 3 times a ball game. This situation must be exploited by *SCORING!*

f. Winner's zone. It is the ten-yard line to the goal line. We *must* score anyway possible when we advance to this zone. This is an area to utilize your best percentage plays as well as be ready to attack a team's goal line defense. Re-

FIELD POSITION CHART

Goal line

Winner's zone
1. Must score touchdown
2. Run or pass
3. Attack goal line defenses

10-yard line

Must zone
(four down area)
1. Keep off balance (run or pass)
2. Toughest area--must control ball--must score
3. 2.5 yards basic requirement
4. Possible field goal

35-yard line

Free Wheeling zone
(3 down area)
1. Keep off balance (run/pass)
2. Entire offense available
3. 3.5 yards basic down requirement
—50 4. Use plays set up in last zone   50 —
5. Punting Zone

40-yard line

First Down zone
(3 down area)
1. Keep off balance (run/pass)
2. Get first down
3. 3.5 yards basic requirement
4. Get better punting position

20-yard line

Danger zone
1. Keep off balance (run/pass)
2. Plays with maximum security - little ball handling
3. Quick kick   Determined by over-all philosophy
4. Early down punt

5-yard line

Critical zone
1. Punt
2. Move ball to 3 yard line to use spread punt
3. Maximum security

Goal line

member what got you here, and don't try to get fancy. Remind the team of the effort it will take to score, and do not commit an offside. *A penalty in this area could prevent a score.* Don't forget the value of a field goal, if you are losing by three points or less. If the score is such that a field goal will win or put you ahead, don't give your kicker a poor angle on your third down play. An interception would mean disaster! Your basic down requirement is 2.5 yards. *SCORE THE SUREST WAY*!!

The quarterback

Some of the elements of successful quarterbacking are:

Leadership

1. You lead by doing.
2. The quarterbacks are as important to a football team as the pitcher is to a baseball team.
3. A quarterback can't be a leader unless he does his job.
4. The great doer is the great leader.
5. Actions speak louder than words.
6. Believe in yourself.
7. Be willing to listen to the suggestions of others.

Goals of a quarterback

1. As the quarterback, you are responsible for moving the team across the goal line.
2. You get an average of thirteen attempts to score, and we feel we have to score 4 times. This is the most important statistic in evaluating a quarterback. If he can take the team across the goal line or produce some sort of score one third of the time, he is doing his job.

How to be a successful quarterback

1. Work hard!
2. Know and accept responsibility.
    a. A quarterback must think like a computer — you only get out of your mind what you put into it.
    b. You have to reduce mistakes and enhance luck.
        a. Luck can be enhanced by concentration.
    c. Everyone gets an opportunity to do something big — only those that put a lot into it can take advantage

of the opportunity when the situation presents itself. You have to be prepared.
3. Once you get the job done, you don't care who gets the credit!

Types of quarterbacks

1. There are winners and there are losers.
2. You can't define what makes a winner or a loser, but you have to be conscious that they do exist.
3. Your reaction to losing can tell if you are a winner or a loser.
4. You can lose and still be a winner as long as your reaction is correct.
5. Consistency is the key.
6. Football is the greatest form of competition.
   a. The object is winning.
   b. You have to have desire. Want to win.
   c. You must have the determination to win.
   d. Hard work is the catalyst for desire and determination that results in winning.
7. Be realistic in setting your personal goals.
8. You don't quit physically until you quit mentally.
9. The essence of good quarterbacking is not letting your mental processes allow you to quit!

Know defenses

1. Every defense has a weakness.
   a. Why? Because the offense knows what is going to happen and can concentrate on that.
   b. The defense has to be prepared for anything!
   c. Your job as a quarterback is to know where the weaknesses are!
2. No defense can stop your offense if you execute.
   a. Counter plays are important to your offense.
   b. The importance of a counter is knowing when to use one.
3. Worry the defense enough about one thing, enough that you create a defensive weakness.
   a. Force the defense to over-compensate to defend what you are known for.
4. Plot your game.
   a. Don't be an impulsive gambler!
   b. Think out every situation before hand.
5. Keep it simple.

6. Learn your personnel.
   a. Know their strengths and weaknesses.
   b. Understand what is being asked of them in their respective positions.

Attacking, stunting, jumping or tough linebacker defenses

1. Go on short count (catch them off-balance).
2. Go on long count (force them to set in their last defense).
3. Run your outside game.
4. Use of multiple formations that will help stabilize the defense.

15

Defense

The defense has four missions:
1. Prevent the score
2. Get the ball
3. Gain vertical field advantage
4. Score

To carry out these four missions, Stanford has exhibited considerable flexibility in its defensive thinking. Our considerations revolve around the knowledge that we have gained regarding all types of defenses and some of the recent trends in football. Coaches in most conferences must utilize both up-to-date knowledge and new trends to succeed against the outstanding opponents that are faced both in league and in intersectional games. With the increasing use of the pass, along with the fact the clock is stopped so many more times now, a great deal of burden is placed on defenses; as a consequence, we have had to make some revolutionary changes.

Notwithstanding the talents of great players such as Jim Plunkett, our philosophy is to win with defense. Previously, our emphasis on offense had a direct negative effect on our defense and our defensive attitude, and that probably was one of the reasons that it took us some time to achieve total success. However, as we examine our success during 1970 and during the Rose Bowl game, it is abundantly evident that the greatest contribution to our victories was our defensive program. We constantly came up with the big plays on defense, and although we won games by scores of 34-27 and 9-7, the defensive plays were responsible more for the wins than any other single factor.

Coaches who play under one-platoon rules or use athletes both ways should spend a great deal of practice time on defense; defensive success and/or emphasis may be very dependent on what is done offensively. The passing game does not dictate a tough, hard-nosed brand of defense because the ball is being thrown so much. We probably were not aware of this for the first couple of years while we were building our program at Stanford; we emphasized the pass primarily on offense, and therefore had to re-examine our thinking and make a definite change during the last couple of years. The most important accomplishment was in the establishment of a new defensive attitude. We emphasized the importance of our defense, and decided that although the passing game had forced us into a passing type of defense, we still would emphasize a different attitude among our defensive personnel by using various alignments and charges. We found that we were placing too much emphasis on pass coverage and pass rush and were not developing an aggressive enough total defensive attitude. With our change to utilize several alignments, we based our defensive principles on attacking the offense and penetrating the offensive line to force it into mistakes. We employ a variety of defensive alignments and charges so the opponent will not be able to zero in on any one defense. We also changed our teaching emphasis on defense by basing it on the ability to run and to pursue; although we still do not employ a lot of full-speed hitting, we emphasize that each defensive player should be in on every tackle on every play.

As we continually emphasize, we constantly try to determine the most efficient manner in which to fit our personnel into our defensive philosophy which is based on stopping the pass and its related actions. This does not mean, however, that we sacrifice our defense when we play a team with a strong running attack. We believe that in evaluating personnel, we can arrive at a system of stopping both the run and the pass. For example, if there are players with great attributes for stunting and exceptional movement, a more efficient system can be built around their talents.

Defense is a total team feeling from the head coach through the assistant coaches and to the individual players. Everyone must understand completely what is attempting to be accomplished in every different situation and the methods of taking advantage of what any one particular team attempts to do. After establishing this philosophy, it is important not to change from week to week. Emphasize and re-emphasize certain aspects of the total philosophy. Don't adjust or change something that is working for you.

Defensive physical preparedness parallels defensive attitude, and we believe that rather than talking about how aggressive we are going to be, it is better to emphasize total all-out pursuit and the responsibility of each player getting a hit on the ball on every play. Teaching and demanding full-speed reactions and pursuit are two necessary elements in pre-game preparedness, and we have satisfied ourselves that this can be accomplished without a great deal of total scrimmage. It is more important for us to have our players mentally ready for a particular game than it is to punish them physically during the week to the point they cannot perform efficiently on game day. A team's physical preparedness is related directly to the confidence and the mental preparedness of the individual players.

Elements of a successful defense

Eliminate mistakes

The burden of achieving perfection is on-the-field teaching. A coach must be certain that players are following his instructions to the letter. This, of course, requires individual technique teaching and reactions to offensive plays. A disciplined defense, where the responsibilities are very well defined, will make possible this perfection, particularly if coaches strive to eliminate mistakes as they occur.

Teaching goals and objectives

A coach must have defensive goals and objectives that involve the players in his defensive philosophy. He must communicate to the players realistically what will occur during a game. Do not set goals too high and give the players the illusion the goals are possible when the percentages are against any chance of succeeding. For example, a coach may instill thoughts in his players' minds that the team will not give up a first down, that there will be no passes completed, or that the opponent will not score. Players may strive for these goals, but they must be approached realistically only with the complete involvement of the team so it can take pride in whatever success is realized. We spend a lot of time with our defensive team discussing the specific areas in which improvement is needed. We also make an effort to involve them in our efforts in achieving these particular goals and find that they then will take the lead themselves. The intelligent coach also might examine the possibility of assigning different members of the defensive team to be responsible for success in some of these specific areas. A suggestion would be to utilize military ranks to add emphasis to certain important phases of defensive play—for instance, "captain," "general," "commander," or "major" for areas like pursuit, gang tackling, playing the ball, or pass rush. The following were our defensive objectives for the 1970 season:

Defensive objectives

Get the ball

1. Force 4 turnovers a game.
2. Give the ball to the offense 4 times a game inside the 40. *Remember*, if the opponent has no long T.D. runs, no long T.D. passes, can't score inside our 10, we have a shutout.

In 1969, the top defensive team in our conference was USC. They held their opponents to 97 yards rushing and 247 yards of total offense. They won the league. We must equal or better this.

The top team in scoring defense was UCLA, limiting opponents to 10.3 points a game (Arkansas gave up 7.6). They tied us for second place. We must equal or better this.

Look over these statistics carefully:

	1968	1969	1970
First Downs			
Rushing	83	77	
Passing	62	84	
Rushing			
Plays	481	421	
Gain	1843	1586	
Loss	247	484	
Net	1596	1102	
Touchdowns	18	12	
Avg. per Play	3.3	2.6	
Avg. per Game	159.6	110	
Passing			
Attempted	241	297	
Completed	98	145	
Percentage	.406	.488	
Yards Gained	1340	1832	
Had Intercepted	19	19	
Touchdowns	4	9	
Avg. per Game	134	183	
Total Offense			
Plays	722	718	
Net Gain	2936	2934	
Avg. per Play	4.1	4.1	
Avg. per Game	293.6	293	
Fumbles			
Number/Lost	36/18	25/19	
Interceptions			
Number	18	17	
Yards Returned	266	188	
Touchdowns	1	1	

Think tackling

It is vital that each player believes that he is going to make a tackle on every play. For this reason, we emphasize it in all of our drills and feel that it instills a very important attitude in each player. We teach a basic tackling technique of putting the head on the ball, and our players practice it every day.

Have a system of terminology and communication

It is essential on defense to have an efficient method of communicating with players to eliminate defensive mistakes. Our defensive personnel include the down four — the two guards and two tackles; the three linebackers — the middle linebacker (the mike man), the left and right linebackers, who will be designated Strike or Whip depending on the offensive set. Our secondary includes the right halfback, the left halfback, the strong safety or mover, and the free safety. We also number the line of scrimmage from the center out from left to right so we have ease in communicating specific areas of responsibility to our defense.

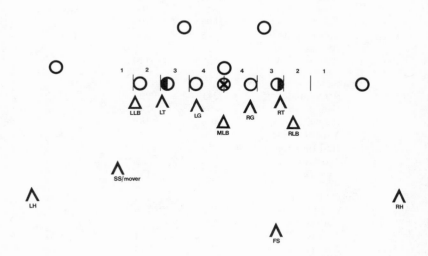

The guard gaps on either side of the center comprise the four areas; the tackle gaps are the three areas; the tight end gaps are the two areas; and the areas outside the tight ends are the ones on both sides of the center.

Following is our Defensive Terminology Sheet:

Defensive terminology

Flanker:	An offensive halfback set out to the left or right. If set inside a spread end, it is called slot back.
Tight End:	One who is split no more than four yards from his tackle.
Split End:	One who is split five or more yards from his tackle.
Fullback:	Remaining back who is behind center or on the tight end side.
Near Back:	The remaining back on your side of center. Could be HB or FB.
Onside:	The side which the play was run.
Off-Side:	The side away from which the play was run.
Strongside:	The side of the line toward the flanker (or slot).
Weakside:	The side away from the flanker.
Bootleg:	The QB fakes to backs in one direction and he goes the other, which ends up in either run or pass.
Roll Out:	The QB runs with the flow of the backs and runs or passes.
Waggle:	The QB fakes a run into the line on one side and runs to the other to pass.
Reverse:	An offensive play that starts out in one direction and develops to the opposite side of the line, either by exchange of the ball or the same ball carrier changing his direction.
Even Defense:	Defense without a man in front of the center.
Odd Defense:	Defense with a man lined up in front of the center.
Key:	A move by an offensive man that determines the move or reaction of a defensive man.
Chucking:	Holding up or changing the course of a receiver.
Blitz:	Penetration of the linebackers in the snap, with coordination of the Down 4.
Rotation:	Movement of the deep secondary and backers, either before the snap, after the snap, or on key to one side.
Invert:	Same as rotation except the safety to rotation takes the underneath route.
Press:	The position of a linebacker or HB head up on a receiver on or near the line of scrimmage.
Screen Pass:	A delayed forward pass behind the line of scrimmage with the receiver led by one or more linemen.
Oscar:	Alert to change total defense.
Belt:	Head up—deliver blow on tight end. Good shoulder bump. No hurry to leave: cut back. Back field pattern can't stay hooked. Cutback, pitch, contain rollout.

Check-Flare:	A remaining back who blocks, forward pass protection block, then slides off and catches a short forward pass.
Draw:	A delayed type of play where QB drops back as a pass and hands off to a remaining back who has faked a pass protection block.
Running Play Pass:	A forward pass that develps from a running play fake.
Contain:	To keep the ball inside or moving laterally.
Absolute Contain:	Stop the ball from moving laterally.
"Ball":	Team call indicating ball has been released on forward pass, lateral, or fumble.
"Fire":	A call indicating an interception or position for interception.
Flow:	Lateral direction of the ball.
Motion:	Lateral movement by an offensive back before the snap of the ball.
Key Stunt:	A stunt executed on key.
"In":	Call to indicate a receiver route.
"Out":	Call to indicate a receiver route.
Fight Pressure:	React back through a block.
Flatten (Flat):	A movement parallel to the line of scrimmage in pursuit.
Play Football:	Instinctive reaction after execution of defensive assignment.
Bench:	From hash mark to short side.
Field:	From hash mark to wide side.
"Crack":	A call to indicate a wide, split man blocking in on a defensive man.
"Cross":	A call to indicate a receiver's route.
Coverage:	Assigned areas or men for pass defense.
Gap:	Area between two offensive players.
Inside Out:	Pursuit from inside the ball to the sideline.
Pursuit:	The proper angle at which the defensive player can get to the ball carrier the fastest.
Relative Hook:	Hook zones in relation to the ball.
Seam:	Space between two pass zones or defensive players.
Stem:	Shifting or resetting the offensive backs before the snap of the ball.
Stunt:	A change in the base defense to gain additional pass rush or to confuse blocking assignments.
Square:	Position with shoulders parallel to the goal line.

Swing Pattern:	A receiver moving laterally in front of your position.
Space:	Man coverage. Cutback man. Pitch man on option.
Quick:	Stunt. Cheat outside. Then becomes box technique. Outside pass rush. QB.
Dog 65:	Even – 3 hole if w. Even line up 3 go 3.
Box:	Back foot away. Box only is flat. No cutback. Contain. Penetrate. Force pitch on option! Pass. 3 back hook.

Teach formation recognition

The entire team should have full knowledge of different formations and formation strengths. We base much of our defensive alignments and reactions on formation strength, and we believe it is extremely important for the entire team to understand exactly what a particular formation alignment consists of and the particular strength of the formation. The accompanying chart illustrates the manner in which we view the opponent's formations and exactly how we categorize them with our terminology.

1. T – 3 backs in tight backfield

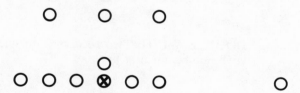

2. RED: Balanced formation – flanker on opposite side of HB

3. BROWN: Flanker on same side as HB — Unbalanced strong

4. GREEN: Fullback in HB position — No back in normal fullback position

5. BLUE: Two remaining backs are in straight line behind C & QB

6. DOUBLE WING: Two receivers on each side of center, with one remaining back

7. TRIPLE: 3 receivers on one side

8. SPREAD FORMATION: QB deep and backs on each side (Shot gun)

9. TAN: Combination of Brown and Blue (3 backs)

10. PINK: Combination of Red and Blue (3 backs)

11. STRONG SLOT: Slot inside of tight end

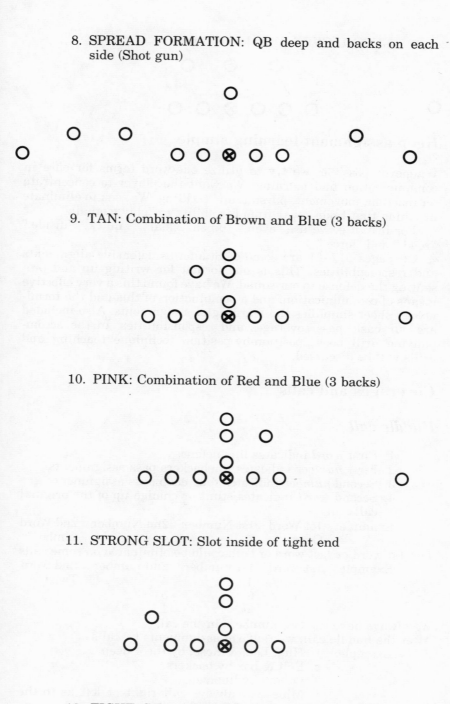

12. TIGHT: Split end is tighter than 4 yards

13. END OVER: Unbalanced line

Keep assignment learning simple

Whenever possible, we try to utilize one-word terms for ease in communication and learning. We want the player to concentrate on reaction, movement, pursuit, and tackling. We seek to eliminate anything that takes away from his ability to "play football."

For instance, we use "even," "pinch," "slam," "quick," "inside," "read," and "force."

On pages 317–21 are some of Stanford's defensive alignments and responsibilities. This is our format for writing up and presenting the defense to our squad. We have found this a very effective means of communication, and a combination of this and the terminology sheet simplifies the learning of assignments. Also included are our basic pass coverages and responsibilities. In the accompanying drill book, position-by-position technique teaching and drills will be discussed.

Coverages and calls

Huddle call

1. First *word* indicates line defense
2. First *number* indicates linebackers pass assignments
3. Second *number* indicates four deep pass assignments
4. Second *word* indicates stunt or change up of the original call

Example:	1st Word	1st Number	2nd Number	2nd Word
	Over	3	4	Limbo

The 1st word or last word or both could be eliminated on some calls

Example:	1st word	1st number	2nd number	2nd word
		4	4	Twist
	Over	6	5	
		3	1	

We always have the two numbers in the call
After the huddle call, we reaffirm assignments by calls

Example:
1. Hug, Lou, & Rose, by the 4 deep
2. Belt & box by backers
3. Others by linemen
4. Mike will always call right or left as to the strength of their formation

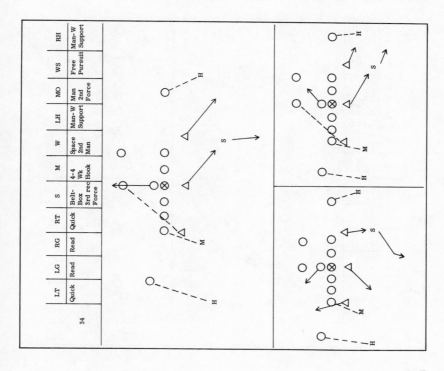

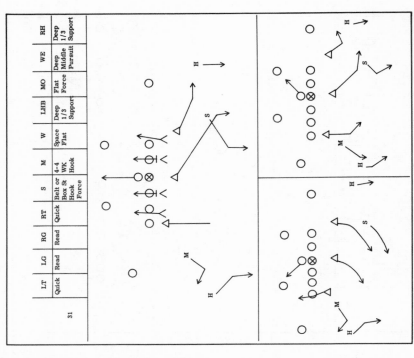

LT	LG	RG	RT	S	M	W	LHB	MO	WE	RH
Quick	Read	Read	Quick	Belt or Box St Hook Force	4-4 WK Hook	Space Flat	Deep 1/3 Support	Flat Force	Deep Middle Pursuit	Deep 1/3 Support

31

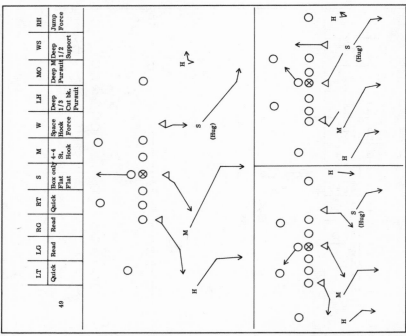

LT	LG	RG	RT	S	M	W	LH	MO	WS	RH
Quick	Read	Read	Quick	Box only Flat Flat	4-4 St. Hook	Space Hook Force	Deep 1/3 Cut bk. Pursuit	Deep M Pursuit	Deep 1/2 Support	Jump Force

49

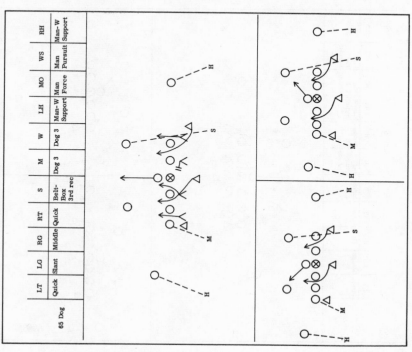

41

LT	LG	RG	RT	S	M	W	SH B	MO	J	WHB
Quick	Read	Read	Quick	Belt Only St curl Force	4-4 St hook	Space 2nd Rec	Deep 1/3 Support	Flat Force	Deep Middle Pursuit Support	Deep 1/3 Support

65 Dog

LT	LG	RG	RT	S	M	W	LH	MO	WS	RH
Quick	Slant	Middle	Quick	Belt- Box 3rd rec	Dog 3	Dog 3	Man-W Support	Man Force	Man Pursuit	Man-W Support

65 Pinch

LT	LG	RG	RT	S	M	W	LH	MO	WS	RH
Inside	Slant	Middle	Inside	Quick	2-2-QB 3rd rec	Quick	Man-W Support	Man 2nd Cutback Pursuit	Man 2nd Pursuit	Man-W Support

65 Slam

LT	LG	RG	RT	S	M	W	LH	MO	WS	RH
Inside	Middle	Go	Inside	Inside QB	1-1 Pitch 3rd rec	Inside QB	Man-W Support	Man 2nd Force	Man 2nd Pursuit	Man Support

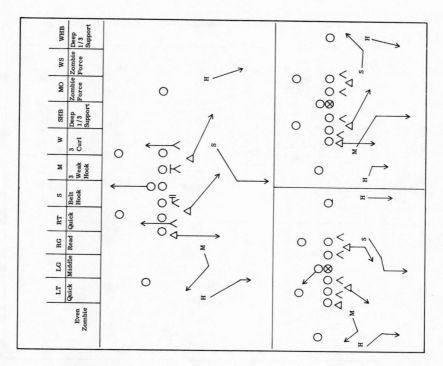

Also, we will be able to change the coverage or parts of it by calls after we see their set

    Example: Change from 44 in huddle to 34 after seeing a *Red* set

Coverages: Linebackers will have six coverages
1. 44 – Backers are coming strong
2. 34 – Backers are coming weak
3. 65 – Two backers are stunting and one covering man
4. 49 – Four means backers are strong, like 44, except 9 indicates zone coverage for the four deep and the backers are playing *zone*
5. 31 – Three means backers are weak, like 34, except 1 indicates zone coverage for the four deep and the backers are playing *zone*
6. 41 – Four means backers are strong, and 1 indicates zone, but to the strong side also and we end up in strong coverage with backers and strong coverage in the 4 deep

4 Deep Have Five Coverages:
1. 5 – means man to man with four deep and one backer (5)
2. 4 – free safety man
3. 34 – free safety man – backers weak
4. 1 – zone strong
5. 9 – zone weak

Sample formats for defensive assignment learning (linebackers and 4 deep):

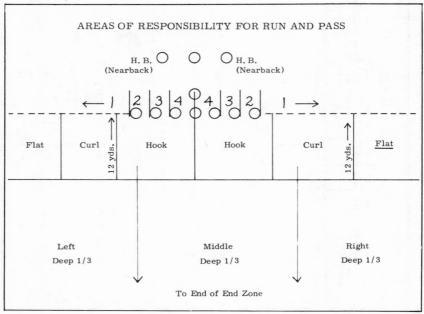

AREAS OF RESPONSIBILITY FOR RUN AND PASS

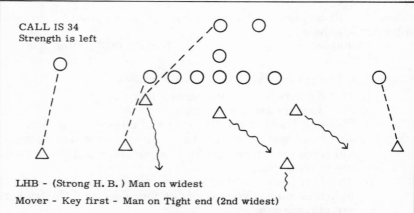

LHB - (Strong H. B.) Man on widest

Mover - Key first - Man on Tight end (2nd widest)

Safety - Free - Key H. B. - Same as 44 except know that backers are coming weak

RHB - (Weak H. B.) Man on widest

Strong L. B. - Man on F. B. - Force T. E. to outside and take strong hook if F. B. blocks

Weak L. B. - Man on out break of H. B. - If blocks or breaks inside go to hole

Mike - Go weak - pick up H. B. on flare, or weak hook if no H. B.

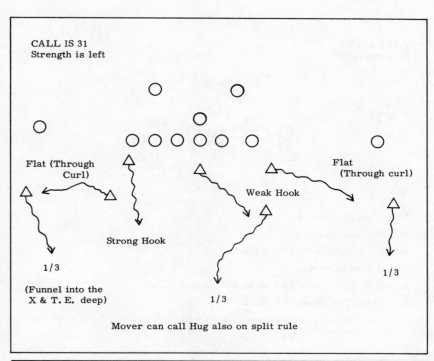

CALL IS 31
Strength is left

Flat (Through Curl)

Flat (Through curl)

Weak Hook

Strong Hook

1/3

1/3

(Funnel into the X & T. E. deep)

1/3

Mover can call Hug also on split rule

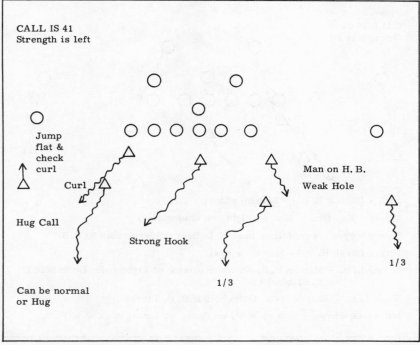

CALL IS 41
Strength is left

Jump flat & check curl

Curl

Man on H. B.

Weak Hole

Hug Call

Strong Hook

1/3

Can be normal or Hug

1/3

CALL IS 65
Strength is left

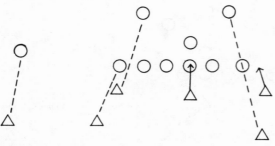

LHB - Man on widest

Mover - Man on 2nd Man (T. E.)

Safety - Man on H. B. (2nd widest)

RHB - Man on widest

Strong L. B. - Drawn as Man on 3rd (F. B.)

Remaining Two Backers - Blitz

    (Could be any combination of stunts with Two backers & man with the
other backer on F. B.)

CALL IS 44
Strength is left

LHB - (Strong H. B.) - Man on widest

Mover - Key first - Man on Tight end (2nd widest)

Safety - Free - key H. B. - protect L. B. er on deep route by H.B.

RHB - (Weak H. B.) - Man on widest

Strong L. B. - Man on F. B. on route outside of Tight end - Go to hole if
        F. B. blocks

Weak L. B. - Man on H. B. Go to hole if H. B. blocks

Mike - Go strong - pick up F. B. on flare, or strong hook if no F. B.

DEFENSE - 44

POSITION	ALIGNMENT	RUN RESPONSIBILITY	PASS RESPONSIBILITY'
STRONG H. B.	2 yds. Outside x 7 - 9 yds. Inside foot back Use split rule	Normal - Support Force - if Mover is cracked (Man must block)	Man on widest
MOVER	2 yds. x 8 yds. Outside T. E. or slot Inside foot back	Normal - Force "Box" call - Cutback Key G your side Option - stall & take Q. B.	Man on T. E. Blocks - your free Key H. B. - comes across & pass shows, use slide coverage
SAFETY	10 yds. deep Varies on H. B.	H. B. straight up on run - hit it H. B. weak - call clear to W. H. B. Pursuit	Key H. B. Free - be conscious of Whip on H. B. route H. B. across & pass shows, use slide coverage
WEAK H. B.	2 yds. x 7 - 9 yds. on outside Inside foot back Use split rule	Force if man cracks Force if safety calls clear Pursuit	Man on widest

COMMENTS:

325

DEFENSE - 65

POSITION	ALIGNMENT	RUN RESPONSIBILITY	PASS RESPONSIBILITY
STRONG H. B.	2 yds. outside x 7 - 9 yds. Inside foot back Use inside position if possible	Normal - Support Force if man blocks	Man on widest Try to take inside & make the Q. B. throw the tougher pass, the out
MOVER	1 yd. x 8 yds. Outside T. E. or slot Inside foot back	Normal - Force Option - stall & take Q. B.	Man on T. E. Blocks - your free
SAFETY	10 yds. deep - Varies on H. B.	Pursuit	Man on 2nd widest on weakside
WEAK H. B.	2 yds. outside x 7 - 9 yds. Inside foot back Use inside position if possible	Force if man cracks - Pursuit	Man on widest

COMMENTS:

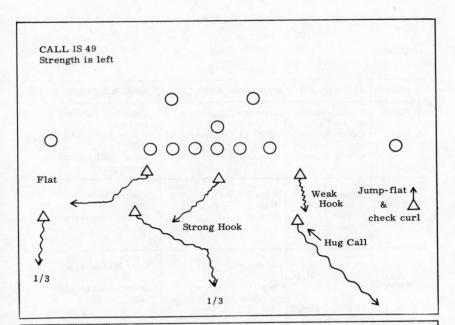

CALL IS 49
Strength is left

Flat

Weak Hook

Jump-flat
&
check curl

Strong Hook

Hug Call

1/3

1/3

DEFENSE - 49

POSITION	ALIGNMENT	RUN RESPONSIBILITY	PASS RESPONSIBILITY
STRONG H. B.	2 yds. outside x 7 - 9 yds. Inside foot back Use split rule	Support - Pursuit -	Deep 1/3 Funnel two deep receivers
MOVER	2 yds x 8 yds. Outside T. E. or slot Inside foot back	Cutback (Box call) Q. B. - Pursuit	Deep middle -
SAFETY	10 yds deep - outside of H. B. Must be able to get to deep out- side.	Pursuit	Deep 1/3 Don't over-run post
WEAK H. B.	2 yds outside x 7 - 9 yds. Inside foot back Try to stay outside	Force Jump	Jump - Flat - Curl & play ball

327

DEFENSE - 31

POSITION	ALIGNMENT	RUN RESPONSIBILITY	PASS RESPONSIBILITY
STRONG H. B.	2 yds. outside x 7 to 9 yds. Inside foot back Use split rule	Normal - Support "Hug" call - Force	Deep 1/3 - Funnel between 2 deep receivers - play ball "Hug" call - Jump techniques
MOVER	2 yds. x 8 yds. Outside T. E. or Slot Inside foot back	Normal - Force "Hug" call - Support Pursuit	Flat - Check Curl "Hug" call - deep 1/3, Funnel receivers
SAFETY	10 yds. deep outside of H. B. Position varies with Set and Field	Pursuit - Clear W. H. B. on run weak	Deep Middle 1/3 Deepest man - play ball
WEAK H. B.	2 yds. Outside x 7 - 9 yds. Inside foot back Use split rule	Pursuit Can get clear call from safety	Deep 1/3 Be aware of 2nd man that can get deep

COMMENTS:

Use varied alignments

Offenses are extremely strong in today's football, and we do not believe we could ever stay with one defense and accomplish our defensive goals. For this reason, we coach several different alignments to confuse or cause a mistake in the opponent's blocking schemes. We think that a defense such as the professional four-three is very adjustable and allows us to accomplish this mission. We use a man on the center if we feel the opposing center is vulnerable to a good strong middle guard. We slide our defense strong and/ or weak; we stack our linebackers if we feel this would give an advantage. We also use an eagle position over the tight end if we feel he is a strong enough pass catcher or if he is not a very powerful run-blocker. Stanford's basic alignments and overall strengths:

BASE
1. COVERAGE
2. RUSH
3. RUN

ODD
1. RUN
2. RUSH
3. COVERAGE

EVEN
1. RUSH
2. RUN
3. COVERAGE

Use different coverages

There are so many well-conceived offenses and an abundance of excellent offensive personnel that we must employ different coverages in our defense to prevent the offense from concentrating on any one in particular. An example of three coverages from the same base alignment.

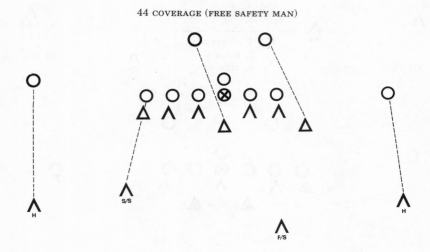

44 COVERAGE (FREE SAFETY MAN)

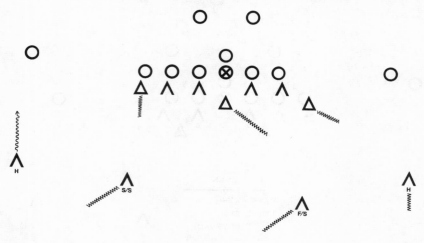

31 COVERAGE (ZONE—ROTATION STRONG—LB'S CAN GO STRONG OR WEAK)

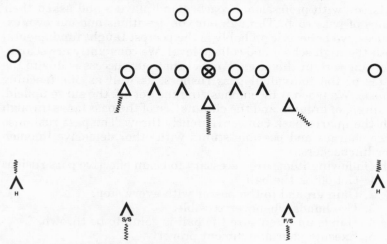

Establish a pass-rush ratio

Defense must have a basic philosophy of defending the forward pass, with a certain number of persons normally rushing the passer and a certain number covering. We have a normal four-seven pass-rush ratio, and if we decide to rush with more or fewer, a total adjustment in our defense is made for that particular play. We examine carefully the type of offense that a team uses, as well as the type of personnel that executes the offense before we determine exactly the approach that will be used against a particular team. Sometimes we use a six-five ratio which we will examine later.

Make practice resemble actual game circumstances

The more a coach can create game-like situations, the more he can impart to the player what is expected of him when the ball is snapped. If these situations are not created, it is almost impossible to evaluate a player's reactions and determine whether he is aware of his assignment and responsibility. We experience difficulty evaluating our efficiency when the offense is not going full speed. This does not mean that we go all out and tackle, but our players must react and pursue at full speed to determine what and where the break-downs are.

Teach pass rush

The added emphasis on the pass, offensively, has resulted in a thorough study of our ability to rush the passer. We have had many discussions with professional coaches and players and asked their opinions of pass rush. Through our conversations and our own experiences, we believe it probably is the poorest taught fundamental at both the high school and college level. We constantly are searching for answers in this area. We feel that our success is due to the abilities of the individual pass rushers, as well as our teaching emphasis. We teach it by emphasizing the get off, the surge upfield, the gaining of ground, and the elimination of the pass lanes through which the quarterback can conveniently throw. The pass rush also utilizes charges and possible stunts with other defensive linemen and/or linebackers.

The following items are necessary to be an effective pass rusher:
1. Get off on the ball.
2. Gain ground to the passer with every step.
3. Use hands whenever possible.
4. Hands up when sure the ball is going to be thrown.
5. Execute your assignment properly.

Tackles, when responsible for outside pass rush, may use these means to get to the passer:
1. Beat blocker with depth and come back to hit.

Example: "run around"

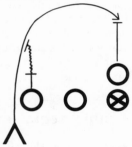

2. Beat blocker by forcing him deep and throwing him the way he is going (be certain you are at *least* as deep as the QB).

Example: "throw"

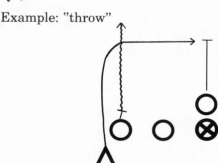

3. Defeat blocker by allowing him to get his weight back and power throw him to QB. (Never allow yourself to be pinned to inside)

Example: "butt and throw"   Example: "pinned inside"

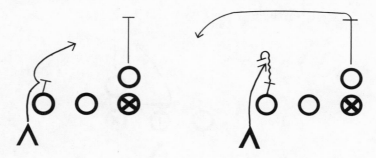

4. Finally, we eliminate blocker by engaging him immediately with our hands to pull him off balance.

Example:

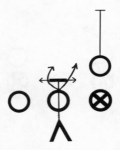

Tackles and guards, when responsible for inside rush lane, may use these means to get to passer.

1. Defeat blocker by engaging him quickly with power and force. When he loses balance, throw him hard in the easiest direction. (Be certain to gain ground)

Example: "butt and throw"

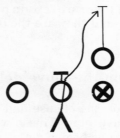

2. Eliminate blocker by avoiding him quickly. Get the mid-point of your force beyond his and go to passer. You must grab him and cross over to that side. It must be a quick coordinated movement.

Example:

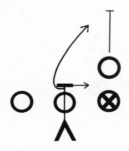

3. Same as 4. for tackles

Example: "grab and throw"

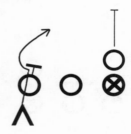

Develop personnel who accelerate to the ball

We would rather have a slow man accelerating to the ball and pursuing one hundred percent of the time than a fast player who is inconsistent. We make specific efforts to teach our players to accelerate to the ball and emphasize the success that can be realized. We have found that there are certain players who can be taught this easier than others, and they are the ones to whom we entrust the responsibility.

Penetrating, read on-the-move defenses

This puts the pressure on the offense and gives an opportunity for more aggressive defensive play. This always is a concern of the passing team because it has been a notion in football that the passing teams sometimes were soft on defense. We believe the trend toward this type of aggressive play has helped our defensive attitude and has been very important in our program.

Execute stunting defenses

Defensively, we attempt to predict the down and distance situations where stunts will be effective, and we try to structure the number of stunts that are proportionate to the abilities of the players who will be executing the stunting. This is extremely important because sometimes there are players who do not stunt well, do not penetrate well. Therefore, it would be a grave mistake to stunt with players who do not possess those abilities. Because there has been so much emphasis and discussion on effective means of rushing the passer, we have tried to incorporate stunts which can be utilized by our defensive linemen. These maneuvers have been very effective, and they allow us to utilize our linebackers and secondary in various coverages.

Know your opponent

The defense must know what his opponent is attempting to accomplish and must attempt to predict what he will do in a particular down and distance situation. In all of our scouting, we try to predict on each down whether the opponent will *run* or *pass*. Although this not always is possible, we try to be as efficient as possible so we can call the most appropriate defense. A thorough knowledge of opponents and their philosophies can be obtained by viewing films in the off season and further substantiated by scouts in season. We further can determine new trends that the opponent introduces. We attempt to get the percentage on our side in terms of defensive calls; therefore, we try to determine what the opponent will do and try to call our defense accordingly.

There are some defenses or defensive alignments and/or coverages that are better in a run situation and obviously are not effective under pass conditions. If a team does keep us off balance, and we are not sure whether they will run or pass, then it is important to prepare our best all-around defense. Defensively, as contrasted with offense, we try to maneuver the opponent into the obvious situations so we can use our strongest defense to take advantage of the percentage call that he must make.

The time and research that we have put into developing our philosophy of down and distance football has been fruitful, and it has been a very important part of our success for the past several years. We will continue to explore and expand in this area so the best possible percentage can be realized when calls are made both offensively and defensively. We strongly believe other coaches would profit by similar exploration and study.

Utilize the best defense for the obvious down situation

We have explained this in relation to the run and pass philosophy, and it becomes more important as we examine each team we play. There are certain defenses and/or defensive alignments that are better in a given situation. One is the revolutionary four-five-two defense which allows four rushers, five underneath short coverage players who will cover either man or zone, followed by a two-deep zone. The three-five-three defense is composed of three rushers with five players playing the intermediate zones and a three-deep zone backing them up. These two defenses, along with the other obvious defenses and defensive alignments that have been developed, should be studied by all coaches who then can determine what is appropriate for their programs in terms of the opponents they face.

3-5-3 Alignment:

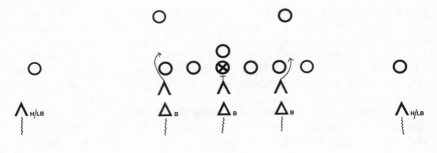

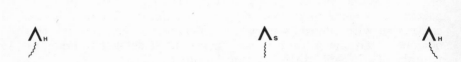

Contain

With the advent and emphasis on the pass in football today, it is necessary to examine at all times the basic structure of our defense in terms of containment. When facing a good drop-back team, we feel we can get by with a four-man contain. On the other hand, when facing a sprint-out or roll-out quarterback, it almost definitely requires some type of five-man system of containment. We believe there will be a definite trend in the next few years to more roll-out and sprint-out actions by the quarterback to force teams to place more men on the line of scrimmage.

Have a run philosophy

A team must have a philosophy of defense to follow in stopping a running play team, and more specifically, in a predicted running situation. It is our philosophy to stop the run by attacking the line of scrimmage, forcing blocking errors, and then allowing our tacklers to pursue in the second and third waves. This is somewhat unique compared with some defensive beliefs, but it fits in nicely with the alignments and coverages we use and allows us to base a good deal of our overall philosophy on stopping the pass. It also permits us to utilize our run philosophy by having the strong second and third wave of tacklers running full speed to the ball. Other considerations in stopping the run include determining whether to assign gaps and attack the offense or stay off the line, read the blockers, and then pursue.

Have a pass defense philosophy

The first considerations in establishing a pass defense philosophy, or stopping a team in a particular passing situation, are whether to rush or cover, whether to use man or zone, or whether to defend field or formation. Depending on the opponent, we usually cover more than half of the time, but we mix in enough rushes to keep the opponent off balance and force him to block our defenses. We also use as much zone coverage as possible, although when we stunt we can utilize man coverage. When we use man coverage, we employ the free safety principle, so the entire pressure is not placed on each individual pass defender. Basically, we defend formations first against the pass, but if formation alignment would get us into bad field coverage, then we obviously cover the field to minimize obvious weaknesses. The alignments that are presented in a pass situation also are extremely important. If a team can present an alignment or alignments to an offense that disguise rush and cover, as well as the type of coverage that is going to be used, then the offense is placed in the most difficult situation possible. For this reason, we use various alignments that prevent the great passer from picking apart one coverage.

Pass defense

The success or failure of a football team probably will depend more on pass defense than on any other element in the game. A coach must teach his players what to do when the ball is in the air and convince them that they must not allow a completion or a touchdown pass. A pass defender probably requires the greatest amount of mental toughness than any other position in football. He must have a tremendous amount of concentration and must be ready constantly to make the big play. Continuous examination of pass defense and its techniques and the importance placed on it probably comprise the toughest coaching jobs in football.

In selecting pass defenders, a coach should consider these qualities in a player:
1. Speed
2. Balance
3. Lateral movement
4. Timing
5. Agility

Be prepared to defense any and all options

The option play probably is the one single play that bothers us the most in defensive football. The exposure to the triple option, the belly option, the swing option, the counter option, and two or three other types has made us realize the importance of having a specific responsibility for the components of each option in our various defensive alignments. Each defense must outline who has the first back through the line, who has the quarterback, as well as the responsibility for the pitch man, or the trailing back. To aid in our preparation, we outline detailed responsibilities to our players in our defensive write-ups. An illustration in this chapter includes some of our thoughts on defensing the triple option and the write-ups in our specific defenses. We also mention the defensive responsibilities on options. Of course, the different types of options might necessitate different types of defenses or responsibilities, and this is one of the many problems in defensing a team that uses more than one type of option.

Defending the triple option

The starting point is actual assignment of responsibility in your defense (s).
a. fullback or first back
b. quarterback
c. pitch man

For example, in our base defense we assign the tackle to the quarterback, the linebacker to the pitch man, and the mike and guard to the fullback.

The defense must stop the fullback first, regardless of the team or the ability of the backs. To accomplish this, a man must be outside the fullback's course.

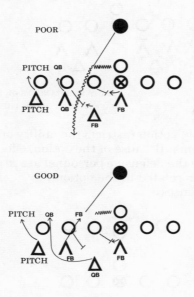

The defense cannot stay in the same alignment against the option because of the many options that are used. Our best defense for the triple option, strong and weak, is:

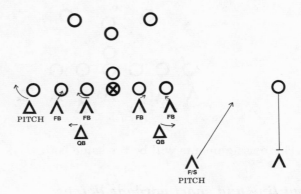

It would be the same coverage weak with the safety or corner man taking the pitch man. A single error can cost the game.

The key is the quarterback assignment and the ability to take up that responsibility if the man assigned to the quarterback is being blocked. Here is an example:

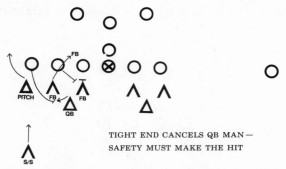

TIGHT END CANCELS QB MAN—
SAFETY MUST MAKE THE HIT

The use of the triple option restricts the ability of the defense to vary certain adjustments. Because of the option, effective pass rush is taken away because the defensive personnel are so geared to their specific responsibilities related to the option.

Other effective defenses:

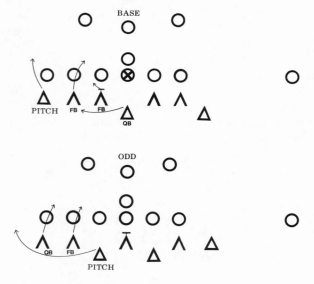

These assignments will be the same both ways.

Goal line and short yardage defense

The goal line defense is used very sparingly in today's football. We believe our basic defenses are structured solidly enough to stop a team in most situations, but we know that there are certain situations where inches or short yardage necessitate additional alignments or the use of another man or two on the line of scrimmage. This becomes very important on the goal line, and although we seldom use our basic goal line defense, we do stress the inches or extreme short yardage defense so we can be in the best possible defense for the situation and/or the predicted offensive call.

The following is our 85 goal line defense, and goal line adjustments appear on page 342.

	LT	LG	RG	RT	S	M	W	SHB	MO	WS	WHB
85 Goal line	Slant	Gap	Gap	Go	Inside	1st Bk 3rd Rec	Inside	Man-W Support	Man-2 Slide Force	Man-2 Slide Force	Man-W Support

Have a good preparation or scout team

We consider this to be one of the most important elements in getting our defensive team ready. We realize it is difficult at all levels to have separate preparation teams. However, if there are not sufficient personnel, a coach might consider utilizing the offense to prepare the defense as is done by the professional teams. The prepa-

GOAL LINE ADJUSTMENTS

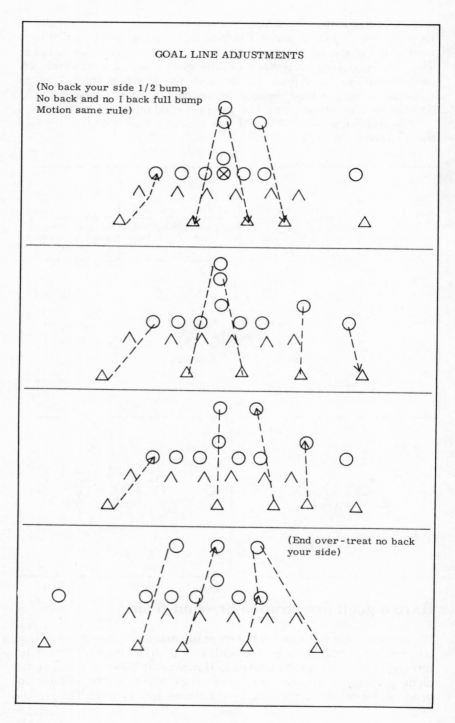

(No back your side 1/2 bump
No back and no I back full bump
Motion same rule)

(End over-treat no back
your side)

342

ration team must be coached from week to week, and it must perform a particularly good job of showing the defense exactly what can be expected of the opponent's offense. We do not believe that a preparation team must run every single play that the opposition uses, but it must execute the five or six most effective rushing plays, along with three or four of its best pass actions. One of the staff's most competent coaches, if not the head coach himself, should be assigned the responsibility of preparation. The defense must have a thorough knowledge of what to expect on game day.

Have a defensive grading system

One of the primary satisfactions of being a member of a defensive team is the constant opportunity for success. On most plays, the athlete has a chance to be part of a tackle, and therefore it is very easy to evaluate exactly how well he performs. For this reason, we have a defensive grading system which gives the players points for their defensive successes and also reflects their miscues. The grading chart is included in this chapter. Players are awarded one point for getting a part of a tackle and two points for an unassisted tackle. We also indicate mental errors and further define them into different types. M_1 is a technique; M_2 is in the pass rush; M_3 is pass coverage; and M_4 is for causing a penalty. The most damaging grade is the D, or Dog play. This is straight from the shoulder and doesn't leave any question regarding what the coach means. The player has committed an error that places him in the category of a loser. Two years ago we had several dogs on every play; now we are down to two or three in an entire game. We believe the emphasis on the grading system has had a lot to do with this improvement.

DEFENSIVE PLAY SHEET

NAME	1st QUARTER PLAYS	%	2nd QUARTER PLAYS	%	3rd QUARTER PLAYS	%	4th QUARTER PLAYS	%	TOTAL PLAYS	%
Labrum	15	93 %	17	94 %	17	94 %	16	88 %	65	92%
Gosnell	15	87 %	18	85 %	14	86 %	14	79 %	61	84%
Becklund	15	80 %	18	83 %	17	76 %	10	70 %	60	77%
Watrin	15	80 %	18	85%	16	88 %	16	75 %	65	82%
Olsen	15	87 %	18		17	88 %	15	67 %	65	80%
Workman							6	66 %	6	66%
Plummer					3	33 %	2	100 %	5	67%
Hutchins	1	100 %					1	100 %	2	100%

DEFENSIVE GRADING SHEET

NAME	TOTAL	FIRST	SECOND	THIRD	FOURTH
Labrum	11	2	1, 1, 1	1, 1, 1, 1, 1, 1	
Gornell	6	2, M_1, 1	1, 1, 1, 1	1	1, M_2, D
Plummer	1			1	
Becklund	13	2, 1, M_1	M, 2, 1, 1	1, 2, 1	1, 1, 1, 1, M_4
Workman	1	1			
Watrin	7	M, M, M	1, 2, 1, 1	1, 1	2, 1
Dunston	3	1	2		
Olsen	18	1	1, 1, 1, 1, 1, 1	2, 2, 1, M_2 1, 1, 1	1, M_4, 2, 1, 1
Hutchins	1	1			
Anderson	11		1	1, 1, 1	1, 1, 1, 1, 1, 1, 1
Christensen	1	1			
Schulz	12	2, 1, M	1, 1, 1	1, M_1	1, 2, 1, 1, 1, 1
Couey	1		1		
Myrick	7	1	1, 1, 1, 1	1, 1	M_3, 1
Detwiler	11	2, 1	2, 2	1, 1	2
Stanfill	5	1, M_3, 2, M_3	2		1, M_3, 1, 1
Peters		M_3	M_3		
Smith				M_3, 1	
Boyer	2	1	1		

M_1 - Technique M_3 - Pass Coverage & Run Support

M_2 - Pass Rush M_4 - Penalty

Know how to defend draws and screens

This area is minimized by many coaches, but with the emphasis
on the passing game and its related actions, it requires a very
sound philosophy and plan for each opponent. We believe that
in our basic four-seven pass rush ratio, the linebackers or second
wave must have both the draw and screen responsibilities. With
only four men rushing, with one man assigned to the draw and

screen, it results, in effect, in a three-man rush. This cuts down any chance for the effectiveness that the down four can have. We believe that if it is a passing situation, the four rushers should be turned loose and nothing else should deter their primary responsibilities. If a team exceeds its base ratio, such as a six-five, then we assign one of our down linemen to the draw and screen responsibility. If the guards are not involved in a particular stunt, then we assign the guard on the side of the predicted draw or screen to take that responsibility. It is obvious that we will not always predict the side of the draw or screen; therefore, we assign one of our guards this responsibility because he is closer to the middle of the ball and can help in either direction. Of course, if the guards are involved in some sort of a middle stunt, then we have to assign one of our tackles to the draw and screen and risk the chance the play will go the other way and eliminate his effectiveness.

Individual position teaching

Defensive linemen

Our defense is based on the principle of "attacking" the offense. In most situations we penetrate the offensive line to force it into errors and mistakes. In all situations we make *every* effort to make *every* tackle on *every* play.

We employ a variety of defensive alignments and charges. This aids us considerably because the opponents cannot zero in on one defense or charge. Our play is determined by a defensive call. The defensive call tells us the following things: 1) alignment, 2) technique, 3) reaction. It is imperative that we do not make a "mental-error," because the lack of them is the single most important phase in winning. Proper execution is a must. You will have to be willing to spend extra time off the field studying football, and also dedicate yourself toward improvement every second you are on the field.

A brief explanation of alignments, techniques, responsibilities and reactions are included on the following pages. It is an impossibility to include all items of importance; be prepared to add or detract information.

Techniques

Quick

Quick is primarily for the tackles. From your alignment call, move quickly into the backfield on the ball or on the offensive lineman's movements.

A. Be ready to "read" the blocker as you move. The offensive tackle is your primary key. Your reaction will depend on how the offensive man attacks you. You must be in the backfield on all "quick" calls.
B. The angle of penetration for a normal charge is slightly less than perpendicular to the line of scrimmage.
C. You will use a 3 point stance with feet staggered slightly. Keep your back straight with head and eyes up. Distribute your weight forward to enable you to penetrate quickly.
D. Your responsibilities are:
    1. #2 area.
    2. QB on options.
    3. Outside pass rush.
    4. Trail all plays away from you.
Examples:

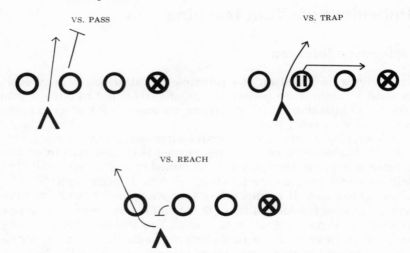

Inside

Inside is primarily for the tackles. From your alignment call, move quickly into the backfield on the ball or on the offensive lineman's movements.

A. The angle of penetration is much greater than when you are in a "quick" technique. Drive hard through the offensive tackle. Be ready to react to him. "Inside" will change your area of responsibility as well as your option assignment. Make certain you do not go in front of tackles face, but through his mid-point.
B. Your responsibilities are:
    1. #3 area.
    2. FB on option.

3. Work to get outside pass rush.

4. Work to get deep on play action away from you.

Examples:

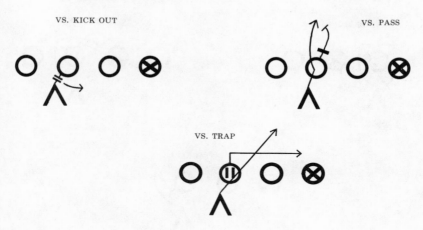

VS. KICK OUT

VS. PASS

VS. TRAP

Slant

Slant techniques may be used by both guards and tackles. The proper execution of a "slant" move must be made from a head up position on the offensive blocker. The movement will always be to the right.

    A. On the movement, we will start with a cross-over step to our right. Be ready to eliminate blocker with your left arm and shoulder and work up the field to the ball. Your primary key is the man you have lined up on.

    B. The closer to the ball the better able to penetrate. Concentrate your weight on your right foot and hand.

    C. You will be in a four point stance. Make certain your back is straight, with your head and eyes up. Do not tip the "slant" movement by lunging or a quick count. Be tensed and ready to explode.

    D. Your responsibility will depend on the call:

Left Guard	1. #4 area.
	2. FB on options.
	3. Inside pass rush.
Right Guard	1. #3 area.
	2. FB on options.
	3. Inside pass rush.
Left Tackle	1. #3 area.
	2. FB on option.
	3. Inside pass rush.
Right Tackle	1. #2 area (C.P. — wide).
	2. QB on option.

3. Outside pass rush.
4. Trail on all action away from you.

Examples:

VS REACH (GUARD)

VS TRAP

VS REACH (TACKLE)

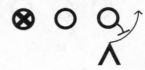

Go

Go is exactly the same as slant, except it is our penetrative movement to the left.

A. Your responsibility is:

Left Guard 1. #3 area.
     2. FB on option.
     3. Inside pass rush.

Right Guard 1. #4 area.
     2. FB on option.
     3. Inside pass rush.

Left Tackle 1. #2 area (C.P. – wide).
     2. QB on option.
     3. Outside pass rush.
     4. Trail all action away.

Right Tackle 1. #3 area.
     2. FB on option.
     3. Inside pass rush.

Examples:

VS REACH

VS PASS

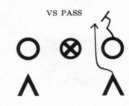

Middle

Middle is primarily a guard technique. Proper execution will require you to be off the ball a little, the distance depending on your ability. On the movement of the offense you will take a controlled jab step to the center. From that position be ready to react to either the center or the guard, depending on the play. You must stop their charge and get to the ball. Generally, you will be responsible for draws and screens.

    A. Your weight should be equally distributed in your balanced 4 point stance. Stay low as you make your controlled step. Be ready to strike the center with your "inside force," and the guard with your "outside force."

    B. Responsibilities are:
        1. #4 area (C.P. help in #3)
        2. FB on options.
        3. Draw and screens vs. pass. (C.P. — Beware, if the center or either guard is attempting to block you.)

    Example:

VS. REACH   VS. OFFENSIVE BLOCK

VS. PASS

Wide

Wide is primarily a guard technique. It is very similar to a "middle" call except the controlled jab step is to the outside, and you will react to the guard or tackle blocks.

    A. Responsibilities are:
        1. #3 Area (C.P. — help in #4).
        2. FB on option.
        3. Inside pass rush.

Example:

VS. TACKLE

VS. PASS

VS. REACH

Read

Read is a technique to be used by both the guards and tackles. To perform effectively you must be in a head up position and possibly off the ball slightly. Your reactions and movement will depend on your primary key. The movement of your key will tell you where the ball is going. You must accelerate to it as hard as possible. Also, it is imperative that you are able to stop the charge of the blocker and rid yourself of him by striking a blow and using your hands properly.

    A. Guards will be in balanced 4 point stance, with weight equally distributed to allow movement in any direction. Tackles must restrict their normal stance (must be more balanced than normal).

    B. Make certain your head goes in same direction as the key. Never go around the blocker.

    C. Never penetrate the line of scrimmage unless you can hit.

    D. Responsibilities are:

        1. The two adjacent areas to the man
            a. Example—left guard has #3 and #4
            b. Left tackle has #2 and #3

        2. Options rules are constant
          Areas #3 and #4—FB
          Areas #3 and #2—QB
          Areas #2 and #1—pitch

        3. Guards—inside pass rush.
          Tackles—outside pass rush.

Examples:

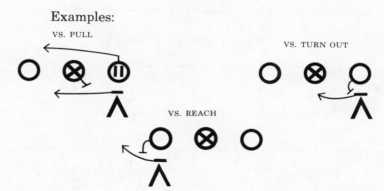

VS. PULL

VS. TURN OUT

VS. REACH

Now that we have discussed in detail the basic linemen techniques, the following is a sample of one of our defensive assignment sheets, for quick and easy reference and memorization of these techniques. On page 352 are illustrations of some of these defensive assignments and charges.

DEFENSIVE ASSIGNMENTS

	BASE	limbo	palm	over	under	slam	pinch	dog
Left T	quick	left slant c. p. right quick	quick	quick	quick	inside	inside	quick
Left G	read	left go c.p. right middle	slant c/p. (wide)	"left" read on guard "right" read on center	"left" read on center "right" read on guard	middle	slant	left slant right middle
RightG	read	Left middle right slant c. p.	gap c. p. (wide)	"left" read on center "right" read on guard	"left" read on guard "right" read on center	go	middle	left middle right go
Right T	quick	left quick right go c. p.	quick	quick	quick	inside	inside	quick

DEFENSIVE CHARGES AND STUNTS

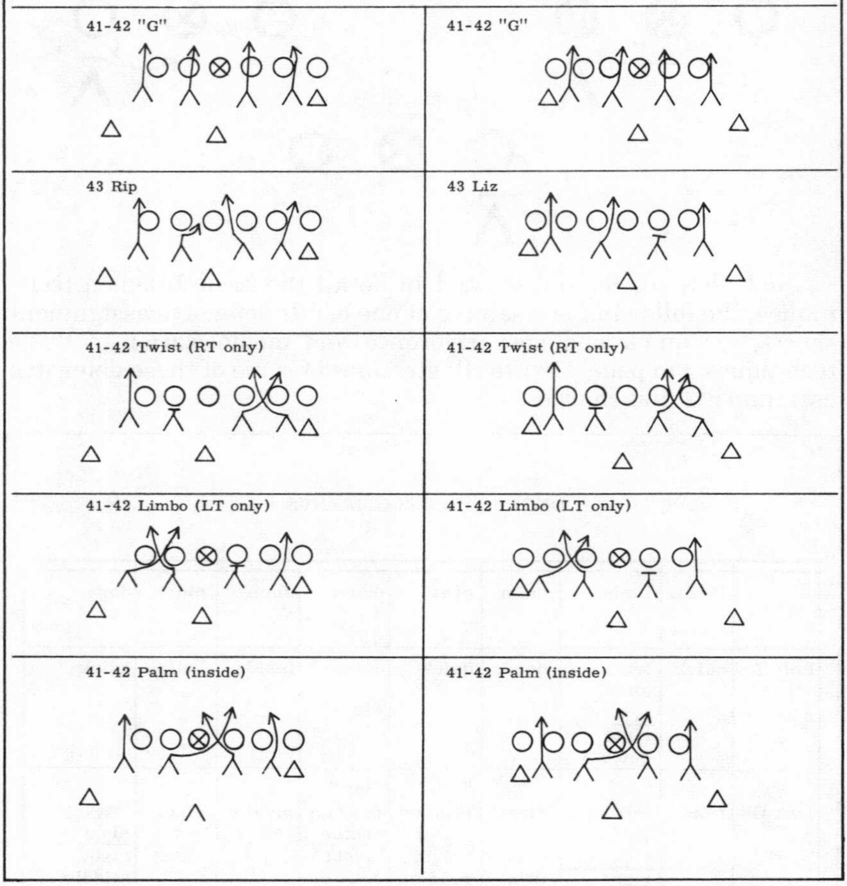

41-42 "G"

41-42 "G"

43 Rip

43 Liz

41-42 Twist (RT only)

41-42 Twist (RT only)

41-42 Limbo (LT only)

41-42 Limbo (LT only)

41-42 Palm (inside)

41-42 Palm (inside)

Linebackers

Terminology

1. Force: Name for one of the outside linebacker assignments. It means:
   a. Hook or seam on drop back
   b. Force all flow his way
   c. Belt on sweeps
   d. Pitch on options

2. Hang: Name for one of the outside linebacker assignments. It means:
   a. Flat on all passes
   b. Belt
   c. Pitch on options
3. Seam: Area between flat and hook and usually on hash
4. Read: Read man or men for reaction and assignment
5. Key: Key man for flow and assignment
6. Bounce: Move square behind line and shuffle
7. Stall: Staying behind ball and checking cutback
8. Strong hook: Hook on side of call
9. Weak hook: Hook away from side of call
10. Lou: Zone coverage roating left
11. Rose: Zone coverage rotating right
12. Push through: Go through blockers with near shoulder
13. Cross hit: Inside shoulder and arm through outside shoulder and head
14. Skate: Ability to stay square and on your feet and keep ball moving laterally in front of you
15. Slam: Changes the outside linebackers assignment to QB, trail and contain
16. Flood: Call by backers when both backs go in one direction, whether it's drop-back or roll

Mike

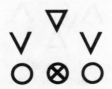

Line up—on heels of the guards
Stance— Knees bent, feet just slightly wider than shoulders so you can step with either foot—head up, looking for tips of the play
Before you assume your position:
1. Indicate strength and make a right or left call (be sure call is right the first time to eliminate confusion—make call loud).
2. Look for the offensive set (red, blue, etc.) so you can make a change or to help in your play recognition.
3. Call out anything that you might suspect or see, like draw, reverse, pass, etc.

4. Go over your assignments in your mind so you will be right.
5. When center puts hands on ball, get set and concentrate on key or read.

Read assignment

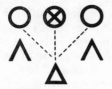

Key center and two guards for your first reaction.

Center comes straight at you, choose a foot and strike him and disengage. Strike to neutralize him and then find ball. Don't look for ball before strike, and don't disengage too fast until you determine flow.

Center comes out right or left, you strike with near foot and near forearm or shoulder, so you don't get cut off; then the ball or flow. (1) Strike and (2) become square again.

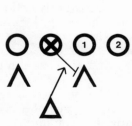

Center blocks on guard. Step up and look for trapper or slam blocker. Strike with good position and body control and then find ball or flow. Step to tail of center, move toward his direction to cut down hole, then find first trapper either 1 or 2 and next the back.

If sweep develops out of this block, or even a pass, you might run it down, or bounce out of blocks and pursue.

Key assignment: Key a man and his movement will give you the flow, or assignment, or both. It could be just a partial move of a man also, like the quarterback's shoulders. An example of key defense:

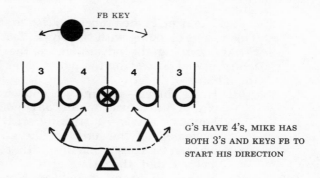

G'S HAVE 4'S, MIKE HAS BOTH 3'S AND KEYS FB TO START HIS DIRECTION

Outside LB's—strike or whip

Although their positions and assignments are usually different, we will deal with them here as one, and on a tight end.

Line up—splitting the tight end's stance, inside knee on his nose, feet parallel, but could get a slight stagger with inside foot up; as low as possible and keying end's hat. Probably use hands, forearm, and shoulder in that order on end, depending on strength and situation.

If end releases, we think pass until action indicates run.

If end blocks, we step and assume run.

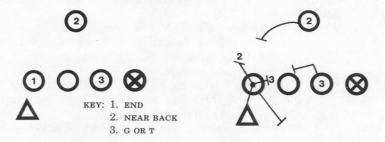

KEY: 1. END
     2. NEAR BACK
     3. G OR T

In order to have a great defensive team, or be champions, we must have great linebackers. They have the full range of assignments, because of the great versatility of our schedule and conference. This means 50-50 run and pass. Tough enough to take on linemen and backs, quick enough to cover a pass receiver man, and smart enough to be a little ahead of the offense.

We want to be able to do six basic techniques on run defense:

1. Stance: getting ready to play, proper position and balance will allow you to have quick and powerful movement in any direction. Stance, alignment, and key are all included in this technique and will vary with position, defense and situation.

2. Attack: getting in the proper position to strike the blocker. This means stepping with the proper foot or feet.

3. Strike: gaining the advantage on the blocker by neutralizing and destroying the power of his block by delivering a blow.
   a. Hand shiver—striking up and out with the heels of your hands, used mainly on cut off blocks or hooks.
   b. Forearm shiver—a striking with an up and out movement of the forearm like an uppercut to an opponent's chest, usually with one arm to near foot so that the other arm is free to throw the blocker. In strong straight on blocks you could use both arms.
   c. Shoulder shiver—the last resort strike, used to stack up a hole and when the going gets tough, usually with an inside out blocker, almost the same as the forearm, only with the shoulder.

4. Hold: this is the maintaining of the advantage on the blocker and holding your area of responsibility. If you try to disengage too early, you could open up holes and overrun.

5. Disengage: If you get rid of blocker too soon and don't hold, you could create holes. Also, if you are so intent on whipping the blocker, which sometimes happens in a challenge on a fight you will become preoccupied and never get to the ball.
   We will use three methods to disengage:
   a. Recoil—stepping laterally, or back and laterally toward the point of attack. If the play is defined, you can hustle and pursue.
   b. Throw—this is using your hands and grabbing the blocker and throwing him away from the point of attack, while stepping to it.
   c. Spin—last resort, spin out from blocker when really caught.

6. Pursuit: While all the others are important, this makes the champion. It is taking the proper path, with quickness and speed, to cut off the ball carrier. We try to never

follow color, and don't go around blocks. Rather give ground. The great defensive games will have no D's on the board on Monday.

Our pass defense is divided into three parts:

1. Zone: When pass develops you must know your area, where the help is coming from, the field position, strength of offensive set, etc. the pass drop should always be fast by LB'ers when they read pass, and especially if they get a slow read. Then when the QB sets and is ready to throw you should set and be ready to react. This does not mean stopping; remember especially the *feet—they must always keep moving.* But it means getting in control so that you can move to the ball fast when it is thrown. Squaring the shoulders and when you read the QB's eyes, arm and motion, you can tell the direction of the pass. Reaction to the ball is the ability to move to ball at the proper angle to break up pass. Don't round the corners and angles. You must develop the ability to go to the ball and intercept it. Catch it at its highest point. Return to nearest sideline and if in traffic cover the ball. If teammate intercepts, block the intended receiver if you are close enough.

2. Man:

    a. *Concentration*—this is really important: look right at receiver's number. Concentration is the secret to man-to-man coverage.

    b. *Position*—position is almost everything in defense, or the pursuit to get position. *Never let a receiver gain a head up position with you.* You should take a strong position opposite your help in the coverage. If no help, it will usually be to the middle.

    c. *Drive*—the toughest thing to do, especially if you have lost position. When receiver makes his final break, drive to catch him concentrating on him. If receiver changes direction, be in a position so that he must make contact with you in order to make that change. If you keep position, you can play the ball. If you lose position then you play his hands and he moves to catch the ball. Most receivers must slow up to catch a deep pass and you can catch him if you concentrate on what you are doing and drive to get him.

3. Pass Rush: on pass rush defenses, you must be ready for run and play like a down lineman. You must feel you will not get through clean, and if you do it will be easy. Assume someone will block you and get ready to strike, staying low, and reading the play. If an offensive man sets up to block you, try to shoulder block him and punish him. Also

try to get by the blocker, with either an arm, leg or shoulder. Don't go in blind, and yet be aggressive, and have that great desire to get home.

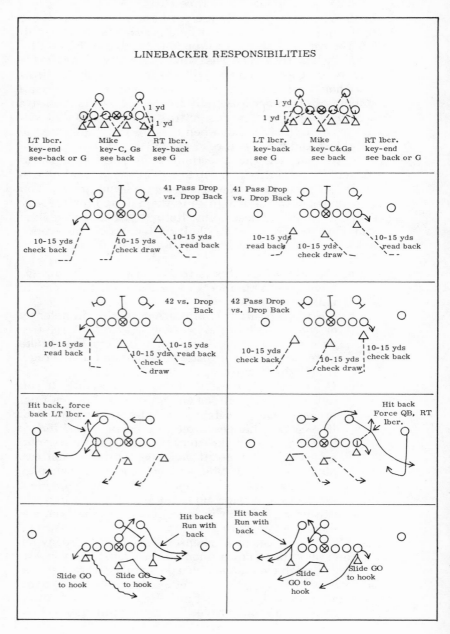

LINEBACKER RESPONSIBILITIES

Four-deep secondary

I. Types of players for these positions
    A. Special players; skilled such as quarterbacks and receivers
        1. Abilities
            a. Speed
            b. Agility
            c. Sense
            d. Toughness (tackling-block protection)
            e. Pluses — strength, height, hands
        2. Athletes — Basketball type
            a. Feel, understanding, anticipation
            b. Pressure type
                (1) Foul shot
                (2) Pinch hit
                (3) Pressure putt
                (4) Last man on a run
        3. Skills
            a. Natural sense
            b. Veteran-experience
            c. Other sports
II. Positions and requirements
    A. Halfbacks
        1. Must have good speed — 4.7 — 4.8
        2. Can cover deep and run with fast receivers
        3. Size not necessarily a factor
        4. L.H. should be strongest
        5. R.H. should be faster and most agile
        6. Confidence
        7. Balance
        8. Might be left or right sided
            a. Give them a choice if important
        9. Good tacklers
    B. Mover (Strong safety)
        1. Good speed (not necessarily like H.B.)
        2. Good strength — tackle and bump
        3. Tough — should be best tackler
        4. Good sense — quick learner
        5. Right and left shoulders
        6. Size would be a plus
    C. Free safety
        1. Good sense; flowing athlete
        2. Good sense or jump
        3. Sure tackler
        4. Should call the secondary
        5. Good speed

6. Probably best athlete; agility
7. Toughness a plus
8. Leader and hustler

Techniques for four-deep

I. Pass drop and run support
    A. Stance and position
        1. Position—varies on set and assignment
           (a) H.B.'s two yards outside of and seven yards off split receiver
           (b) H.B.'s four yards outside of and five yards off when there is no split receiver
           (c) Mover one yard outside of and four-seven yards off second receiver
           (d) Safety one yard outside of and eight yards off second receiver
        2. Stance—Varies some with individuals
           (a) H.B.'s—outside foot up, slightly pointed in, knees bent, shoulders forward, arms down, head down (eyes up).
           (b) Mover and safety—outside foot back, same stance as H.B.'s except could be taller for vision and assignment
    B. Pass drop
        1. Shuffle
        2. Key—run or pass
        3. Receiver
        4. Pass drop: stay low, head down, shoulders forward; Arms and feet work fast (short steps); Keep position (two or three yards); look at belt buckle. Be ready to support on a running play.
        5. Position
           (a) Man—end up in position at the end of the pass drop; outside (or inside) and two or three yards off the receiver;
           (b) Zone—could end up the same as man, or the players' position in the zone. This should be defined and well in mind
        6. Ball
           (a) Man—when man becomes receiver, the player should play the ball. This, of course, is based on keeping the position.
           (b) Zone—always be aware of the man or men in your zone, but play the ball and the QB much faster.

C. Drills
  1. Reaction—run or pass

  (a) Coach indicates run or pass
    (1) use rolls
    (2) later use draws
  2. Receivers—one-on-one; three yards

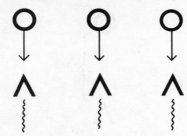

  (a) keep position; stay low
  (b) individual and in groups
  3. Receivers—one-on-one; six yards

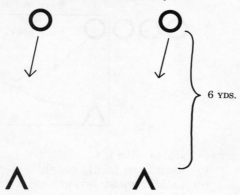

6 YDS.

a. Receivers go to 13 yards hard
b. Keep position
4. Receivers — no ball
    (a) tall defender cut
    (b) build confidence in movement
    (c) watch receivers
5. One-on-one — ball
6. Search
7. Overhead catch (no receivers)
    (a) add receiver in the behind position

II. Tackling
    1. Form
        (a) Command hit — both move forward
        (b) form tackle; good pop 4 drive
        (c) points
            (1) head up; bull neck
            (2) back straight
            (3) knees bent
            (4) butt ball and continue movement
            (5) thrown arms and wrap

3 YDS.

2. Move to angle — square up after hit
3. Square tackling

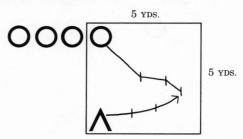

5 YDS.

5 YDS.

(a) starts with hit
(b) form first; tackle tough
(c) tackler must bring him down and force him out
    of square

4. Sideline tackling

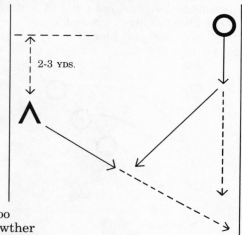

2-3 YDS.

    5. Smoo
    6. Crowther
III. Block protection
    A. Form
        1. Stay low; knees bent
        2. Arms protecting lap
        3. Strike with flipper or shoulder
        4. Have hands ready
        5. Change shoulder

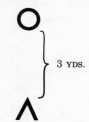

3 YDS.

    B. Hook
        1. Move to outside position
        2. Use hands on head and pads
        3. Look right at blocker, not ball carrier
        4. Keep inside leg free after strike by pulling out and
           regaining ground again.

C. Recoil—three vs. 1
   1. Command go—first man and others follow
   2. Don't give too much ground wide
   3. High, low, and roll blocks
   4. Same as #2.

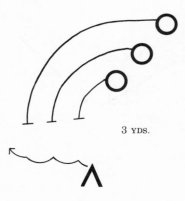

3 YDS.

D. Defeat stalk
   1. Must keep position, usually outside
   2. Get to man fast on recognition in order to disengage
   3. Grab and throw the blocker
   4. Try not to lose ground

IV. Playing the ball
   A. The secret of pass defense
   B. We utilize "ball" days to emphasize going for the ball
   C. Drills for playing the ball can be found in the drill book

Defensive secondary check list

   1. Great pride
   2. Pass 75 percent; run 25 percent. Always think pass first
   3. No one deep
   4. Talk to each other
   5. Know the opponents
   6. Patterns
   7. Run or pass
   8. Inside out
   9. Force (squeeze)
   10. Force (cutback, support)
   11. If wrong, sell out
   12. Confidence

Training the defensive signal caller

We have indicated previously that we like to make our defensive calls from the sideline during a game. We are aware of the importance of the defensive signal caller on the field and we spend considerable time making sure the signal caller understands the game plans so he can make any necessary on-the-field game adjustments. No matter who makes the defensive calls, here are some helpful hints to the prospective signal caller:

There are three primary players on a football team whose leadership qualities will help to determine the degree of success the squad will achieve. These are the captain, the offensive quarterback, and the defensive signal caller.

It can be seen, therefore, that leadership qualities are vital to the young man in charge of directing the team's defensive strategy. Being a good leader depends upon many aspects of the player's character and certainly most important is that he leads by example — both on and off the field. Any team leader who violates training is providing negative leadership and is directly contributing to the weakening of the team.

Good leadership is represented as a "way of life" rather than by merely being forceful and commanding. Good leadership on the part of the defensive signal caller will inspire in his teammates confidence in his calls. From confidence comes enthusiasm; and from enthusiasm comes the type of play which spells victory. It is a vital role of the defensive signal caller to inspire a winning attitude.

Poise is a quality which the signal caller must have. Anyone can lead well when everything is going right. The good defensive signal caller keeps his head when faced with perplexing offensive problems and when faced with an opponent who is physically tough. It is *poise* which can help to win upset victories, and it is *poise* which keeps the favorable balance, even though for a while the tide seems to be turning. Even more important than making the correct call is the ability to maintain composure and to have teammates *believe* you are making the correct call. Great leaders will never panic!

While qualities of leadership are essential, they alone are not enough to make you a fully qualified signal caller. For your leadership to be effective over the long pull it is essential that you have a very thorough knowledge of *defensive and offensive* strategy. Such a knowledge is gained only through experience and through conscientious study on your part. There is no short cut! There is no "easy" road to excellence!

There are plenty of armchair quarterbacks, but they have neither the authority nor responsibility of directing a team in action. To the defensive signal caller will fall both that authority and that responsibility. He will take a vital *physical* part in the execution of defensive calls, and as a result will be expected to exhibit tremendous physical and mental toughness. He can lead *only* by example. He never can allow himself to show fatigue! He can never allow himself to show discouragement! He must have the driving pride to play with greater abandon and intensity than anyone else on the field! He must be perfectly conditioned! He must never be late for a practice; he must hustle all the time! These things must be done when winning and when losing.

Finally, he must remember that the calling of defensive signals is merely a *battle of wits* between him and the offensive quarterback. If he is to be the winner in this battle, it is essential that he has a very thorough knowledge of *offensive* strategy and tactics as well as of defensive strategy and tactics.

The experience of being a signal caller should be one of the most rewarding ones in an athlete's life. It will be a brief experience packed with responsibility, pressure, study, work, and other demands. A signal caller represents the key to success for the entire team. Being a good athlete is not enough. It takes a real man to shoulder this job.

The objectives of defense

A. To prevent a score
B. To maintain field position
C. To force the opponents to make a mistake
D. To gain ball possession by:
  1. Forcing a punt
  2. Forcing a fumble
  3. Intercepting a pass
  4. Stealing the ball
E. To consume time by:
  1. Running out the clock
  2. To give up ground on occasion, but not scores
F. To demoralize the opponent by:
  1. Hard hitting
  2. Confusing them
  3. Thwarting their offensive plans
G. To score by:
  1. Interception
  2. Recovered fumble
  3. Punt return
  4. Blocking a punt
  5. Stealing the ball
  6. Forcing a safety

Meet strength with strength

This is the fundamental axiom of sound defensive deployment. It is essential that the signal caller recognize distribution of strength.

Defensive structures will match defensive strength to that of the offense. Below are diagrams indicating the meeting of strength with strength.

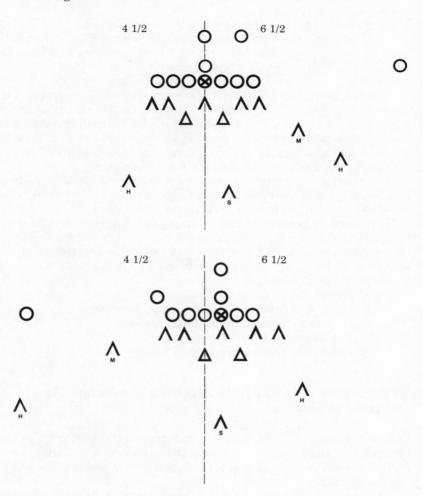

The team role in pass defense

Of all the areas in defense, there is none so important as those related to pass defense. In the broadest sense of interpretation, there are only two types of situations with which a player will be faced. One is the likely or obvious passing situation; the other is the situation where a pass is not necessarily expected.

In the obvious pass situation, it must be remembered there is also a strong likelihood of a "trick" from a fake of a pass. These "tricks" involve screens, draws, statue of liberty plays, etc. You must keep your team alerted to these "trick" possibilities. There are two ways basically in which you will have to deal with the obvious passing situation:

    a. *Coverage:*   Call a containing type of defense.

    b. *Rush:*   Call a defense which uses a 6 or 7 man sell-out. Man to man pass coverage is adaptable to this type of rush.

It must be remembered that the rush is used as a surprise element and is meant to destroy the "rhythm" which the passing QB hopes to have in order to complete his pass. The rush can result in forcing a sizeable loss or in causing an interception. It is a tactic which is more daring in nature but is a bit more risky and is vulnerable to the tricks which develop from the passing game.

In situations whereby the pass is not necessarily expected, there can be no specific instructions other than to employ the type of defense deemed logical for the total tactical situation.

It is most important to realize that pass defense is a *total* team function and it is the defensive signal caller's responsibility to thoroughly ingrain all team members with the knowledge of the importance they play as pass defenders. In actuality, pass defense is comprised of the following components:

    a. Rush (line and linebackers)

    b. Hold up receivers (linemen, ends, linebackers)

    c. Coverage (backs, linebackers, ends)

    d. Punishing receivers (everyone)

    e. Returning interceptions (everyone)

Summary of how to apply defenses to combat the offensive problems

Defenses which are *containing* in nature are the best ones to use for pass coverage and for stopping the attack to the flanks. Generally, *penetrating* defenses meet internal power and confuse blocking assignments.

There is a proper time to call certain defenses. *Mastery* of when and how to apply our defenses will make a successful signal caller.

The tactical situation

After becoming thoroughly familiar with the system of defense and the purpose for the use of each call, there are certain variable factors which always must be considered to most effectively apply the defensive plan. It should be noted that these are the identical variable factors which the offensive quarterback is evaluating in his attempt to make a call. These factors help shape what is known as the "Tactical situation." Full understanding of these variables and knowing how they will affect the call being made by the offensive quarterback will make possible the correct defensive call most of the time. The factors which comprise the tactical situation, in order of importance, are: score, time, field position, down and distance, wind and weather, game plan.

Let's study these variables one at a time:

1. Score: The general rule here is that you gamble more when you are behind than when you are leading. It is not wise, however, to become so conservative when ahead that the opponents are able to generate rhythm and turn the tide in their favor. The amount of gambling to be used is very much related to not only the score, but the time remaining as well. Late in the game, when a team is trailing and must have the ball, it is essential to utilize a forcing defense even at the expense of a considerable gamble. It is foolhardy to gamble wildly, even though losing by a small margin, when there is considerable time remaining to play in the game.

2. Time: It is important first of all to remember that time running out at the end of the half is vastly different from that at the end of the game. Even though trailing near the end of the half, it would be foolish to gamble wildly and thereby run the risk of giving up a touchdown which might put the game out of reach and which could help provide a tremendous psychological advantage to the opponents. At the end of the half the defense should play to consume time and prevent a score.

   When trailing at the end of the game, it is essential to gain possession of the ball. The defensive signal caller should now gamble more and should remind teammates that they must secure possession of the ball by jarring it loose when tackling the ball carrier. When trailing, it is vital that the defensive signal caller know how many times-out remain and that he use them only to conserve time and stop the clock in order to help regain ball possession. Every effort should be made to use the clock to favor a particular situation. If leading, a team wants to run out the clock and not stop it. When trailing, it is important that to employ every possible method to conserve time and to stop the clock. Opponents, of course, also will be aware of this time consideration, but a team must be better prepared to use it according to its needs. (See section on two-minute offense) This is where level-headedness on the part of the signal caller is the key. A great percentage of games are won or lost in the last few minutes of the contest.

The clock can be stopped and time conserved in the following ways:
1. Incomplete pass
2. Out of bounds
3. Time out
4. First down
5. Measurement

When ahead very late in the game the defensive signal caller should remember that the offense must move a long distance and will seek to utilize the time-conserving weapons. Also the offense likely will need to resort to a passing attack to move the ball this distance. Prevent defense may be utilized although we have had some painful experiences with the use of the prevent defense too soon or in the wrong situation. The idea here is to allow the offense short gains but to keep it from throwing a touchdown. Every attempt should be made also to keep the ball carrier in bounds when he is tackled so the clock will not stop. Also in such a situation the defense must be ready for a quick lineup when the offense has used up all its time-outs.

3. Field Position: In order to know what to call, the defensive signal caller should have a general understanding of how offensive quarterbacks are instructed regarding field position. It is important to remember that this is a general guide and will vary somewhat from team to team, QB to QB, and coach to coach.

The offensive QB is often instructed as follows:

Own goal to 20:	Conservative plays. Pass unlikely. Possible quick kick on any down. Punt on early downs with long yardage to go.
Between the 20 yard lines:	Your entire attack is available. (3 down area)
Opponents 20 to the goal:	Try to march to a TD passing when deemed necessary. (4 down area)

On the basis of the general instruction given to the offensive QB there are certain salient points to remember:

a. On any possible punting situation, make a call which would allow you to employ the proper "scrimmage" defense and which calls for a method of defensing the punt also.

b. Be ready for anything between the twenty yard lines.

c. When you have your opponent deep in the hole, use a penetrating, forcing type of defense in an effort to force a mistake on the part of your opponent.

d. When employing goal line defenses, be aware of the obvious sneaks and power off tackle plays. Also know when the down and yardage situation calls for a goal line defensive stunt which strengthens your flanks and rollout pass containment.

Thus far the field position discussion has dealt with the vertical field position (yard line). It is also important that your call be based on lateral field position (hash mark) as well. We categorize hash mark tendencies in terms of *field* and *bench*. When an opponent is on a hash mark, it is not likely that he can run wide or rollout pass into the bench. Many teams will run reverses off tackle into the bench, however. Scouting reports will give you thorough information on what the hash mark tendencies of an opponent are, and this will help you with your calls.

4. Down and Distance: It is first important to be able to classify the down and yardage situations, and we place these in the category of either run, pass, long or short. As was explained previously, it is extremely important for us to try to predict a team's run and pass downs.

In order to know intelligently how much an opponent must average per play, it is vital that you be aware of what we refer to as the "three down area" and the "four down area." The "three down area" is that area between the opponent's goal line and our thirty-five yard line and is thus called because usually the opponent has *three downs* in which to make a first down when he has the ball in this area of the field. Should he not make the first down after three tries, it is likely that he will punt on fourth down. Therefore, the required yardage in the "three down area" is approximately 3.4 per play. You should apply your calculations accordingly, realizing that in most instances the opponent's yardage per play requirement does not include usage of the 4th down.

The "four down area" is that position on the field between the thirty-five yard line and the goal line. In this area it is very unlikely that the opponent will punt on fourth down. Fourth down is available to him, therefore, as an added opportunity to move the ball in an attempt for a first down or a score. Since the offense now has *four* plays in which to move for a first down, the required yardage is now only 2.5 yards per play. This is a consideration which you must be alert to in order to evaluate correctly the down and yardage situation.

The approach to down and yardage situations, therefore, undergoes a definite change when the opponents move from the "three down area" to the "four down area."

An extremely important point to remember is that the truly vital situation is the one which develops on third down. If successful here, a team can halt the opponent's drive. By the same token the offensive QB knows that this is the "must" down for him, also. You and all your teammates must be dedicated to making this a successful down on your part. This is the showdown! We use the term "Geronimo" for these big downs.

5. Wind and weather: When unusual wind or weather conditions prevail, they affect both teams and the good signal caller will actually turn these circumstances to his own favor. When a strong wind is with a team, it wants the ball and a defensive gamble which is designed to force opponents to punt is one which should be definitely considered. When the offense has a strong wind at its back, a quick-kick is a possibility for which to be alert. It is important to keep teammates alerted to this possibility.

When receiving a punt *from* a strong wind, it is wise to call for a return since the likelihood is there that the opponents will outkick their coverage. When the offense is kicking *into* a strong wind, there will be little chance to muster a planned return and so a punt rush should be stressed.

Wet conditions tend to favor the defense because ball handling problems are made even more difficult. Keep teammates alert to trying the forcing of a fumble by jarring the ball loose.

6. Personnel: Very often opponents will have outstanding players who must be stopped, or they will have particular backs or receivers upon whom they tend to call in specific situations. By studying the scouting report thoroughly, you will be better equipped to use calls at the correct time.

7. Game Plan: Throughout the week, information will be supplied about the opponent's strengths and weaknesses. This information and the plan in combatting the opponent should be studied by the defensive signal caller under the guidance and direction of the coach. In actuality, the game plan should be detailed in very simple terms. Defensive

callers should become acquainted with the opposing team's favorite plays, their tendencies in crucial situations, and the quarterback whom he will be facing. In applying defenses it is well to remember that you need not be elaborate, nor need you use the entire repertoire of defenses. Utilize the proper defensive calls to keep the offense off balance and keep them from zeroing in on one alignment or coverage. The coach can instruct you all during the week, but on the day of the game the coaches and players must make the game decisions and adjustments that will provide success. At times it might become necessary for you to implement a change in the basic game plan. Herein lies a true test of how thoroughly you have learned all aspects of sound defensive signal calling.

We have now extensively reviewed the factors which go into making up the Tactical Situation. It is well to remember that these factors are all inter-related. By merely considering one factor, while not being aware of the others, you could get a very distorted idea of the true Tactical Situation. One example follows:

You have a five point lead and the opponent has the ball third and one at midfield. So far you have information only of SCORE — FIELD POSITION — DOWN & DISTANCE. In such a circumstance you might call a forcing, short yardage defense.

However, by adding the TIME factor and saying only two seconds remain in the game, it is likely that you would call another form of defense.

There are countless other examples which could be used for illustration, but it is obvious that *all* factors enter into the decision to be made. It is not expected that on every play you will have to go through the process of weighing each and every one of these factors. They have been outlined as a guide for you, and the good signal caller will gain a command of the TACTICAL SITUATION, which allows him to apply the proper call quickly without going through a systematic evaluation process on every down.

In actuality a number of these factors will not change appreciably from down to down. The score, weather, time, personnel, and game plan will remain relatively constant and are not likely to undergo radical changes often during the game. Even field position will not change to a great extent very often. The one truly dynamic factor is the down and distance, and in this area you will have to be sharp and alert in applying the down and distance factor in its relationship to the other factors. Your knowledge and predictability of a situation being run or pass will be critical to your ultimate success. When the other factors do undergo a change (score, weather, etc.), these usually will be of such a nature that the change could seriously alter the tactical situation.

Responsibilities of the signal caller

1. The Huddle: Maintain a sharp huddle. Keep order and quiet in the huddle.
2. The Call: When making your call, there is certain information along with the actual defense that you must convey to your teammates. In order, these are the "ingredients" of your call:
   a. Tell them DOWN & DISTANCE
   b. Call the defense.
   c. If called for, warn about any tricks or plays to expect. This information you should have on the basis of the scouting report and on the basis of your general knowledge as a signal caller.
   Two hypothetical calls are listed below:
   a. "First and ten—."
   b. "Third and fifteen—(watch for a screen or draw.)"
3. Be a leader in word and action; mentally and physically.

Summary

This information is extensive and has exposed you to many facets of signal calling. We have thoroughly detailed and examined the game of football, but in the final analysis there are three points taken from all the preceding material about which the great signal caller is most aware. These points are repeated below because they form the heart and soul of the winning signal caller's thinking and leadership:

1. The game of football revolves about the third down. This is the showdown!
2. All members of the team are kept constantly informed of the situation. They are kept aware by the *signal caller* of the down and distance, of how much yardage can be given up, and of what tricks or plays to expect. Because of the signal caller's leadership and knowledge, his teammates actually gain a true insight into the total defensive plan, tactics, and strategy. When they become aware of these elements, it is much more likely that they will become better defensive players.
3. The toughest, most hard-nosed, most hustling, most dedicated defensive player on the team is that man who is leading the team defensively—the signal caller.

Defensive game plans

A very important aspect of game preparation defensively is preparing the defensive write-ups each week. The head coach makes two or three pages of comments relative to the upcoming opponent, and they will be followed by individual position game plans. These defensive write-ups are given to the defensive players on Friday night after the squad attends a movie. The players read this information prior to going to bed. A sample of two of these defensive write-ups appears in the drill book. The coach on the field, who will be assisting the defensive signal caller, simplifies his information in the enclosed form for ease in communication. His field chart contains the actual defensive game plan based on the opponent's down and distance tendencies.

SAMPLE DEFENSIVE GAME PLAN

1-10	PASS	RUN
BASE 44 41 31 52 EVEN (MOVE) 44 52 ODD (OPPOSITE) 31 52 pinch RUSH BASE 65 slam odd 65 slam EVEN 65 pinch	COVER 31 (PRESS) 41 52 } EVEN BASE limbo palm 44 31 } Odd 52 Rush 65 DOG } EVEN DOG 4 65 palm } Odd limbo	BASE 44 31 EVEN 52 (MOVE) 31 Odd (opposite) 31 44 pinch SLAM RUSH BASE 65 slam odd 65 slam EVEN 65 pinch
	LONG	SHORT
	BASE 45 52	85 (inches)

16

Kicking Game

Throughout this book, we have attempted to show the younger coach, particularly, just how much of an open mind he must keep in all phases of football. Probably the most consistent area, however, is in the kicking game.

The entire complexion of a football game can depend upon a field goal or through yardage gained or lost in the exchange of punts and their returns. For these reasons, successful coaches and football programs throughout the country at all levels should have a very well thought out and thoroughly coached kicking game. It receives attention in clinics and in professional journals, where it is universally acknowledged for its importance in winning close football games.

The primary requisite for a successful kicking game is to allot the necessary practice time to develop and refine it. However, most coaches are extremely interested in how well their offense and defense perform, and too often are more than willing to add more practice time to become proficient in those areas at the expense of the kicking game. We believe that with all of the information available on this phase of the game, the mistakes and inconsistencies of the kicking game can be greatly reduced. These errors lose more football games than any other single factor in the game today.

Because so much yardage on kicks is concealed, it is easy to overlook that aspect of the game. A coach should keep statistics for every game on yardage of kicks, and the returns of punts, and kick-offs—both offensively and defensively, in addition to the net distance of the actual kick. Analyzing these statistics, a coach will have good indication of why he won or lost.

In this age of specialization, the kicking specialist probably is the most important single person in the football program. The best advice that can be given to a new coach is to find those players who have kicking talents and emphasize both to them and to the entire squad just how important their contributions can be to the overall success of the entire program. Too many coaches structure their thinking according to archaic approaches to the game. They seek the total, all-around football player who can play sixty minutes a game. They rely upon their players to out-condition, out-hit, out-work, and have a better overall attitude than their opponents. This is an admirable approach to the game, but it must be remembered that courage and toughness can be displayed in many ways. The coach who still is adhering to this concept many times will not open his eyes to seek talent at all levels that will assist him in the kicking game.

An efficient kicker often may be found on the soccer field where the stress on kicking is emphasized to a greater degree than any other sport. The glamour that surrounds the kicker through the television media has opened the doors for a new, revitalized attitude among young athletes. Kickers are in every school and in every program; it is the responsibility of the coach to find them. Preliminary testing of a prospective kicker includes assessing leg power and form, and coaching techniques will perfect those natural attributes. The kicker's ability in most cases will be enhanced when it is emphasized how important he can be to the total success of the program. An additional bonus is provided for the athlete who is not blessed with great size or overall athletic ability, but nonetheless can be a valuable member of the team.

A unique kind of concentration and courage is required of a kicker. For example, the pressure on a field goal kicker on the twenty-five yard line, with his team behind by two points with less than a minute remaining in the game, is much like the pressure felt by a golfer who is trying for a three-foot putt to win a major tournament. The best way to get a kicker used to this situation is to create pressure conditions in practice. The point is: don't avoid it or it will be too late when the kicker is under fire in game conditions.

In all areas of kicking, it is our belief that a coach should establish a well thought out, consistent system. As in all phases of football, a team should force its opponent to beat what it does best. For example, if a team plans to win with its defense, a coach always must think in terms of where the ball is *positioned* on the field. He should not take chances when the ball is in his own territory. He should establish a quick-kick in his repertoire of plays and not be afraid to kick on third down if it means getting the ball deep into the opponent's territory.

Too many coaches attempt to do too much in the kicking game. This can be as disastrous as following the same philosophy in the offensive and defensive planning. A team does not need two or three ways to return the ball, four or five punt rushes, two or three point after touchdown or field goal rushes. As a matter of reality, most coaches do not allot enough time to practice these areas. When the time is available, assignments should be well defined and there should be a very minimum of change from week to week or from game to game.

Have a specific system

In our years of coaching and observing the kicking game and evaluating kicking programs, several factors become very apparent. First, there are many, many ways to approach the kicking game or to perform its various aspects. Although there are several effective ways, it is obvious that the successful kicking coach has a definite "system" that he has utilized in a basic form for many years. Therefore, the first objective is the establishment of a specific system in all areas of kicking. Secondly, the effective kicking games have standard methods of drilling and in teaching fundamentals. Kicking has some very definite fundamental skills involved, and drills can be set up to teach these skills. Drills should undergo a minimum number of changes from year to year. Third, the successful kicking program places a major emphasis on that phase of football. Stanford's head coach takes charge of the kicking game and is responsible for the introduction and follow through plan from week to week. When the head coach places this much emphasis on that part of the total program, its importance becomes obvious. Fourth, a coach must exert a very strong disciplinary approach to this phase of the program — perhaps more than any other — because it is an area in which players tend to become careless. Unlike the flexibility that we recommend in other aspects of football, the kicking game must be consistent in every regard. Some of the more important areas are:
1. The snap of the ball
2. The height of the ball
3. The time it is in the air
4. The snap on the point after touchdown
5. Protection of the inside gap by a point after touchdown or field goal protector
6. Holding the ball for the point after touchdown
7. The coverage lanes in punt, punt coverage, coverage lanes in kickoff.
8. "Shoulder relationship" on the ball in all coverages. Shoulder relationship is defined as using the proper shoulder or angle approach to the ball to maintain efficient field coverage. The long return is caused more often than not by an

over-balance of coverage men on one side of the ball or
the other.

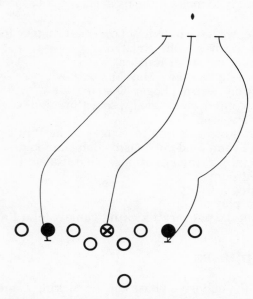

   Fifth, a coach can utilize special teams to carry out some of the
different aspects of the kicking game because of substitution rules
and the specialized nature of today's football. This makes it possible
to have special kickoff coverage teams, punt return teams, or other
units that are advantageous. This gives the athlete who normally
does not play a great deal of opportunity to display the energy and
enthusiasm that is an integral part of the program. We definitely
want to emphasize, however, that this is not always the answer to
a successful kicking game. A coach should not necessarily let everyone off the bench just so they'll be able to say that they played in a
game. He must sensitively evaluate this aspect of the program because sometimes the kicking game affords the opportunity to rest
skilled players. They will be, therefore, that much more effective
when they return to the game. If a coach ever sacrifices a decrease
in performance by those who perform the kicking game and it causes
breakdowns, he may be wiser to take the better players and coach
them in the kicking game.
   Before embarking on a discussion of the coaching of individual
skills, the areas of team teaching should be noted. They include:
punt return, punt rush, kickoff coverage, kickoff return, P.A.T. and
field goal protection and coverage, punt protection and coverage,
P.A.T. and field goal rush, tight punt, taking a safety, punt play,
and special kicking situations such as kickoff game and punt game.
   We break down our kicking game into offensive and defensive
areas for specific responsibility and communication. We give each

coach the specific responsibility in every area of kicking. We have found that he will take additional pride in his specialty and conduct research and study to make it the most successful aspect of that part of the game.

For example, we have individual coaches assigned to these areas:
1. Punt return—John Ralston
2. Punt rush—John Ralston
3. Kick off coverage—Max McCartney
4. Kick off return—Roger Theder
5. P.A.T. and field goal protection and coverage—Jack Christiansen
6. Punt protection and coverage—Mike White
7. P.A.T. and field goal rush—Bob Gambold
8. Special kicking situations—John Ralston
9. Tight punt
10. Taking a safety
11. Punt play
12. In charge of overall kicking game—John Ralston

Offensive phases

Following are the offensive phases of the kicking game:
1. Punt and coverage
   a. Center, kicker, timing (2.1 second, 14 yard snap)
   b. Protection and release (recoil)
   c. Coverage relationship (spacing)
   d. Kick inside your coverage
   e. Kill man, contain man, and safeties
   f. Each man must make the tackle
2. Kickoff return
   a. Field the ball
   b. Wedge relationship or return relationship
   c. Front three (upset coverage with your block)
   d. Proper setting of wedge in relationship to the caught ball
   e. Get the ball out to 30 yard line if possible
3. P.A.T. and Field Goal
   a. Center snap, holding, and kicking timing (1.3 to 1.4 sec., 7 yd. snap)
   b. Your line techniques (Never move outside foot; player is responsible for inside gap.)
   c. Halfbacks or wingbacks position
   d. Coverage if a field goal
4. Poocher Punt and/or Tight Punt
   a. Have a philosophy of when to use either one; familiarize your team with downing the ball rules to eliminate a ball rolling into end zone.

5. Plays from kicking formations
    a. Punt Play
    b. P.A.T. and field goal play
6. Onside kickoff return
    a. Substitute good "fielders" in your front nine men.

Defensive procedures

Defensive kicking procedures include:
1. Punt rush
    a. Getoff
    b. Go to the blocking point
    c. Handle the ball in fair catch
    d. Start return course to either side
2. Punt return
    a. Force a fast kick
    b. Field the ball
    c. Pin down the corner
    d. Be quick in getting to the ball
3. P.A.T. and field goal rush
    a. Quickness in get off
    b. Put pressure on the corner
    c. Have coverage if a fake
4. Kickoff coverage
    a. Speed downfield
    b. Get back on course
    c. Have 2 distinct waves
    d. Make the tackle
5. Poocher return
    a. Alert left end for a contain or spy man
    b. Force kick quickly
    c. Handle the ball
    d. Have a blocking protector for the man fielding the punt
    e. Do not ever field the punt inside the 10 yard line
6. Onside kickoff
    a. Get the ball
    b. Block the "fielders"

Basic diagrams will follow that will illustrate all aspects of the kicking game. They will explain the exact details that go into our kicking game at Stanford and also will include brief explanations of exactly how we have arrived at the systems we are using. We in no way are attempting to imply that this is the only way to handle each particular phase of the kicking game; but we do feel that we have been able to iron out some of the coaching points and specific elements that are necessary in each area. The drill book contains more detailed explanations of the various drills with suggested outlines for practicing kicking in pre-practice and practice as well as methods of warming up before a game.

Spread punt

We have tried several forms of punt formations at Stanford and have settled on the standard spread punt with two backs in the center-guard seams. The most unique feature of our punt formation takes advantage of the fact that it is virtually impossible to determine whom a player will block when he comes to the line of scrimmage. Because protection is the number one goal of our punt alignment, we became impressed with the recoil technique used by the University of Washington. The basis for this theory of punting is that standard splits are established at the line and the linemen recoil, and the backs fire out to establish a consistent wall of blockers at the moment that the coverage pattern is formed. The recoil gives any defensive rushes or stunts a chance to materialize; therefore, it gives us a chance to pick up the dangerous rushers by a very disciplined release after our recoil. The most important aspect of the punt formation is the center snap, and we feel that the ball should be snapped from the center to the kicker in nine-tenths of a second. The kicker, who is fourteen yards back, should have the ball released from his foot in 2.1 or 2.2 seconds, thus giving him from 1.2 to 1.3 seconds to kick the ball. The details of teaching these particular techniques are contained in the drill book. The following is our spread punt alignment and some of the principles, position assignments, and coaching points:

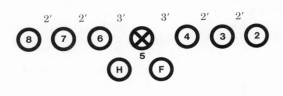

General principles

1. Huddle Call: spread punt on the snap—"ready break"
2. Stance: assume a two point stance with your elbows on your knees. Upbacks will use three point stance with either hand down.
3. Blocking Principle: recoil and block through an area or man if he is in your assigned area. "Pop" the man with the forehead through the man's numbers and get into your coverage lane. Release outside the man if possible.
4. Snap Count: the FB will give a "set" command after checking with the punter. The ball will be snapped anytime after a one second pause following the set call. All adjustments stop with the set command!

Position assignments

1. Center: make the perfect snap anytime after the one second pause following the set command.
2. Guards: recoil, driving off the inside foot. Block through your area and get into your coverage lane. Never block inside off your outside foot!
3. Tackles: recoil, driving off the inside foot if blocking outside and off the outside foot if blocking down in a "load" situation (2 man threat to G-T seam). Call down if blocking down to notify end. Block through your area and get into your coverage lane.
4. Ends: same as tackles. Be alert for overload situation inside!
5. Upbacks (halfback & flanker): line up one yard deep. On snap of ball step to center with inside foot, drive off inside foot. Block through your area and get into coverage lane.
6. Fullback: check with the punter to see if he is ready, at the proper depth and what foot he is kicking with. Block the first dangerous rusher. Be alert for overloads. Call "set" when punter is ready. Release into safety coverage lane. Fullback can never step back!
7. Kicker: after kicking ball cover opposite FB.

Spread punt coverage

One of the first questions a coach must ask himself when studying the punt game, specifically the coverage, is whether he is looking for a punter who can punt for distance or for height. Obviously, it would be ideal to have a punter who could accomplish both. However, successful punt coverage is based on the punter's ability not to outkick his coverage, thus giving the great backs a chance to get underway. During the 1970 season, our punters averaged slightly over thirty-five yards per game. However, in the sixty punts involved, our opponents returned the ball only a total of 61 yards. We are confident that this return percentage was among the best in the country, but we don't feel it was achieved by accident. We spend an appreciable amount of time on punt coverage, and probably the most important elements we emphasize are:

After recoil, it is important to release outside if possible to get in the proper coverage lane; the initial ten to fifteen yard sprint after release from the line of scrimmage is crucial to coverage; and someone, either the kicker or the two containing ends, must find the ball as soon as possible so we can maintain the coverage relationship (approaching the ball with the proper shoulder). "Every coverage man must know where the ball is."

These are the general principles that we follow in spread punt coverage:

General rules

1. Never follow a teammate downfield—relative spacing.
2. Stay in your assigned lane regardless of what happens.
3. Converge on the ball through your inside shoulder (left side—right shoulder) (right side—left shoulder).
4. The first man down is free to take a "shot"—kill man.
5. Keep your shoulders square to the football.
6. Fair catch signal—first man down should sprint right past the receiver.
7. Come to balance 3 to 4 yards in front of the football. The "balance" position will depend on each player's individual abilities.

Assignments

1. Line (3-4 6-7) recoil and strike through your area. Fan out gaining relative spacing to the man inside you, then locate the football. Don't cover looking for the ball; locate it as you sprint to cover. Don't run, sprint!!! Come to balance 3 to 4 yards in front of the football. Approach the ball with the proper shoulder.
2. Ends: contain the football by sprinting for a course that would put you 5 yards outside and 5 yards in front of the football. Be ready to converge on the football from the outside in if it "pops" our forward wall.
3. Center: release straight for the ball. Stay *head up* on the ball as it moves laterally.

4. Upbacks: release straight ahead and go for the ball. Run past a fair catch man. Keep the ball on your inside shoulder.
5. Fullback: become a safety on the side you line up on.
6. Kicker: become a safety opposite the FB.

Coaching points

1. Change personnel to more effectively get coverage.
2. Be ready to use upbacks as contain men and ends as "kill men."

Below is a coverage diagram with explanations:

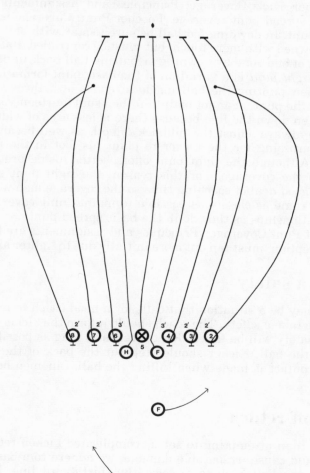

Poocher and tight punt

The *poocher* is more of an emphasis rather than an alternate formation. The poocher punt is used when we want to place the opponent inside its own ten-yard line. It indicates a regular line formation and coverage with the emphasis on the rules involved in downing the ball before it rolls into the end zone. The ability to be successful with a poocher punt rests primarily in the ability of the kicker. He must be able to kick a reasonable distance and to have the ball land dead on the ground or with a minimum of roll so the coverage men can place pressure on the prospective receiver. It must be remembered that artificial turf may cause the ball to make unpredictable bounces.

Poocher Kick Coverage: Principles and assignments are the same as spread punt coverage. Poocher Punt: Coverage is same as spread punt. In downing football be sure to stay with ball. Football is not downed with mere touch, but must be controlled. Ball must be kept out of end zone by downing or batting ball back in play.

The *tight punt* is a variation of the basic punt formation and is used when punting the ball inside a team's own three-yard line. Because the punter cannot maintain the usual fourteen-yard depth, we tighten down the line because there is less area of width to protect. We always adjust the fullback's depth as well because it is a bit embarassing for the kicker to plant his foot in the fullback's pocket. Although the tight punt offers better inside protection, it restricts the coverage. For this reason, the tight punt should be given a good deal of coaching time so the coverage men will spread out and come as closely as possible to maintaining coverage lanes and relationships as they do in the basic spread punt.

Tight Punt Coverage: Principles and assignments are the same. One exception: must fan out more initially due to tighter alignment.

Take a safety

There may be a situation that calls for a head coach to make a decision to take a safety. The coach should inform the kicker and team that a safety will be taken. Kicker takes as long as possible before killing the ball. Kicker should step out the back of the end zone before contact is made when killing the ball. Linemen hold blocks longer.

Kickoff return

Rather than attempting to set up complicated kickoff return plays that could cause irreparable damage, we adhere to a basic goal of getting the ball back to at least the thirty-yard line. Maximum security is the most important prerequisite in structuring our return because we are able to account for all of the opponent's key coverage men with our front five blockers. Then our wedge of four men personally escort our return man as far upfield as possible. We vary the type of blocks used by our wall men and give them a definite side to peel back to assist the runner. Choosing return men should be of primary importance because he must be strong enough to make his own way when the coverage men converge, and to hold the ball when he is hit by an open field, full-speed tackle.

Illustrated below is the wedge return diagram:

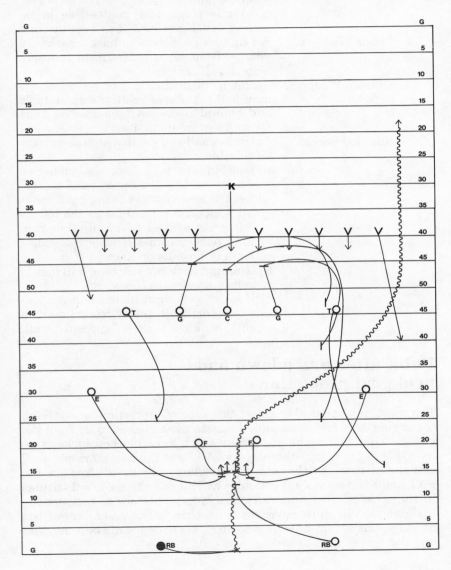

Rules:

Call:	We call "wedge right" or "wedge left" which will indicate peel area. Direction may change depending on kick direction.
Wall:	Pick out three of inside five coverage men (excluding safety) and block them aggressively.

    a. Outside wall, pick out designated most dangerous rushers on outside and block man.

    b. Middle three after aggressive block, peel to designated side and set up wall.

Inside Wedgers:	Set-up wedge between hash marks 10 yds. in front of ball. Maintain relationship to ball carrier.
Outside Wedgers:	Sprint to near shoulder of inside wedge man and get proper relationship (outside and behind inside wedgeman). Be alert for tacklers from outside.
Running backs:	Catch football and get to wedge as quickly as possible.

    a. One running back becomes catcher as determined by the direction of return. Return left: right running back takes all kicks from his right as far left as left point of goal post and other running back becomes blocker on wedge, looking for outside man.

    b. Running back not catching ball makes call to accelerate the wedge.

    c. If kick is off right or left and is opposite return call, inside wedge man on side of kick makes "opposite" call.

Point after touchdown and field goal protection

The most important element of this type of protection is to stretch the corner as wide as possible because most rushes come from the outside, and this is the area from which most blocked kicks originate. We suggest that the players who have the necessary physical equipment to make the widest possible corner be utilized for the PAT and FG if possible. Your rules will dictate the use of substitutes in these cases. Two important coaching points are to instruct the lineman that he must never move his outside foot and to know that he is responsible for anyone who attempts to penetrate between him and the player next to him.

The center, holder, and kicker must spend as much time together as possible to perfect their timing.

Below is illustrated the Stanford formation for points after touchdown and field goals:

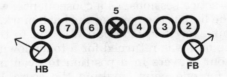

1. Stance: three point stance
2. Assignments
   a. Line: step with your inside foot, keeping your shoulders square and seal off the inside gap.
   b. HB and FB: line up splitting the ends alignment position with the inside foot, facing out at a 45 degree angle. Seal the inside gap and protect to the outside without moving the inside foot.
   c. Holder: call "set," place the ball. Huddle call—P.A.T. on the snap.
   d. Snap Count: same as spread punt
3. Field Goal: same; now include coverage responsibility. Line: fan out and cover field—HB & FB—contain Holder: when calling field goal on the snap, remind the team to *cover*—then ready—break!

On-side kickoff

This is an area of kicking that is given very little attention but is very predictable. Because the situation usually is predictable, there is no excuse for not having the most effective and dependable personnel on the front line who can handle the ball. I learned this lesson the hard way when I was coaching at Utah State in 1960.

We went ahead of Wyoming 17-6 with about one minute and fifty seconds to play. On the face of it, Utah State had the game wrapped up. Because it was a championship game, we wanted to give our third team players an opportunity to get in some playing time, so we substituted them along with Jim Turner, a great kickoff man. Our kickoff procedure was to kick from the middle of the field. However, because we were playing on wet grounds, the middle of the field was very soft and Jim decided on his own to move the ball to the hash mark to get better footing. This possibility never had been covered in our practice sessions; as a consequence, we had five men on each side of the ball at the point of the hash mark. Turner kicked deep into Wyoming territory, the ball was run to the wide side of the field, and the ball was returned for a touchdown because there were so few of our players in a position to even make an effort. Wyoming went for one point, making the score 17-13 with one minute and forty-three seconds left on the clock.

Wyoming still had plenty of time to win if it could get its hands on the ball, so it was obvious that the onside kick would be exploited. To add to our problems, we had spent little time on fielding an on-side kick. Instead of substituting players who were used to handling the ball, the regular Utah State tackles lined up in their normal positions. The kickoff was well placed to one of our tackles, who bobbled the ball, and Wyoming had possession on our 43-yard line with a full minute-and-a-half to play. They moved to a first down on our twenty-eight yard line and from there threw four passes into the end zone, any one of which could have resulted in a Wyoming win. The passes were batted around, and were touched by Wyoming men, but fortune was with us and none connected.

It doesn't take a football expert to know that the kicking game, or lack of practice in it, almost cost us a championship. Needless to say, I did some intensive analysis of our kicking game as I left the field. Too often it is lessons such as this that make an indelible impression on the importance of the connecting link between offense and defense.

Page 391 shows our on-side kick alignment and return.

Rules:
   Lineup:
      1. Wedge move up inside 45 yd. line
      2. Wall moves up tight to 50 yd. line
      3. Running backs remain in return position
   Return:
      1. If ball is not onside kick we will have an automatic wedge right return. Wedge and wall men execute the wedge return right the best possible way.

Punt plays

It is important to incorporate a play or two from the base punt formation. These may include reverses, sweeps, passes or other well executed surprises. The fact that you are known for plays from punt

ONSIDE KICK ALIGNMENT

```
G  _____
5  _____
10 _____
15 _____
20 _____
25 _____
30 _____
                              K
35 _____▽_____
40 ___▽____▽____▽_▽___▽_____▽___▽___▽___▽___▽
45 _____
50 _____
45 ___Ⓣ_____Ⓔ____Ⓖ_ⒻⒷ_Ⓒ_ⒻⒷ_Ⓖ_____Ⓔ____Ⓣ___
40 _____
35 _____
30 _____
25 _____
20 _____
15 _____
10 _____
5  _____
G  _____ⓇⒷ_____ⓇⒷ_____
```

formation can be of value to cut down rushes and allow for more
effective coverage. Below are illustrated two of our fake punt plays.

FAKE PUNT RUN

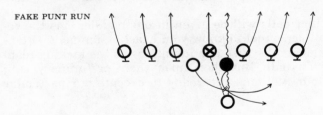

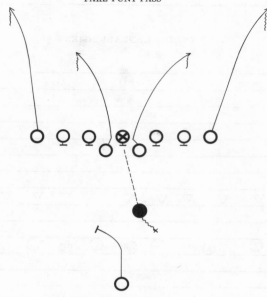

Defensive punt game

In defensing our opponent's punt game we will break down into
five separate categories. It should be remembered at the outset,
however, that you never neglect the four basic don'ts in the kicking
game. We will be continually selling these as we are going along.
They are: 1) don't be off-side, 2) don't rough the kicker, 3) don't
clip, and 4) don't let the ball hit the ground.

Our five categories will be broken down into two from our base
alignment and three from our odd alignment or return position.
Our calls will be as follows: 1) *base — hold-up,* 2) *base — go get it
outside,* 3) *odd — return right,* 4) *odd — return left* and 5) *odd —
go get it inside.*

These particular calls will be given in our huddle; it is the responsibility of all personnel to know your exact assignment. Oftentimes we will want to disguise our intentions as the kicking team
approaches the football. But then upon their preliminary call,
we must be in our positions and ready to execute our particular
assignment.

Base — hold-up

With a nine-man punt, we will align on every man along the line.
Mike will be aligned on the center, our guards on the upbacks, our
tackles on the offensive guards, our strike and whip on the offensive

tackles, and our halfbacks will be aligned on the offensive ends. We will have our two safetys in a deep position.

All linemen should be aligned slightly on the outside, and on the snap of the ball crab inside with your head to the ball and hold up the particular man you are aligned on as long as possible. Halfbacks will play man for man on the offensive ends. Harass them downfield as long as possible. Be sure you are conscious of whether or not the ball is kicked.

All linemen scramble up when your man gets away from you and hustle back to your side to form a wall. Safety's handle ball properly and get what you can, probably up the middle.

K

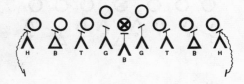

SAFETYS 40 YARDS
DOWNFIELD

Base – go get it outside

From our base alignment, on the snap of the ball, we want our two
outside halfbacks to jump inside of the offensive ends and rush aggressively to the kicking spot. Strike and whip will take over the
man coverage on the ends and will harass them down the field from
an inside out position as we will be returning the ball up the middle.
Guards and tackles charge as aligned. Mike pick one side or the
other, and drive the upback guard seam.

Safetys handle the ball properly and return up the middle.

K

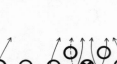

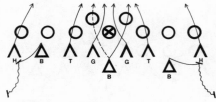

SAFETYS 40 YARDS
DOWNFIELD

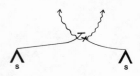

Odd—return right

We will want to disguise our intentions somewhat when we are in our odd alignment. Our Mike backer should cover the guard to his side and then come out late on our returns. Our strong safety and ship linebacker should move in and out to disguise their intentions from either a return or an inside rush. In our return, we will be operating with a single safety and two deep halfbacks able to field a short kick by fair catching should the ball come in their direction.

We will slide our line to the right as diagramed for all of our odd returns or rush.

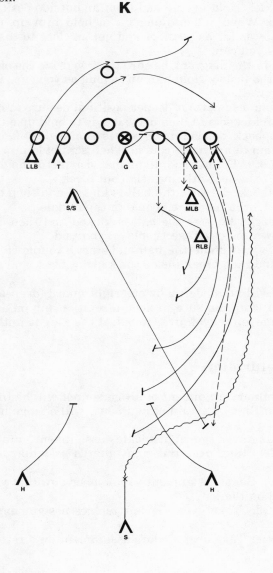

Strike: Rush outside the general protector and try to block the kick. If you do not block the kick, then be sure you block the kicker.

Left tackle: Rush inside the general protector and you will be our man who comes down outside the wall ready to clean up.

Left guard: From a position on the nose of the center you will be charging aggressively into whichever of the middle three is their first man down. Once you have charged through him, get into the wall at the proper position.

Right guard: From an alignment on the tackle, force him to the inside and then hustle as deep as possible in the wall.

Right tackle: Hold up the end from an outside position as long as possible. When you no longer can hold him up, drive straight downfield as far as possible and get as close to the ball for your block as you can.

Mike: As in the diagram, be sure that we drive the offensive tackle well to the inside. Hold him up as long as you can. Then scramble into the wall.

Whip: From a somewhat deeper position, be sure first that the ball has been kicked and then drive inside to hold up either the guard or the upback, depending on who is coming downfield. Be sure you force them to an inside course. Then scramble into the wall.

Strong safety: From your alignment, drive crossfield and kick the contain man out with an inside out block.

Right halfback: Be sure the ball is kicked and then drive inside to slow down the coverage people in the middle.

Left halfback: Be sure the ball is kicked and then drive inside to slow down the coverage people on your side.

Single safety: Handle the ball and start a couple of steps straight ahead and then break inside the kickout block and get behind the wall.

Our wall will be made up by our right guard (deepest), left guard, Mike, and whip. Be sure to keep a relationship on each other and be set to move the wall over to ball if the kick is to the far side.

Odd – return left

The preliminary alignment of all personnel will be the same as for the Return Right. Certain assignments will change however.

Strike: Take over the right tackles assignment on a return right.

Left tackle: Take over the right guards assignment on a return right.

Left guard: Same assignment – remember now that you will set up the wall on the left.

Right guard: Take over the left tackles assignment on a return right.

Right tackle: Take over strike's assignment on a return right.

K

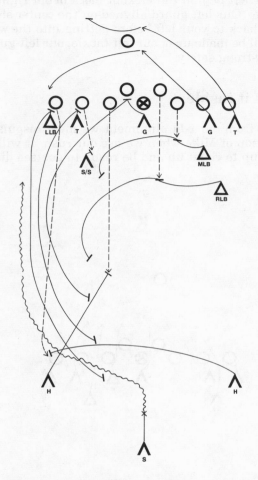

Mike: Execute the start of your return right assignment, but pass up the tackle and block the guard. Scramble quickly and get into the wall on our left.

Whip: Execute your same assignment as in a return right blocking the most dangerous coverage man and then scramble up and get in the wall on the left. (You will probably hit the right up back.)

Strong safety: Drive the offensive tackle to your side to the inside. Stay with him.

Left halfback: Be sure the ball is kicked and drive to the inside to block, probably the guard to your side.

Right halfback: You will assume the kickout block on the defensive end similar to the strong safetys assignment on a return right.

Safety: Handle the ball and take two steps straight upfield and then
    break to your left behind the kickout block of our right halfback.
    Special Note: Our left guard aligned on the center should drive
through the upback to your left before getting into the wall.
    Our wall will be made up of our left tackle, our left guard, Mike,
Whip, and our strong safety.

Odd – go get it inside

All personnel – from our odd alignment we must disguise particularly the intention of Mike when we use our rush. It will be necessary also for whip to cheat up and be ready to go. (see diagram)

K

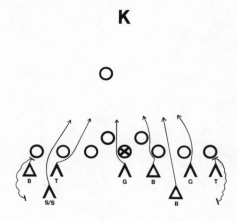

SAFETYS 40 YARDS
DOWNFIELD

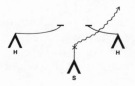

398

Strike and right tackle: Draw the block of the offensive ends and hold them up as long as you can. Stay with them downfield, harassing them whenever you can.

Left tackle: Charge as diagramed.

Left guard: Charge as diagramed.

Mike: Charge as diagramed.

Right guard: Charge as diagramed.

Strong safety: Rush as is diagramed.

Whip back: Rush as is diagramed.

Left halfback: Be sure ball is kicked and then block first man down to your side.

Right halfback: Be sure ball is kicked and then block first man down to your side.

Safety: Handle the ball and chances are your best return opportunity will come to your right.

General rules on our return:

1. We must know who their best coverage personnel are.
2. We must force the tackle to the inside on the return side.
3. We must delay the end on the return side as long as possible prior to driving downfield for a block, in the area of the ball.
4. We will always have two men forcing a punt on our return and they should attempt to block the kick. Also, be sure to rush with one inside and one outside the general protector.
5. Mike and whip should roll block the first men downfield.
6. The halfbacks must always be conscious to block first men downfield which will allow the safety to catch the ball.
7. All linemen should be conscious when the ball approaches the wall and you do not have a blocking assignment to turn upfield and run with the ball carrier.
8. Be sure we are setting the wall at least ten yards from the sideline.
9. The end man on the line away from the return has the assignment of blocking the kicker.

Remember again our four basic don'ts in the kicking game: 1) don't be offside, 2) don't rough the kicker, 3) don't clip and 4) don't let the ball hit the ground.

The kicking game always results in a win or loss, particularly in the close games. Let's win with our kicking game. *Let's block a kick! Let's return all the way!*

Blocking PAT's and field goals

Because of increasingly good defensive efficiency, the only real opportunity to block a point after touchdown or field goal is from the outside. Following is our rush if the opponent is in a kicking formation:

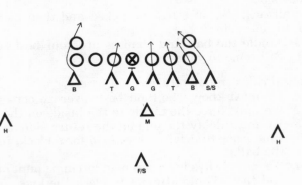

LLB – Position – outside blocking back
   Responsibility – #1
 LT – Position – outside guard
   Responsibility – #4 (hands up)
 LG – Position – nose on center
   Responsibility – deliver blow on center (hands up)
 RT – Same as left
 RG – Position – outside tackle (on side of rush)
   Responsibility – block kick
RLB – Position – nose on blocking back
   Responsibility – block kick (#1)
MOVER – Position – nose on tight end (on side of block call)
   Responsibility – block kick
MIKE – Position – inside guard on side of block call
   Responsibility – 1 man coverage with HB on
    1. short side of field
    2. side of block
HB'S – Responsibility – outside receiver
  S – Responsibility –
    1. field short attempts
    2. man coverage with HB on:
        1. wide side of field
        2. opposite block call

Kickoff coverage

Kickoff coverage is probably one of the most important aspects of football because it directly determines where a team will begin the opening series of offensive plays. The success of coverage, of course, will be determined by the abilities of the kicker; but most teams are not blessed with kickers who can get the ball into the end zone, so it is an area of the game in which we must do a good job. Because unlimited substitution is available, a coach has the opportunity to utilize the most effective players on his team to perform this important function. We do not advocate that a coach use this as an opportunity to substitute second and third team players because his only result would be a costly breakdown that could possibly influence the outcome of the game. Here are some of the important elements that we consider in determining our coverages from week to week:

1. Evaluate your own kicker, whether or not he has the ability to be an active tackler or should be a safety.
2. Evaluate position of safetys. It is important to determine the position of safetys to provide adequate field coverage.
3. Evaluate the opponent's returns. The type of return that is utilized will have a great deal of bearing on what the coverage men are asked to do. Techniques included in defeating their return will include destroying the wedge, getting behind a wall, getting through a picket set-up, and awareness of crossing blocking patterns.
4. Evaluate weather and field conditions. These include types of turf as well as the effect of playing under artificial lights.
5. Determine the direction of the kick, if possible. It might be advisable to kick to, or away from, certain personnel on the opponent's team.
6. Review elements of our pitch-fork coverage
   a. accelerate to the ball
   b. don't follow a team-mate
   c. get back into your lane
   d. always approach the ball with proper shoulder
   e. always keep toes toward goal line when converging on the ball.

Stanford's basic kickoff coverage is broken down into three primary elements. Six players are designated as lane men and are responsible to sprint in their assigned lanes until the return route is determined. Three players are sprinters and have the sole responsibility to go immediately to the ball. They must penetrate the blocking pattern, and they have the option of taking any chances to get the hit. Two safetys are responsible to stop the long return. They sprint at least fifteen yards and then back up the ball.

Following is a detailed diagram of the assigned men, lanes, and direction of pursuit:

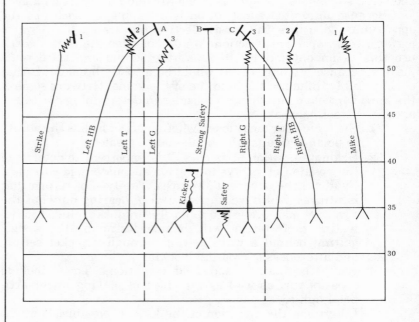

KICK OFF COVERAGE

Sprinters (A - B - C):
A. Continue to ball and tackle everything with right shoulder.
B. Continue to ball and tackle everything from a front position.
C. Continue to ball and tackle everything with left shoulder.

Lanes (1 - 2 - 3 left; 1 - 2 - 3 right):
1-2-3 left shoulder lanes: Come to balance about 10 yards in front of ball and converge to inside.
1-2-3 right shoulder lanes: Come to balance about 10 yards in front of ball and converge to inside.

Kicker: First safety, be ready to force ball to nearest sideline.

Safety: Work with kicker to pin runner to sideline.

On-side kick

We kick the ball on the top right corner in an attempt to get a sideways spin that puts the ball on our left side just over the ten-yard required area. The five men on the kicker's left become full-speed sprinters and make an effort to recover the ball as quickly as possible. The five men on the right side of the kicker should become safeties and immediately back up the left side in the event of a poor kick. It took us close to twenty years of coaching before we realized the importance of the safeties in an on-side kick. During the 1966 UCLA game we had an on-side kick returned for a touchdown because of poor preparation and design of our on-side kick coverage.

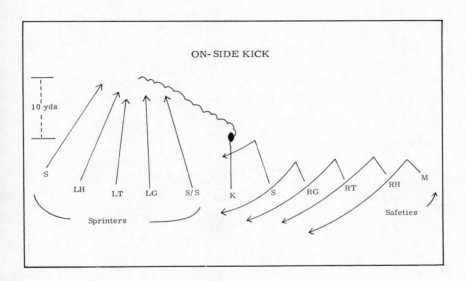

Drills for the kicking game

We have attempted to point out the importance of the kicking game to the total success of a football team. Because this is the case, we also emphasize the importance of drilling individual techniques that comprise a successful kicking game. There are obvious individual skills related to the center and/or kickers, but coaches constantly should examine the other individual techniques such as covering a punt or kickoff as well as the technique of blocking a point after touchdown, field goal, or punt.

The following diagrams illustrate examples of drills:

Punt coverage drill

1. Teach punt coverage to the individual coverage men.
2. Two men covering at a time for emphasis on relationship to ball and field. Full speed or form drill.
3. Any player or players can be singled out to cover.
4. No defense is used except the punt receiver.

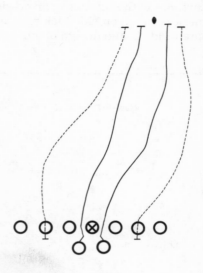

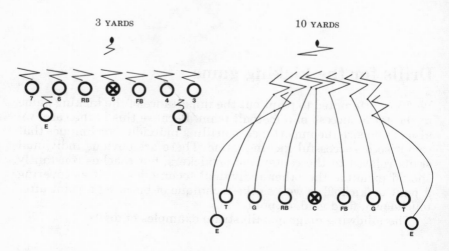

Punt or PAT-field goal blocking drills

1. Teach the blocking point and stress the importance of aiming for this spot to prevent roughing the kicker penalty
2. Drills should be utilized with one player at a time with his proper relationship to the ball
3. No offense is needed except for the center and kicker, as well as appropriate markings for offensive spacing

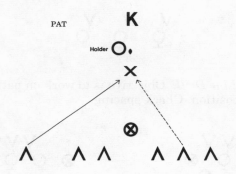

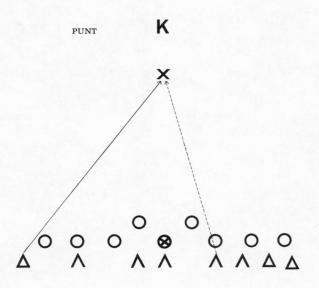

Punting drills

1. Stance Splits
2. Recoil and Blocking Position
3. Coverage
4. Tackling

One on one: Objective is to develop good stance-split-set up, understand technique and blocking position, start the path of coverage.

One-Half Line Drill: Objective is to work on path of coverage blocking position. Check spacing.

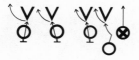   

17

Scouting

Throughout the history of football, head coaches have been faced with the task of trying to determine what every opponent has planned for him. The frantic questions that are uppermost in the minds of coaches in every league, from Pop Warner to the sophisticated professional ranks, are:
1. What must we stop?
2. How can we gain?
3. What must we do to win?

Untold hours and money are spent in an attempt to arrive at a solution that will provide the tools for a winning effort.

We are going to discuss the manner in which our philosophy at Stanford has changed, the choosing of an efficient scout, the use of films, methods of organizing and evaluating both the off-season and in-season scouting evaluation systems, total staff involvement, selective scouting forms and their use; what to ask the scout when he returns to campus, sample scouting reports, preparing the scout for his assignment, *and* some of the new scouting trends, including computerized scouting, and our opinions of its effectiveness.

Scouting obviously is different depending upon the coaching level. However, knowing what the opponent is going to do, or at least making a concerted effort to determine what he is going to do, is something every coach wants to know. The methods and procedures that are used obviously will depend upon the available money as well as the abilities of the scouting personnel.

Many young coaches point to their lack of funds or lack of available scouting personnel as a reason for decreased scouting emphasis and success. However, we believe these excuses are unnecessary, and that a coach at any level can organize a workable system.

Scouting, as is true in so many other areas of football, has undergone a great change in the past few years. At Stanford, we always are looking for methods of improving our evaluations of opponents. We have arrived at the conclusion that a competent scout can be sitting in a football stadium, or he can perform his responsibilities in a film screening room. We believe that the combination of the two techniques supplies the best possible information. However, if we had to make a choice, we believe that a better evaluation can be obtained through the use of films. Every aspect of the opponent's offensive and defensive system can be studied and analyzed in detail by using audio-visual aids. Plays and defenses can be run back and forth many times to determine whether there is some key to aid us in our preparation. In our league, as well as in a good many other college and university conferences, there are provisions for certain film exchange programs. These usually are more than adequate to provide thorough examinations of the opponents.

The problem may be harder to solve at the high school level; however, most high schools do take films and should be able to provide an exchange with a given opponent. In many small communities, there are amateur or professional photographers who are interested in sports and will perform the service for little or no cost to the school.

When exchanging films it is important to have a well organized system of procurement as well as an efficient means of keeping track of your own films. The letter we use is on page 409.

Even though we prefer the use of films, we also are aware of the importance of having a staff member scout each opponent. Our current scouting program consists of a two-man approach which allows our personnel to observe each opponent the week prior to the scheduled game. This technique provides a necessary continuity and basis for comparison. One scout concentrates on the opponent's offense, the other on the defense. There is a definite disadvantage to this approach because the scout does not always see the upcoming opponent in the toughest game or in the toughest possible situation. However, as we pointed out earlier, this can be compensated for by using selected films. Another advantage of using the two scout system is their aid in the subsequent week of practice when they supervise the scout teams to prepare your offensive and defensive players. With their knowledge and insight of the opponent's game plans and style of play, they have an opportunity to be a coach in charge of their own program. These scouts also are responsible for written and oral reports to be presented to the other staff members as well as to the squad. In all good scouting procedures, it must be remembered that it is not only the amount of knowledge to be gained by the coaches that is important; it is how much of this knowledge can be translated and communicated to the players. All of the opponent's tendencies are meaningless unless they can be utilized in the actual game.

FILM REQUEST LETTER

DEPARTMENT OF PHYSICAL EDUCATION AND ATHLETICS

STANFORD UNIVERSITY
STANFORD, CALIFORNIA 94305

We are extremely interested in exchanging films with you during the coming football season. If agreeable, please send the movies of your game(s) with:

_____   _____

_____   _____

_____   _____

The above film(s) will be returned to you by:

_____

_____

_____

We will be happy to send you film(s) of our game(s)
with: to be sent on:

_____   _____

_____   _____

_____   _____

The above film(s) to be returned by:

_____

_____

_____

If you prefer any other films, please let me know, and we will make every effort to accommodate you.

Sincerely,

John Ralston
Head Football Coach

Scouting at Stanford begins sometime during the month of May when preliminary scouting directives are issued for the following Fall. Probably the most important individual in a scouting program is the staff member who is assigned to the film exchange program. We have one coach who is assigned that responsibility, and he must formulate a very detailed, organized procedure to handle both our own films and those of our opponents. The film man's problems are increased because he must keep one film circulating from week to week, or in some cases, two or three times a week to make the necessary and beneficial exchanges.

The preliminary scouting directive is issued to the staff late in the Spring, and assignments are made regarding who will be responsible for reviewing the films and who will perform the on-the-scene scouting.

One of the most important elements in scouting is to familiarize oneself with the opponents before the scout team actually observes the opposition play. It obviously is impossible to scout an early season opponent, particularly the first or second teams on the schedule. Therefore, the first part of our staff directive is a review of past season games, Summer film studies, and specific information regarding Spring game scouting. As we progress in the season, we realize adjustments have been made by our opponents in personnel and style of play, so the actual "man-looks" become more and more necessary and important both offensively and defensively. We have found, however, that a number of our opponents usually follow some distinct pattern year in and year out.

On page 411 is our summer film study directive. The organization of film procurement and study is extremely important so each staff member knows exactly the area for which he is responsible. On page 412, our 1970 scouting schedule appears.

We are aware that most high school coaches are very conscious of the importance of scouting and like to do as much of the actual man-looks themselves as possible. The hard-working coach will see as many as three or four games a weekend to try to keep up with his opponents' progress. This, of course, isn't always possible, and the coach who plans ahead usually will find the best possible substitute. He may be able to rely upon a fellow teacher who has a basic knowledge of football in terms of formations and basic patterns as well as defensive alignments and coverages. Oftentimes, a former teammate or a former player who has a knowledge of the coach's program will perform excellently and volunteer to see the most important opponent several times. Frequently, there are former college or professional players in the community who would be happy to return to the game through this avenue of observation. Whether it is a member of the coach's regular staff or a volunteer, this is the basic outline he should follow:

1. Study the scouting forms and refer to them as a check on what to look for.

SUMMER FILM STUDY

ARKANSAS: ENTIRE STAFF
    A.   Study - All 1969 game films
    B.   Breakdown - 1969 Okla. State (opener), Texas Tech and Mississippi (Bowl Game)

    Secure films: Arkansas - Frank Broyles
                  (by previous agreement)

SAN JOSE STATE: Scouts & GAMBOLD
    A.   Study - 1969 Stanford-San Jose
    B.   Study - 1969 California-San Jose
    C.   Breakdown - 1969 Pacific-San Jose

    Secure films: California - Ray Willsey
                  Pacific - Homer Smith

OREGON: Scouts & MC CARTNEY
    A.   Study - 1969 Stanford-Oregon
    B.   Study - 1969 UCLA-Oregon
    C.   Study - 1969 Oregon State-Oregon
    D.   Study - 1969 Hawaii- Oregon

    Secure films: UCLA - Tom Prothro
                  Oregon State - Dee Andros
                  Hawaii - Dave Holmes

PURDUE: FEHRING & THEDER
    A.   Study - 1969 Stanford-Purdue
    B.   Breakdown - 1969 Indiana-Purdue

    Secure films: Indiana - John Pont

U.S.C.:   Scouts & WHITE & PEASLEY
    A.   Study - 1969 Stanford-USC

WASHINGTON STATE: Scouts & CHRISTIANSEN
    A.   Study - 1969 Stanford-W.S.U.

U.C.L.A.:   Scouts & MC CARTNEY & THEDER
    A.   Study - 1969 Stanford-UCLA

OREGON STATE: Scouts & GAMBOLD
    A.   Study - 1969 Stanford-OSU

WASHINGTON: Scouts & PEASLEY
    A.   Study - 1969 Stanford-Washington

AIR FORCE ACADEMY: Scouts & CHRISTIANSEN
    A.   Study - 1969 Stanford-Air Force

CALIFORNIA: Scouts & WHITE
    A.   Study - 1969 Stanford-California

SCOUTING SCHEDULE

Sept. 12th: ARKANSAS - Staff (White & Gambold)
        A.   Summer Film Study
        B.   Spring Game Film
        C.   Scout Spring Game - May 2nd - Theder

Sept. 19th: SAN JOSE STATE - Currey & Cardin (Gambold -- 2 man team)
        A.   Summer Film Study
        B.   Scout - Santa Barbara vs. San Jose State at Santa Barbara
              Sept. 12th.

Sept. 26th: OREGON - Currey & Cardin (McCartney)
        A.   Summer Film Study
        B.   Scout - Illinois vs. Oregon at Champaign Sept. 19th

Oct. 3rd: PURDUE - Fehring (Theder)
        A.   Summer Film Study
        B.   Scout - T. C. U. vs. Purdue at Lafayette Sept. 19th
        C.   Scout - Notre Dame vs. Purdue at South Bend Sept. 26th

Oct. 10th: U. S. C. - Currey & Cardin (White & Peasley)
        A.   Scout - O. S. U. vs. U. S. C. (night) at Los Angeles Oct. 3rd.

Oct 17th: WASHINGTON STATE - Currey & Cardin (Christiansen)
        A.   Scout - Arizona State vs. W. S. U. at Tempe Oct. 10th

Oct. 24th: U. C. L. A. - Currey & Cardin (McCartney & Theder)
        A.   Scout - Cal vs. U. C. L. A. at Berkeley Oct. 17th

Oct. 31st: OREGON STATE - Currey & Cardin (Gambold)
        A.   Scout - Washington vs. O. S. U. at Corvallis Oct. 24th

Nov. 7th: WASHINGTON - Currey & Cardin (Peasley)
        A.   Scout - Oregon vs. Washington at Seattle Oct. 31st

Nov. 14th: AIR FORCE ACADEMY - Currey & Cardin (Christiansen)
        A.   Scout - Oregon vs. Air Force at Eugene Nov. 7th

Nov. 21st: CALIFORNIA - Currey & Cardin (White)
        A.   Scout - San Jose vs. California at Berkeley Nov. 14th

IMPORTANT: ORDER YOUR NEWSPAPERS FOR SCOUTING AND RECRUIT-
ING THROUGH BOB GAMBOLD NOW! ! ! !

2. Seated one-half hour before game time.
3. View every play only as an opportunity to gain certain information. If you're enjoying the game, you're not conscientiously doing your job.
4. Report must be definite. Omit anything that has not been checked.

412

5. During warm-up, memorize names and numbers of backs and ends who'll start the game to aid you in learning their pass plays.
6. Don't try to write too much. When the team is in the huddle, note the yards to go, down, and what you're going to look for in the next play.
7. List details you are looking for, in order of importance.
8. After game, check your notes before leaving your seat. You will have time while waiting for statistics. Be sure that you pick them up, and have a complete set.
9. Anything that isn't clear should be straightened out while the game still is fresh in your mind.
10. List the points to be checked at the next game.
11. Fill out Scouting Report as soon as possible after the game.
12. Include newspaper clipping of game, give any play-by-play account, if possible.
13. In all diagrams, denote offensive players by O, defense by V.

Scouting the opponent's defense

In order to make an effective analysis of the opponent, film analysis and on-the-scene scouting should provide answers relative to both offense and defense. These defensive elements must be determined to properly prepare a team's offensive strategy:

1. Base defense
2. Any alternate defenses
3. Base coverages
4. Alternate coverages
5. Short yardage defenses
6. Long yardage or prevent defenses
7. Goal line defense
8. Major stunts
9. Pass rush ratio
10. Pass rush contain
11. Specific personnel, that is, their techniques and ability
12. Defensive analysis
    a. Down and distance analysis — normal, long, short
    b. Field position
13. Punt defense — on third or fourth downs, rush or return
14. Kick-off coverage — the distance of the kick, crossing men, safeties, and best coverage men
15. Plays that have hurt their defense
    a. Specific runs
    b. Specific passes
16. Strongest phases of their defense

17. Weakest phases of their defense
18. Analysis of their defensive philosophy and thinking
19. Evaluation of their defensive attitude
20. General suggestions offensively, or the answer to one of the three most important scouting questions, "How can we gain?"

Scouting the opponent's offense

The following are questions that should be answered for the benefit of the defense, based on what the opponent's offense is in the habit of doing:

1. Their base offense
2. Their goal line offense
3. Short yardage offense
4. Primary formations
5. Six best running plays
6. Four best pass plays
7. Offensive analysis
   a. 1-10 tendency-run or pass
   b. Run downs
   c. Pass downs
8. Strong phases of offense
9. Weak phases of offense
10. Punt formation
11. Second and third down punt formations and any runs from that
12. Kick-off formation
13. Pass or run plays from field goal formation
14. Things that have hurt them, such as stunts, rotation
15. Key personnel
16. Offensive team attitude and successes
17. Suggestions defensively or the answer to the third question, "What must we stop?"

It is imperative to seek, and respect, the scout's opinions and recommendations for attacking the opponent both offensively and defensively. It is very easy to become so bogged down with facts and figures that the scout never has the opportunity to give his own opinion of what the best procedures should be. Most of what the opponent does is very obvious; it is the not-so-obvious or well-concealed attacks that require preparation to realize the most success.

The high school coach may not have the personnel or funds to carry out the scouting procedures that will be outlined in this text. It is very possible that he will have to depend upon one man to scout both the offense and defense of the opponent. In that event, he can follow a much more simplified approach which should include these facts:

1. Huddle, shift, cadence.
2. Remarks on offensive and defense personnel; best players, possible worst players.
3. General remarks on offense; multiple formations, basic plays, passing formations, short yardage plays.
4. General remarks on defense; basic defensive alignment, over-shifts, deep secondary coverage, goal line, short yardage.
5. Strongest and weakest phases of opponent's offense and defense.
6. Recommendations for offense and defense that will be effective against opponent.

This information, coupled with the staff's previously acquired knowledge, should be ample to prepare a squad for a particular opponent. It should be remembered that too much information can be dangerous; the only information that is important is that which can be used effectively. A coach should be certain that the least knowledgeable assistant and player knows what he is talking about. A sample of this scout report will be found in the drill book.

General scouting procedures

1. All coaches should consult with the in-office film man to be sure that arrangements have been made to obtain the required films and the times that they will be available for study. Films should not be kept for too long a period of time. If two or more persons are scheduled to work together, it is important to block out the necessary time for effective use of the film.
2. Check with other staff members who are assigned to order newspapers from the communities of upcoming opponents. Newspapers generally write very factual information regarding injuries and other information that can be interpreted and integrated into the over-all scouting report.
3. One man on the staff should be in charge of all the necessary scouting supplies so they can be contained in one central file; each coach, therefore, does not have to be responsible for all of the various necessary forms and information.
4. Those in charge of scouting should arrange with the athletic department secretary during the Summer for travel arrangements and reservations, thus avoiding the Fall

rush of business. This includes making use of school cars, etc.

5. If at all possible, the scout should return to the home school immediately following the game he views. Copies of his written report should be ready by 7 p.m. on Sunday following a Saturday game. The scout should be prepared to undergo a thorough question and answer period between 7:30 and 10 p.m. on Sunday. The written reports for squad members should not be distributed until Monday evening, but they should be completed on Sunday so that work will not interfere with the Monday schedule. The reports for the squad should be distributed at the Monday evening training table.

Preparing for scouting assignment

Whether evaluating a team live or on film, we suggest the "Scouting Book" that is contained on pages 417-24. The scout or scouts are able to keep all of the important facts and will be able to answer the questions posed by the coaching staff. The book also can be used for notes and diagrams, along with the summaries he will need to make his reports to the coaches and players. It contains space for the scout to note pre-game warmup procedures, information concerning punters, passers, and personnel involved in point after touchdown, field goal, and kickoff. It also affords the scout an opportunity to mention specific information such as injuries and the physical condition of individual players or the team as a whole.

Taking the play-by-play

The most effective manner in which to take the play-by-play during the game is the format that follows which contains space for four diagrams per page. Each scout takes an ample supply of these blank forms on his assignment. The offensive play-by-play is a very difficult assignment, and any previous knowledge of the opposition that he can acquire will be very useful. If the defensive scout or a volunteer person is available to keep up with the down and distance and hash marks and play gain, it will greatly aid the person recording the information. We don't usually require a defensive play-by-play, but we do require a summary of defenses in normal long and short yardage situations. A scout should have specific opinions and a "feel" for the team scouted rather than just volumes of information. There are coaches who are often suspected of weighing the reports to determine the efficiency of the report! It is not the size of the report; it is what it contains.

SCOUTING HANDBOOK

PERSONNEL

Name	No.	Hgt.	Wgt.	Characteristics and Ability

LEFT END:
   Offense:
 	
   Defense:				

LEFT TACKLE:
   Offense:
 	
   Defense:				

LEFT GUARD:
   Offense:
 	
   Defense:				

Note: In column for characteristics and ability, describe style, speed, method, and direction of charge on defense, and ability as an offensive runner, blocker, receiver, etc. (Squares should be made for every position on the opponent's team)

SUMMARY OF DEFENSIVE FORMATIONS

Draw with accuracy and explain in detail the various defensive formations used. Number of men in line and their positions with respect to offensive line-up? positions of backs? distances from line? etc.

The following represent the minimum types of defense that should be carefully drawn up and explained in detail:

A. Regular defense (that employed most of time)

B. Defensive formations (punt)

C. Defensive formations (goal line)

    1. Point conversion defense

D. Defensive formations (in passing situations)

OFFENSE

Do they huddle?   How?

Shift after huddle?

Do they hurry into formation after huddle?

Call signals?

PUNTING

Are ends strong?

Do linemen go with snap of ball or protect kicker?

How many steps does kicker take?

Does he kick straight toward middle of line or out of bounds?

Do they quick kick?

Right or left footed kicker?

Kicks high or low?

Favor kicking on which down?

Who on kicking side does most tackling?

General comments on their punting game:

PASSES

Do they throw passes in own territory?

Who is star receiver?

Who does most of passing?

Right or left handed?

Are passes covered?

Are they consistent on down and distance to be gained in use of passes?

Passes quick or delayed?

Are running passes well covered?

Note direction receivers take.

What is favorite pass and who is favorite receiver?

Use of screens?

Diagram pass protection.

RUNNING PLAYS

Was offensive effective:_____because of_____

        1. Good interference

        2. Speedy and hard driving backs

        3. Weak opposition

What linemen come out to lead interference?

Are they fast_____Run low_____Do they point_____

Diagrams: (enclosed)

KICK DEFENSE

Do ends rush kicker?

Do ends and tackle open themselves up to a fake kick or run?

Drop back with opposing end?

Check opposing ends?

Do they allow offensive end to line up outside of them?

Any set formation to block kick?

Which way does safety man return punt?

Diagram defense formation when punt is expected.

Comment:

DEFENSE AGAINST RUNNING PLAYS

Show charge of linemen.

Do linemen use straight arm shiver?_____Slice and when?_____

Submarine_____Drift_____Position of hands_____

Do ends come in fast?

Is defensive center active outside his own tackles and ends?

Is tackle easily blocked?

Do halves come in and meet running play?

Is man backing up line quick in diagnosing play?

Does he meet it with determination?

Does weak side half pull out of position on strong side plays?

What is ability of backs to tackle in the open?

Do they use team defensive pattern?

Do linebackers and linemen team?

Penetrating line backers?

Who can be trapped?

Where should we concentrate our running attack?

Comments:

DEFENSE AGAINST PASSES

Do they use: Man-to-man

                Zone

                Combination

Are any particular backs weak on pass defense - short stature, slow, etc. ?

Does line rush passer fast?

Who drops back on weak side to cover on passes?

Where do linebackers cover?

Do they hold up ends?

Where can passes be completed? What kind? Where is their pass defense weak?

How do they cover on a running pass?

Are they vulnerable to this?

Diagram:

Comment:

GENERALSHIP

OFFENSE

1. What is their favorite first down play?

2. Do they like end runs from hash mark to wide side of field?

3. Do they like to run into sidelines from hash mark?

4. What is their short yardage first down play?

5. What is their short yardage touchdown play?

6. What is their bread and butter play?

7. Are they a passing or running team?

8. What is their favorite play to get out of trouble in their own territory?

9. Do they run from punt formation?

10. What is their style of attack inside the ten yard line?

11. Do they counter midway between hash marks?

GENERALSHIP

DEFENSE

1. What is their first down defense?

2. What is their passing situation defense?

3. What is their short yardage defense?

4. If defense is sliding or looping, do they move to wide side of field or to man in motion? Consistently, or now and then?

5. Can we run ends from deep punt on third down?

6. What defense can we expect when we have ball on our own ten-yard line? Opponent's ten-yard line?

```
┌──────────────────────────────────────────────────────────────┐
│                                                                │
│              SUMMARY OF OFFENSIVE FORMATIONS                   │
│          (Indicate personnel and composite offensive chart)    │
│                                                                │
│                                                                │
│   Diagram all formations and defenses used by _____   │
│                                              Opponents         │
│                                                                │
│                                                                │
│   DIAGRAM PASSES  (Indicate routes and depths)                 │
│                                                                │
│                                                                │
│                                                                │
│                                                                │
│   DIAGRAM FAVORITE RUNNING AND PASSING PLAYS                   │
│         (Indicate scoring plays)                               │
│                                                                │
│                                                                │
│                                                                │
│   GENERAL COMMENTS (Strengths and weaknesses)                  │
│                                                                │
│                                                                │
│                                                                │
└──────────────────────────────────────────────────────────────┘
```

Following is a simplified play-by-play offensive work sheet that would be particularly useful to the high school coach who does not enjoy the luxury of a scouting team. We had used these forms up to the time we started our two scout system.

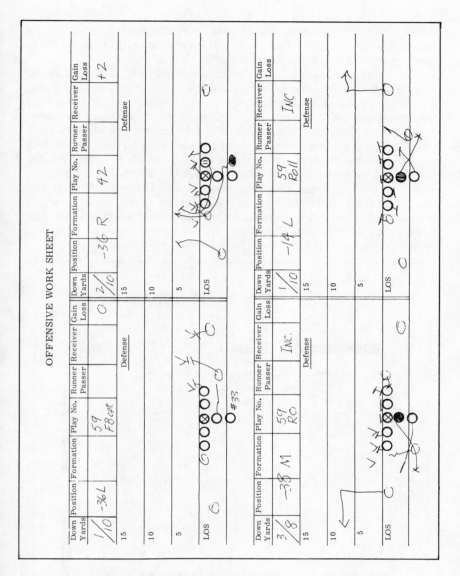

OFFENSIVE WORK SHEET

Key sort card

The only drawback to these forms is the time involved in compiling the information sought by the head coach. Because of this, we have developed a somewhat different procedure, a very basic form of an IBM key sort card. (See sample) All of the necessary information used by the scout for both offense and defense is listed around the four edges of the card. The actual drawing to be filled in on each play, as well as any blocking or pass patterns and courses, appears in the center of the card. We use common numbering terminology for all offensive series. This saves valuable recording time whenever our scouts are working as a team.

The scout should punch his cards immediately after the game while all details are fresh in his mind. A regular paper punch can be used, with one hole punched at a time, beginning with the down, then the distance, the hash, etc. Although it may appear that some of the material is duplicated, all of the headings are essential for a detailed report. An ordinary long ice pick or knitting needle can be used to separate the cards. If the scout or coach is searching for third-down play, he inserts the pick into the third-down hole and shakes out all of these plays in a neat pile. If he wants only the third-down-and-short-yardage plays, one to three yards, he inserts the pick into the third-and-short hole and shakes loose the cards. This eliminates the necessity of going through sixty to eighty cards looking for a specific play.

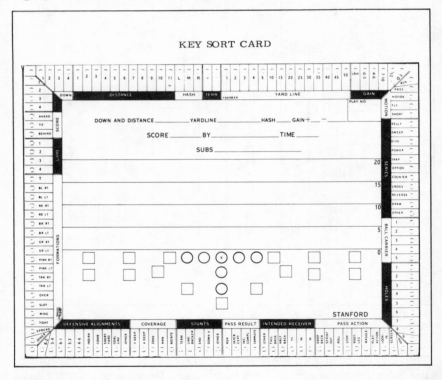

Reporting back

After returning to the campus, our scouts are required to submit written reports to both coaches and players as soon as possible. Following is the schedule we follow:

SCOUT REPORT SCHEDULE

TYPICAL SUNDAY PROGRAM

1:00 PM to 5:00 PM	Coaches study game films the previous Saturday.
5:00 PM	Dinner with the squad.
6:00 PM	Squad meets with coaching staff. Head coach reflects on game of the day before. Game films shown and coaches make constructive comments.
7:30 PM	Squad meeting adjourns.
7:30 PM to 10:00 PM	Coaches meet with the scout and begin to assemble a working knowledge of next opponent. One scout will be with the defensive coaches and the other will be with the offensive coaches.

TYPICAL MONDAY EVENING

6:30 PM	Training table dinner.
7:00 PM to 7:30 PM	Written reports handed out and an oral report given by either the scout or Coach Ralston. This half-hour report may be given before the training table dinner or between the hours of 6 and 6:30 PM. The squad is divided and one scout will take the defense and the other the offense. The bulk of the information may be given on the field, but this meeting should help to hit the high points as well as giving out the written reports.

SCOUT REPORT CONTENT

Coaches copy will include:

1. Title sheet (game scouted, etc.)
2. General summary and recommendations
3. General remarks...Offensive and Defensive
4. Personnel (Offensive and Defensive)
5. Formation and field position - hit charts
6. Tendency sheet:
   A. Personnel
   B. Field Position
   C. Formation
   D. Signal calling or down
7. Diagram all runs vs. our defensive (indicate expected blocking pattern)
8. Diagram all passes vs. our defense (indicate expected blocking pattern)
9. Diagram all trick plays vs. our defense (indicate expected blocking pattern)
10. Basic defenses should include:
    A. Adjustments or stunts
    B. Goal line and short yardage
    C. Secondary coverages
    D. Prevent or long yardage
    E. Down or field position tendencies in usage
11. Punting game
12. Kick off game

The scout report contents are transmitted by the appropriate coaches to the players, and the squad members additionally receive this written information:

1. Title sheet
2. Personnel (Offensive and Defensive)
3. Formations (basic)
4. Favorite runs vs. our defense — (1 page)
5. Favorite passes vs. our defense — (1 page)
6. Basic defenses
   a. Goal line and short yardage
7. Punting game
8. Kick off game

Additional scouting forms and completed scouting reports appear in the drill book.

Here are some tips to be followed in the coach-scout relationship:

Offensive scouting — Don't ask the scout too much. Ask him to supply basic information concerning alignment, basic action of the backfield, any key players. Don't expect the inexperienced scout to obtain a lot of the opponent's different tendencies. He either is incapable of gathering the information or his conclusions very well might not be valid.

Defensive scouting — A coach can consider it a major accomplishment if the scout determines the opponent's alignment, whether it is an odd or even defense, and if a three or four-deep coverage is used. That information, along with key personnel, will supply a coach a sound basis for setting up his attack.

Kicking game — These reports should be as simple and as easily read as possible. However, it is extremely important to have full knowledge of an opponent's capabilities from both a punting and return standpoint. A thorough understanding of when and how a team makes fullest use of its kicking abilities will assist a team in setting up its game strategy and approach to its own kicking game. (A full discussion of the kicking game is contained earlier in this text.)

Computerized scouting

With the development of new and improved computers and other time-saving devices, we are examining the feasibility of a sophisticated scouting system both from the efficiency and financial points of view. The most highly developed computer programs have been developed in professional football. Computer programs produce reports for prospect scouting and game preparation. The first effort by professional teams in the National Football League to use computer produced reports in the evaluation of college prospects was initiated in 1963 by the Los Angeles Rams, the San Francisco

49'ers, and the Dallas Cowboys. They formed a cooperative group which pooled scouting information to produce better quality information on college players faster and more economically. Other cooperative groups of professional football teams have been formed since that time.

Computer programs also have been used to analyze offensive and defensive tendencies of professional teams. As far back as the early 1950's, colleges — notably Princeton — had developed straightforward computer listings of their opponents' offense tendencies. A design of a computerized reporting program was developed for use by the Washington Redskins during the 1965 season. These computer programs process information obtained from game films and generate detailed reports regarding which offensive plays were used by the opponent in specific situations. They detail all of the running and passing plays executed from a specific formation. A description of each passing play is listed in detail and separated by game. A frequency chart is computed for each offensive formation run by an opponent.

The information that can be obtained from a computer is virtually endless. In the final analysis, the real value of this technique is time. A computer can process in about two minutes what normally would require an entire staff several days to compile.

We have spent a lot of time and research in this area, and we still are examining both the mark sensing (the old graphite pencil marking system) along with the more universal key punching process used by college and professional teams. We have computers available, and we suggest that if a coach is in a similar situation that he examine the possibilities personally.

On p. 430 is another style of computerized scouting form which we have been researching and developing. This form is not practical for our purposes because each page represents only one play, and it would be impossible for one man to complete during a game. We do feel, however, that the readers would be interested in the research that has gone into formulating a card of this detail and the information that it contains. It may offer some suggestions for future scouting forms.

Scouting summary

No matter how mechanically efficient a computer is, remember that you only get out of it what you put in. Football still is played by people who are not as consistent as computers. Random fluctuations in performances can mislead coaches' evaluation of opponents. And this is where the value of a competent scout shows up. Notwithstanding the various aids that a scout has at his command, he is subject to a great deal of pressure. The ability to record all of the information, whether from a film or on the scene, is extremely

PLAY ANALYSIS PROGRAM INPUT SHEET

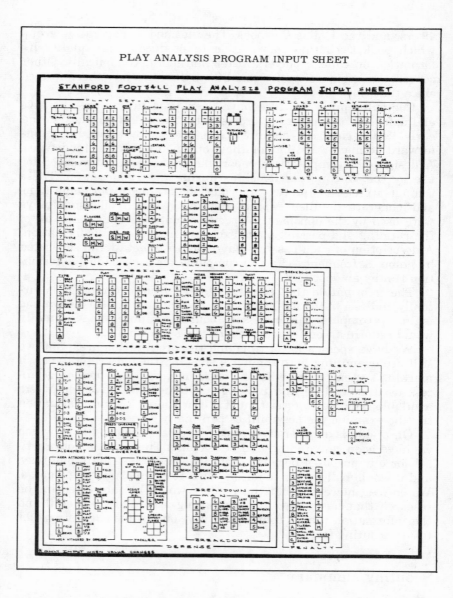

necessary and calls for a firm background on the opponent that is being scouted. The two-scout system used by Stanford is advantageous because the scout responsible for defense can assist the scout who is responsible for offense. There are only so many seconds between plays to gather all of the necessary information, and it is virtually impossible without assistance. In this case, the scout responsible for each area should indicate to the other exactly what he wants him to look for. After the entire information is gathered,

430

the scout should compile it immediately and begin formulating answers for questions that he will get from the coaching staff. Once again, the more a scout is prepared before a game, the easier it will be for him to make his analysis at its conclusion.

Obviously it is not possible, nor perhaps desirable, for every coach to follow Stanford's method of scouting. We merely have delineated our procedures, forms, and charts that different coaches with different needs might adapt. As was mentioned earlier, one never should hide behind the excuse that he does not have enough money or available personnel to get the job done.

Secondly, we believe that it is important to select a scout who can see several of the opponents so a continuity is developed and comparisons can be drawn. A coach must realize that his scout probably will not see the home team play because of his primary duties. In this case, he should attend Spring practice, early Fall practice, and actually go through scouting procedures during a scrimmage of his home team.

Third, the head coach should make a thorough evaluation of the opponents before outlining to the scout exactly what is expected of him. A head coach who is well organized and understands his opponents will have the necessary information on most of the teams he plays, so the scout merely will be a vehicle for him to substantiate what he already knows or to determine if any new wrinkles have been introduced by the opposition.

18

The Trainer

He receives no write-ups in the newspapers. He seldom, if ever, is interviewed on radio or television. He gets no standing ovations. Few persons in the stadium can point to him.

He is the trainer, the one who ranks with equal importance with the highest level of coaches. He is the one who keeps the wheels turning.

Athletic training is an auxiliary function of medicine, and it is involved with the prevention and care of injuries associated with competitive athletics. In addition to the prevention and care of injuries, the trainer carries the responsibility of rehabilitating an injured athlete so he can return to service in the shortest, yet safest, period of time. The trainer also is often the team psychologist who will aid the troubled athlete. Many times mental anxieties or real or imaginary bumps or bruises are left in the training room because of the expertise and practical psychology of the trainer. The athlete then goes to the practice or playing field with only his team responsibilities to consider.

Here are a few of his primary training duties:

Administration of first aid to injured athletes; preparation and utilization of a program of conditioning for athletes in cooperation with the coaching staff; administration of therapeutic methods and techniques under the direction of the team physician; application of devices including strapping, bandaging or bracing to present or protect against injury; development and supervision of rehabilitation programs; proper selection, care, and fitting of equipment in cooperation with the coaching and equipment staffs; supervision of all training menus and diets; and supervision of the safety factors involved with all athletic playing areas by insuring that all hazards are eliminated.

By their very nature, sports invite injury. The all-out effort required, the rapid change of direction, and the intensity of contact that is compounded by emotion are among the hazards that are inherent in sports activities.

According to the National Athletic Trainers Association, there is no comprehensive estimate of the number of athletes who are injured annually in athletic competition. However, insurance companies report that tens of thousands of athletes suffer fractures, sprains, strains, abrasions, and contusions annually. Statistics indicate that the annual number of injuries resulting from athletic competition, especially from football, has been increasing. It is pointed out, however, that the blame for his increasing number of injuries does not rest with the nature of the game alone. The increase is due, at least in part, to the increased participation of youth in today's sports programs. It is estimated, for example, that more than 810,000 young men in over 14,000 high schools alone participate in football each year. If the risk in competitive sports such as football is to be justified, every sports program is obligated to do everything within its power to prevent injury, to minimize the severity of the injury, and to treat each injury promptly and properly, with total rehabilitation as the goal.

Considerable progress has been made in the athletic training field at the collegiate and professional levels; however, much remains to be done at the junior high school and secondary school levels. Too few high schools have professionally trained men on their staffs to fill the position of athletic trainer. First, the coaching staffs at the high school and junior high school levels are smaller in number. This limits the time they have to cover the day-to-day services of an adequate athletic training program. Second, many high schools in smaller communities, and even some colleges, have problems because of the lack of physicians experienced in athletic medicine. In addition, the younger athlete is less mature and developed physically than college players. Therefore, they require closer observation.

One of the most serious problems, which received little notice until recent years, is serious heat illness. Statistics show that sixteen percent of all football fatalities from 1960 to 1963 were attributed to heat stroke. Numerous reportings of near-fatal heat stroke also were reported. It has been estimated that the number of cases of heat exhaustion exceeded a thousand. After reviewing the statistics, coaches might become extremely discouraged concerning early training. Fortunately there are precautions to take which will cut down the chance of serious heat illness of squad members. The first, and perhaps most important preventive measure, is acclimatization. It is done through *work* and *exposure*.

Most authorities suggest running activities which tax the cardio-vascular systems to operate. The running and exposure should begin very moderately and work toward higher work loads. An athlete should be able to handle an hour per day of heavy exercise during exposure before attempting football practice. Acclimitization occurs relatively fast. One can be eighty percent acclimated in five days, fully acclimated in two weeks.

Coaches also can exercise discretion by scheduling morning practice at 8 a.m. and late afternoon practice at 3:30 or 4 p.m. These times usually work out satisfactorily with meal and meeting schedules. Later in the autumn, when the days shorten and temperatures are much cooler, the coach may change his hours of practice. During practice, it is recommended that water and salt pills be made available for all players. We have used water breaks in the middle of our practice sessions to replace these fluids and salt in the players' systems. (The water we use contains a salt solution.) Recently, light, mesh-type jerseys, which allow much better ventilation than the old cotton jerseys, have appeared on the market. There is absolutely no place for the rubber or plastic sweat suit on the football field. Even under moderate environmental conditions, the use of such suits is extremely dangerous because of the complete blockage of necessary evaporation.

Physicians urge that rest periods in a shaded area be allowed, usually at a rate of five to ten minutes per thirty minute work periods. Physical examinations carefully scrutinizing players for incapacities to function under conditions of heat stress should be carried out by the team physician.

The NCAA has recognized the dangers of full-scale workouts at the beginning of Fall practice, and colleges now must practice without pads for at least three days. Some high schools have instituted similar rules; however, there still exist the "hard-nosed" coaches who insist on lengthy running drills and early contact work.

Whether an athlete becomes ill from heat or is injured, his first place for observation or treatment is in the training quarters. The trainer then should make a preliminary diagnosis, and, if possible, a very preliminary prognosis. Trainers should know exactly what their professional limitations are, and consult the team physician if the injury or illness is beyond their capabilities to diagnose. The team trainer and the physician's positions with the coaching staffs in most schools are in advisory capacities; however, final decisions should be made by the team physician.

When the daily programs are set up by the coach, the trainer's time involving athletes should be taken into consideration. It also is important that a daily reporting time be mutually arranged for the trainer to consult with the coaches on the current physical status of the squad. This status should be easily communicated between trainer and coach. We have used this injury report form.

DAILY INJURY AND PLAYER STATUS REPORT

I   RED CROSS WITH PADS. (NO CONTACT ABLE TO RUN AND ENGAGE
    IN SELECTIVE DRILLS.)

1._____	6._____	11._____
2._____	7._____	12._____
3._____	8._____	13._____
4._____	9._____	14._____
5._____	10._____	15._____

II RED CROSS WITHOUT PADS. (NO CONTACT, NO DRILLS, ABLE TO DO
    THERAPUTIC RUNNING ONLY.)

1._____	6._____	11._____
2._____	7._____	12._____
3._____	8._____	13._____
4._____	9._____	14._____
5._____	10._____	15._____

III NO PADS, NO RED CROSS. (OBSERVER, CANNOT HAVE CONTACT OR
    RUN.)

1._____	6._____	11._____
2._____	7._____	12._____
3._____	8._____	13._____
4._____	9._____	14._____
5._____	10._____	15._____

IV TRAINER AND COACH TO CONFER

1._____	6._____	11._____
2._____	7._____	12._____
3._____	8._____	13._____
4._____	9._____	14._____
5._____	10._____	15._____

The trainer submits the form by 2:00 p.m. each practice day so the individual coaches can prepare their practice plans with the available personnel. We also assign an assistant coach to provide additional conditioning drills tailored to the extent and type of the individual's injury.

Tardiness or failure of an athlete to report for treatment or appointment with the trainer or team physician should be regarded as an absence or tardiness to a squad practice or meeting.

When coaches are considering ordering equipment, the trainer and team physician should be consulted, especially for protective equipment and footwear.

The trainer should be on the field at all times during all contact sports practice. If there is sufficient personnel, the trainer's assistant should be assigned to the training room.

The selection and employment of a qualified trainer not only will provide professional medical care for the squad; he will enhance the entire program through his association with the players. Choose him with care, and then listen to what he has to say.

The trainer can perform has duties with complete efficiency if he has the appropriate equipment and an adequate training room. Most colleges and universities are well equipped in these areas; however, in many instances, the budgets available to high school coaches do not permit adequate facilities. Through our experience at the high school level, we would suggest that a coach who is working with a limited budget get together with the faculty members in the industrial arts departments and arrange for the construction of certain equipment and facilities.

Basic equipment in the training room should include:
1. One large storage cabinet
2. One first-aid cabinet and dressing table combination
3. One dressing table. (This could be built in the school shops.)
4. An electrical refrigerator.
5. Three training room tables (Could be built at school)
6. Whirlpool bath (Could be built at school)
7. Two heat lamps
8. Weight scale
9. Ventilating fan.

It should be established that the trainer is the master of his domain; a professional attitude by the trainer will enhance this attitude, and he can enhance this atmosphere by posting signs such as these:
1. No horseplay in training quarters
2. This room is yours — keep it clean
3. No undressing in training room
4. Before treatment for minor cuts and scratches, you must shower
5. No spikes allowed
6. No foul language

Student trainers

Colleges and universities that have medical schools can draw upon them for student trainers who will work with the professional trainer and gain practical knowledge that also will help in their medical careers. In some cases, credit is given for this work. At all times, they should be under the supervision of the team physician and give treatment *only* to the point of their capabilities.

At the high school level, the duties that can be assigned necessarily are much more limited. It is necessary to work closely with a young man chosen to work in the training room, but he should be able to fulfill a vital function in the more routine chores. It must be assumed that the student trainers know nothing about the care and prevention of athletic injuries. However, they can be trained in the arts of strapping, massage, and the use of certain electric equipment such as a whirlpool bath. In our experience the coach himself often has the responsibility of performing many of the trainer's functions. We urge these coaches to study and keep up with the trends in this area just as conscientiously as he does in the other areas of football.

Some of the necessary supplies that are needed in every training room, in addition to tape, band aids, and wraps, include:

Tourniquets, wood applicators, sterile gauze, felt, sponge rubber, ice bag, analgesic balm, benzoin compound, green soap, smelling salts, "hot stuff," athletic powder, rubdown liniment, salt tablets, and firm grip.

Every coach should leave to the discretion of the professional trainer the ordering of medical supplies. He will consult with the team physician because each state has its own medical codes in relation to drugs and medical supplies.

The Stanford trainer is in charge of weight reduction programs and the training table.

Weight reduction

Following are three accepted diets that provide the minimum requirements of the body of vitamins, proteins and minerals. They can be used with safety individually or are interchangeable by meals.

Remember, it is far easier to lose two pounds than twenty pounds. Get a player down to his best playing weight and make him stay there by self-discipline. Excessive weight gain and laziness tend to go hand in hand.

Rules

1. Beverages may be sweetened if dietary non-caloric sweetening are used.
2. Breads must be cut out.
3. No soft drinks between meals, except dietary non-caloric drinks.
4. No eating between meals, especially candy, peanuts, pies, etc.
5. No alcoholic beverages.

Breakfast	Lunch	Dinner
	tossed salad/dressing	salad/dressings
1 lg. glass of juice	1 bowl soup/crackers	10-12 oz. portion meat
2-3 eggs	1 8-10 oz. portion of	1 4-oz. portion potatoes
1 bowl of cereal,	meat	2 other 3-oz. portions
preferably cooked	3-4 slices of bread/	of vegetables
3-4 oz. portion ham,	butter & jelly	3-4 slices of bread/
bacon or sausage	2-3 oz. portions of	butter & jelly
3 slices toast/jelly	vegetables	2 glasses of milk
2 glasses milk	milk	dessert
A fresh fruit	dessert	A fresh fruit

The athlete in strenuous training needs close to 6,000 calories of food per day. The above diet will furnish you with approximately 6,000 or more calories, depending on whether or not you increase or decrease your intake of some of the various items. You will be primarily guided by your appetite.

If you should still have difficulty gaining weight while on a diet such as the above, there are other items that can be used along with your meals to promote a gain in weight.

1. *Lipomul*—Oral; Upjohn Co. A liquid formula of concentrated calories containing corn oil and other ingredients. Dosage is 1-4 tablespoonfuls one or two times daily after or between meals. Along with Lipomul, we recommend Sigtab tablets also by Upjohn. This is a special vitamin tablet made to help meet the metabolic requirements of stress.

2. *Nutrament* and *Hustle* are two different liquid meal products which are nutritionally-balanced in ready-to-drink form. These products, used as a beverage with meals and for between-meal snacks, gives the extra calories needed for weight gaining. More important, they provide a balanced ration of the nutrients used by the body for muscle building, allowing weight gain to take the form of muscle gain rather than undesirable fatty tissue.

3. The Hilcoa Corporation in San Jose has done extensive research and has developed several products available only to athletic organizations. Their vitamin and mineral tablets along with their *Natural Gain* and *High Protein Powder* products have been very popular with our players.

1,005 Calories	1,023 Calories	1,019 Calories
Breakfast	*Breakfast*	*Breakfast*
1 medium grapefruit	3 medium size prunes	1/2 glass orange juice
1 egg (poached)	without sugar	1 thin slice toast
1 slice toast	1 thin slice toast	1/2 sq. butter
1/2 square butter	1/2 sq. butter	omelet (1 egg)
1 glass skim milk	2 thin strips bacon	1 glass skim milk
coffee or tea	1 glass skim milk	coffee or tea
	coffee or tea	

Lunch

Ham omelet (1 egg &
2 tbsp. lean, diced
ham)
3 heaping tbsp. squash
Celery and radishes
(1 large heart celery;
4 small radishes)
3 tbsp. apple sauce
1 glass skim milk
tea or coffee

Lunch

1 large serving white
meat of chicken
1/2 cup of peas
Salad: 2 leaves lettuce,
1 med-sized tomato
2 asparagus tips, 2 3/4
inches long
1/2 cup frozen orange
juice
1 glass skim milk
tea or coffee

Lunch

Plain broth (fat
skimmed off)
2 crackers
Salad: 2 leaves lettuce
1/2 cup salmon or tuna
2 stalks celery, 2 tbsp.
peas, 1 hard-boiled
egg
2/3 cup spinach
Fruit cup: 1/4 grapefruit
1/2 med-sized orange;
1/2 banana
1/2 glass skim milk or
buttermilk
tea or coffee

Dinner

Med. serving chicken
2 tbsp. mashed potato
3 heaping tbsp. beets
or greens
Cucumber and lettuce
salad; 2 leaves
lettuce; 12 slices
cucumber; 1 slice
tomato with lemon
or vinegar
1 med. sliced banana
coffee or tea

Dinner

1 average serving cold
sliced tongue
Salad: 2 lettuce leaves;
1/3 cup shredded
cabbage; 1 tbsp. each
pimento & green
pepper;
mayonnaise
2/3 cup beets
2 stalks celery
1 thin slice graham
bread
1/2 sq. butter
1 medium-sized peach
1 glass skim milk
coffee or tea

Dinner

1 large serving lean
roast beef
2/3 cup cauliflower
2/3 cup string beans
1/2 cup salad; 1 pkg.
lemon jello; 1 cup
grated raw carrots;
4 stalks chopped
celery; 2 lettuce leaves
1/2 cup apple sauce
tea or coffee

Equipment

Many coaches who assume new positions believe that they should immediately order all new field and player equipment to create a changed atmosphere or new squad image. We are the first to advocate first class equipment for the protection and safety of players; however, the on-the-field equipment is just as important to a program's success, particularly when budgets are limited and every expenditure must prove its worth.

One of the first considerations should be the proper lining of the practice field. If space is available, a regulation field should be lined up to forty or fifty yards. It should be divided in segments of five yards with regulation hash marks. These markings and spacings are necessary for the development of the passing game and to create down and distance, kicking, and field and hash-mark situations. The coaches and players must experience a total "feel" of the football field to become properly prepared for game conditions. Five-yard squares are useful in administering certain drills, along with target jerseys or some other marking mechanism to utilize basic movement and agility exercises. (Our grounds supervisor, Mel Nelson, does an excellent job with the maintenance of our field and equipment.)

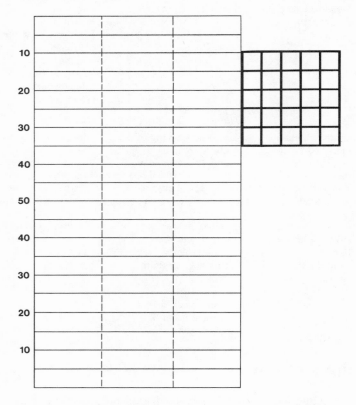

If the entire outline of the field is not visible, sidelines can be marked with target jerseys, towels, or conventional highway fluorescent cones. Our staff places such great premium on the setting of our formations, utilizing the field, and defensing the entire field that this is an important element for us to consider in detail.

We also mark our defensive team teaching squares at the side of the field to teach defensive assignments against a properly spaced, simulated team.

Although a coach normally does not have the responsibility of maintaining the field, he should be conscious of its use. Excessive use of one portion of the field will make it virtually useless either during the rainy season or when the weather is hot and dry. A coach may resent having to view the field through the eyes of a gardener, but a restricted practice space can become a concern of major proportions during extreme or unusual weather conditions.

Basic equipment that is needed includes:

1. Seven-man sled: This is probably our most valuable piece of equipment; although it probably is the most expensive item, it is an integral part of our training program. The seven-man sled, or crowther, is used in drills that are outlined in the drill book, and it is used by both offensive and defensive teams.

2. Two-man crowthers: We recommend the conventional two-padded crowther for use in movement drills and for teaching offensive blocking techniques.

3. One-man crowther: It is a new piece of equipment, and we use it extensively in offensive blocking. It is based on the one pad principle, and if the block is not properly executed, it will turn the crowther indicating a mistake in technique has been made.

4. One-man shmoo: Although this is the elder statesman of field equipment, it is the best piece of machinery for defenses. It consists of a one-man pad that comes off two cylinders and is pushed along the ground much the same as a one-man crowther. The pad is at a convenient slant and provides an excellent surface for teaching tackling techniques.

5. Big dummies: We don't use the large dummies as much as in the past because they do not portray the many moving and varied defenses that we face. However, we do find them useful teaching tools for assignments in a team situation and for the individual shoulder block.

6. Hand shields: We have adopted the arm and hand shields used by the Dallas Cowboys. They are fluorescent colored arm guards used by defensive linemen to protect themselves and allow mobility while being involved in a full-speed drill. Although they are somewhat cumbersome, a full-speed drill is possible without suffering the usual bumps and bruises. We also continue to use the conventional light air bags, which make possible full speed drills. These particularly are useful for linebackers and safety men downfield, because full-speed blocks can be made without risking injury.

7. Large shields: These are effective in teaching offense because they allow enough give during one-on-one blocking that a strain is not placed on the blocker's neck.

They also are very helpful for our blocking on the move and downfield blocking techniques. The primary drawback is their size, three feet high and from one-and-a-half feet to two-feet wide. Consequently, the player holding it has difficulty controlling it because the contact spreads over the entire area of the shield.

8. Chutes: This is a piece of equipment, sometimes a series of pipes, that forces linemen to get off in a low blocking position, and it probably is one of the best teaching aids in football. We became acquainted with it when we were associated with Pete Elliott at the University of California and were exposed to the split T coaching philosophy of Bud Wilkinson. One of their secrets was the ability of their teams to come out of the huddle, get up to the line and get off better than any team has in the history of football. Their players came off the line low and hard, and much credit for this blocking position was due to the use of chutes.

FOOTBALL CHUTE

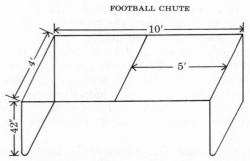

IT IS MADE OF 1″ EMT ELECTRICAL CONDUIT. THERE IS A SEPARATION AT MIDWAY (5′) FOR SUPPORT. THE BOTTOMS ARE ROUNDED.

9. Two-by-twelve boards: One of the most effective pieces of equipment in teaching individual blocking techniques is the standard two-by-twelve piece of lumber. The ideal board is ten feet in length, and is used to emphasize the wide base which is so important in our one-on-one blocking technique. They can be utilized with other equipment such as large dummies, and/or shields, or light air bags to create an actual blocking situation. The bags are placed at one end of the board, the player responds to the starting count, performs his blocking technique, and pushes the bag off the board by using the all-important wide base. If the player steps on the board, his feet will slip and he will realize he is not performing the technique correctly.

442

10. Netting: This is placed behind one set of goal posts and extends from the ground to the crossbar. It obviously saves a lot of ball shagging by our managers. Included with the netting is a tire which is strung from the crossbar to the approximate height of a receiver. The quarterbacks use this every day in their warm-up drills, so it serves as both a time-saver and a teacher of technique. Our kickers also use the net to work on both place-kicking and punting. While Stanford was practicing in Long Beach for the Rose Bowl, we noted that the Los Angeles Rams used a portable baseball backstop for the same purposes.

11. Reactor: This is an important and necessary piece of equipment for the defense because the coach can stand behind it and release a spring which will disengage either the right or left pad at the player using it. The player, from a squared up position in front of the reactor, then must reset the pad and return to his normal position. The machine reflects reaction time, strength, and quickness.

12. Hand shiver board: This is a permanently staked padded board that is elevated in two different heights. The player proceeds in either direction, first shivering the board and then regaining his balance before going to the next position. It teaches balance, movement, and the ability to use hands and arms to ward off blockers who will come at a player from both heights.

There is an abundance of field equipment on the market, and we are not advocating that the average school requires all the facilities mentioned above. Football still is based on fundamental blocking and tackling, and a coach should evaluate fully his department's finances and needs before an investment is made.

Following is an offensive check-list for the use of available equipment:

Functional use of equipment and objectives

1. Get off base, balance, follow through, blocking height, blocking angle, head position, understanding of blocking techniques, understanding of total play, target, explosiveness, hitting a moving target, polishing of plays, stance, and quickness.

Equipment drills:
Seven-man crowther. Main objectives of the seven-man crowther.
1. To develop explosiveness from the offensive stance.
2. To develop great get-off.

3. To develop the proper steps.
4. To develop good blocking position and angle.
5. To develop great follow-through.
6. To develop eye and head position when blocking.
7. To develop quickness.

Main objectives of chutes:
1. Develop proper height of all blocks.
2. Develop proper blocking angle and body lean.
3. Develop low center of base and balance when blocking.
4. Develop explosiveness from stance.
5. Develop the get-off.

Main objectives of boards:
1. Develop proper base.
2. Develop good get-off.
3. Develop proper steps.
4. Develop proper angle of release from line of scrimmage.
5. Develop good stance and get-off.
6. Develop understanding of target area.
7. Develop the quickness to offensive's snap count.

Main objectives of heavy bag work:
1. Develop explosiveness from stance.
2. Develop understanding of target areas.
3. Develop understanding of blocking techniques.
4. Develop the ideal head position when blocking.
5. Develop proper stance and quickness.
6. Develop good blocking base and balance.
7. Develop height and angle of blocking.

Main objectives of light air bags:
1. Develop understanding of the rules.
2. Develop understanding of blocking techniques.
3. Develop understanding of total play.
4. Develop the ability to hit a moving target.
5. Develop a precision in polishing all plays.
6. Develop great follow-through.
7. Develop proper stance, steps and target.
8. Develop great get-off.

It is of paramount importance to combine as many pieces of equipment to speed the result we are trying to obtain. For example, the boards and bags are very easily combined. The boards, bags and chutes are easily combined, and the objectives are overlapping. It will be advantageous to combine as many of these skills and equipment and objectives in our early workouts during two a day so that we can move on to the polishing and total play picture at the earliest date possible.

Player equipment

A player's attitude on the field begins with his equipment. First-class equipment that is well taken care of will have a very positive effect on the total football program. We credit much of our excellence in equipment, as well as the organization of the equipment room, to Virgil "Doc" Marvin.

In all levels of football, large sums of money are spent every year on player equipment. Equipment, like other areas of football, is subject to change and it is important to keep abreast of the improvements and innovations in every area from shoes to helmets. Most of this equipment, which is produced by quality manufacturers, is designed to last for a long time if it receives the proper cleaning, care, and maintenance.

Here is a list of rules followed by Doc Marvin:
1. Utilize proper methods for out-of-season storage.
2. Equipment should be stored, repaired, and maintained in accordance with manufacturer's recommendations.
3. Athletic equipment must be cleaned and laundered frequently. It must be dried after use.
4. There must be a clear understanding of the equipment manager's duties in relation to the coaching staff.
5. Establish a definite policy regarding the care of equipment.
7. The head coach should be directly responsible for the care of equipment.
8. An accurate record must be kept of all equipment, including condition, size, and age.
9. All athletic equipment must be marked for size and identification.
10. A definite system must be used regarding the issuance, use, and return of athletic equipment.

On page 446 is a suggested format to be used by the equipment manager in categorizing players' sizes and keeping track of items checked out by players.

The manager

A good manager is as important to a coach as a highly efficient secretary is to a business executive. The three basic qualities that he must possess are to be responsible, a good organizer, and prompt. If a team can carry only one manager, it might be well to select a lower classman and train him so he will be able to aid the program for several years. In colleges and universities, it is the practice to have several assistant managers who are lower classmen, one of whom will work his way up to become head manager during his

EQUIPMENT CHECKLIST

Form No. 65 224

FROSH 1970

LOCKER 308	NAME		PLAYING NO.	POSITION	HEIGHT	WEIGHT	HELMET	SHOES	SHOE SIZE	SHOULDER PADS	HIP PADS	WAIST	PANT SIZE
2507	AUSTIN	LENARD	59	T-G	5-10	245	7½C		10½E	R44-46	XL-C WIL	42	XL
~~2509~~	~~BAKER~~	~~RICKY~~ x	~~QUIT~~	~~B~~	~~5-9~~	~~148~~	~~6¾~~	~~OWN~~	~~9½E~~	~~WIL-R~~	~~M-C RAWL~~	~~30~~	~~M~~
~~2348~~	~~BAMATTRE~~	~~BILL~~	~~QUIT~~	~~D-B~~	~~5-11~~	~~175~~	~~7¾~~	~~OWN~~	~~8~~	~~WIL-R~~	~~M-C WIL~~	~~34~~	~~L~~
2483	BEATTY,	BOB	x53	C-LB	6-0	185	6⅞C		9½E	A41-92	M-C WILSON	32	L
2333	BLACKSTONE,	BRUCE	66	G-LB	6-0	212	7¼C	OWN	10EE	A40-44	M-C RAWL	34	L
2334 x	BROHARD,	CURT x	75	T	6-3	210	7⅛C	NEW	12½E	A42-44	L-C WIL	34	L
2335	BURKE,	BILL	69	T-LB	5-10	220	7⅜C		11½E LRT	A44-46	L-C RAWL	36	XL
~~2511~~	~~BUSSE,~~	~~CURT~~		~~B~~	~~6-3~~	~~173~~	~~7½~~	~~OWN~~	~~11D~~	~~A40-42~~	~~M-C RAWL~~	~~32~~	~~L~~
2336 x	CERNOCK,	BARRY	86	E-QB	6-5	212	7⅜		13½E	A40-42	L-C WIL	34	L-L
2517	COLLOM,	DOUG	10	QB	5-8	150	7½		8½E	A38-40	M-C WIL	30	M
~~2513~~	~~CONWAY,~~	~~TIM~~		~~E-HB~~	~~5-10~~	~~165~~	~~7⅜~~		~~9½E~~	~~A40-42~~	~~M-C RAWL~~	~~32~~	~~M~~
~~2515~~	~~COOK,~~	~~PHIL~~	~~QUIT~~	~~TE-LB~~	~~6-2~~	~~175~~	~~7½~~		~~10½D~~	~~A40-42~~	~~M-C RAWL~~	~~34~~	~~L~~
2337	DELLA PIETRA,	DICK	63	T-G	5-11	200	7⅜C		9EE	A42-44	L-C RAWL	36	XL
2311	ESPARZA,	MARIO	50	QB	5-10	180	7¼		10E	A40-42	L-C WIL	34	L
2343 x	FERGUSON,	JIM	31	HB-S	6-1	180	7⅜U	OWN	10D	A38-40	M-C WIL	30	M
2339 x	FERGUSON,	JOHN	74	T-TE	6-5	215	6⅞C	NEW	13E	A42-44	L-C RAWL	36	XL-L
2390 x	FERGUSON,	MARK	71	T-LB	6-4	210	7C	NEW	13E	A42-44	L-C RAWL	36	XL-L
~~2514~~	~~JAMES,~~	~~ART~~ x		~~TE-LB~~	~~5-11~~	~~190~~	~~7⅜~~		~~9EE~~	~~WIL-L~~	~~M-C RAWL~~	~~34~~	~~L~~
~~2317~~	~~GIUSTI,~~	~~RICK~~	~~QUIT~~		~~6-0~~	~~188~~	~~7¼~~		~~11½E~~	~~WIL-L~~	~~M-C WIL~~	~~32~~	~~L~~
2315 x	GOLDSTEIN,	MAX	24	QB-DB	6-2	190	7½		12E	A42-44	L-C WIL	32	L
~~2521~~	~~HAMMERICH,~~	~~WARREN~~ x	~~QUIT~~	~~LB~~	~~5-10~~	~~155~~	~~7½~~		~~9½D~~	~~A38-40~~	~~M-C WIL~~	~~30~~	~~M~~
2523	HANKAMEK,	RANDY	44	FB-E	6-0	195	7¼C		11E	S38-40	L-C WILS	34	XL
2342 x	ISHMAN,	REGGIE	23	SE-HB	6-3	180	7¼W	OWN	10E	A40-42	M-C WIL	32	M
2313 x	JORDAN,	JIM	54	FB-LB	6-1	210	7⅜C		10½E	A42-44	L-C WIL	34	L
~~2525~~	~~JOHNSON,~~	~~FRED~~	~~QUIT~~	~~T~~	~~6-0~~	~~170~~	~~7⅝C~~		~~10EEE~~	~~A38-40~~	~~M-C WIL~~	~~30~~	~~M~~
2527	LASATER,	TOM	80	E-HB	6-0	175	7		9E	A40-42	M-C RAWL	32	L
2537	MANUEL,	MEL	67	FB-LE	6-1	198	7⅛C	OWN	12E	R40-42	M-C RAWL	32	M

senior year. Thus the system is self-propagating, and there always will be an experienced manager available to help the coach train a new one. He should aid the coach in the pre-season inventory, compile lists of prospective squad members, and help in mailing of invitations to early practice. During the season, he must be sure all dummies are on the field, keep balls inflated, keep unauthorized personnel away from the practice session, have kicking tees available, take daily attendance, check all equipment to insure cleanliness and proper working order, and collect all equipment after practice. One important function of our manager is to signal, with a small air horn, the time changes in our daily practices.

A manager's duties at home games include assisting in equipment and uniform issue, collecting valuables, directing opposing teams and officials to dressing rooms, and having parkas available in bad weather. Following the game, the manager must keep all unauthorized personnel out of the locker room, return wallets and valuables to teams; and in some instances, call newspapers and report the results of the game.

Before leaving for away games, the manager should check all uniforms, check practice balls, and statistic charts. Upon arrival at the away field, he should get equipment to the proper locker area, obtain towels from the home team, collect valuables, find the short-

---

REMINDERS TO MANAGERS

1. Managers in charge are responsible for picking up equipment placement slip from coaches room each day by 3:15.

2. Football shacks should be open at 3:15 with balls out for the quarterbacks therefore, at least two managers should come at 3:15 ... the manager in charge and one other.

3. Utters must be filled up as early in the practice as possible. (Faucet is in the corp. yard). Check each day with Coach Ralston for water break times.

4. If by some very legitimate reason you cannot make practice on a certain day, call Bob Mattson - 328-8937 at least one day before the practice, if no answer, please call Dorothy Potts in the Athletic Office - Ex-4591 ... If something comes up that will keep you from coming on the day of the practice, call the manager in charge that day.

Chris Morrison	327-2920	Ext. 107
Frank Carasco	327-2920	Ext. 431
Mark Wardenburg	327-2920	Ext. 1314
Hal Baer	327-2920	Ext. 1332
Dave Barber	327-2920	OTERO
John Wright	328-6144	
John Sullivan	328-8937	
Bob Mattson	328-8937	

The most important thing is to plan all that is possible ahead of time. The managers in charge should check with Coach Ralston at the start of the practice to see if anything special should be done... "Quote of the Quarter"..."It's a good life, I think."

est route to the field, and get parkas, kicking tee, water, and balls to the field.

After arrival at home, the manager's duties include unloading the bus, checking for loose equipment, collecting uniforms, and assisting the coach in winding up other details.

The student manager should not be asked to perform these and other tasks without appropriate recognition. He should be included in all of the team dinners, award ceremonies, and social gatherings, and should receive a certificate or school emblem for his services.

Illustrated are basic instructions and schedules that coaches should supply to their managers. Written communication aids in maintaining time schedules and distributing appropriate equipment and supplies when and where they are required.

19

Football Rules

We have dwelled on the elimination of mistakes to prevent a team from beating itself; one of the most neglected, but most important, aspects of this is the knowledge and application of football rules. We realize that rules are slightly different at all levels of play, but every coach owes it to himself and his team to be certain that everyone on his staff and squad is familiar with all of the rules and the manner in which they are applied.

We have instituted a procedure at Stanford whereby a Pacific 8 official visits us during one of our pre-season practices. Jimmy Coffis, a local high school administrator as well as a conference official, has spent part of an afternoon with the squad acquainting it with any new rule changes. He also conducts a question and answer period. This has proved valuable because the players want to be involved in a knowledge of the rules, and through the question and answer period they understand a better application of the rules. We generally have had Mr. Coffis or one of our staff members acquaint the squad with the mechanics of officiating so they will have an appreciation for the officials' problems as well. We attempt to acquaint out squad with the proper approach to officials and officiating, and when our team captain or captains are elected, we offer them a little extra insight into officiating and instruct them on their responsibilities as our team leaders. We follow up with a written test similar to the following to insure a complete knowledge and understanding of all of the rules.

FOOTBALL RULES EXAM FOR PLAYERS

Given below are 50 true-false statements which pertain to the 1970 NCAA Football Rules. Some of the statements are true, others are false. The letters "T" (true) and "F" (false) are printed in the left margin opposite each statement. Select the answer you think most applicable by circling your choice.

T   F   1. A player may participate while wearing a cast as long as the cast is covered with one half inch of slow recovery foam padding.

T   F   2. During a free time-out one or more players may confer with the coaching staff at the team area.

T   F   3. After the ready for play signal is given by the referee the team in possession has 25 seconds in which to put the ball in play.

T   F   4. Three eligible substitutes of either team may enter the game at any time before the ball is put in play.

T   F   5. An incoming substitute must report to a designated official when substitutes are limited.

T   F   6. A player is out of bounds when any part of his person touches anything which is on or outside the boundary line. This includes officials or another player.

T   F   7. A kickoff may be made from any spot on or behind the kicking team's restraining line.

T   F   8. On a kickoff all players of the kicking team must be behind the ball and in bounds until ball is kicked.

T   F   9. All players of the receiving team on a kickoff must be in bounds and behind their restraining line with at least five of them within five yards of that line.

T   F   10. A player of the kicking team who has been in bounds on a kickoff, recovers the kicked ball which was not touched by the receiving team on the 20-yard line. It is legal and the ball belongs to his team.

T   F   11. The kicking team only may advance the ball if during a punt the ball does not cross the line of scrimmage.

T   F   12. On a punt the kicking team illegally touches the ball on the 15-yard line. The ball rolls to the 3-yard line where it is declared dead. Should the receiving team so choose it will be their ball 1 - 10 on the 15-yard line.

T   F   13. A player of the receiving team is about to catch a scrimmage kick, is tackled before the ball arrives but catches the kick while he is falling. RULING: Illegal interference.

T   F   14. During a scrimmage play prior to the snap, a defensive linebacker charges into neutral zone and retreats with no contact resulting. RULING: Legal.

T   F   15. Same as above only this time his act draws instant reflex charge by an offensive lineman causing contact. RULING: Foul by the defense.

450

T   F   16. Defensive lineman charges into neutral zone prior to the snap. While he is retreating an offensive lineman makes a delayed charge and makes contact with the defensive player. RULING: Offsetting fouls.

T   F   17. A player after signaling for a fair catch shall not carry the ball more than three steps.

T   F   18. Any player signaling for a fair catch and does not touch the ball shall not block during the remainder of that down.

T   F   19. A defensive lineman charges into neutral zone prior to the snap and before he can return to a legal position an offensive lineman makes a delayed charge and causes contact with another defensive player. RULING: Foul by the offense.

T   F   20. It is legal for all offensive players to lock legs on the line of scrimmage.

T   F   21. A backward pass that strikes the ground may be recovered and advanced by the defense.

T   F   22. A backward pass or fumble that goes out of bounds between the goal lines belongs to the team last touching the ball prior to going out of bounds.

T   F   23. The neutral zone is established when the ball is ready for play.

T   F   24. A defensive back intercepts a legal forward pass while he is in the air deep in his end zone. His shoulder hits goal post while in the air but his feet come down in bounds. RULING: Touchback.

T   F   25. The penalty for ineligibles downfield on a legal forward pass is 15 yards from previous spot and loss of down.

T   F   26. During a forward pass no ineligible player shall be beyond the neutral zone until a legal forward pass is thrown.

T   F   27. After a score the player in possession of the ball must return it to an official immediately.

T   F   28. It is a foul if the passing team deliberately bats a backward pass forward out of bounds in an attempt to gain yardage.

T   F   29. A member of the passing team on a forward pass play is restricted from blocking an opponent beyond the neutral zone from the time the ball is snapped until the pass is touched by any player.

T   F   30. A player receives a legal forward pass in the air and lands on or outside the boundary line. RULING: Incomplete.

T   F   31. On a field goal attempt the ball is kicked into the shoulder of an offensive lineman then continues over the cross-bar and through the uprights. RULING: 3 points for the kicking team.

T   F   32. A ball carrier is hit and fumbles the ball on his opponent's 3-yard line. The ball rolls into the end zone where it is recovered by a defensive player. RULING: Touchback.

T   F   **33.** Defensive back intercepts a legal forward pass in his own end zone and attempts to run it out, but is tackled and downed behind his own goal line. RULING: Safety.

T   F   **34.** After a safety is scored the team scored upon will put the ball in play at its own 20-yard line by a free kick which may be a punt, drop kick, or a place kick.

T   F   **35.** After a safety the ball is put in play by a punt. The kick rolls to the receiving team's 35-yard line where a member of the kicking team recovers the kick. RULING: Illegal touching by kicking team. Ball goes to receiver 1-10 on their 35.

T   F   **36.** Clipping is illegal anywhere on the playing field.

T   F   **37.** On a kickoff the ball falls from the tee and the kicker kicks the the ball from behind the 40-yard line. RULING: Legal kickoff.

T   F   **38.** On a kickoff the kicked ball strikes a member of the receiving team after it has traveled 15 yards. The ball rebounds into possession of a player of the kicking team who advances the ball. RULING: Legal advance. 1-10 for team who kicked off.

T   F   **39.** An opponent turns his back to a legal side block, making it impossible for the blocker to avoid running into the back of the opponent. RULING: Clipping.

T   F   **40.** On a legal forward pass a defensive back has his back to the ball and is waving his arms in the face of an eligible receiver. The receiver, in attempting to catch the pass, runs into the defensive back. RULING: Pass interference by the defense.

T   F   **41.** During an attempted field goal no opponent shall rough the holder of a place kick.

T   F   **42.** The limit lines are located 6 feet outside of the sideline and end line. No person shall be within the limit lines except when permitted to be on the field.

T   F   **43.** During a shoulder block the hand must be in contact with the blocker's body. The hand and arm must be kept below the shoulders of the opponent during the entire block.

T   F   **44.** A teammate of a runner may assist him in gaining yardage by pushing, lifting or charging into him.

T   F   **45.** The holder of a field goal attempt has his knee on the ground when he receives the snap. He may legally pass or run with the ball.

T   F   **46.** A player shall not deliberately kick a free ball.

T   F   **47.** Defensive lineman breaks through on punt, partially blocks the kick and his momentum carries him into the kicker, knocking him to the ground. RULING: Roughing the kicker.

T   F   **48.** Ball is kicked legally on kickoff. Kick is muffed by receiver on his own 15-yard line. It then rolls into the end zone where another member of the receiving team falls on it. RULING: 1-10 for receiving team on their 15-yard line.

T F 49. Defensive back intercepts ball on 3-yard line and the intercepting
          momentum carries him into the end zone, where he is tackled.
          RULING: Defensive team's ball 1-10 on the 3-yard line.

T F 50. Eligible offensive end steps on sideline as the result of a
          defensive block. He comes back in bounds and catches forward
          pass for a touchdown. RULING: Legal catch and 6 points are
          awarded.

KEY TO PLAYER RULES EXAM

No.	True or False	Reference	No.	True or False	Reference
1.	F	Rule 1-4-5b	26.	T	Rule 7-3-10
2.	F	Rule 3-3-8	27.	T	Rule 9-2-1d
3.	T	Rule 3-4-2a Rule 4-1-5	28.	T	Rule 9-4-2
4.	F	Rule 3-5-1	29.	T	Rule 7-3-8
5.	T	Rule 3-5-2d	30.	T	Rule 7-3-7
6.	F	Rule 4-2-1	31.	F	Rule 8-4-1
7.	F	Rule 6-1-2	32.	T	A. R. 40
8.	F	Rule 6-1-2	33.	F	A. R. 41
9.	T	Rule 6-1-2	34.	T	Rule 8-5-5
10.	T	Rule 6-1-3	35.	F	Rule 6-1-3
11.	F	Rule 6-3-1	36.	F	Rule 9-1-2d
12.	T	Rule 6-3-2	37.	T	R. I. 26 (2)
13.	T	A. R. 22	38.	F	R. I. 26 (4)
14.	T	A. R. 26	39.	F	A. R. 44
15.	T	A. R. 26	40.	T	A. R. 34
16.	T	A. R. 26	41.	T	Rule 9-1-3
17.	F	Rule 6-5-2	42.	T	Rule 1-2-3
18.	T	Rule 6-5-4	43.	T	Rule 9-3-3
19.	T	A. R. 26	44.	F	Rule 9-3-2
20.	F	Rule 7-1-3b2	45.	T	Rule 4-1-3b
21.	F	Rule 7-2-2	46.	T	Rule 9-4-3
22.	F	Rule 7-2-3	47.	F	Rule 9-1-3
23.	T	Rule 2-17-1	48.	F	Rule 8-5-3
24.	F	Rule 4-2-1	49.	T	R. I. 46 (e-1)
25.	F	Rule 7-3-9	50.	F	Rule 7-3-4

20

Conditioning and Weight Training

Conditioning

Our approach to off-season conditioning is much the same as our total football philosophy: we have moved away from mandatory off-season programs that require the same kind of program for all players. We feel that conditioning is definitely an individual thing. We realize that our situation is much different from the high school program because most college players are very self-motivated and already have been exposed to some type of weight program. We also realize that most of them have a good idea of exactly the direction in which they want to go in their weight training program; therefore, we try to provide each individual with the necessary program and equipment that are tailored to his needs. Once again, we are indebted to coaches and trainers from the professional ranks who have assisted us appreciably with our players' individual needs. Our good friend, Larry Gardner the trainer of the Dallas Cowboys, has given us a lot of help in off-season conditioning programs as well as advice concerning diet; a good share of his information will be contained in the drill book.

We also are indebted to Paul Wiggin, former Stanford All-American and currently an assistant coach of the San Francisco '49ers. Paul, along with the entire 49er organization, is very helpful in talking with our players concerning all forms of off-season training from gaining to losing weight, increasing speed, and suggestions for agility programs. Paul's insight and knowledge concerning explosive football, contained in his book, *Off Season Football Training,* 1967, in collaboration with Floyd Peters and Dr. Harvey E. Williams, are used by many of our players.

Explosive power

The authors place considerable emphasis on explosive power, explaining that because football requires not only strength, but speed and alertness in the application of that strength, a weight training program should emphasize explosiveness. Violent body movements, as well as sheer muscle power, are included in this approach.

Although the workout for explosive power is similar to many popular weight training programs, every exercise has been thoroughly evaluated for its application to football. A vast number of exercises must be considered that are most beneficial for football, but they must be performed so the muscle activity is as similar as possible to that exerted in playing football.

It is contended by many that by increasing the strength of an athlete, it is increasing his explosive power, and for the most part, this is true. However, strength is not necessarily explosiveness, and the strongest lineman on the field may not be the most explosive.

The strongest lineman often relies upon his power alone without combining power with explosion. Only a superior athlete has the necessary strength and still uses his strength in an explosive manner to overpower his opponents.

Football has evolved more and more into a game of quickness of movement, especially in line play. The same transformation should take place in the weight training program. In this activity, each athlete may use a different weight, but the imperative factor is the explosiveness with which he lifts the weights.

According to Wiggin, Peters, and Dr. Williams, a good guideline in achieving explosiveness is *make the barbells ring*. If they do not ring, the athlete is not exercising in an explosive manner.

A typical workout should average about forty-five to fifty-five minutes. It should not exceed one hour because the amount of activity prescribed has been planned purposely for this shorter period of time. The total program of weight training, agility, and sprint would be too lengthy if the weight training period lasts longer than one hour. It could be possible for eight athletes to work with one set of weights and still complete the suggested workout within the allocated time. This means that as soon as one lifter completes his lift, the next man must be ready to start work. Ideally, between four and six participants should work on each bar, and it is helpful if they are grouped according to strength as much as possible.

For every minute devoted to weight conditioning, an equal amount of time, or perhaps more, should be given to the development of agility. This time should be devoted to enjoyable, competitive athletic activity such as basketball, handball, volleyball, or tennis. Solid diet and rest programs are equally important for continual improvement.

An athlete on this program must work out three times per week

—no more, no less. Regularity is the key; *never miss a workout.*

We recognize that some high schools are unable to afford weight equipment or a facility to house them. Vic Rowen, head football coach and athletic director at San Francisco State College, has made available the following plans and directions for making weights for use by the budget-minded institution:

How to make weights

The making of a set of weights is relatively simple and inexpensive. To make them you need the following items:
1. A four foot length of inch boiler pipe
2. Two tin cans
3. One bag of ready mix concrete

If you wish to start out with a weight of approximately 35–40 pounds, use one gallon cans. If you desire the weights to weigh about 50–60 pounds, use five quart cans. (Oil cans are good.)

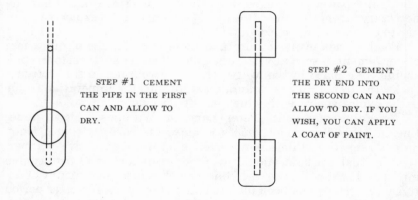

STEP #1 CEMENT THE PIPE IN THE FIRST CAN AND ALLOW TO DRY.

STEP #2 CEMENT THE DRY END INTO THE SECOND CAN AND ALLOW TO DRY. IF YOU WISH, YOU CAN APPLY A COAT OF PAINT.

Sandbags also can be improvised for use in a weight training program.

Agility drills

1. COKE CASE JUMP—This drill is done by jumping (25 times—four sets—for a total of 100) over a coke case or folding chair. Jump off of the toes laterally. Do not stop, but make it continuous. This exercise helps develop agility and balance.
2. WAVE DRILLS—Three to four boys move right, left,

front, back — according to the instructor. Never cross the feet and keep body low. Do this drill from both a two point and a four point stance.

3. QUARTER EAGLE — Assume a good football position. On the instructor's command of left or right, the boy turns $1/4$ turn in the direction of the command. Don't go more than 15-20 seconds.

4. WALL RUNNING — Place your hands on the wall with your feet well back and begin to run. Emphasize high leg action.

5. MONKEY ROLLS (3 man figure eight on mat) — Three boys are on hands and knees facing the instructor. On the signal the middle man rolls to his right. The man on his right dives over him and under the third man. The boys continue to do this until stopped by the instructor.

The authors wish to especially thank Don Cochren and Larry Gardner, co-trainers of the Dallas Cowboys, who have been very instrumental in outlining the following information regarding off-season conditioning:

Functional strength

Three of the goals for our off-season program are to increase strength, power, and explosiveness. Our coaching staff has encouraged doing the functional strength program to: (1) make the athlete functionally stronger in muscles used for blocking, tackling, and running; (2) strengthen the muscles, ligaments and tendons that support and surround the joints of the human body; (3) help the athlete "explode" from a starting position or when meeting an opponent.

Facts about functional strength

Part of this program is derived from the Russian Olympic weight training program. Russian weight lifters are slim, lanky athletes who are tremendously strong, quick and agile. This is the type of football player we hope to develop with the Indians.

The use of weights as a means of increasing athletic ability is a concept that is well recognized and accepted by those interested in developing the maximal potential of an athlete. It stimulates the circulation, helps maintain flexibility, increases appetite and neuromuscular control and tends to enhance the sense of well-being. This program is designed to increase strength, flexibility, explosiveness, speed and quickness rather than build bulky bodies that we have associated with weight lifters in the past.

Half-hearted and irregular practice will produce nothing and be a waste of valuable time, as well as being a personal disappointment. Extend your efforts at all times to improve your current capacity. "Wind" endurance and agility must be developed specifically by running. Everyone should be tested when reporting to Fall practice and categorized by his physical condition.

Training routines

The Functional Strength program is done four days a week (M-T-Th-F) and the first cross-country run is done on Monday or Tuesday; the second is done on Thursday or Friday. It is good to participate in activities that require a great deal of running and agility such as handball, paddle-ball, tennis, volley ball and basketball. These are outstanding activities that will help build your "wind" endurance as well as aid in developing quickness; they can be done on the days that cross-country running is not scheduled.

If not accustomed to this type of program, start slowly with light, easily handled weights. Gradually add more weight as the muscles become adjusted to the training and as the athlete gains familiarity with the exercise. When performing exercises, execute in a rapid forceful movement during the lifting stage. Always perform the exercise through the full range of motion.

Terminology

Repetition: An execution of an exercise from starting position, back to starting position.
Set: Execution of an exercise a given number of repetitions. (A 2-3 minute rest between sets is recommended.)

Exercise routines

An exercise routine will be assigned individually depending on what we want to accomplish (weight gain, weight loss, maintenance). When, after repeated trials at a given exercise, it seems impossible to improve or increase either the repetitions or weight, you have encountered a "sticking point." A change in routine or exercise may be indicated. It should be stressed that our program is designed for you to use the weights that you can handle and take through the range of motion rapidly the required number of reps. If you have a "power rack" where you work out, this is also beneficial to get through "sticking points," but normally use the amount of weight that you can handle.

Calisthenics or warm-up

Calisthenics, which generally are referred to as "warm-up" exercises in athletic activity, have a definite purpose in competitive sports. They are exercises that are used as a warm-up preliminary to more strenuous activity, and to obtain this purpose they must be carried out energetically and with complete dedication.

It has been found that muscles are more effective after the initial warm-up and are less susceptible to injury. This is because of a mild rise in body temperature and a moderate stretching of the muscle fibers. By increasing the body temperature through activity, the circulatory process becomes accelerated, carrying the needed oxygen supply and the stored energy-producing materials to the muscles, while carrying away carbon dioxide and other by-products of muscular activity. Gradually stretching the muscles causes the muscle fibers to become more extensible and elastic. Greater extensibility of a muscle brings about more forceful contractions. (Increases length of muscles through stretching.) In other words, the more extensible your muscles, the quicker and more violent you will be able to carry out your athletic assignments.

Although the elasticity of a muscle is sufficient to withstand the strains of moderate contractions, it is not unusual for an athlete not only to tear a tendon but also to rupture muscle fibers, causing muscle strain. In other words, muscles react like elastic material when a moderate resistance is applied to them. When, however, a muscle contracts with great violence or is otherwise opposed by a force which overcomes its elasticity, it becomes breakable. This is what we try to overcome through stretching while doing calisthenics.

The value of calisthenics is lost if you simply just go through the motions, and you are hindering only yourself. If not properly warmed-up, the body will not function at a high rate of efficiency. Also, each day you might miss due to injury from pulling a muscle decreases your opportunity of making the team.

The subject of "stretching" is being examined very closely by our Stanford coaching staff. We plan to devote 15 full minutes to stretching exercises during each practice as we begin our 1971 season. Coaches interested in this important phase of football would do well to talk to local gymnastic or track coaches who recognize the importance of the "flexible" athlete. Space prohibits detailing of our individual stretching exercises, but we will be anxious to share our findings with any interested coaches.

Warm-up

1. Jog three-hundred and forty-six yards or one lap around a football field if one is close to the work out area.

2. One and one-half minutes total of the following exercises (change exercises every fifteen seconds):
    A. Toe hop—push off of the ground with both feet straight up for about four to six inches and after landing go right back up again in a bouncing motion—hands on hips.
    B. Fore and aft hop—this is done with a side straddle hop cadence, but the feet go to the front and rear instead of out to the side—hands on hips.
    C. Side straddle hop—hands on hips.
3. Backward run—run backward for two hundred yards.
4. Bunny hop—with both feet together hop to the right and then back to the left of a straight line for fifty yards.
5. Standing broad jumps—broad jump for ten yards trying to complete the ten yards in three jumps.
6. Squat jumps—start with knees bent, fingers touching the ground; jump straight up and touch the goal post cross bar or some other object of approximately the same height and return to the ground in the same starting position. Jump ten times.

Functional strength exercises

These exercises are to be done with each workout when exercising with weights.

A chart that will help as you record your weights each month appears on page 461.

CLEAN AND PRESS

1. Clean and press: From a crouch position (tail low) with heels on the floor and the head up, lift bar with a very fast pull from the floor employing the legs and hips. When the

FUNCTIONAL STRENGTH EXERCISES

These exercises are to be done with each workout when exercising with weights.

Below is a chart that will help as you record your weights each month.

EXERCISES		SETS		DATE			
		1	2	March	April	May	June
	Dead Lift						
	Clean & Press						
	Power Clean						
	Stiff Legged Dead Lift						
	Bench Press						
	1/4 Squats						
	1/2 Squats						
Power	(Low Pull						
	((Dead Lift						
Racks	((Low Press						
	(High Press						
	Knee Extensions						
	Knee Curls						
	Sit-ups						
	Cross Country	2 - 3 miles, 2 days per week					

bar reaches the knees, rise up on the toes. Keep the bar close to the body all the way up to the chest. Keep elbows in close to the body. As the legs are straightening, thrust the weight from the chest by extending the arms to the overhead position. Then return to the starting position on the floor. This movement is done very quickly.

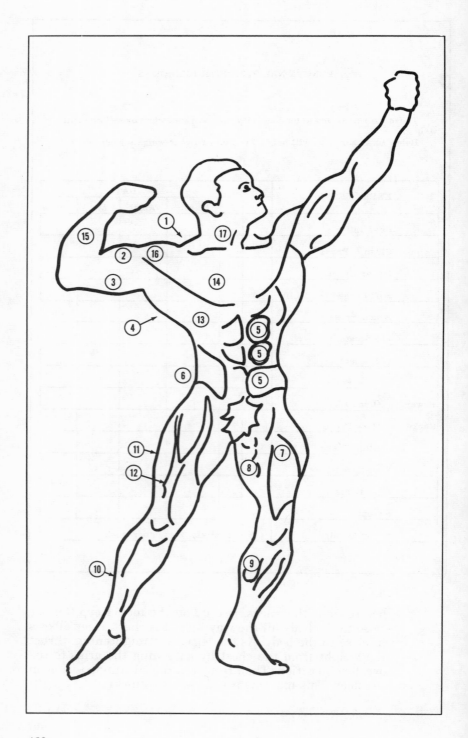

1. Trapezius: Upright Rowing Motion and shoulder shrugging while holding weight. All forms of overhead pressing.

2. Biceps: Heavy Curl and Concentration Curl. Chinning the bar. All forms of chinning and curling. Curl very effective.

3. Triceps: French Curl. All forms of pressing and push-ups such as parallel bar dips.

4. Latissimus dorsi: All forms of Pull-over with barbell. Bent Over Rowing Motion.

5. Abdominals: Leg Raises and Sit-ups. All forms of bending forward against a resistance.

6. External obliques: Side to Side Bending holding weight and Sit-ups. Coming erect from bent to side position against resistance.

7. Sartorius: Squats and Leg Raise to front with Iron Boot. Standing Leg Curl with Iron Boot.

8. Adductor: Squeezing legs together against a resistance.

9. Calf: Raise on toes while holding heavy weight. All forms of springing and jumping off toes with weight across shoulders.

10. Peroneal: Raising toes against resistance. Jumping and springing, particularly recovery after jump.

11. Vastus lateralis: Half Squats and Leg Raises to side with Iron Boot. All forms of squatting, springing and jumping with weights.

12. Quadriceps femoris: Leg Raises to front with Iron Boot and Half Squat. All forms of squatting, springing and jumping with weights.

13. Serratus magnus: Flyes and Lateral Raises while lying. Two Hands Pullover and all forms of supporting a heavy weight overhead. Handbalancing.

14. Pectoral: Heavy Bench Presses and Lateral Raise while lying. All forms of dipping. Bringing arms together against resistance.

15. Forearm: Wrist Curls and Reverse Curls. Using Squeeze-grips and all forms of Wrist Wrestling. All forms of gripping and holding of heavy weights. Lifting thick handled barbells.

16. Deltoid: Lateral Raise and Forward Raise while standing. All forms of muscling out heavy dumbbells to sides and front. All forms of pressing dumbbells and barbells.

17. Sterno-cleidomastoid: Wrestler's Bridge and bringing head forward against resistance.

POWER CLEAN

2. Power clean: Same form as first part of the clean and press; knees should be straight at the top position. Lower barbell to floor and repeat.

POWER PULL

3. Power pull: From a crouch position grasp the bar with the hands about shoulder length apart. Straightening the knees, head, and back vigorously, stand erect and pull the bar up to the chin in one continuous motion. The elbows should remain higher than the hands throughout. Lower barbell to floor and repeat.

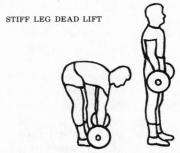

STIFF LEG DEAD LIFT

4. Stiff leg dead lift: Grasp bar about shoulder-width apart and stand to an erect position. Lower the weight to the floor keeping the knees straight so that the muscles of the low back and the back of the legs will be stretched. No attempt should be made to increase the weight with this exercise.

Other related weight training exercises

NEIDER PRESS

1. The Neider press or incline press: Standing erect or leaning against an incline board, the barbell is held as in the
   military press. The difference in this press is the angle to
   which you extend your arms. This angle being 1:30 by
   the clock. (The exercise may also be performed with dumbbells.)

BENT FORWARD ROW

2. Bent forward row: Standing with the upper part of your
   body parallel to the floor, knees slightly bent. Place hands
   knuckles out,—pull or lift the barbell to your chest, keeping elbows high. Place hand . . .
   1. Shoulder width
   2. Medium
   3. Very wide for the three different sets

CURLS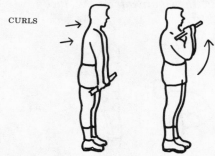

3. Curls: Stand erect with a barbell hanging at arms length
   in front of you. Grip the bar alongside your legs with

knuckles facing back. In curling the weight to your shoulders, allow your trunk to assist in the lift by bowing forward and heaving back as you lift or curl the weight.

4. Bench press: Lying on a bench on back, place hands on the barbell resting at head. A partner hands the barbell to your extended arms over your chest. Lower the bar to your chest, then press to arms length. Place your hands— 1. Very wide. 2. Medium, and 3. Arms parallel for the three different sets.

SQUATS

5. Squats: Standing erect, with barbell held across the back of shoulders, bend the knees and sink down to approximately a 90 degree angle at the knees, and return to an erect stance. *Do not go into a full squat because you might possibly damage the ligaments of the knee.*

DEAD LIFT

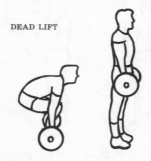

6. Dead lift: Start in a crouch position with the head up; keep the shoulders back, the chest up and stand to an erect posi-

tion lifting the bar bell. Keep the arms straight throughout the exercise — lower to the starting position and repeat.

7. Neck raises (head-strap): From leaning position raise
and lower head. This exercise can be done laterally bending head from side lying position from top of table with
head extended from edge of table.

UPRIGHT ROWING

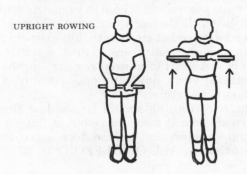

8. Upright rowing: Place your hands three inches apart
in the middle of a barbell with the knuckles facing out.
Stand erect, with barbell hanging at arms' length in front
of you. Raise or pull the bar to your chin, keeping the
elbows above the bar. (Point them toward the ceiling)
Then allow the bar to sink to arms length.

Isometrics

Since the arrival of Billy Cannon on the campus of L.S.U., much
has been written about his success as an athlete in college and
professional football because he participated in a training program
which included isometric contraction exercises. This is another
means of overloading the muscle, and it's through the "overload
principle" that a muscle will gain in strength and size.

When the Stanford Indians decided to initiate an off-season
conditioning program, a combination of weight training and isometric exercises was employed. While both methods build strength,
it seems that Isometric builds strength more rapidly with less effort,
but the body bulk, or weight gain seems to increase more when on
a weight training program. When the two are combined, excellent
results occur.

Rules for isometric muscle training

1. Gradually increase the force of the contraction. (Do not jerk from a relaxed position to one of maximum or near maximum contraction.)
2. Each exercise is held in static contraction (maximum or near maximum) for about ten seconds.
3. Before each exercise, take a deep breath and exhale slowly through the ten seconds of contraction. Take more breaths if needed. Do not hold breath *particularly* if dizziness, headache, nausea or other side-effects occur.
4. In each exercise the muscle is held in isometric contraction at a length just a little less than normal resting length. Strength can be gained at any length, but existing research indicates that best results are gained when the static contraction is just short of normal resting length.
5. Do each exercise every day, only once per day, and only one repetition per exercise.
6. Isometric muscle training should be the last thing done in a practice session. It takes more out of the participant than he might realize and may reduce speed for a few hours after exercise. ALL OUT EFFORT IS REQUIRED.

SHOULDER SHRUG

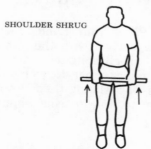

1. *The shoulder shrug:* When performing this exercise, the bar is placed at a height even with the hands when you are standing straight up between the racks. From this position, you pull up on the bar by shrugging the shoulders.

TOE RAISE

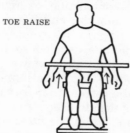

2. *Toe raise:* For this exercise you will need a 2 × 4 about

2 feet long, a bench and some padding material. You sit on the bench with your toes resting on the 2 × 4. The bar is placed at a height a few inches above the knees, with padding between the knees and the bar. From this position the bar is pushed upward by extending the toes. One day the toes are pointed slightly in, the next day, slightly out, and the next day straight ahead.

HIGH PRESS

3. *High press:* For the high press the bar is set at a height slightly less than maximum reach when the arms are extended simultaneously. Grasping the bar with the hands about shoulder width apart, looking straight ahead; tighten your leg, hip and back muscles; and push on the bar as hard as possible.

LEG CURL

4. *Leg curl:* When performing this exercise you take a prone position on a bench with the backs of your legs striking the bar just above the heel. You may want to put a towel under your knees for padding. The legs during the exercise are only slightly bent. You attempt to force the bar upward by curling (or flexing) the legs.

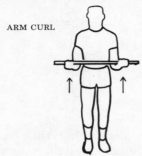

ARM CURL

5. *Arm curl:* When performing this exercise, the bar is placed at a height slightly below the elbow joint when you are

standing straight up between the racks. From the standing position you put both arms, at the wrist, under the bar and pull up on the bar.

LEG PRESS

6. *Leg press:* You place the bar at a height just short of maximum extension for the legs (when you are lying on your back on the bench). The bench is grasped with your hands, and your head is held up as you attempt to move the bar upward by pushing against it with your legs.

BENCH PRESS

7. *Bench press:* You place the bar at a height just short of maximum extension for the arms (when lying on your back on the bench). Bar is directly above armpit level. Push upward on the bar as hard as possible.

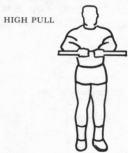

HIGH PULL

8. *High pull:* When performing this exercise the bar is placed at elbow height or slightly above, when standing straight up between the racks. From the standing position, hands on the bar close together, palms down, pull up on the bar.

Running

1. The off-season functional strength program should last at least three months and possibly longer. The first month should be devoted to using lighter weights and concentrating on the correct form. Little or no attempt should be made to increase the weight loads until the third or fourth week. In *addition* to cross-country running — playing handball, paddle ball, basketball or any type of agility drills is certainly encouraged. The running program to be started six weeks before reporting for practice is to be done in conjunction with the functional strength program; cross-country running is incorporated in this program. If isometric facilities are available and you feel that you need extra work to get certain body areas stronger, do these just prior to your shower.

2. Should you have sustained a joint injury the past season, be sure to concentrate on the muscles surrounding the joint structure because the strength of the particular joint can be increased through resistive exercises.

3. Be sincere when you start your running program or "roadwork." It has been proven time and time again in athletic competition that performance is governed by the condition of your legs.

4. To help eliminate the blister problem, try to wear football shoes which are well broken in. Also do a considerable amount of walking and running barefooted on the grass because this will tend to toughen the soles of your feet.

5. Try to have a sun tan when reporting in the Fall, for this will eliminate any chances of getting a painful sunburn on your arms, legs, neck and face.

6. Be sure to take salt and potassium tablets as prescribed by the trainer to maintain a proper salt water balance within the body. This will tend to lessen fatigue and the possibility of having a pulled muscle.